ELEMENTS OF SOFT TREATMENTS

FUNDAMENTALS OF WINDOW TREATMENTS, BEDDING, AND SOFT ACCESSORIES

Kirk B. Axelson

Barbara Talmadge

Published in the United States by

Precision Draperies Education

Denver, Colorado

Copyright © 2006 Precision Draperies Education

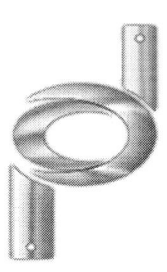

The specifications and information represented by the charts in this collection are acceptable industry standards, but by no means, the only acceptable standards. Every effort has been made to present complete and usable formulas, charts, and rule of thumbs.

The publisher and author can not be held liable for any problems and / or expenses, direct or indirect, that might be incurred as a result of using these materials.

All Rights Reserved. No part of this publication may be produced, stored in a retrieval system, or transmitted in any form or by any means, electronic, mechanical, photocopy, recording or otherwise, without prior permission of the copyright owner.

ISBN 1-933768-04-5

How to reach us:

Phone: (720) 837-3290

www.draperyeducation.com

info@draperyeducation.com

Illustrations: Tara Lindsay, Duncan K. McPherson, and Kirk Axelson

Assistant Editors: Barbara Talmadge, Glenn Axelson, and Kirk Axelson

Editor in-Chief: Helen Bell

Layout & pre-press support: Glenn Axelson

Cover: Floyd R. Chapman

Pre-Press: PrintShop PLUS, Denver, Co.

Dedication

We dedicate this book to our Moms, Ethel and Irene,
two wise women who had the good sense to teach us a trade we can always fall back on. We know they are together somewhere in heaven today sipping margaritas over lunch, and they are smiling.

FOREWORD

What a knockout!

Finally, educational material for designers and decorators in the field of window coverings and bedding.

Kirk Axelson, the workroom professional, has teamed up with long time designer, Barbara Talmadge to author the *Elements of Window Treatments, Bedding, and Soft Treatments*.

Kirk has combined his 25 years manufacturing knowledge with Barbara's extensive design experience to create a one of a kind book. It was created with the desire to provide quality educational material on the basics of the design industry that deals with window coverings, bedding, and other similar soft treatments. This book is for anyone who desires more knowledge about soft window coverings, bedding, pillows, shams, and much more. It is a must read for anyone who makes their living designing custom window coverings.

Glenn Axelson

ACKNOWLEDGEMENTS

We wish to express our special thanks to Floyd R. Chapman for the cover design; to Helen Bell who patiently kept us on track, and to Glenn Axelson who diligently kept us on task. Without the efforts of these generous souls, this book would still just be an idea.

TABLE OF CONTENTS

Chapter 1	Draperies	1
Chapter 2	Rod Pocket Panels	19
Chapter 3	Toppers	33
Chapter 4	Drapery Valances	47
Chapter 5	Rod Pocket Valances	57
Chapter 6	Cornices	65
Chapter 7	Traditional and Open Swags	77
Chapter 8	Window Scarfs	101
Chapter 9	Fabric Shades	111
Chapter 10	Sunbursts	127
Chapter 11	Bedding	137
Chapter 12	Pillows and Pillow Shams	155
Chapter 13	Soft Treatment Accessories	167
Chapter 14	Add ons	175
Appendix A	Fabric Direction	191
Appendix B	Technical Specifications	199
Appendix C	Thumbnails	211
Appendix D	Work Orders	313
	Glossary	331

INTRODUCTION

What is it about windows? Ever since humans emerged from their caves and started building dwellings, those houses always included some kind of opening. Perhaps this happened because while being protected from the elements, they wanted to know at the same time what was going on outside. Cut a hole in the wall and problem solved, with a view and the ability to see what was going on outside their shelter. However, there was a problem with the hole in the wall. The rain came in and belongings got wet. The wind blew out the fire, and it was cold and draughty. What would a solution be? Hang an animal skin over the opening to keep out the elements. It was movable, kept things dry, and the wind and cold were blocked. And there you have it: the birth of the custom window covering.

Somewhere along the line someone invented glass, which eliminated much of the reason for the original intent of the window covering. But by then the idea of hanging things over the windows was ingrained in our genetic psyche and the window covering was here to stay. This desire is primal, and will be around as long as there are Homo sapiens.

Things have continued to evolve, and window coverings have gone from simple to ornate and back again, depending on the social and economic trends at a given time. The basic idea remains however, and the job of designing and manufacturing them is a very secure one.

The purpose of this book is to give the modern interior designer a basic understanding of the elements that make up certain kinds of window coverings and soft furnishings, so they may understand the mechanics of putting together a soft treatment. The work of designing the treatment should remain the task of the designer, while the process of manufacturing the design can be accomplished by an appropriately skilled craftsman. The ability for these two to communicate effectively is dependent on the manufacturer understanding the role of the designer, and the designer comprehending the terminology and role of the manufacturer. The fundamentals and tips within this book are an attempt to move the current window covering and soft treatment advancement in that direction.

DRAPERIES

Window coverings in the drapery family are probably the most basic method for decorating the window and controlling temperature and light, and they have been in existence ever since there have been windows. They are defined as a panel, or panels, of fabric that cover the entire window, and they may be set up as decorative stationary treatments. They have some kind of constructed top that allows for attachment to a rod, and there are countless ways of varying the style and look of this treatment and its function. The constructed top might consist of pleats, tabs, attached rings, grommets, snaps, or other unusual headings. Outlined within this chapter are some of the most common drapery styles along with methods of measuring, construction, and design, which are time tested and generally accepted among drapery professionals today.

There are business rules when talking about draperies. When the term "drapery" is used, it is expected that some kind of constructed top will be used. These constructed tops are often referred to as the drapery "heading", and the type of heading generally determines the style of the drapery. When no specific heading style is specified, a pleated top is assumed. However due to the recent increase in the popularity of drapery in design, specifying a heading style is a necessity. With the rapid rate of evolution in this area, current practice dictates requesting a sewn sample of a particular style from the workroom prior to production to be sure designer and client agree on the design and construction. Rod pocket panels can also be used as a drapery, but in this book they are treated in a separate chapter, since they have their own set of criteria.

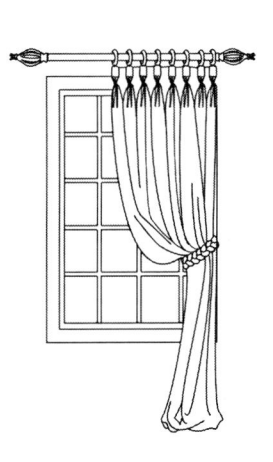

Elements of Soft Treatments

Draperies

HEADING STYLES

Draperies can have many types of headings. The styles will usually fall into one of five categories: pleated tops, soft tops, tab tops, unusual headings, and special setups. Listed below are some of the most common styles and some of their variations. Drapery construction methods will vary, but the resulting appearance of the drape and heading should appear as described.

Pleated drapery "fullness" refers to the amount of fabric width used. Fullness is usually expressed in ratios such as 2:1 or 2x. This means that there will be twice as much fabric width than there is rod width being covered by the drapery. Fullness varies by design from 2x to 3½x and most designs require a particular amount of fullness in order to look right. The workroom will usually have specific instructions regarding how much fullness is required for a particular style.

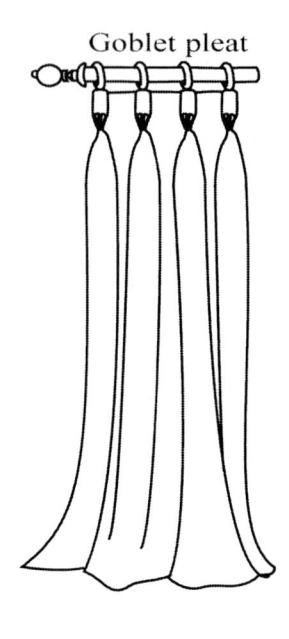

Goblet pleat

5-finger pleat

Pleated tops

This category of drapery heading is manufactured with some type of sewn pleat creating groups of fullness separated by flat spaces. Pleated headings are usually made with buckram, crinoline, or some other type of stiffener. When buckram is used, the top becomes crisp and formal looking. Pleated draperies typically use a drapery hook, which is placed behind the pleat or tape heading. It is used to attach the drapery to rod slides or rings. To see a list of pin settings, refer to Appendix B.

Variations are created by changing the location of the tack or gather in the fullness from top to bottom. Varying the amount of the fullness, fanning it (goblet pleat at left), or tacking with different multiples of pinches (known as "fingers"), are other methods to vary the pleat style. The pleats can also be sewn flat as in a box pleat, or made so there are scallops between the pleats.

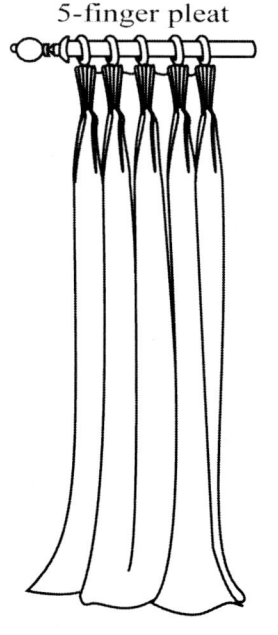

> When the top is scalloped, the hooks that are used to attach to the rings may show due to the scallop at the top. Consider using sewn on rings instead of hooks.

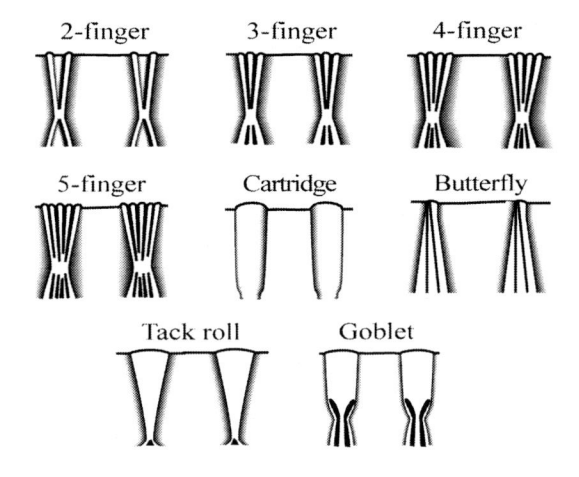

Some of the more common pleat styles are illustrated here. The cartridge pleat, tack roll, and goblet do not traverse and stack as nicely as the finger styles and the butterfly, so those may be more suitable as stationary panels, rather than working draperies.

The fullness required for each pleat style will vary with the design chosen. Typically the 2-finger style requires 2x fullness, whilst the 3-finger, 4-finger, butterfly, cartridge, goblet, and tack roll require 2.5x fullness. The 5-finger requires 3x fullness. Some styles can be made a little more or a little less full to create a certain effect, but the look will differ with changes in fullness, and this is why seeing a sewn sample from the workroom can be so critical.

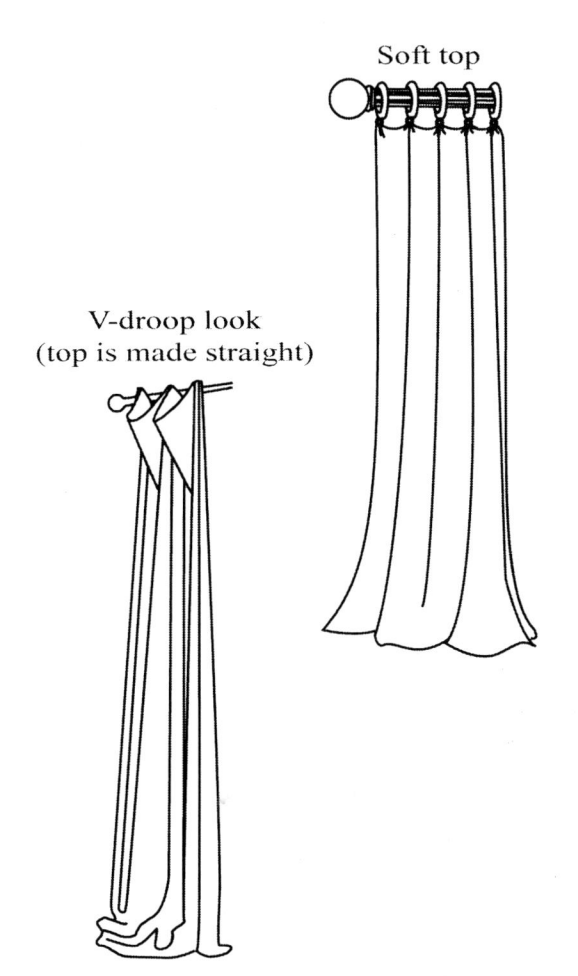

Soft tops

For this drapery style, the heading of the drapery is manufactured so the top has no stiffener (buckram). Without the buckram or crinoline stiffener, the look of the drapery changes to a softer and more casual effect. The basic soft top is straight across and flat with the rings sewn directly onto the top of the drapery. The finished top can have a knife edge "pillowcase" top or a facing on top as much as 6"–8", depending on the design.

Many soft top styles are not suitable for use as full working draperies because the fullness in the panel is not maintained when these draperies are drawn, and therefore the appearance will change dramatically. Often these varieties need to remain stationary, as soft top panels require dressing of the spaces and pleats at the top each time the drapery is opened and closed. Sometimes a "memory" stitch can be added to the top to help with this. The memory stitch helps keep the spaces in place when the drapery is being hand drawn to its closed position. This is known as a top memory stitch. Depending on the style of drapery, the memory stitching will not be seen.

Elements of Soft Treatments

Variations of soft top draperies can also have sewn in pleats and be tacked in various ways, simply eliminating the stiffener. Fullness can be varied and the top can also be constructed with scallops between the rings or pleats. To achieve a contrasting cuff effect at the top, place some facing along the top back edge. When the drapery is dressed on site, the top edge is folded to the front to reveal the top reverse side of the contrasting fabric.

Single wide strap

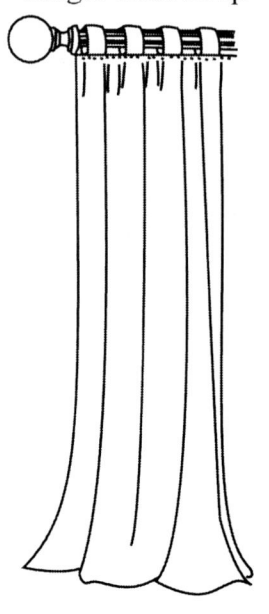

Tabs - long

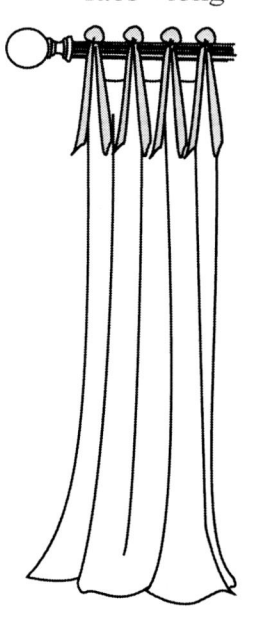

Tab tops

This style is constructed with a tab of some description at the top. These tabs loop around, or are tied to the drapery rod. Tabs can be constructed in a variety of ways, such as ties from cording, single wide straps, shaped straps, or shoe string ties. The top of the drapery may have scallops or be straight.

Tab styles usually require less fullness, closer to 2x. The fullness can vary depending on the type of tab used, and tabs are considered to be add-on items. Consult with the workroom as the tabs come in a variety of styles, and confirm their policy regarding fullness and any additional yardages needed for making the tabs.

Tab panels also make better stationary panels than full working draperies, because fullness is not maintained when drawn closed and fabric tabs do not slide easily along many of the rods. This is especially true if the rod being used is wrought iron. When using a tab drapery as a full working drapery, it will require dressing of the spaces at the top each time the drapery is opened and closed. A memory stitch can be used with tab styles but this is not an ideal solution.

Diamond pleat tape

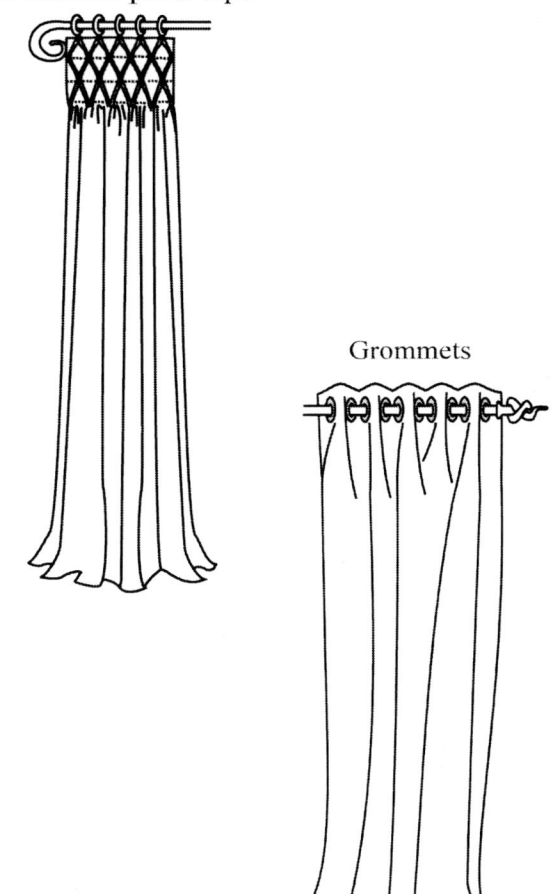

Grommets

Unusual headings

There are some unusual heading styles, such as tops that require a shirring tape, snap tape, or grommets, that can be added to the top of the drapery to create the different looks. The fullness will vary by specific style. Check with the workroom regarding their requirements for these, and request to see a sewn sample.

Shirring tapes are usually used for stationary panels, but depending on the style, they can also be used for full working draperies. Shirring tape styles can have tabs or string ties added for attachment to the rod but the stack of the drapery when open will be very large in this instance. This type of drapery is hard to operate as the top will bind on the rod, and is especially problematic if the drapery is long.

Variations using snap tapes can provide benefits such as reducing stack and ease of operation. These styles will also require special hardware designed specifically to operate with the snap style drapery headings.

Ripple fold using snap tape
(shown with butt masters)

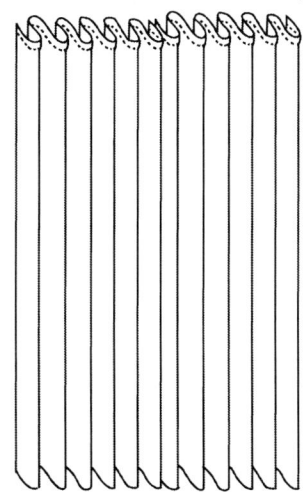

Accordian pleat using snap tape
(shown with overlap masters)

Elements of Soft Treatments

5-finger pleat with petticoat square

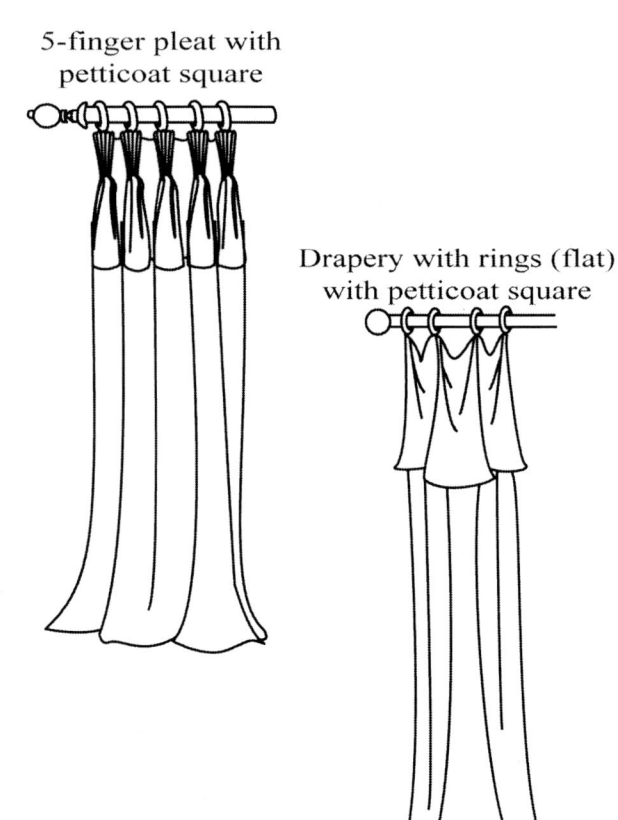

Drapery with rings (flat) with petticoat square

Special set-ups
In this category of drapery style, multiple layers of fabric are used to create different effects. They are created through the use of add-on units such as a petticoat or swag. In these situations the attachment is sewn or attached directly to the drapery as opposed to being a separately installed component. These types of set-ups are usually stationary and rarely used as full working draperies. When used as working draperies, they are hard to open and close due to the weight of the fabric and will bind on the rod, and are especially problematic if the drapery is long.

MEASURING AND ORDERING DRAPERIES

There are a number of different factors that need to be considered in designing a drapery treatment. Begin the process by taking complete window measurements including the dimensions of the walls above, below, and to the right and left of the opening. Make notes regarding the width and thickness of any window casings, trims, and aprons. Also note any obstructions surrounding the window such as wall switches, light fixtures, heating vents, and so on.

> Heating and air conditioning vents located on the floor in close proximity to floor length draperies can be particularly problematic, as air blowing up a drapery panel will cause it to billow and hang badly. Avoid stacking draperies over vents whenever possible.

After measuring, begin designing the drapery treatments taking the following factors into account. Consider such questions as will the draperies be stationary or full working? If they are full working, in which direction will the drapes stack and draw? How much wall will be covered and how much window will be exposed? What length will the draperies be?

Stationary versus full working draperies
It is very important when ordering draperies that either full working or stationary is specified. This specification has a significant impact on the final cost of labor and yardage. It also has a tremendous bearing on the type of hardware that will be needed.

A **full working** drapery will open and close by means of a traversing rod or hand baton, covering the window. The function is to provide light control, privacy, and/or temperature control.

A **Stationary** (or side hang) drapery means the drapery does not operate and it is for decoration only.

DRAPERY OVERLAPS AND RETURNS

What are returns and overlaps?

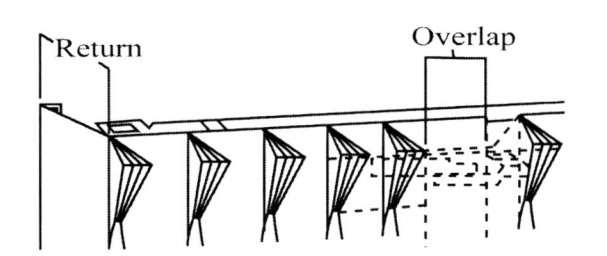

Returns
This is the distance from the face of the drapery rod to the wall. Workrooms think of this measurement as being the distance from the finished edge of the panel to the last pleat, ring, tab, snap, grommet, or other attachment to the rod. Order the return from the workroom ½" larger than the rod projection to allow for some fabric "relax" in the return when the drapery is hung.

Overlaps
This is the portion of the panel that crosses over on a pair of draperies. This is also the case on stack left or stack right drapery where it is attached to the master carriage on a one way traversing rod. Workrooms think of this measurement as being the distance from the finished edge of the panel to the first pleat, ring, tab, snap, grommet, or attachment to the rod. Order the overlap from the workroom ½" larger per panel than the actual overlap of the fabric to allow for fabric relax when the drapery is hanging.

DRAW AND STACK CONFIGURATIONS

When designing a drapery treatment, a choice needs to be made regarding the direction the drapes will draw, if functional, and the location where they will be stored when not in use, or "stacked". Draperies can be set up as split draw, double traversing, one way stack left, and one way stack right.

When ordering panel draperies, it is very important to indicate in which direction the drapery will stack, and in which direction the drapery will draw if it is to be an operable panel. Here are some examples of stack directions.

Draperies

One way stack left

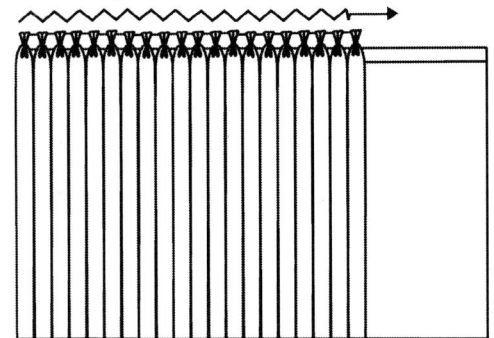

One way stack left (SL)
This indicates that the drapery will stack on the left and will draw to the right. When an SL panel is specified, the drapery "return" or outer edge will be made on the left side and the "overlap" (leading edge) will be on the right

One way stack right

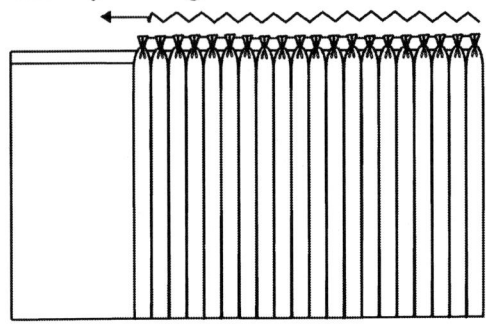

One way stack right (SR)
This indicates that the drapery will stack on the right and will draw to the left. When an SR panel is specified, the drapery "return" will be made on the right and the "overlap" will be on the left.

Split Draw

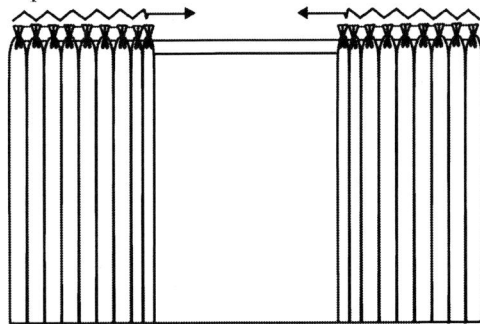

Pair or split draw (PR)
This indicates that the drapery will be split in the middle with two equal halves, with stacking to the right and left, and both sides drawing toward the center. When a PR is specified, the "overlaps" are in the center and the "returns" are made on the two outside edges.

Off set panel

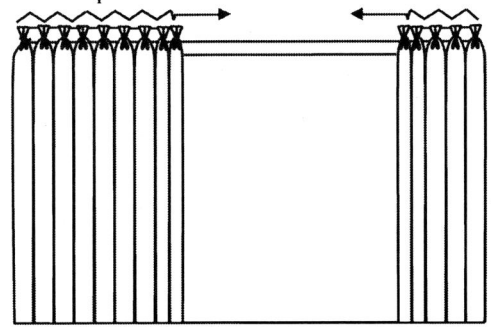

Offset pair (OSPR)
Sometimes a pair of draperies will not have equal width dimensions for both sides. This is called an "off set" pair. These pairs are usually ordered as separate panels and a notation is made on the work order indicating that they will hang together as a pair so that the workroom will make the fullness, pleating, spacing, and pattern match.

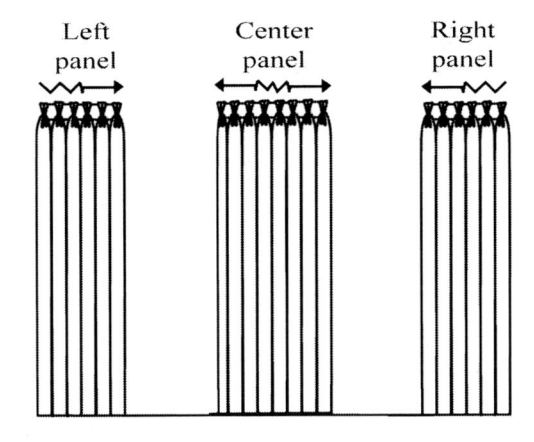

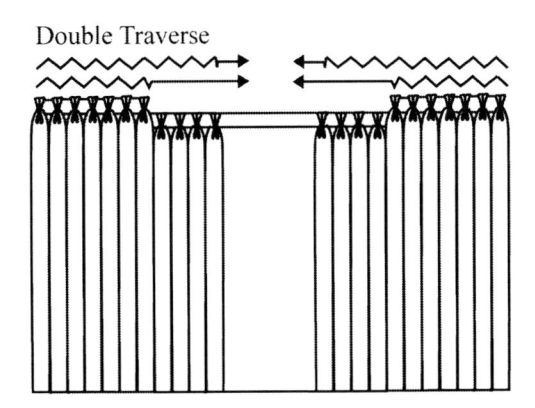

Center panel (SC)
This indicates that the drapery will be used in between two windows. It will stack toward the center, and the "overlaps" (leading and outer edges) will draw outward to the left and also to the right.

Double traverse (DT)
This is where two drapery rods are used on the same window, one behind the other. These rods can be utility rods, iron poles, or wood poles. Usually both rods are suspended from the same brackets, but separate brackets are also acceptable. Double traversing sets of wood, iron, or utility track can also be interchangeable, for instance, using a wood or iron pole in front of a utility traversing rod.

The purpose of the double rod set is to be able to use two different drapery materials on the same window. The most common application is a sheer fabric on the back rod (the rod closest to the wall and window) and some type of decorative fabric on the front rod. Another popular application would be a heavy liner on the back rod and decorative sheer on the front rod.

Drapery stacking space requirements
If the drapery is full working, determine if the drapery is to clear the window when open or if coverage of some of the glass is acceptable. This is usually a matter where the client will want to have input since the loss of light or view from a window covered by drapery is an emotional decision.

Draperies that stack off the glass or opening and stack over the wall will make the room appear larger and more open while gaining maximum benefit from the light and view the window allows. The drawback of this is that drapes stacked on the wall require longer rods, more fabric, are therefore more expensive and can cover valuable wall space.

Elements of Soft Treatments

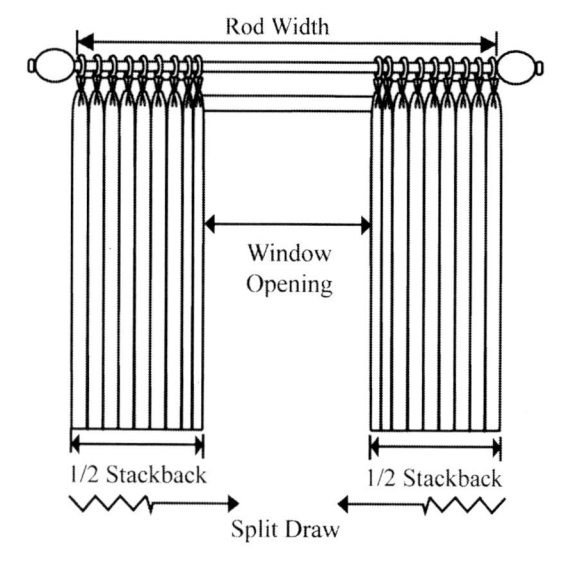

Draperies that stack over the widow or glass tend to be less desirable as they will often obstruct views and block light. If the drapery is to clear the window, an allowance for "stack back" must be made. It is the designer's job to determine the client's preferences and strike an acceptable balance between the client's wishes and the stack requirements outlined below.

Use the following stack back formula to find the approximate stack back width. Once this is determined, add it to the width of the window opening. After applying the formula, ensure that the finished width includes the stack back on each side of the window.

Stack back formulas
For pair: rod width ÷ 6 = approximate stack back width per side.

For panel: rod width ÷ 3 = approximate stack back width per panel.

Examples:

Pair:
If rod width = 100, then 100 ÷ 6 = 16.66. This is the approximate stack back width on each side of the window. The rod width needed to clear the window would be the window width plus 16.6" on each side.

Panel:
If rod width = 100, then 100 ÷ 3 = 33.33. This equals the approximate stack back width when the drape is fully open. The approximate rod width needed would be the window width plus the stack back plus the extension of the rod past the window on the non-stack side.

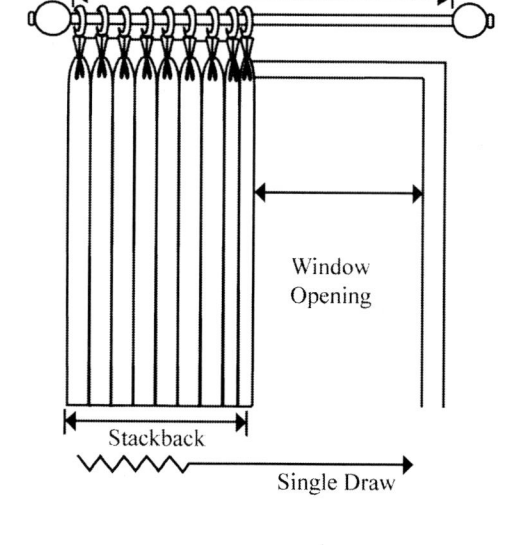

> These general formulas work in most cases. Figuring drapery stack is not an exact science, and it is necessary to keep in mind a few variables such as thickness of fabric, interlining, type of heading, and type of hardware, and to adjust the results up or down accordingly.

DETERMINING DRAPERY LENGTH

Drapery length is a matter of client preference and the desired impact of the window treatment. Standard minimum drapery coverage for a full working drapery is 6" above the opening, 5" below the opening, and, 5" to each side of the opening. Less than this is sometimes done, however less is usually considered to be below custom standard. Occasionally, architectural factors require adjusting this. Drapery width will be adjusted based on the consideration of the factors above. Drapery lengths can be made to minimum coverage, sill length, apron length, floor length, breaking length, puddle length, or café length.

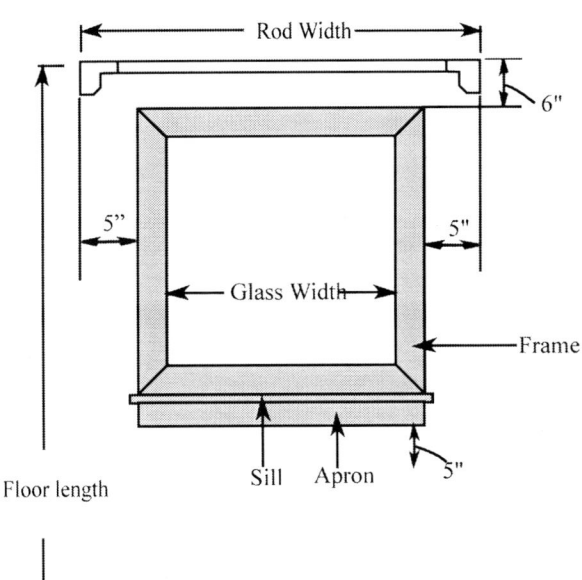

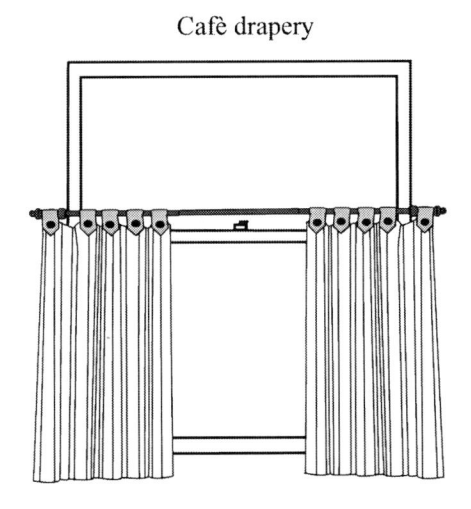

Sill length is where the bottom of the drapery sits above the sill approximately ½" or so.

Apron length is where the bottom of drapery is set approximately 5" below the wood molding or sill.

Floor length draperies are usually allowed to clear the floor or carpet by about ½". Sometimes these draperies are shorter in order to not cover heat registers or other architectural features. Floor length drapes can be to minimum coverage above the window, or they can go all the way to the ceiling, depending on the hardware used and the desired impact of the drapery design.

Breaking length will break on the floor, usually by 1"-2".

Puddle length can be as small as 3"- 10" or as much as 20".

Café length is a short drapery that is made to sill or apron length at the bottom, but the top only covers to half way or two thirds of the way up the window. The resulting effect leaves the top of the window uncovered allowing light to come in while still providing privacy. Café length drapes are often paired with valances of a similar design.

Elements of Soft Treatments

Draperies

In determining the drapery length, a few rules do however apply.

Full working drapes should not be made to break or puddle. The additional fabric sweeping the floor when the drape is opened and closed will cause excessive wear on the hardware or cause the hardware to fail or fall down. Dragging fabric will also become very dirty and wear excessively. If the design requires breaking this rule, be sure the client is aware of these drawbacks.

Stationary side hangs are only decorative and are not meant to function, so therefore length determination can be based entirely on the desired impact of the design. They can break or puddle as much or as little as the tasteful appearance of the fabric will allow. Some heavy fabrics do not break well. Stationary panels can also be drawn back with tie backs or can have a bishop sleeve effect as described below.

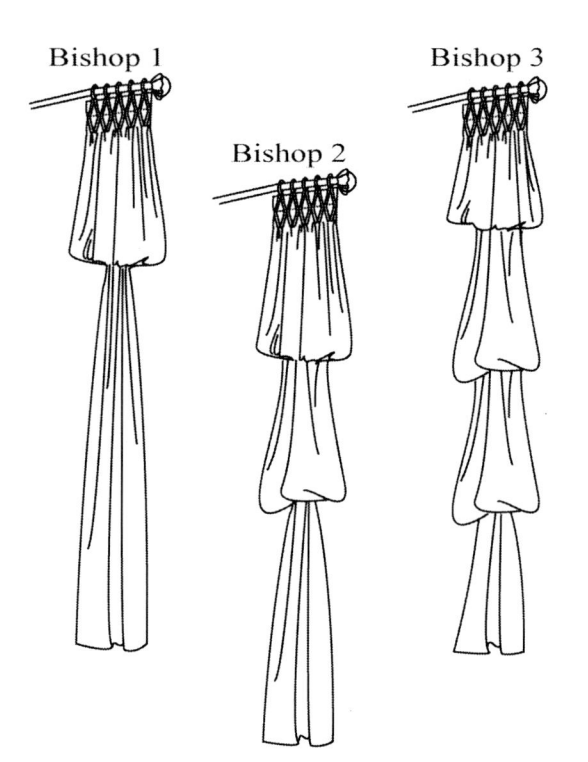

The "bishop effect" is a puffed look which is created by stringing a drapery cord behind the panels and tying extra fabric fullness up at different intervals to create the effect. Hidden tiebacks are then added at the base of each puff. There can be three or more "bishops" depending on the desired look. The bishop effect can also be created with certain types of hardware and tieback holders, but the extra length to do this needs to be added to the finished length of the drapery panel when it is ordered. Usually an extra 12"-20" inches of length is needed for each bishop puff.

> Remember to indicate on the work order the extra inches needed to the finished length for breaks, puddles and bishop sleeve take-up.

DRAPERY CLEARANCE

It is important for the designer to understand the formulas for clearance because clients often require an explanation when they realize how much space their draperies will take up. Some operating drapery combinations will occupy up to 18" of space. Clients will often be alarmed when they think they are giving up that much of their room, and sometimes this clearance factor can preclude the placement of pieces of furniture. When installed, draperies require space in which to hang. The typical front to back stack of a drapery panel is around 4" if the drape is of an average fullness. More fullness will require more room to stack. Drapery clearance should be calculated at the bottom of the drapery where the fullness of the fabric will hang freely.

For an inoperable stationary drapery or side hang, typically no more than 4" of projection will be required and less is possible if it is acceptable for the drape to lean against the wall somewhat. For working or functioning draperies that must open and close, more space, or clearance, is required to prevent the fabric from rubbing or dragging on walls and adjacent panels, when multiple layers of drapery are installed. For the best results, allow 1" of clearance between the wall and the drape, 4" for each layer of drapery, and 1" in between each layer.

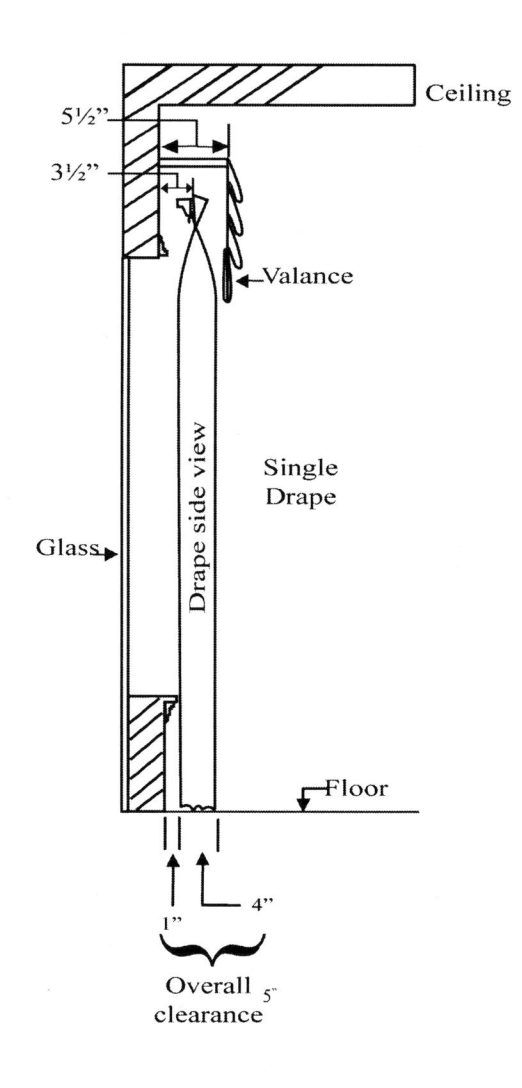

Example:
One layer of sheer unlined drapery requires 5" of clearance space (4" drape stack + 1" wall clearance). Since the drapery rod hangs at the center of the drape stack, subtract 2" (½ of the drape stack). Clearance to the wall is 1", so rod placement is at 3" from the wall. Order the drapery return ½" larger than rod projection to allow for some relax in the fabric. The return order size on this drape will be 3½" inches. Motorized draperies require additional clearance due to the fact that the motors move the drape more slowly than a hand drawn or cord traversing drapery. Allow 1½"-2" between layers for the drapes to clear.

> If the window trim is very thick, window sills project out from the wall, or there are door knobs, window cranks, and handles to clear, include these in the wall clearance calculation.

LININGS

Drapery lining is an element which is often overlooked in the design of the window treatment. It is however a crucial factor in the final outcome and look of the finished product. A suitable lining can often have an impact on client satisfaction. Sometimes the lining choice should be made first, even before the decorative fabric that will cover it is chosen, as the lining selection can have a bearing on the style that should be used and the fabric that will be chosen. For example, black-out, or room darkening lining should always be offered in a bedroom, even before fabric is chosen as these linings are not compatible with many face fabrics. Interlining will often be appropriate for its thermal properties, but it can be problematic when used with otherwise bulky fabrics.

Elements of Soft Treatments

Lining draperies will add years to the life of fabrics. It protects them from fading and damage and it gives most fabrics more body and weight, causing them to have a more elegant drape. Lining will provide a uniform appearance of the same color from the exterior of the house. Draperies should always be lined, except in cases where the fabric is sheer, and is being used specifically for its transparent qualities.

Linings play an important part in controlling light and providing thermal protection. Familiarity with the basic lining types and their function is a necessary element for consideration in designing any drapery treatment. It is best whenever possible, to match the weave and fiber content of the drapery lining to the face fabric. Mixed and matched fabrics and linings will separate and repel one another causing flaring, wrinkling, and an overall messy appearance. In some cases, such as with a delicate fiber like silk, a compatible lining type should be used, and/or interlining should be added for additional protection and optimal drape.

Many linings today have added thermal and light blocking properties which can be an excellent solution in some design situations. The lining supply industry is changing and responding constantly to design needs by making available many lining choices. Interlinings are now available as laminates to black outs and other types of basic linings, so being aware of industry trends through trade publications is a useful tool in remaining aware of the types of linings available for various uses.

SPECIAL WINDOW SHAPES

In the course of design work with windows, it is likely that widows with shapes other than the basic rectangle will be encountered, and in fact, odd shapes and configurations are quite common. Draperies are probably the most versatile type of covering used to fit these situations. A thorough understanding of the rules governing drapery design and construction makes fitting drapery to uniquely shaped windows a fun and satisfying part of the designer's task.

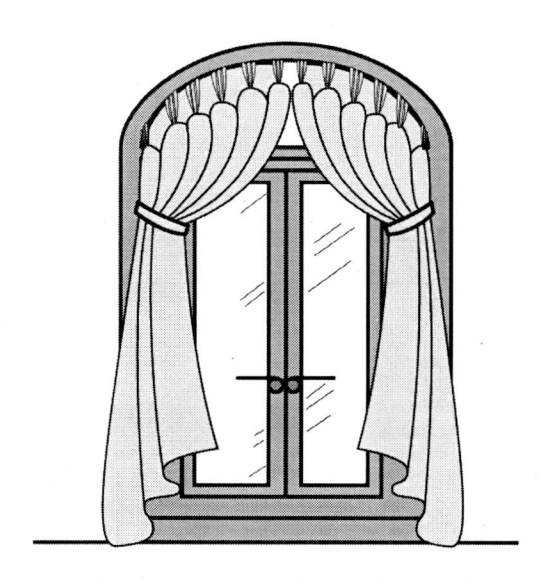

Arched windows

Many drapery styles can be configured to fit an arched shape window. The primary constraint that will be encountered when doing this is that the drapery top will need to remain stationary. Some type of tie back, hold back, or special cord operated mechanism may need to be used in order for a drapery to open and close over an arched window configuration.

Adapting the drapery styles so that the drapery hangs correctly is quite a time consuming and labor intensive accomplishment for the workroom. Expect the labor costs in these situations to have a considerable up-charge. Templates of the arch shapes will be required by the workroom for drapery production.

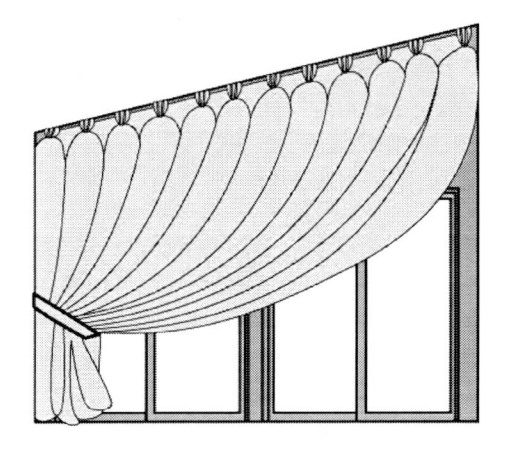

Slanted windows

Draperies can also be adapted for windows with slanted tops. Again, the constraint in these situations is that the drapery will not be operable or the drapery must stack to the longest side of the slant, otherwise the fabric will bind and pool on the floor when operated. This will usually require the panel to stack all in one direction and precludes the use of a two way operating pair. These draperies are also quite labor intensive to manufacture, and expect up-charges comparable to arched top draperies. Templates are not required in these cases, but precise measurements are, including the degrees of all angles.

Cathedral windows

Similar to the slanted top, draperies will also work in these configurations. Operable panels here would have to stack to the center of the opening, which may not be the best design solution. Tiebacks, holdbacks, or stringing mechanisms will allow operation of these as in the arched window. Expect labor up-charges, and provide precise measurements, including the degree of all angles.

Draperies

GENERAL INFORMATION

- Full working means draperies will open and close by means of a traversing rod or hand baton.
- Stationary (side hangs) means they do not operate and are set-up for decorative purposes only.
- Always clearly specify if the draperies are to be lined, unlined or interlined.
- Lining selection is part of the drapery design.
- Check with the workroom regarding their policy on pattern matching if using a fabric with a printed or woven repeating pattern.

PRICING

- Draperies are priced per width of fabric, sometimes called "width of measure" or WOM.
- Some workrooms bill in even numbered widths only: 2,4,6,8, etc. Check with the workroom regarding their policy on this.
- Some workrooms have a minimum width charge.
- Railroaded fabric will need to be converted into widths in order to find the cost.
- Depending on the workroom, there may be a maximum width of fabric to determine the per width charge. For example, if the fabric is 132" wide and the maximum width of fabric is 54", 132 ÷ 54 = 2.444, round up = 3 widths. The billable widths are 3.
- Banding, trims, ruffles, and similar decorations added to draperies are billed separately from the per-width base charge and are usually per foot or each.

RECOMMENDED FABRICS

- Most fabric types can be used for drapery. Medium weight usually provides the most desirable drape, hanging in nice, even folds.
- Bulky or upholstery weight fabric is usually not recommended (check with the workroom).
- Light weight fabrics will hang softly and flare. Sometimes interlining will need to be added to achieve a desirable drape.
- Lining gives light weight fabrics more body.
- Interlining gives the fabrics a more luxurious look.
- Voile sheers will not form a continuous pattern of the folds along the lower hem.
- Batiste sheers or heavier sheers will have a more definite pattern of the folds along the lower hem.

FABRIC FULLNESS RECOMMENDATIONS

- Light weight fabrics: 3x or fuller.
- Laces: 3x or less.
- Medium weight fabrics: 2.5x but usually suitable at any fullness.
- Bulky fabrics: 2x.
- Upholstery weight fabrics: 2x.

- Balance the above recommendations with the requirements for style fullness recommended by the workroom.
- If using a patterned fabric keep in mind that more fullness will hide the pattern. For example, if using a lace, reducing the fullness may better show the lace pattern.

TIPS WHEN MEASURING

- To ceiling – make sure hardware will allow drapery to go to ceiling.
- If sill length, measure just above sill approximately ½".
- Apron length – recommended 2" below wood molding under sill, or 5" below sill if there is no molding.
- To clear floor – ½" off floor is standard.
- Break on floor – add ½"-1".
- Puddle – add 2"-15".

Review

1) What are the characteristics of draperies and what are their primary functions?

2) What are the differences between full working and stationary drapes, detailing considerations for each when suggesting them to a client.

3) A client has a cathedral window in a west facing bedroom. Describe the treatment you would recommend, and give reasons for your suggestion.

4) Your client has a stunning mountain view and a wall of ceiling to floor length windows. What drapery treatment (if any) would you recommend and why?

5) If you are installing working sheer draperies and working pleated draperies on a DT, how far will the draperies project into the room? Show your working.

6) What are the benefits of lining draperies, and when should each type be used? Give examples.

7) Why is a floor length drapery stacked over a heating and air conditioning vent a problem? How can treatments be styled to avoid this problem?

ROD POCKET PANELS

The rod pocket panel is what has traditionally been known as a "curtain". Draperies are sometimes called "curtains" but by definition this is not correct. A rod pocket panel is an un-pleated, but shirred panel, while a drapery is a panel with a pleated or constructed top. Since the term "curtain" has become a somewhat interchangeable term for fabric panels and window covering products in general, it is defined here as rod pocket panels.

Rod pocket panels are shirred or gathered, usually onto a rod. Depending on the style one wishes to create with these panels, there are many different kinds of rods that can be used and they are sometimes even board mounted or mounted using hook and loop tapes. The most basic method used to hang them is through the use of a plain oval curtain rod, which is then covered by other curtains, drapes, or valances. Decorative and wide rod treatments can also be used.

Rod pocket panels are usually set up as stationary panels or side hangs because the shirred fabric is difficult to move across the rod. Sometimes they are set up as full panels covering an entire window, and in these cases there is often some type of tieback device to hold the panels open. In some instances, the panels are tied back during the day and closed at night. The drawback to this is that they can become quite wrinkled from being tied back, and when released and allowed to close, the creases then show and deform the hang of the panel.

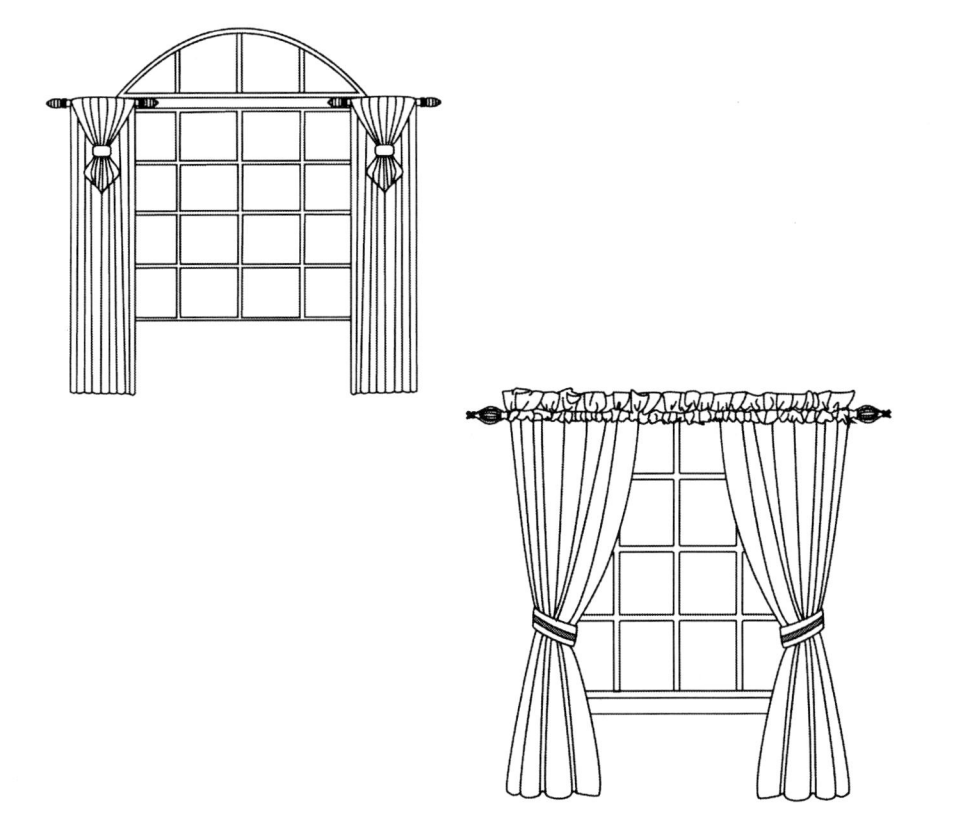

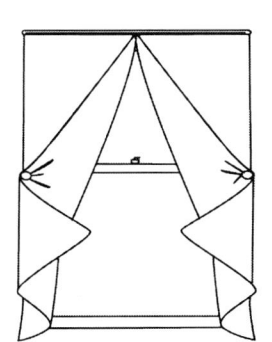

Elements of Soft Treatments

Rod Pocket Panels

Curtain lengths start around 36", and shorter treatments of this type are usually called valances. These panels can be café, sill, apron, or floor length. They can also be made as bishop sleeve panels, or they can break or puddle. All of these length variations allow this class of treatment to be versatile as a decorative element in a room. Curtain side hems will vary from being pillowcased in some cases to small shirt tail hems in others, all depending on the expected use and function of the panel. Bottom hem sizes can also vary, but are typically 4" double hems in a standard custom made curtain panel. Rod pocket panels will also be found with shirring at both the top and bottom instead of having a bottom hem.

There are business rules when talking about rod pocket panels. As with the other categories, when using the term "rod pocket panel", the designer is indicating to the workroom that the panel will be shirred, gathered or flat. Rod pocket panels can have a number of different mountings which, when installed, create the different curtain styles.

There are four basic gathered or shirred style set ups. These characteristics are the key element which all of these have in common.

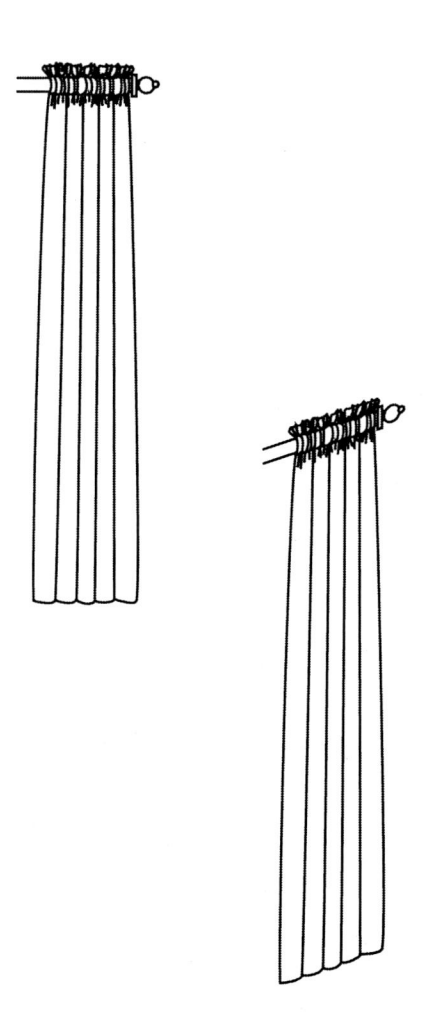

Rod pocket top only
These panels are gathered or shirred onto a rod, and this is the most common application for a rod pocket panel. The top of the panel has a sewn casing or pocket that is made to accommodate the insertion of a rod. The rods used for this style can vary. Depending on the rod used, the pocket or rod casing will be made in different sizes.

Rod pocket panels can be lined or unlined. This style can also be made with a "header" which is a flap of fabric which remains above the rod pocket and creates a ruffle when gathered onto the rod. The header is always above the rod, and is optional. Rod pocket headers can be used to close light gaps between the rod and ceiling in situations where the panel is mounted at the ceiling.

> A very narrow header of only ⅛" can be used to prevent the pocket from having a rounded effect. When installed, the panel appears not to have a header, but the pocket effect is more tailored and squared in appearance.

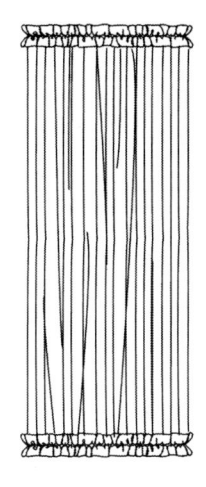

Rod pocket top and bottom

This type of panel is gathered or shirred onto the rod at both the top and the bottom. These types of panels are used in situations where the free movement of the panel at the bottom is not desired, such as on French doors, side lights, and transom windows. Rod pocket top and bottom panels can be lined or unlined, and they can be made with or without headers. The header is always to the outside of the rod.

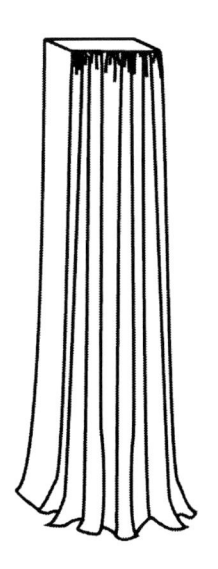

Unusual headings

There are some cases were the panel is shirred and mounted directly onto a board. These panels can be lined or unlined.

Occasionally, because of installation constraints or because the look of a rod is undesirable, the panel may be made without a rod pocket, and will be shirred and mounted directly onto a board, or sewn to hook and loop tape instead. By installing the panels in this manner, hardware and installation costs can be reduced. This method can also be useful when installing panels in tight situations where a curtain rod will not work, such as inside and ceiling mounts.

> Bear in mind, that the direct board mounted version is more difficult to clean as it can not be removed from the board.

Board mounts can be made so that there is a header effect if needed. In these situations some fabric is left above the board and the panels are attached to the face of the board. The board is installed with L-brackets, or the panel with loop tape sewn on can be attached to a "hook angle". This is a type of right angled PVC stock which comes with a hook tape already formed onto it. Hook angle and loop mounted panels are very tidy installations as side panels underneath board valances.

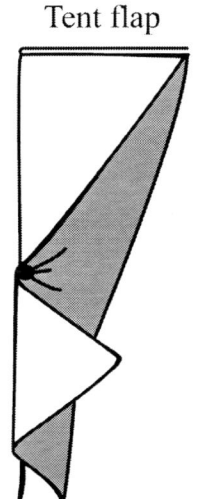

Tent flap

Flat panels, such as the tent flap style are also sometimes mounted in this way, and while they are not gathered or shirred, their classification is closest to being an unusual rod pocket curtain. When using board mounted panels, be careful if the treatment can be seen from above, such as in an open two story area. In this case, request that the top of the mounting board be covered in the main fabric. Check with the workroom as there is usually an additional charge for doing this and additional yardage will be required.

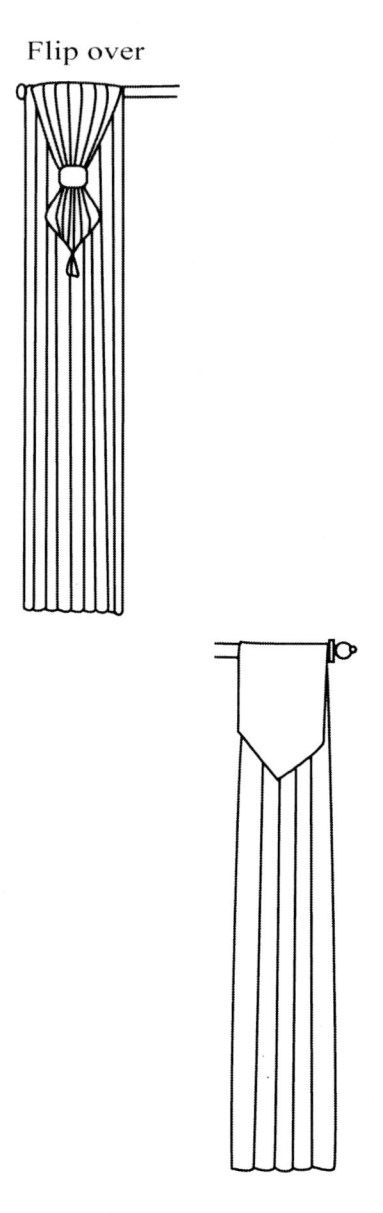

Flip over

Special set-ups

In this category of rod pocket panel styles, multiple layers of fabric are used to create different special effects. The panels are shirred and have an attached petticoat, flat panel, or shaped and reversed header which creates a self-valance effect. These embellishments are considered add-on units. In these situations, the attachment is sewn or attached directly to the panel as opposed to being a separately installed component.

There are three ways these can be mounted. Depending on the final appearance desired, one of these methods may work better than another.

First, using a rod pocket, whereby the petticoat, header, or flat pelmet is sewn to the rod pocket in such a way that it looks as if it was thrown over the rod. This method of mounting may allow the shirred panel to creep or spread open and not stay in place on the rod.

Second, the panel and petticoat or pelmet are seamed together, and then shirred to a piece of loop tape for attachment to the rod, giving the finished appearance of the panel as being shirred onto the rod.

Third, having both the panel and the pelmet made separately, attached to loop tape and then fastening them separately to the rod one behind the other. This method may be bulky.

ROD POCKET STYLE VARIATIONS

Rod pocket panels are extremely versatile window treatments and there are a vast number of ways to create different looks. Part of the reason these treatments are so popular is because they are relatively easy to manufacture when compared to drapery panels, which can often have complicated pleated tops.

Rod pocket curtains do not have the same restricted width as most pleated drapery styles, as the panel width can easily be changed simply by gathering the panel more tightly or loosely on the rod. Recognizing the simplicity of manufacture and versatility of the rod pocket style, hardware manufacturers have increased the variety of decorative curtain rod types available to add to the existing palette of rod pocket style possibilities.

While these rod pocket styles are easier and less labor intensive to make, the custom designer who provides installation with the treatment needs to keep in mind that they are usually more difficult to install. To some degree, the wide range of style choices in this window dressing category have been driven by the ready-made market which sells the treatments, but does not provide installation expertise. For this reason, there is a perception in today's market that these treatments will be inexpensive, and unfortunately the custom rod pocket is often no less expensive once installation is added into the formula. The interior designer must understand this evolution of the curtain, and often explain to clients the reason for the expense.

Some of the many variations are described below.

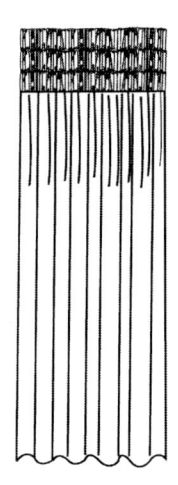

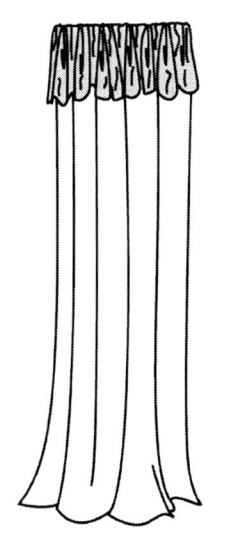

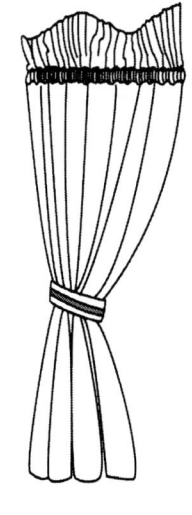

Multiple rod styles
This variation has been around for some time and combinations of this are still in use. When multiple rods are installed close to one another and the panel is made with multiple rod casings, the installed treatment takes on the appearance of a smocked panel. Several wide rods can be installed close together, with the panel sewn with one large pocket, and the resulting curtain appears to create its own shirred top treatment.

Header variations
Different looks can be obtained by changing the size and shape of the header. An extremely large, oversized heading will fall forward and create something of a soft valance effect. By putting a contrasting fabric on the reverse side, the "valance" is then quite attractive. Sometimes a stiffener, welt cord, or small wire can be encased into an oversized header to give the panel top a very full ruffled appearance. If the top of the header is shaped with a scallop or diamond pattern, the curtain will appear to have spires or tulips on top once it is shirred onto the rod. These types of variations work well on the flip over styles, as well shaping the pelmet for interesting effects.

Elements of Soft Treatments

Rod Pocket Panels

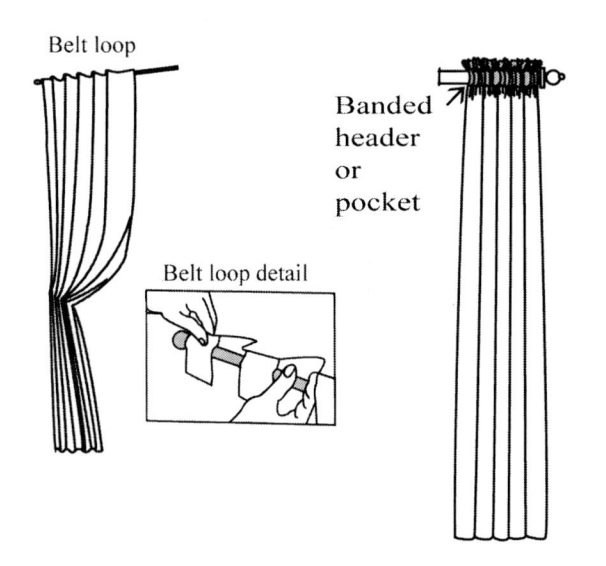

Belt loop

Banded header or pocket

Belt loop detail

Pocket variations

The pocket or pockets that encase the rod(s) can be different colors than the main fabric to make the panel heading or pocket appear banded. Belt loop style tabs can be added to the front of the casings allowing rods to show through and these can also be used to incorporate other colors.

ROD POCKET PANELS AND TAKE-UP

When rod pocket panels are gathered or shirred onto a rod, the overall drapery length will shrink or become shorter. This is because the fabric expands to encase the full circumference of the rod, and also the bulk of the fabric gathering causes the panel to become shorter. An allowance for this "take-up" needs to be added to the drapery's finished length when it is ordered so that the drapery panel, once hung is not too short. Appendix B has a chart showing the amount to be added to the finished length of the drape. This fabric take-up becomes especially critical in cases where the rod pocket panel goes from the ceiling to the floor, when the panel is inside mounted, or when there are rods at both the top and bottom of the panel.

> Do not use the rod size as the pocket size when rod pocket panels are ordered. Rod casings must be made larger than the rod to accommodate its full circumference and the bulk of the shirring. Information on rod pocket sizes for ordering is also included in Appendix B.

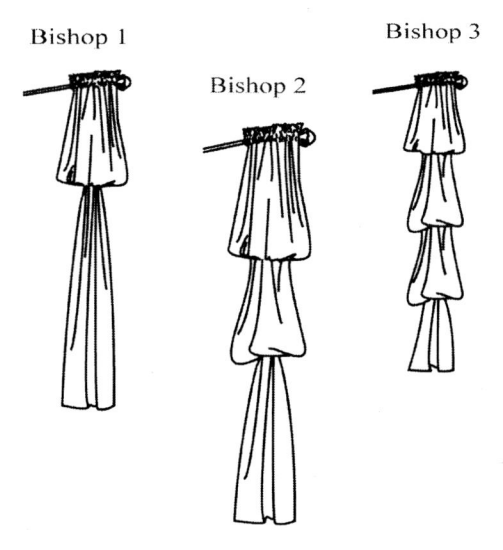

Bishop 1
Bishop 2
Bishop 3

Alternatively, there is a "bishop effect", which is a puffed look at approximately where the tieback goes. There can be multiple bishops, depending on the look that is desired. The bishop effect can be tied up using drapery cord, which is a small rope hidden by the bishop, or by creating a fabric covered tie. You will need approximately 12"- 20" for the allowances of each bishop

MEASURING FOR ROD POCKET PANELS

Measuring for rod pocket panels is done in much the same way as measuring for draperies. Measure the window opening and wall spaces around the window in a similar fashion to other treatments. After measuring, determine the panel's finished width and length. The finished panel length should always include the header if there is one, plus take-up (Appendix B).

Determining panel width

To begin designing the rod pocket panel treatment, first figure out how far past the window or trim to place the outside edge of the panel. Keep in mind that gathered panels remain stationary at the top and do not move like other drapery panels, so stacking space is not such a critical element.

For side panels, place the panels so they will appear to have the correct proportion to the window opening. Start with placement approximately 6"-10" past the window on each side and make the panels just wide enough to cover the trim, but no glass. This size panel will usually just frame the window nicely and works most of the time. If the aim is to make the room feel larger or smaller depending on the design, this extra width is discretionary. For panels that will cover the entire window, usually placement no more than 6" beyond the opening or trim works best. A scale drawing of the window helps to visualize panel placement and this is recommended any time proportion is in doubt.

The dimension from outside of the panel edge to outside of the panel edge will be the rod width. The panels may only cover a portion of this rod, so the panel width may be different from the rod width. For inside mounted curtains, take measurements inside the casing, one at the top and one at the bottom.

Finished length

After the panel width has been established, figure out how long to make the panels. Decide where the top of the panel will be mounted. Outside mounted treatments can be placed so the rod is just above the opening if minimum coverage is desired, but 4"-6" looks best. Adding the header will give the panel an appearance of being mounted higher, so knowing if a header will be used helps to determine height placement. If mounting close to the ceiling, allow for hardware, headers, and the bulk of the shirring process. If a tight fit against the ceiling will be required, the board mounted panel may be best option, and adjustments in length need to be made. Inside mounted curtains will require inside measurements. These are taken inside the window casing, one at each side of the window and middle measurements every three feet. Use the shortest dimension for the curtain length. Determine the panel length by measuring from the established point above the window and use the following guidelines for length.

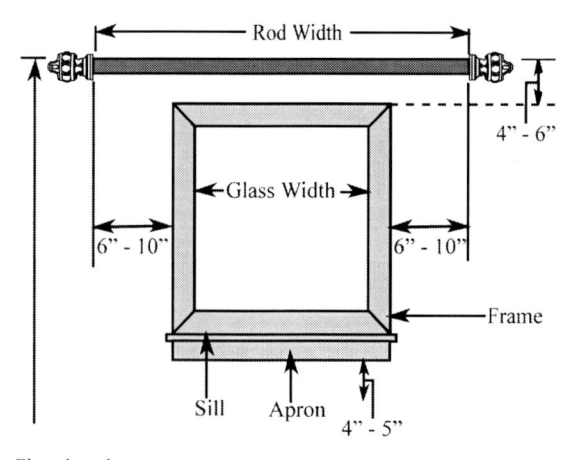

Rod Pocket Panels

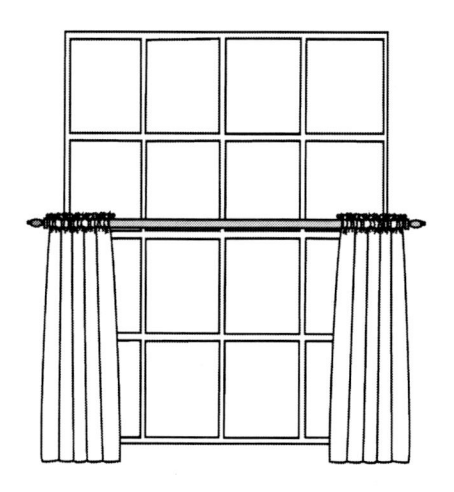

Sill length panels need to be measured to just above the sill, ½" or so. This length is typically used for an inside mounted panel. If outside mounted, a sill length will have some light leakage and can also look too short if the window is located above eye level.

Apron length panels should be measured to approximately 2" below the wood molding under the sill, or 4"-5" below the opening if there is no molding below the window. This length is most commonly used for shorter, more casual panels that are outside mounted.

Floor length panels should be measured to the floor, with a standard deduction for clearance of floor length panels of ½". If panels are ordered longer, there is the risk of having the drapery drag on the floor. Be clear with the workroom regarding their policies for deductions and correcting finished lengths.

Break on the floor requires adding an additional ½"-1" to the floor length measurement. Breaking lengths are most appropriate for soft fabrics, unlined curtain panels, or unstable fabrics such as crushed sheers which will not maintain an even length.

Puddle on the floor requires an additional 2"-15" to the floor length measurement to achieve an acceptable puddle.

> When ordering a rod pocket panel the finished length will always include the header, pocket, and rod take-up.

Café panels can be sill or apron length at the bottom but they cover a half or two-thirds of the lower portion of the window opening, thus creating privacy from below and still allowing a good deal of light into the room. Café length curtains are often coupled with a similarly styled valance at the top of the opening.

ROD POCKET PANELS ORDERING DETAILS

Below is a diagram of a typical rod pocket or gathered panel set up. When the work order is written for rod pocket panels it is helpful to be familiar with the terms used and what their meaning will be to the workroom.

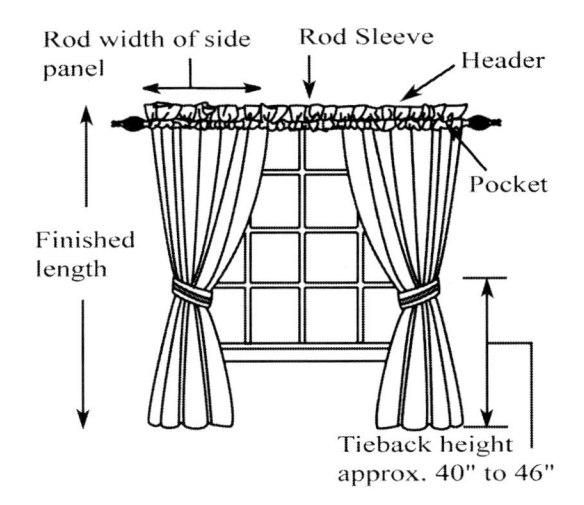

Panels, pairs, and fullness

When ordering a rod pocket panel, state the rod width as only the portion of the rod that will be covered by the panel itself. If there are two panels of exactly the same size they should be ordered as a pair, but remember to state the rod width x2, so there will be coverage for both halves. The workroom will know to divide by two in order to create the pair.

Deciding upon the desired fullness of each panel is necessary. Typical gathered panel fullness is about 2x for lined or heavy weight fabrics, 2½x for medium weight fabrics with lining, and 3x for sheer and light weight fabrics.

It is vital to instruct the workroom where the panel will be hanging at the window. The "stack" terminology is the same as for drapery panels even though gathered panels don't actually stack but are gathered and just hang in one place.

> A rod sleeve is a gathered fabric tube sometimes used to fill space on the rod (see rod pocket valances). Order these as if they were a curtain panel, except the finished length will be equal to the header, pocket, and rod take up only.

GATHERED PANELS AND RETURNS

Rod pocket panels and board mounted panels follow the same basic rules as drapery panels and other board mounted treatments and projections and clearances are the same. The difference that is important to remember is that rod pocket panels will have fullness that goes around the corners and on the returns as well as on the face of the board or rod. Sometimes this extra fullness will cause the treatment to require more fabric than a pleated panel.

The exception would be when using a decorative rod that has a finial on the end. In this case, special consideration must be taken with the planning of the return because the curtain fullness can not go around the corner as the pocket will not allow it. The curtain can be made without a return, but there may be a significant light gap, privacy issue, or problem of under treatments showing if there is no return on the panel. There are two different ways the return can be altered to allow the return to go around the corner: the buttonhole method and the return cut out.

Elements of Soft Treatments

Rod Pocket Panels

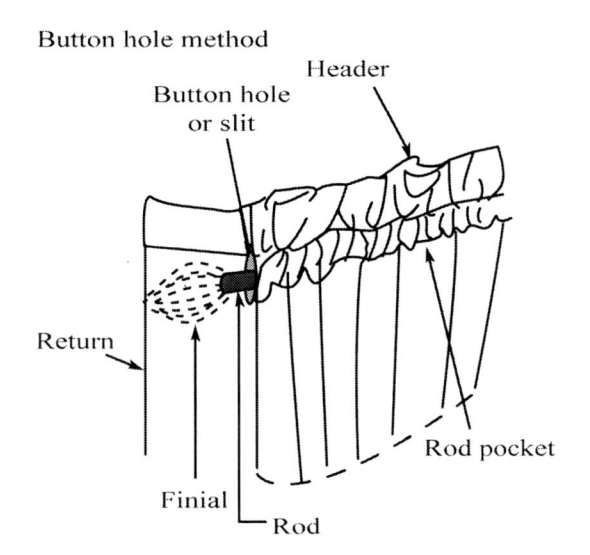

Buttonhole method

The workroom will cut a slit or buttonhole in only the front of the rod casing, which will allow the rod to pass through the casing and then the fabric, to continue around the corner to create the return. The return of the panel will still be flat with no fullness, but the panel will still appear to have a continuation of the header if there is one. In most cases, there is an additional charge to add this detail.

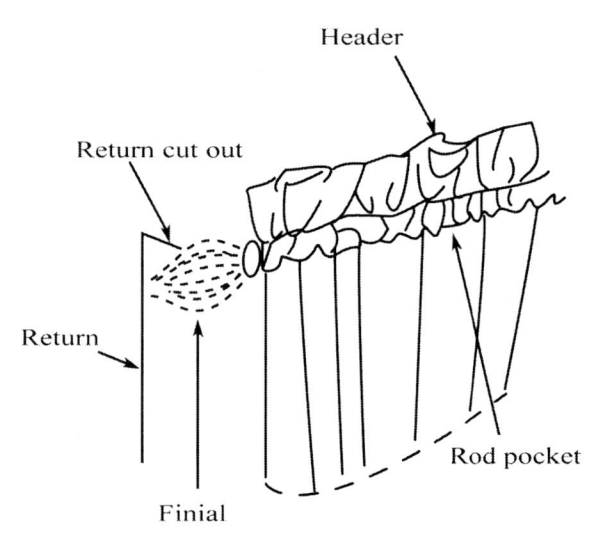

Cut out method

This method of creating a return will have a notch cut at the top of the panel which ends at the base of the casing and is the width of the return. The cut out creates a fabric flap that will fold around the corner and can be attached to the wall with a drapery hook thereby creating a return. The return will be flat, without any fullness. This method will also likely carry a labor surcharge.

Always be sure to discuss the various return detailing choices with the client. There are a wide variety of expectations with regard to light gaps and privacy issues because rod pocket panels usually do not have much stack allowance and they sit closer to the window. The return becomes especially critical if the curtain rod has a large projection or if the panel is expected to cover an under treatment.

LINING

Rod pocket panels should be lined much in the same way as other draperies, and for the same reason that a drapery panel would be lined. Panels from fabrics that are sheer, lace, or some light weight fabrics may be made unlined to serve certain design effects. Some styles, such as the tent flap, will require self or contrast lining as the reverse side is made to be exposed.

When adding lining, or interlining to a rod pocket panel, the additional layers of lining will add some bulk to the rod casing and may make the panel more difficult to gather onto the rod. To compensate for the extra bulk, order the rod casing a little bigger than the chart size shown in Appendix B.

SPECIAL WINDOW SHAPES

Rod pocket panels can always be adapted for special window shapes in much the same way as drapery panels. Sometimes the gathered panel can be a better solution than a drapery. They can often fit into smaller spaces than many of the drapery styles because they can go on smaller rods, be board or hook and loop mounted, abut directly against ceilings, or mount inside casings that are too small to accommodate a drapery rod.

Transom windows
Rod pocket panels can be a good solution for covering some odd shaped window openings. They will not be operable, but will do a good job of filtering light. Slanted top or slanted bottoms done as rod pocket panels can be a less expensive alternative for light control in these situations.

French doors
Because door windows are located in places where privacy is often an issue, rod pocket panels are often used to solve the problem. These panels are attached at the top and bottom of the door window and therefore do not interfere with the door operation as some other coverings might do.

Elements of Soft Treatments

Rod Pocket Panels

Swing arm rods

Rod pocket panels can be hung on special hardware which can be mounted onto doors, allowing the rod to swing open, and permitting the curtain to open and close independent of the door. This works well in situations where occasional privacy is desired and a full drapery is more coverage than may be needed.

GENERAL INFORMATION

- The header, pocket, and take-up are always included in the finished length.
- Fabrics are always pattern matched from width to width.
- Common heading sizes are 1", 2", or 3".
- Short headings work best with light weight fabrics, such as sheers.
- Add for take-up - when the fabric is gathered or shirred onto the rod, the overall drapery length will shrink Appendix B
- When shirring panels for pole type applications, do not expect the panel ends to wrap around the return unless a return cut out or buttonhole is specified.

PRICING

- Pricing for rod pocket panels is per flat fabric width not rod width.
- For railroaded fabrics, convert into widths in order to find the total labor cost.
- Add-on items such as ruffles, banding, and trim are charged for separately.

RECOMMENDED FABRICS

- Bulky or upholstery weight fabrics may not be suitable for some styles (check with the workroom).
- Medium to light weight fabrics work the best for rod pocket panels.
- Heavy fabrics increase the rod pocket size to accommodate the thickness of the fabric.
- Panels ordered with fullness greater than 3x may require a larger pocket, and will have more take-up. This is a critical point when inside mounted.

FULLNESS RECOMMENDATIONS

- Laces: 3x, 2x, or less if the pattern is to be prominently displayed.
- Medium weight fabrics: 2.5x.
- Bulky fabrics: 2x.
- Upholstery weight fabrics: 2x or less.
- If the fabric has a pattern, keep in mind that increased fullness will hide the pattern. For example, if using a lace, reduce the fullness to better show the lace design.
- Upholstery fabrics or chenille may have no fullness if a "flat pelmet" effect is desired (see Add-ons chapter 14).

Review

1) What characteristics of this type of panel distinguish it from drapery type panels?

2) If a curtain panel is to open and close, what add-on item must be included and why?

3) What is the major benefit of a header?

4) Is the header included in the finished length? Explain.

5) Rod take-up will have what effect on the finished curtain length?

6) In what situations is a rod pocket top and bottom panel more appropriate than a rod top only?

TOPPERS

Toppers are similar to drapery valances and rod pocket valances, except they are mounted onto a board by either stapling or by the use of a hook and loop tape across the top edge of the board. They are normally mounted above the window, and usually go all the way across the top of the opening. The hardware required to hang them are L-brackets or angle irons.

There are business rules when talking about toppers, just like the other categories. When using the term "toppers", you are instructing the workroom that the valance will be board mounted.

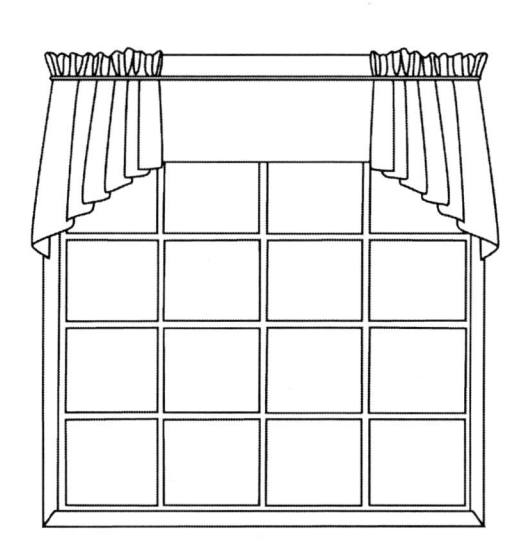

Elements of Soft Treatments

Toppers

TOPPER STYLES

Toppers are divided into six basic types. Whilst toppers are a non working valance, some types have the same names as fabric shades. The basic types are as follows:

Balloons
This style has a pouf effect along the bottom, and fullness is added in both width and length similar to a balloon shade. The fabric will wrap around the mounting board on the ends.

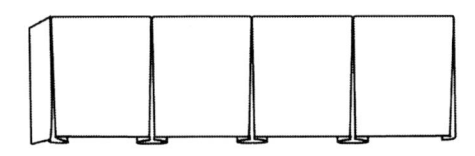

Pleated
This topper has a pleated effect, with fullness in the width only. The fabric wraps around the mounting board on the ends.

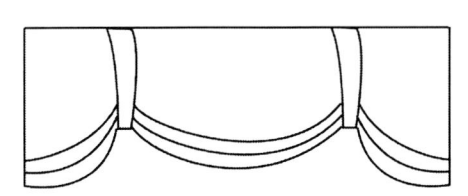

Pull-ups and Roll-ups

Pull-ups
These are either tied up from the bottom with ties or are hand stitched from the back side. This creates a swag or droop effect. This style will have end boards called hard returns in order for the valance to hold its shape.

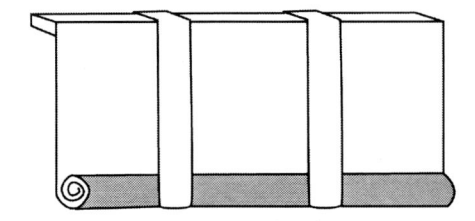

Roll-ups
These toppers are where the fabric is rolled at the bottom, usually onto a tube or dowel. Typically some type of tie is added. The fabric does not wrap around the ends of the board with this style and if made to do so, it will change the look of the valance. Sometimes a fabric flap called an end cap can be used to cover the ends of the mounting board.

Chapter 3

Roman
This style is more flat without any fullness in the width. Fullness is added in the length of the valance. With the flat Roman style, folds are at the bottom only and are stitched in place from the back, or rings are stitched to the reverse side and the fabric is drawn up by strings to the finished length. The fabric may or may not wrap around the mounting board on the ends. If it does, then a hard return is needed.

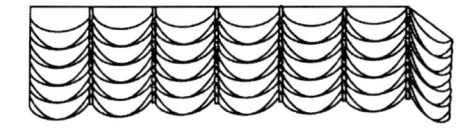

Austrian
These are frequently made from a sheer or light weight fabric, and this style is very soft and formal in appearance. The fabric will wrap around the ends of the mounting board on this style. The use of a hard return is usually required for the valance to hold its shape. The minimum mounting board projection on this style is 3½".

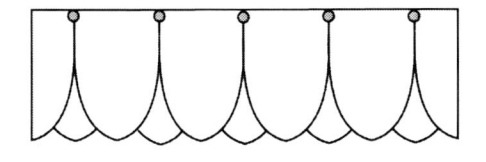

Specialty
This category describes any topper that has a distinctive appearance. These designs require more effort to figure yardages, and often will need patterns drafted before construction. Depending on the style, the returns may wrap around on the ends. A hard return maybe needed depending on the style, or the use of an end cap will be required to cover the mounting board. Expect additional workroom charges for these types of designs.

STYLE VARIATIONS

There are many ways to change the appearance of the basic topper style by varying some aspect of the construction. Some common variations are as follows:

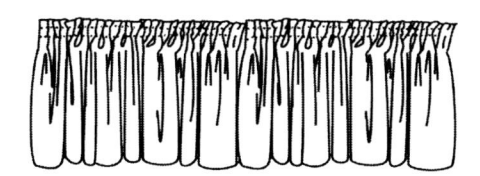

Heading tapes
A variation of the balloon, this topper is made by using some type of shirring tape along the upper edge, which can sometimes also have a header. Shirring tapes can add interest to the topper style, such as smocking or deep gathered headers. When board

Elements of Soft Treatments

Toppers

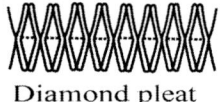

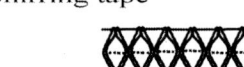

Shirring tape
Diamond pleat
Double diamond pleat

mounted, the header or part of the header is often above the board and is included in the finished length. The part that is shirred or gathered is stapled onto the edge of the board, or there can be loop tape sewn onto the topper which then attaches to the edge of the board which has hook tape on it.

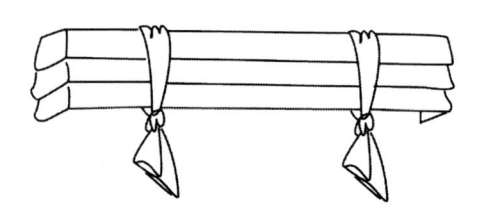

Hobble
The Roman style can be varied by adding multiple folds which are horizontal, fixed, and evenly sized. This is similar to a hobble shade, except it is stationary. The fabric may or may not wrap around the ends of the board. If it does, then a hard return is needed so the valance will retain its shape.

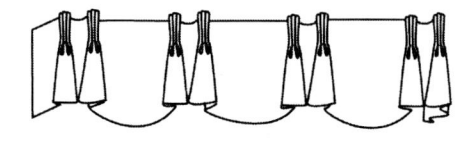

Varied pleat sizes
Different combinations of pleat spacing and sizes can also be used to change the look of the topper and many interesting effects can be achieved.

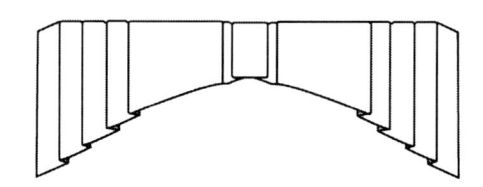

Shaped bottoms
The bottom of the topper is shaped along the lower hem. This variation can be specified on the work order.

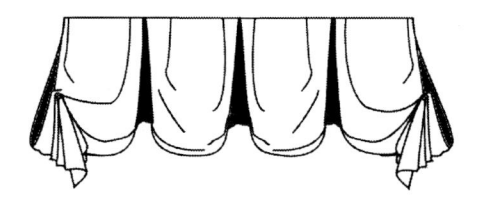

Add-on items
Like all categories, topper styles can be varied through the use of add-on items. Pictured is a box pleated balloon topper with contrast color insets. This is an ingenious way to incorporate an additional fabric into the design. Trims, cording, banding, bows, buttons, and rosettes are just a few of the common add-ons used with toppers.

SHAPED BOTTOM DETAILS

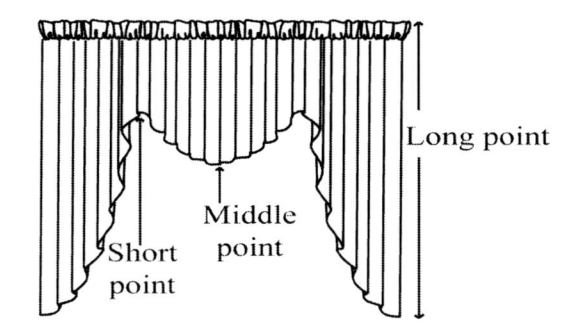

If the topper is shaped along the bottom, a long point, middle point, and short point will need to be specified on the work order.

If there are more than three points of varying lengths, a diagram showing the dimensions is recommended. Indicate the dimensions in the fashion shown on the diagram below.

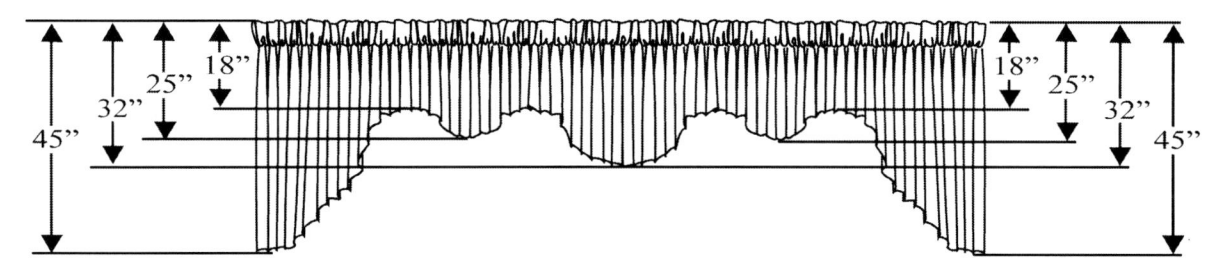

LINING AND FACING OPTIONS

There are four different methods for finishing toppers that are shaped along the bottom. Each method has advantages and disadvantages, and it is the responsibility of the treatment designer to decide which method is the most appropriate for each design.

Self-lined is where the face fabric is used on the reverse side. This is the most commonly used method and will be suitable in most design situations. There are some scenarios where this would not be an appropriate method. These would include cases where the fiber content or the color of the face fabric were not sun tolerant or if it would not be suitable to see the design and color of the face fabric from the back side. In these situations, it is better to use a different fabric for the lining. This is called "contrast lining".

> When a valance is contrast lined, the face fabric may change color due to what is called "bleed through". This can also happen if the contrast fabric has a pattern which may then show through. To avoid this, interline the valance. However the drawback to this is that it can make the valance bulkier and may not drape as nicely as a result.

Elements of Soft Treatments

Shirt tail hem

This is where the bottom edge is turned under approximately ¼"-½", and is then top stitched along the edge. This method is most appropriately used when the topper is unlined and the face and reverse side of the fabric look almost the same. With this method, the bottom is cut to the required shape which can be on the bias grain of the fabric. When the edge is rolled over and top stitched, a ripple effect can occur due the bias cut. This is called "roping" and is generally an undesirable effect.

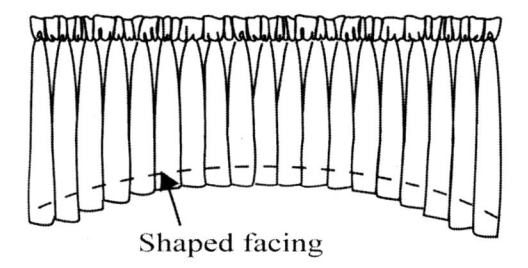

Shaped facing

On the reverse of the valance, there is a strip of fabric approximately 2" wide following the shape of the valance hem. The length of this strip is determined by the long, short, and middle points of the valance. This option is the best choice when a high quality custom finish is desired, or in situations where the valance will be visible from both sides and self lining is not appropriate. A window facing the front of the house would be an example of this. Because this method is labor intensive, there will usually be significant additional labor charges for manufacture, and additional fabric yardage will be required.

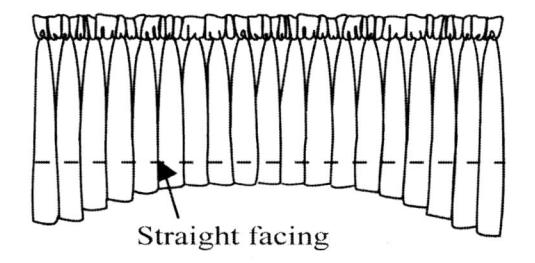

Straight facing

On the reverse, there is a strip of fabric approximately 2"-3" above the shortest point of the valance that extends horizontally and is parallel with the top of the valance. This method would be ordered in a situation where it is not appropriate to self-line the topper. A light or sun sensitive face fabric such as silk, or a bright color that would fade over time due to sunlight, would be two examples of such a situation.

> Be careful when using this method for a thin or light colored fabric because the shadow line of the facing can be obvious. Interlining can minimize this effect but the bulkiness might become a problem depending on the topper style.

MEASURING FOR TOPPERS

The information here represents industry minimum or suggested requirements. Asses the individual situation and adjust the measurements according to the desired impact of the design and the preferences of the client.

When determining proportion, all of the elements of the treatment should be considered. If the topper is mounted over ceiling to floor length draperies, include the length of the draperies in the formula; if mounting over blinds or shades, include the shade length in calculating the desired topper length. As with all design, this is only a guideline, and the proportions can be varied for dramatic effects or if architectural elements in the room dictate its being different.

To specify a topper treatment, first determine board face width, topper finished length, and required projection.

To find the board face width

Measure a minimum of 2" beyond each side of the opening, window trim, drapery rod, blind, or under treatment. If there are any under treatments be sure to allow enough room for them to operate without interference from the fabric topper.

To determine the finished length

Two good rules to follow to find the finished length of the toppers are as follows:

Ceiling mounted

Overall finished length of the window treatment (including undertreatments) ÷ 5, + 2".
This will equal the recommended topper finished length.

> Example: 108 ÷ 5 = 21.6 (round up) = 22 + 2 = 24".
> This is the recommended finished length of the top treatment.

Above the window

Overall finished length of the window treatment (including undertreatments) ÷ 6, + 2".
This will equal the recommended topper finished length.

> Example: 84 ÷ 6 = 16.8 (round up) = 17 + 2 = 19".
> This is the recommended finished length of the top treatment.

To re-measure for accuracy, take a tape measure and place it where the top of the topper was measured from and recheck the length to ensure it looks balanced and is in proportion to the room.

> If re-measuring is not possible because the project is only in the planning stages and work is being done from blueprints, a scale drawing is recommended to check balance and proportion.

Elements of Soft Treatments

TOPPER RETURNS AND PROJECTIONS

There are two types of returns used with toppers.

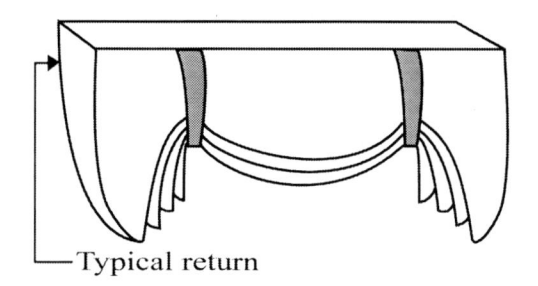

Typical return
This is on a topper consisting of a fabric flap that wraps around the end of the board to cover the gap between the valance face and the wall.

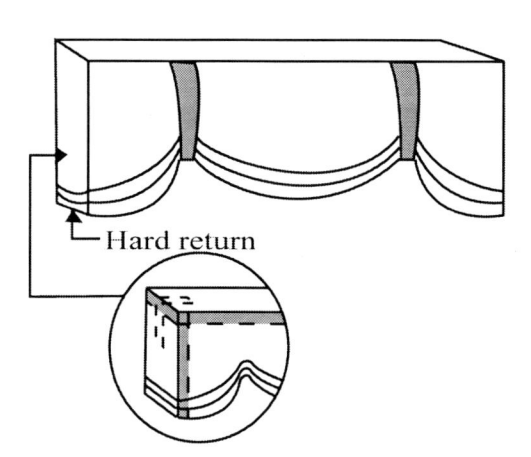

Hard return
This is created by adding a side board that is the same width as the top board, and which is held in place with screws and L-brackets on the inside. This helps the return hold its shape. A hard return would be used when the topper is going over another outside mounted product which requires the full board width to allow it to operate, or if the style dictates the use of a hard return. Most of the time, the workroom will have a labor surcharge for making hard returns.

To determine the required projection (return)

In determining the projection needed for the topper design, the first thing that needs to be considered is the absence or presence of any under treatments. The topper projection needs to be 1½" greater than the maximum projection of the under treatments. In other words, under treatment projections must be calculated first, then 1½" is added to that measurement to get the topper projection. In the case of some hard treatments, such as vertical blinds, be sure to consider the projection of the item in all operating positions: open, closed, louvers tilted, and closed.

The desired projection once calculated will normally be the "return" measurement that will need to be ordered. Remember, the workroom will think of the return in terms of the fabric used to cover the mounting board projection. This distinction is important to understand because sometimes, in order to fit in and around window and cabinet moldings, the return may be larger or smaller than the board projection. In these instances this distinction needs to be made clear to the workroom on the work order.

Topper style should also be considered. If it is one that will lay fairly flat once constructed and installed, the projection will not need to be as great as a topper that will be bulky, such as a balloon type.

When calculating projections, always remember that more is better than less. Extra room can always be filled by adjusting hardware. If there is not enough room for the under treatments to operate under the topper, the item may need to be completely re-made resulting in a lot of unnecessary expense.

> Use caution when determining the finished width of a topper with hard returns because the inside width will be approximately 1½" smaller than the face width due to the thickness of the boards used for the hard returns.

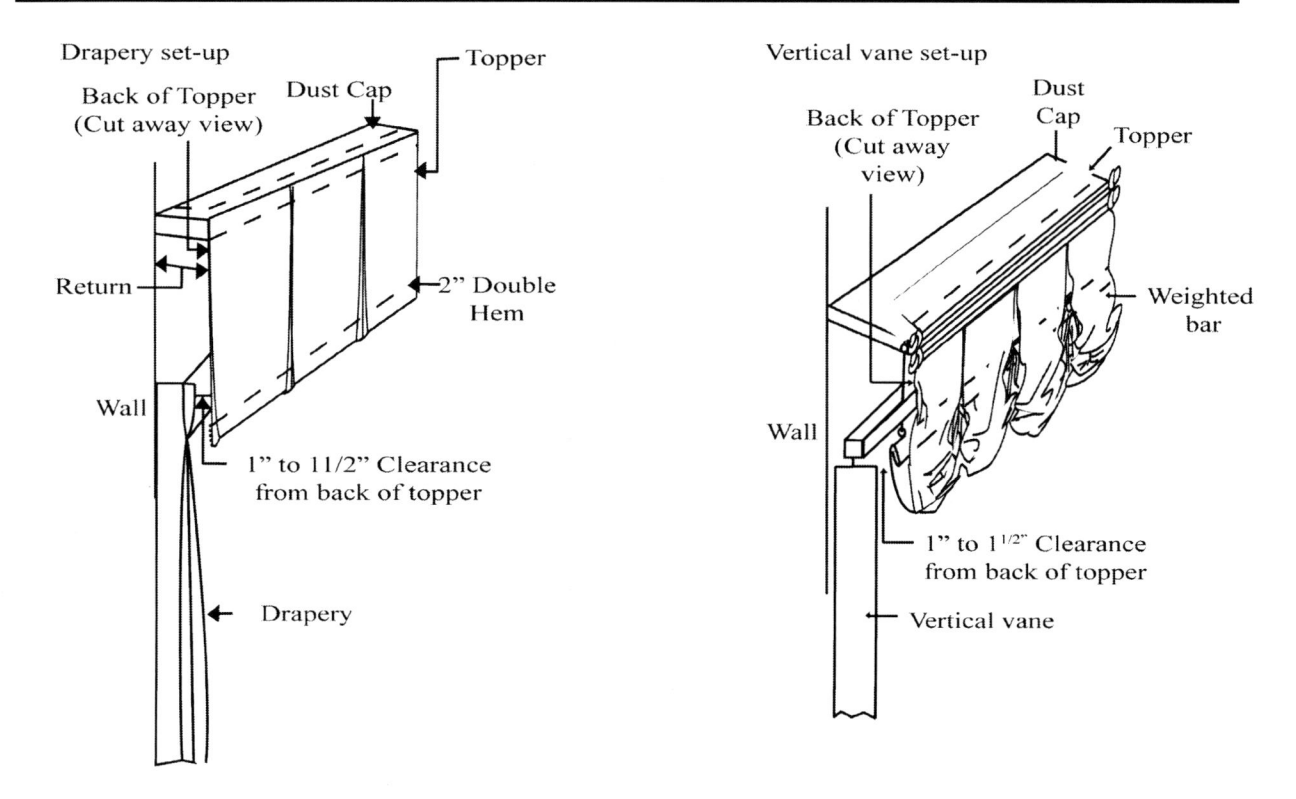

TOPPER MOUNTING METHODS

There are four methods by which toppers can be mounted onto the board.

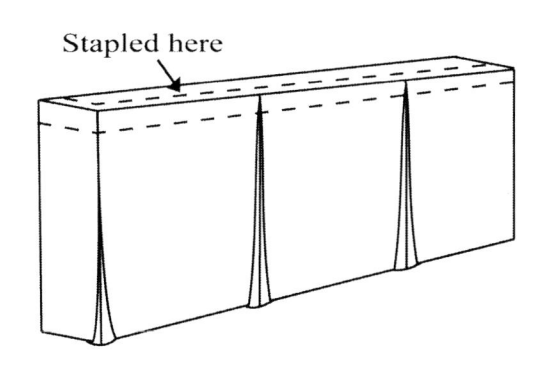

Typical board mount
This is where the treatment is mounted onto a board, and is stapled to the top. The white lining from the board is then wrapped and stapled to the top, approximately ½" from the edge of the board.

Elements of Soft Treatments

Toppers

> If the top of the board will be visible from above, such as over a stairwell, instruct the workroom to cover the top of the board with the same fabric as the face of the valance. Additional yardage will be required for this. Ask the workroom for yardage requirements.

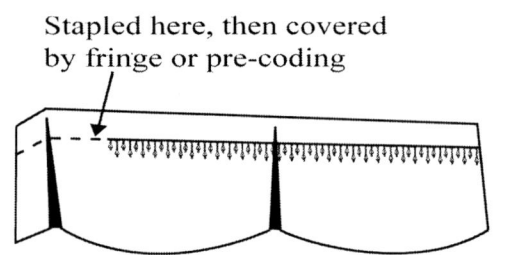

Stapled here, then covered by fringe or pre-coding

Typical edge board mount
The treatment is stapled to the leading edge of the board and the staples are visible. The staples are then covered by a welt, pre-cording, or fringe.

> With this style of mounting, some of the topper face width will usually project above the board. This can be very little, or a lot, depending on the topper style. Be sure to take this into account when measuring and figuring for installation.

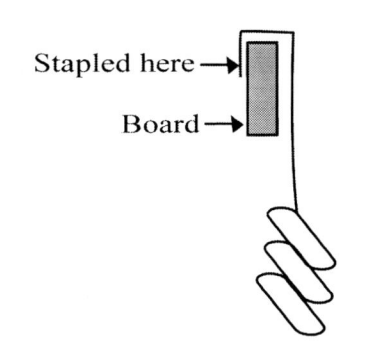

Stapled here
Board

Flat board mount
The topper is mounted onto a 1×2 which is laid flat. The true size of the board is ¾"x1½". This mounting method is used when minimum clearance from the wall is desired, usually when there is no under treatment, or if the under treatment is mounted inside the window casing and does not need room to operate.

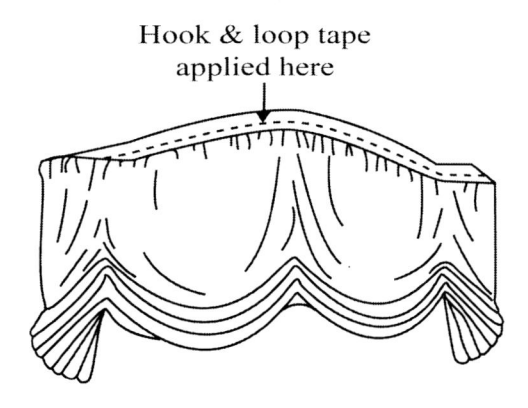

Hook & loop tape applied here

Hook and loop board mount
The valance is attached using the methods described above, except hook and loop tape is used instead of stapling. The loop side of the tape is sewn to the top of the treatment and the hook side of the tape is stapled onto the board. This type of mounting is used in situations where the permanent attachment of the valance to the board is not desirable, such as for frequent cleaning, or ease of installation. Not all styles will work with this type of mount. Check with the workroom to be sure this method will work, and be aware that there is usually a labor surcharge for using this mounting method.

Chapter 3

SPECIAL WINDOW SHAPES

In the course of design work, it is likely that windows with shapes other than the basic rectangle will be encountered, and in fact odd shapes and configurations are quite common. Most of the time, the topper can be adapted to fit these odd shapes. All of the same basic rules regarding toppers apply even when the window shape changes. Once the basic rules have been mastered, it becomes quickly apparent when a situation is encountered that excludes the use of a certain style.

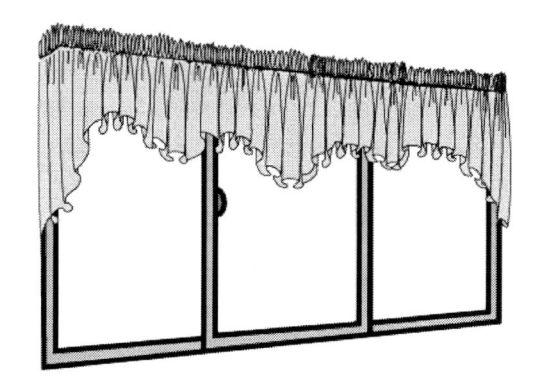

French doors and sliding doors
When designing a treatment with a topper to be installed over a door be sure that the long point of the topper allows sufficient clearance from the floor to allow an average size person to walk through the opening without brushing their head on the valance. Also be sure the long point of the topper does not interfere with the opening and closing of the door.

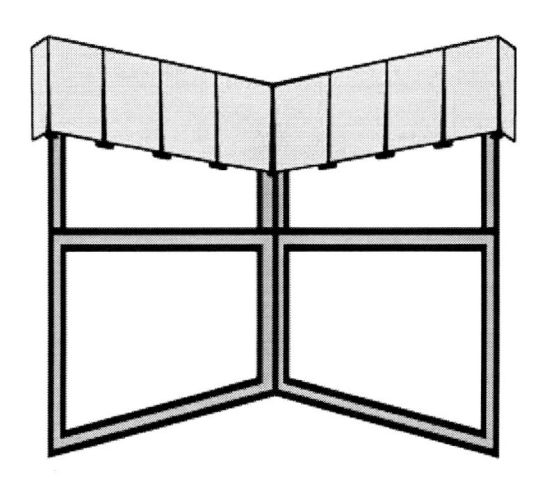

Bay and corner windows
Corner window configurations have a lot of variables with regard to size and available wall space for toppers. When designing a topper treatment for a bay or corner window measure all of the dimensions carefully. Sometimes the dimensions of these windows can limit the type of topper treatment that can be used, or the topper construction may require some extensive modification to achieve a satisfactory result. These situations will become apparent when a scale drawing of the treatment is made.

Arch windows
Most types of toppers can be adapted to go over an arch top opening. Check the dimensions carefully, and do a scale drawing of the intended topper. When the design is drawn to scale, problems such as patterns or style elements being lost in the arc of the arch will quickly become apparent.

Elements of Soft Treatments

GENERAL INFORMATION

- Not all topper styles wrap around the returns. Use end caps to cover the return ends of the board in these cases.
- State on the work order if the topper is wall to wall mounted.
- State on the work order to make allowance for the welt if wall to wall mounted.

PRICING

- Toppers are usually priced by the linear foot.
- There is usually a minimum charge per linear foot (per unit).
- Face width of board + both returns ÷ 12, round up = number of linear feet and also is the billable footage (e.g. 100 + (3.5 × 2 =7) = 107 ÷ 12 = 8.91 round to 9').
- Topper style add-ons such as banding and ruffles are billed separately, usually per linear foot of the specific add-on (not linear foot of topper).
- Topper style add-ons such as bows and buttons are billed separately, usually per each item.

RECOMMENDED FABRICS

- Soft-handed satins, polyesters, laces, and sateen weaves work the best for most toppers.
- Stiff chintz, harsh linens, or crisp cottons will sometimes have handling wrinkles. This is caused by sewing and turning of the fabric during manufacturing.
- Use crisper fabrics for Roman styles.
- Use light-weight fabrics for Austrian styles.
- Heavy weight and upholstery fabrics are not suitable for most styles.

FULLNESS RECOMMENDATIONS

- Ask the workroom to provide fullness recommendations for individual styles.
- Ask to see a sewn sample of the style being requested from the workroom.

TIPS WHEN MEASURING

- Measure 6" above the window to mount toppers.
- When mounting above a drapery (full working or stationary), measure a minimum of 1" above the drapery or hardware that is being used.
- When mounting over a blind only or an inside mounted shade, mount the topper at least 6" above the window or under treatment so the topper will have enough length to look proportionate and not cover too much of the window opening.
- If the topper is to go to the ceiling, make sure the hardware that is being used will allow it to fit against the ceiling.

- If hardware or shirring tape has been attached that will project above the mounting board, be sure to allow room for them to fit when installing the topper close to the ceiling, beams, or other obstructions.
- Be cautious with treatments that require hard returns.
- Allow face width to extend 1½"-2" on each side of the under treatment.
- Allow returns to extend 1½"-2½" to clear the under treatment.
- For shaped bottom toppers provide a labeled diagram for the workroom.

Review

1) Describe what differentiates a topper from other kinds of valances.

2) When measuring for a topper, which measurements are the most important and which is the least critical and why?

3) Describe the two ways toppers are normally mounted. When would there be an exception?

4) When would a hard return be necessary? Discuss.

5) A customer has chosen a shaped bottom topper from a delicate silk fabric. Which finishing method would you select and why?

6) If the ceiling to floor measurement is 10' and the window treatment is from ceiling to floor, what length of topper should be ordered? Show your working.

7) Outline the steps for adapting a topper style to fit into a bay window.

DRAPERY VALANCES

A drapery valance is a panel or panels of fabric used above the window primarily to create a decorative effect. They can also sometimes be used for the function of hiding the hardware of under treatments and to help close light gaps. Drapery valances are mounted above or around the window, are made to enhance the shape of the window and they will typically go all the way across the top.

The heading, or top, has some type of constructed detailing, consisting of pleats, tabs, rings, or other unusual features that allow attachment to mounting hardware. The hardware used can be as creative as the designer and client desire. It can be any sort of rod, medallions, knobs, twigs, finials, or other creative items can be used or converted for attachment to the wall or window to support the valance. The bottom of a drapery valance can be shaped or tied in many different ways to create a virtually endless variety of styles.

Business rules governing the term drapery valance dictate that when this treatment is specified, the fabric will be hung from some type of rod, hooks, or other supplemental hardware attachment. On occasion due to practical or installation necessity, a drapery valance can be supplied with a board for mounting, but the specification would then become a drapery valance converted for board mounting. The drapery valance hangs straight from its attachment much like a drapery and does not have a swag effect.

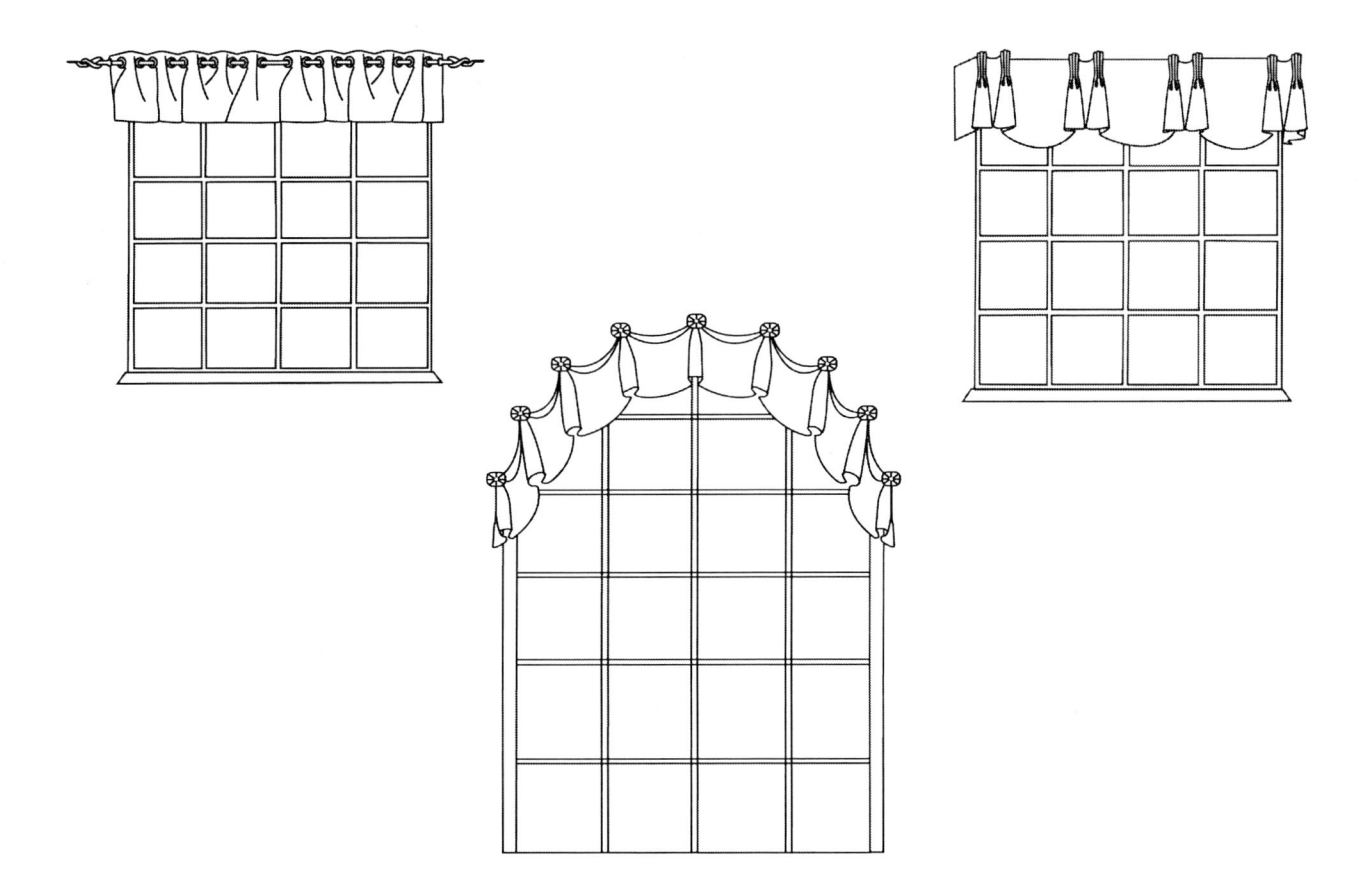

Elements of Soft Treatments

Drapery Valances

DRAPERY VALANCE HEADING/BOTTOM STYLE COMBINATIONS

Drapery valance headings are essentially shorter versions of the drapery heading styles and are divided into the same basic categories: pleated tops, soft tops, tab tops, and unusual headings. The special set ups version of the drapery is also available as a drapery valance, again with the fabric layers being proportionately shorter. The drapery valance takes on its sense of style mainly through variations in valance bottom detailing combined with interesting heading styles and hardware. Drapery valance hems can be straight, scalloped, arched, M-shaped, or any combination of these. Hem shaping details, lining, and facing options are essentially the same as for topper bottoms. Some examples of the currently more popular drapery valances are shown below.

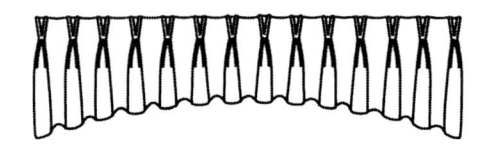

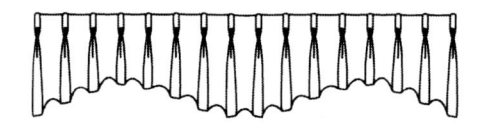

Pleated tops/shaped bottom

Any of the pleated tops can be made with bottom shaping to make an interesting valance style. The ever popular arch and M shape are some examples, and reverse arches and reverse M shapes can be a fun variation of these two popular styles. To get an idea of what they would look like, imagine the valances pictured on the left with their bottom shapes upside down.

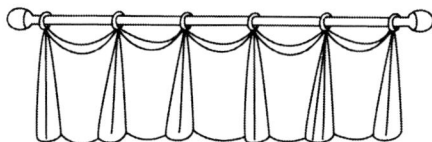

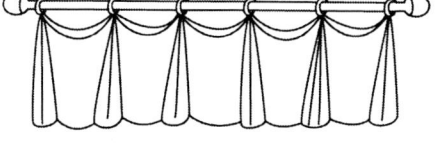

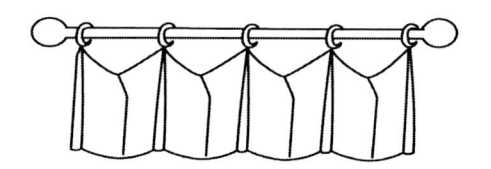

Soft top/straight bottom

Some of the soft top styles create their own hemline shaping simply due to the fabric drape when hung. Because the fabric is shortened to a valance length, this droop will affect the length, creating something of a long and short point even though the valance is actually manufactured straight across the bottom, Depending on the spacing of the pleats and rings, a gap will be created between the rod and top of the valance as well.

When mounting the valance, ensure that the mounting height is high enough to cover under treatments, window moldings, and trim that may show through this gap. These gaps and the amount of the droop can be varied on soft top styles, so they should be considered casual, and expect less structure when using these for valances.

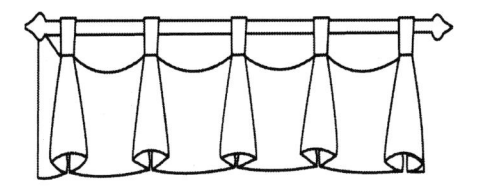

Tab top/scalloped bottom

Tab styles can have scalloped spacing with plain or fancy tabs. In these examples, the scallop is created from a pattern. When the scallop or droop is manufactured this way, it is easier to control the amount of gap between rod and valance, and also long and short points are more manageable. These styles tend to be more tailored than the soft tops.

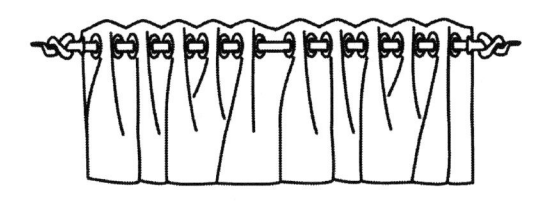

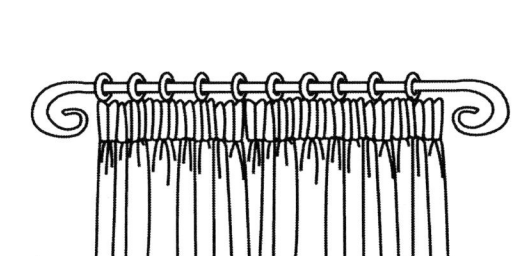

Unusual headings and special set ups

Drapery valances can be made with all sorts of unusual headings in addition to the ones mentioned above, through the use of add-on items such as sewn on rings, grommets, shirring tapes, petticoats, and so on. Generally speaking, when a drapery style is created, the same thing can be done with a valance.

MEASURING AND ORDERING DRAPERY VALANCES

Measuring for drapery valances is done in much the same way as one would measure for toppers. The valance face width, finished length, and projection must be determined.

Once the dimensions are determined, drapery valances are ordered in much the same way as drapery panels, except a drapery valance is almost always a center panel. Specify the desired heading and bottom style. If the bottom is shaped, specify the short and long points, along with lining or facing options as would be done for a topper.

> Many drapery workrooms will have pre-established names and/or numbers for many of the popular drapery valance styles. If the workroom can provide style names and samples, use their trade descriptions when ordering.

Elements of Soft Treatments

49

Drapery Valances

To find the valance face width and rod width

Measure out 3" from each side of the opening or trim if the treatment will be hung over a window with no under treatments, or an inside mounted under treatment. If the drapery valance will be going over an outside mounted under treatment, 2" beyond either side of the under treatment should be adequate.

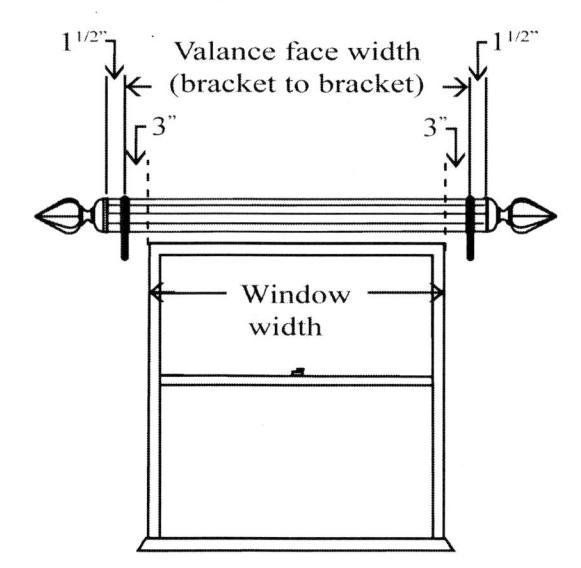

The dimension will be the valance face width, and also the "bracket to bracket" measurement if a decorative rod is being used. This is the dimension that will be required for ordering the valance, plus returns if any.

For the rod width, add 2"-3" to the face width if a decorative rod is being used. This allows space for rod end brackets to be mounted. Consideration of the face width, rod width, and length of finial, are important at this point, so be sure there is sufficient wall space to fit everything in.

To find the finished length

Follow the same rules applicable to measuring for a topper. In review, this procedure is basically the same for all top treatments and is used in many circumstances, but remember that these are still only guidelines. Adjust for client preference, architectural elements, or design impact as needed.

First, when determining proportion, all of the elements of the treatment should be considered. If the drapery valance is mounted over ceiling to floor length draperies, include the full length of the draperies in the formula; if mounting over blinds or shades, include the shade in its lowered position when calculating the desired valance length.

Second, the two basic rules to follow to find the finished length of the valance are as follows:

For ceiling mounted

Overall finished length of the window treatment (including under treatments) ÷ 5, + 2". This will equal the recommended valance finished length.

> Example: 108 ÷ 5 = 21.6 (round up) = 22 + 2 = 24".
> This is the recommended finished length of the top treatment.

For above the window

Overall finished length of the window treatment (including under treatments) ÷ 6, + 2". This will equal the recommended valance finished length.

Example: 84 ÷ 6 = 16.8 (round up) = 17 + 2 = 19".
This is the recommended finished length of the top treatment.

To re-measure for accuracy, take a tape measure and place it where the top of the drapery valance was measured from and recheck the length to ensure it looks balanced and in proportion to the room.

> If re-measuring is not possible because the project is only in the planning stages and work is being done from blue prints, a scale drawing is recommended to check balance and proportion.

Drapery valance projection

When calculating the projection for a drapery valance, begin as with toppers by considering any under treatments. The drapery valance needs to project approximately 1½" beyond the under treatment. Check that available drapery hardware will accommodate the needed projection. Sometimes decorative hardware will not allow for as much projection as may be desired over some treatment combinations, and in these cases, the projection and return sizes of all treatment components may need to be altered to accommodate the hardware. When doing these types of adjustments, remember to discuss any potential clearance issues with the client, as using less clearance may create difficulty in operation with some items, such as vertical blinds. Critical clearance issues may cause this to be an instance where a drapery valance may need to be board mounted rather than using a rod. If there is any doubt about whether a particular drapery valance style can work as a board mount, ask the workroom. Many soft top styles can't be done as board mounted valances and another style may need to be specified.

SPECIAL WINDOW SHAPES

As with most other treatments, drapery valances can be made to fit most special window shapes. Drapery hardware and its limitations is one of the main considerations when trying to fit some odd shaped windows. Drapery rod manufacturers tend to think in terms of small rectangular window shapes and sometimes some very clever design work is needed in order to make certain types of hardware work. This is particularly the case with decorative rods.

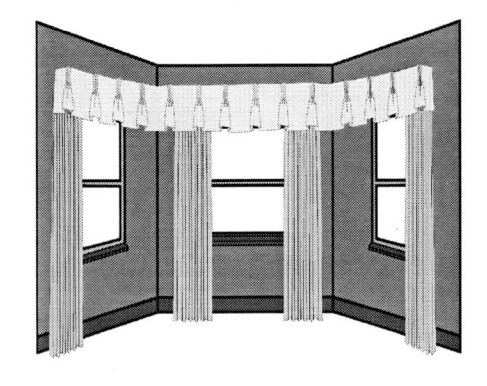

Drapery Valances

Bay windows
Plain curtain rods are probably the most odd shape friendly type of rod because they come in long lengths and can be bent with a fair amount of ease. Valance rods can be ordered custom bent to fit bay and corner configurations, or an extremely good installer will be able to bend them on site at the time of installation. Once the rod is configured to fit the shape, the valance is easily hung as if on any other window.

The potential draw back to a plain rod, is that they are unattractive and the valance style will have to be one which conceals the rod. These types of styles tend to be a more structured and if a casual look is desired, a plain rod installation may not be to the client's liking.

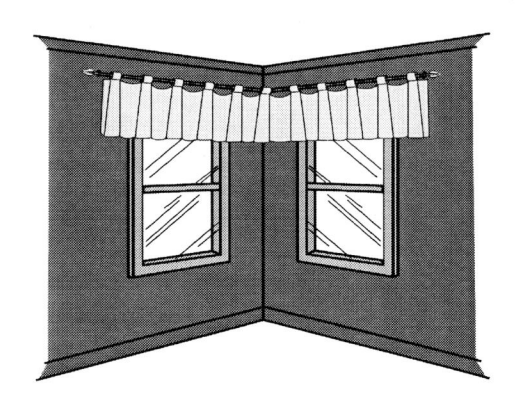

Corner window
When using decorative hardware in a drapery valance application, it is necessary to be very familiar with the hardware being used and to know exactly what kinds of brackets, splices, joints, and accessories are available to go with the rod selected. Before purchasing decorative hardware, quiz the manufacturer at great length to be sure the parts and pieces needed to successfully complete the installation are available in a given line. These situations may call for working very closely with the installer as well, as sometimes the rods will need to be angle cut, welded, or otherwise adjusted at the job site in order to achieve a successful installation. While these treatments can be beautiful, they do require special planning.

Arched window shapes

To simplify the process of installing a rod on an odd shaped window, consider hanging the drapery valance from medallions or hooks. This will work well in a situation where there are no under treatments, or the under treatment is inside mounted. These do not work well over outside mounted under treatments because most of the time, medallion hardware will not have sufficient projection to clear an under treatment. Again, it is wise to work closely with the installer if there are outside mounted items going under the valance, and be very familiar with what the hardware manufacturer has to offer.

GENERAL INFORMATION

- Fabrics should always be pattern matched from width to width.
- Order valances as center panels.
- Specify lining method and facing option on work order (Chapter 3 – Toppers).
- Use style names or numbers established by the workroom if provided.
- State if valance is to be lined, unlined, or self-lined.
- Pin settings for drapery valances are the same as for draperies. (Appendix B)

PRICING

- Drapery valances are priced per width.
- When using fabric railroaded, convert into widths in order to find the total labor cost.
- Drapery valances are usually charged for by full widths only.
- Add-on items such as trim, cord, banding, and tabs are charged separately usually per flat linear foot or per each.

RECOMMENDED FABRICS

- Most fabrics work well for drapery valances, and medium or "drapery" weight fabrics are best.
- Lining gives lighter weight fabrics more body.
- Interlining gives thin fabric a more luxurious look.
- Heavy fabrics can be used if the style is appropriate (check with the workroom if there is any doubt).

FULLNESS RECOMMENDATIONS

- Laces: 3x.
- Medium weight fabrics: 2.5x.
- Bulky fabrics: 2x or less.
- Upholstery weight fabrics: 2x or less.
- For patterned fabric, if more fullness is used, the pattern may be hidden. Use less fullness to show more of the pattern. Spaces between pleats may be larger, and sometimes this affects the style. Check with the workroom if there is any doubt.

TIPS WHEN MEASURING

- To ceiling – make sure the hardware will allow the valance to go to ceiling.
- Don't forget about the finials on the ends if there are any.
- For multi-length shaped valances, draw a diagram and label the short, middle, and long points on the work order.
- Always check that the hardware will accommodate large projections for valances over multiple layers.

Review

1) Specify the lining options for drapery valances and give an example for each situation.

2) How far out on each side of the trim or under treatment should you mount a drapery valance?

3) A customer has chosen a drapery valance style to go over a sliding glass door. What precautions should be taken?

4) What is the approximate projection for a drapery valance to clear the under treatment?

5) When a drapery valance will be mounted over a working drapery pair and working sheers, in a bay window, what is the first and most important consideration?

Drapery Valances

ROD POCKET VALANCES

Rod pocket valances are simply shorter versions of the rod pocket panel, and they will always be hung from a rod or similar hardware. They can be shirred, gathered, or hung flat with no fullness. A shirred or flat valance, when board or hook and loop mounted, is classified as a "topper". As with the other types of valances, they are commonly mounted above the window, and usually go all the way across the top of the window. The hardware used to hang a rod pocket valance can be a decorative pole or an iron rod, wood rod, curtain rod, or even tree branches and twigs, but keep in mind that whatever is used, it needs to be fabric friendly and accommodate the valance being shirred or gathered onto it.

Most of the time, a rod pocket valance will be no longer than 36" in length. Longer lengths are considered a panel. Rod pocket valances with shaped bottoms can have longer tails, but the body length should average 36" or shorter to be considered a valance. Rod pocket valance hem detailing is approached in the same manner as for toppers and drapery valances, with lining and facing options being the same.

There are business rules when talking about rod pocket valances, just as there are with the other categories. When the term "rod pocket" is used, that is an indication to the workroom that the valance will be hung on a rod by means of a pocket or casing.

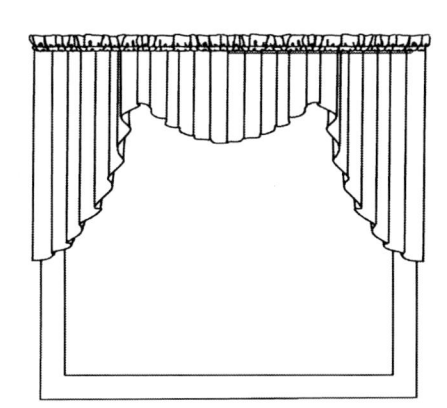

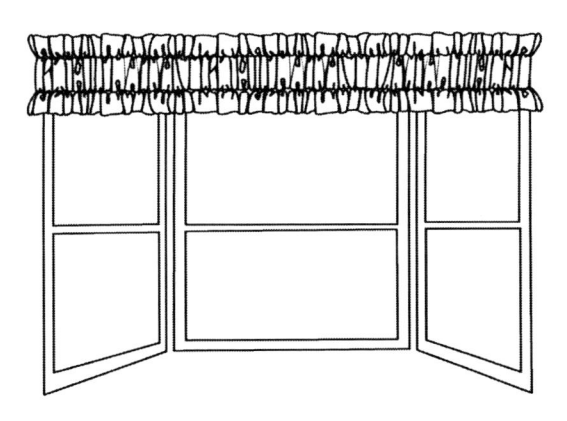

Elements of Soft Treatments

BASIC ROD POCKET VALANCE STYLES

Rod pocket valances are very basic, and typically consist of a header, a rod sleeve or casing, and some kind of skirt. With the exception of the rod pocket or casing any of these elements can be multiplied or eliminated. The basic progression of these styles is illustrated in the following examples.

Rod sleeve
This is the simplest form of a rod pocket valance. They are simply a flat fabric tube or shirred sleeve used to cover a rod intended to be used for decoration or filling space on a rod/panel combination treatment.

> Use these sleeves as a decorative element to cover poles in combination with other treatments such as open swags.

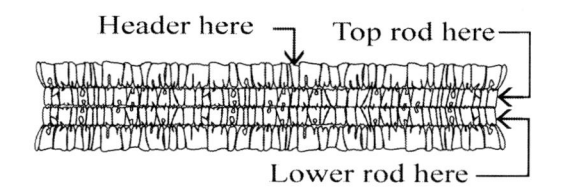

Rod sleeve with header
This type of valance adds a header only to the sleeve application described above. These are usually seen as fillers for spaces between side panels on larger window applications. Different looks can be created by placing the header on the lower end of the rod pocket. Doubling up rods to achieve a stacked look is also possible.

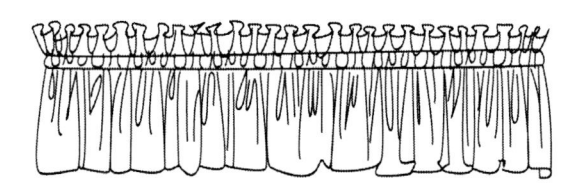

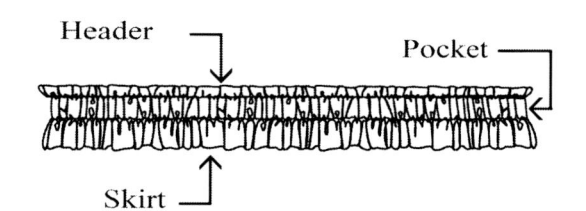

Rod pocket valance with header and skirt
This is probably the most widely used rod pocket valance style. Shown here are two versions of the basic header, casing, and skirt combination. Headers and skirts can be short or long, and casings can be wide or narrow resulting in very different looks while encompassing the same basic style.

Chapter 5

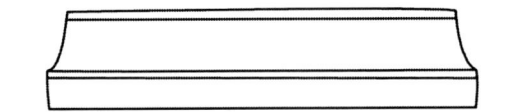

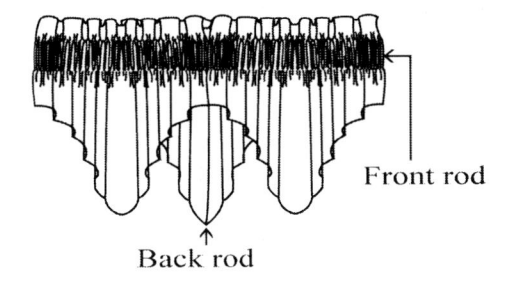

Specialty rod pocket valances

These valances are examples of the kind of styles that can be created when the valance is hung flat on the rod, or shirred with multiple rods. In these cases they may require multiple casings (pockets) and clever positioning of the rods at installation in order to obtain the desired effect.

Front rod

Back rod

> When the rod pocket valance is applied flat onto a rod, it will not be tight looking due to the pocket and rounded ends of the rod and limp fabric. If a firm appearance is desired, a try a cornice or soft cornice style. (See Cornices chapter)

STYLE VARIATIONS

There are a vast number of ways to spice up the basic rod pocket valance. Start with these basic styles and progress from here.

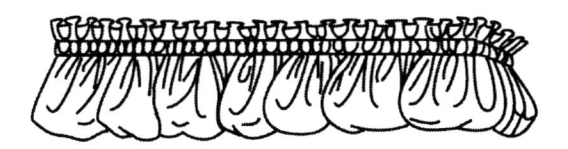

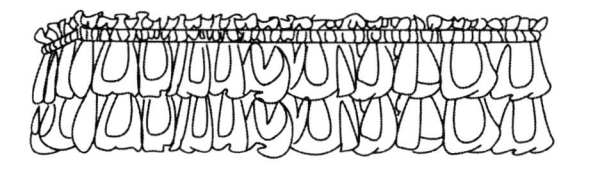

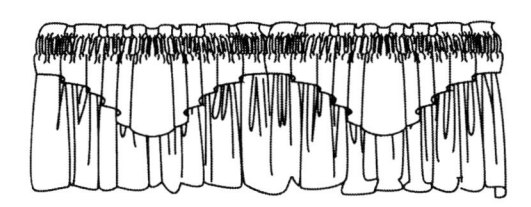

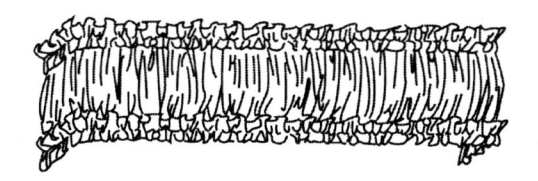

Skirt bottom variations

The balloon bottom effect can be created by adding a second rod casing at the bottom, installing the lower rod closer to the top rod than the skirt's length and allowing the extra fabric to balloon out creating this puffed effect. Adding a second skirt below the bottom rod gives the appearance of an attached ruffle. Adding another skirt and a third rod creates the effect of a double tiered pouf. Another variation of a skirt bottom would be to overlay a shaped skirt on top of a straight skirt for a petticoat effect. By adding another rod after the skirt, a sort of shirred cornice effect can be created as shown in the diagram at the bottom on the left.

> To make the valance puff fuller on the balloon types, add some small bubble wrap or tissue paper filler to the bottom poufs.

Elements of Soft Treatments

59

Rod Pocket Valances

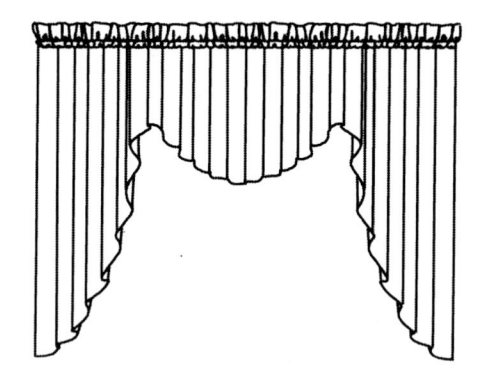

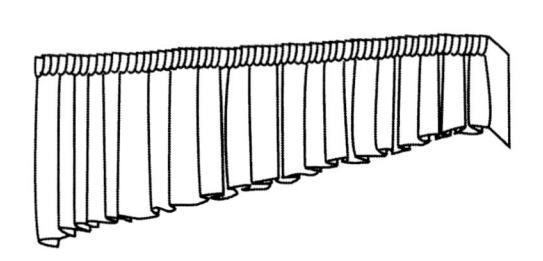

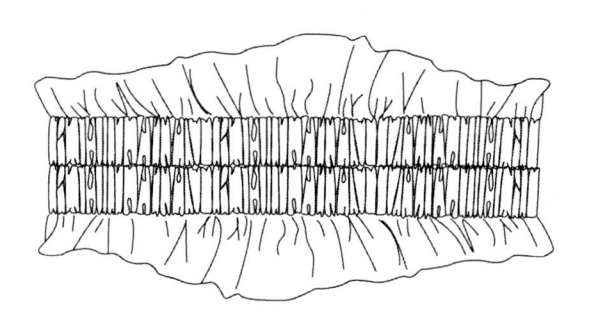

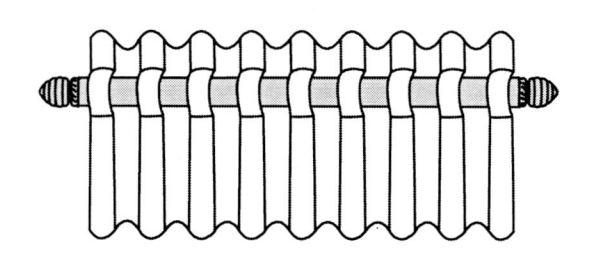

Shaped skirt bottoms

Making the valance skirt with shaping is very common and the typical arch or M-shape is the most popular. For yet another idea, try a reverse arch bottom, scallop, or slant bottom. Shaped bottoms need to follow the same rules for lining and finishing details as toppers and other valances. Headers for these valances are optional.

Header variations

Rod pocket panel header variations can apply to rod pocket valance headers. Large, floppy headers, shaped headers, and even headers of different colors or contrasting fabrics can be used.

Pocket/casing variations

As is the case with headers, valance pockets can have the same variations as for rod pocket panels: contrasting fabrics or belt loop effects, for example. For another "twist", make a rod sleeve with one color on the front and a different color on the back. When installing, twist the fabric around the rod or pole for a candy cane effect.

> If doing a twisted sleeve, allow a larger casing (pocket) size to accommodate the twisting when installing.

MEASURING AND ORDERING ROD POCKET VALANCES

All of the same rules for rod pocket panels apply to rod pocket valances when measuring and ordering. Here is a quick review of those guidelines:

- Rod casings need to be ordered larger than the rod. See Appendix B for the chart of common casing sizes.
- Take-up in valance length will occur. This factor is not as critical with most valances, but be aware of it in situations where valance length might be significant, such as for covering under treatment headers and similar situations. (Appendix B)
- Measure for rod pocket valances the same as for a topper or drapery valance. The same formulas for proportion and clearances apply here. Finished width, finished length, short points, long points, and projection remain the same as for prior chapters.
- If using a decorative rod with finials, discuss the return options with the client. Order a return cut out if one is warranted.

SPECIAL WINDOW SHAPES

Rod pocket valances can be installed onto any window shape to which a rod can be configured to fit. Custom curtain hardware manufacturers have already created a number of solutions. Many curtain rods and even some decorative types of poles can be purchased in sets for bay windows, and hardware such as elbow joints and corner connectors can be ordered. Generally speaking, if the hardware will fit, the rod pocket valance will work.

Doors

When installing a rod pocket valance over a door, the rules regarding head clearance apply in the same way they do for other valances. Rod pocket valances can be a good way to soften a door window because they can be installed directly onto the door and there are curtain rods available with very small projections. This is something to consider because some other treatments with larger projections may hit the wall or other doors when opened.

Rod Pocket Valances

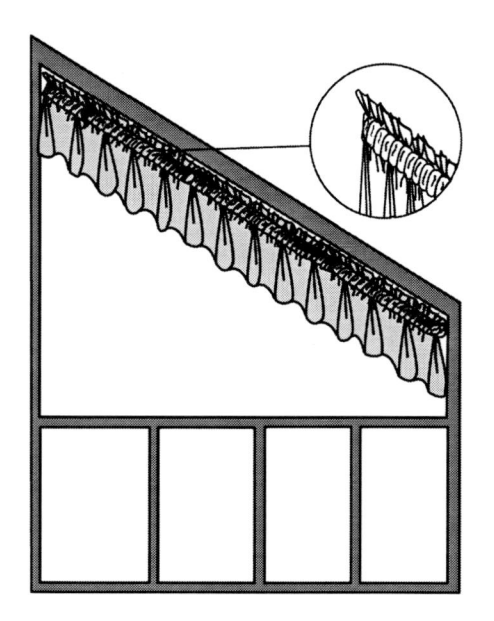

Angled windows

When designing a rod pocket valance to be installed onto a window with an angled top, be aware of the degree of the angle. If the window has a fairly steep angle, the shirring of the pocket will follow the angle of the window and the valance skirt will then hang straight. This can be an attractive design if it is expected, but if unexpected, it can look very odd. If the desired effect of the valance is to have the whole valance appear to hang straight, a gathered topper style may be a better choice.

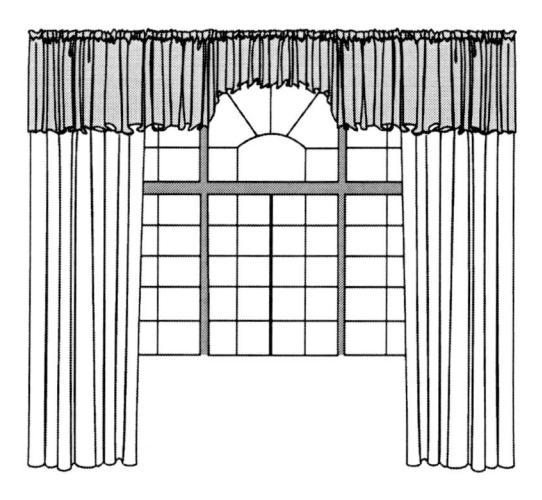

Arched windows

Rod pocket valances can be used on arched windows, but not in an arch shape. In this case, the valance will need to be made straight and the shape of the arch will be lost. Curtain hardware rarely comes in an arch shape. If it can be found or made, it will be quite expensive, and the rod pocket curtain will not gather onto these and hang straight. The effect of the shirring at the rod would follow the curve of the window similarly to the angled window. Gathered arched tops usually do better when ordered as a topper. If a rod pocket valance must be used over an arch, consider tracing the arch shape with the hem of the valance and covering negative space instead.

GENERAL INFORMATION

- The header, pocket, and take-up on a rod pocket valance are always included in the finished length.
- Fabrics are always pattern matched from width to width.
- Valances can be made with the fabric railroaded if the design permits it.
- Common heading sizes are 1", 2", or 3".
- Short headings work best with light weight fabrics, such as sheers, unless a floppy heading effect is desired.

PRICING

- Rod pocket valances are priced per width.
- For railroaded fabrics, convert into widths in order to find the total labor cost.
- Add on items such as banding, trims, ruffles, and so on are billed separately per flat linear foot (the flat width of the fabric before it is shirred).

RECOMMENDED FABRICS

- Most fabrics work well for rod pocket valances - medium to light weights are best.
- Bulky or upholstery weight fabrics may not be suitable for some styles. These can be attractive when used flat on the rod and not shirred (check with the workroom).
- When using heavy fabrics, roughly textured rods, or more than 3x fullness, order the rod casing larger than the chart size to ease installation. (Appendix B).

FULLNESS RECOMMENDATIONS

- Laces: 3x.
- Medium weight fabrics: 2.5x.
- Bulky fabrics: 2x.
- Upholstery weight fabrics: 2x or flat.
- If the fabric is patterned, fullness can be reduced in order to show more of the design. For example, if a lace is being used, less fullness will allow more pattern to show and not get lost in the folds.

Elements of Soft Treatments

Review

1) In what situation/s would a cornice or soft cornice be used in preference to a rod pocket valance?

2) A client has ordered a shaped bottom rod pocket panel to cover a 72" wide window. There will be 2 short points and 3 long points and a contrast band for the hem. The short points will be 20" and the long points will be 30". The hem contrast will be 3". A 2" header is required. Draw a diagram with all labeling necessary.

3) When using a rod sleeve, what is the part that is below the rod pocket called?

4) Detail and illustrate if necessary, how a candy twist casing would be measured and ordered.

5) With rod pocket valances is there take-up involved in the width or the length? Explain.

6) Describe two situations where a shirred topper would be a better solution than a rod pocket valance.

CORNICES

There are two types of manufactured cornices which look similar, but upon closer inspection, differ in a few critical areas. They are known as the cornice and soft cornice.

A cornice is a padded frame made of plywood or particle board for the face. The top, or dust cap, and sides are constructed from ¾" solid board, which is then padded and upholstered.

Soft cornices are constructed in a similar fashion to cornices, except there is no plywood or particle board for the face. The face is soft and has some type of stiffener between the fabric and the lining to give it something of a cornice effect.

There are business rules when talking about cornices, just like the other categories. When the term "cornice" is used, the workroom is advised that the face, top, and sides are made from solid wood and then upholstered. If the face needs to be soft, call it a "soft cornice". The soft cornice is not a widely used manufacturing method, and therefore it is advisable to check with the workroom regarding their policies for manufacturing them. Cornices are installed with angle irons or L-brackets.

Fabric allowances are the same for both types of cornices, but the quality of the construction is totally different from one to the other, and therefore prices vary from hard to soft.

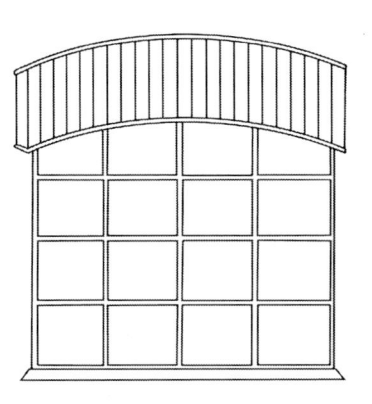

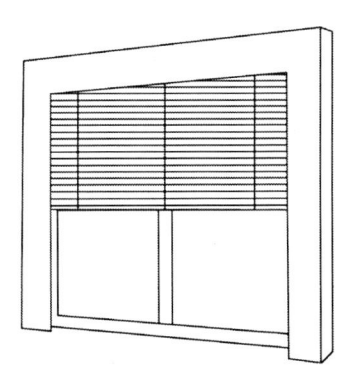

Cornices

CORNICE STYLES

Cornices are probably the most versatile of all of the different kinds of window coverings that can be made. Because of their wooden frame, they can have many creative shapes and forms. There are eight different, basic cornice structures.

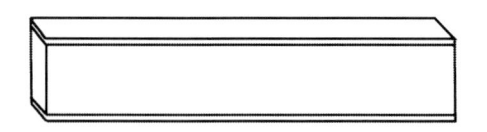

Plain straight
This is the most basic style, where the top and bottom of the cornice is straight and it has straight sides. The face and sides are padded and covered with fabric. Typically a welt cord of some kind is added along the top and bottom edges. If not corded, the fabric and padding continues around the corners, giving the cornice a softer, less upholstered appearance. The cording detail is not standard with all workrooms and there may be additional labor charges for it.

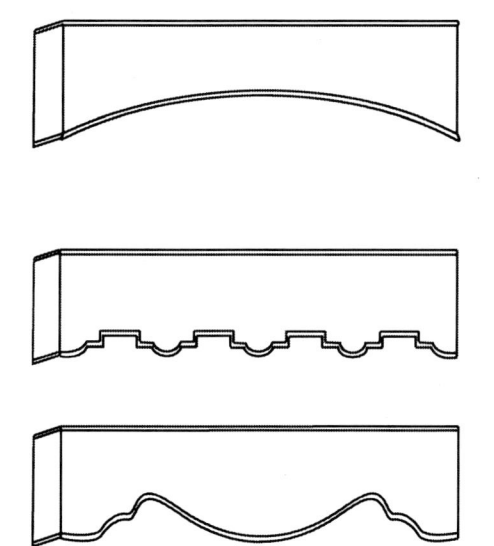

Shaped bottom
This cornice style still features a plain straight top but the bottom edge is cut into some type of a pattern. There are two generally accepted types of bottom pattern cuts - the "repeating pattern" and the "proportional shape".

A repeating pattern is where the bottom pattern is always the same and repeats itself along the width of the cornice.

A proportional shape cornice has a bottom pattern is always the same at each end of the cornice and the shape is designed to scale up or down in proportion to the length of the cornice.

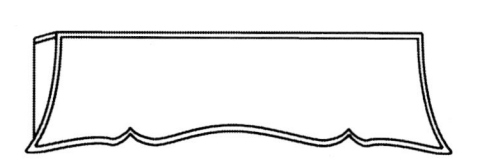

Shaped sides
With this style, the bottom usually has a shape of some sort and the ends of the cornice are designed to protrude outward. Sometimes only the face will have a shaped side and the sides of the cornice box will be straight. When communicating with the customer and the workroom be specific about exactly how the shaping is to be done.

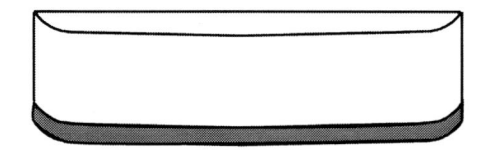

Rounded ends

This style usually has a straight bottom but the ends of the cornice are rounded to a radius of approximately 3"-6", depending on the size of the returns.

> Be cautious when using this style of cornice if there are any under treatments. Be sure that the under treatment/s can still operate properly under the rounded corners.

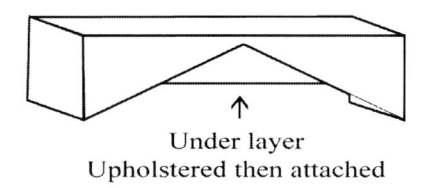

Under layer
Upholstered then attached

Specialty cornices

These are custom designs which require multiple layers and framework. These unique styles will likely require templates and/or patterns being made. Expect there to be workroom up charges for these types of styles.

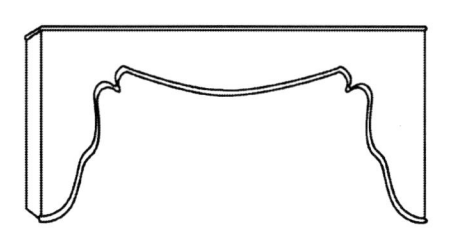

Cantonniere

These are made so the sides, or legs, extend most or all the way to the sill or apron of the window. The face shape then has some sort of artistic cut out that frames the window.

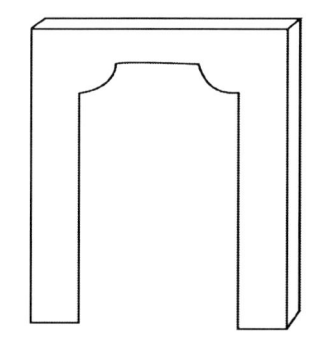

Lambrequin

This is similar to the cantonniere except the sides, or legs, extend all the way to the floor.

STYLE VARIATIONS

Designing cornices can be lots of fun. There are few limitations to the number and types of ways to change the look of a cornice, because it starts with a wood base and the base makes it possible to cut virtually any shape and mold the fabric to that shape. The entire look of the cornice will change just by making simple changes. Some examples are shown below.

Elements of Soft Treatments

Cornices

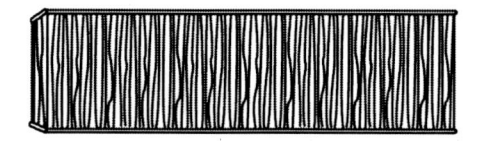

Shirred or pleated

The look of the plain straight cornice can be dramatically altered by shirring or pleating the fabric onto the board rather than upholstering it flat. The fullness for a gathered or pleated look varies from 2x to 3x. The fabrics used can be contrasting colors, or applied in different patterns depending on the desired impact of the design. Doodle a design inside a rectangle, and it can most likely be put on the face of a plain cornice.

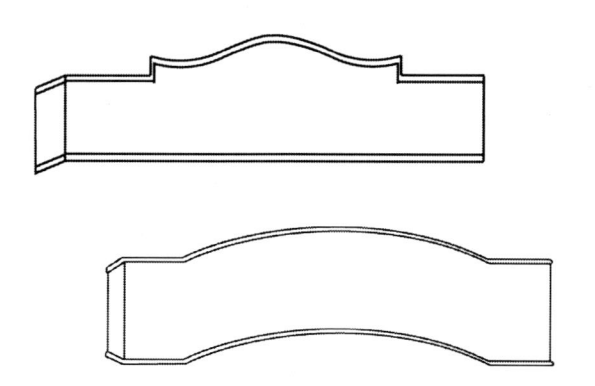

Shaped top or shaped top and bottom

The top of the cornice has a shape to it. The top shape can be the same or different from the bottom. As with shaped ends, communicate carefully with the workroom about whether the top board is to be shaped as well as the face board.

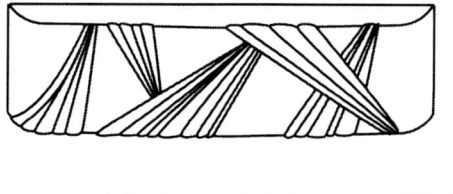

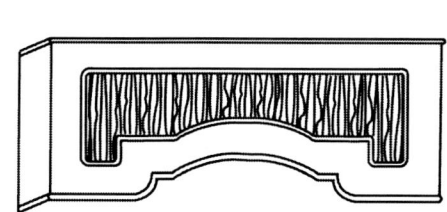

Add-ons

Through the use of add-on accessories such as banding, overlays, cascades, rosettes, bows, and so on, the number of ways one can change the look of a cornice are seemingly infinite.

MEASUREMENT AND PROJECTIONS OF CORNICES

The same basic information is required for measuring and ordering cornices as is needed for other treatments: a width, length, and projection. With cornices however, it is necessary to include more detail. Because the frame is made from wood it has no give, and measurements and specifications must be more exact. Also, once the frame is built and the fabric is applied it is very difficult to make changes of any kind. As the fabric will have no give or play, it likely will not be re-useable if an error is made.

Anatomy of a cornice

To begin understanding how to go about designing a complete and functional cornice unit, it is important to first learn the associated terminology and its components. Knowing the names of these parts will help immensely in communication with the workroom about specific dimensions.

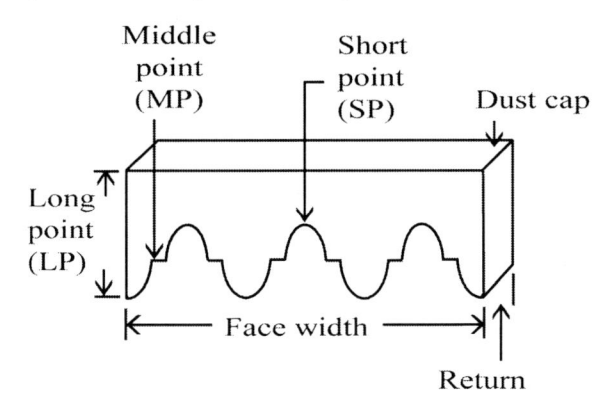

Shaped cornices will have long points, short points, and middle point lengths. When a shaped bottom cornice is specified, supply a diagram to the workroom indicating the dimensions and locations of these points.

Cornice width

Unlike many other fabric treatments, cornices are built on a padded frame which has dimension. Individual workrooms will craft cornices with different thicknesses of padding and side boards, so specify the finished cornice dimensions according to the directions below, to ensure clarity. Let the workroom make the necessary addition or deduction for the materials it uses. Be sure the workroom understands what is being specified: inside dimensions or face width.

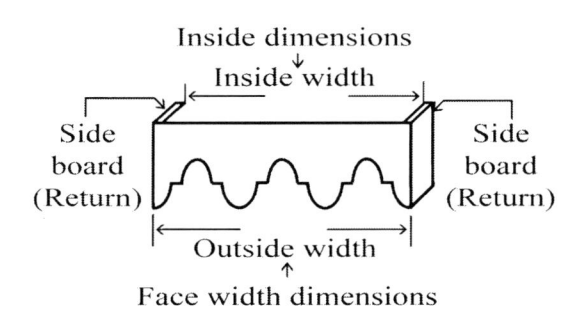

Inside dimensions
These are the width dimensions inside the cornice box between the side boards. The cornice width, if mounting over a window or under treatment should be specified by the inside cornice measurement. Measure the width of the window opening, trim to trim width, or the maximum operating width of any under treatments. Add 2" to this measurement (1" on each side), and specify this as the inside width dimension.

Cornice face width dimensions
These are the dimensions of the cornice measured across its face including width of side boards, padding, and welt cord if there is any. If the cornice will be mounted between two projections, such as walls, book cases, cabinets, and similar tight places, the cornice should be ordered to be made to the face width dimension, and usually ½" smaller than the actual measurement, to allow for ease of installation.

Elements of Soft Treatments

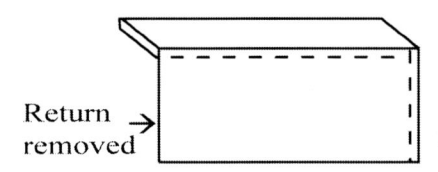

In some situations, as in the case of a cornice that is being installed over wood trim next to a wall, both the face width and inside width can be critical if less than 2" of mounting space is available. A plumper padding or thicker side boards could cause the cornice not to fit. In tight situations like this, specify both the inside width and the face width. These situations may call for the elimination of the side board entirely, and the cornice would then be constructed without one or both sides. Because this could make a significant difference in the finished product that is received, communication regarding these dimensions is critical, both to ensure that the cornice fits when installed and that designer and client have the same expectation of what the mounted cornice will look like.

> When ordering cornices to fit tight in places (such between walls), be sure to measure at the elevation of the installation. Most of the time, vertical surfaces are not perfectly perpendicular to ceilings and floors, or parallel to each other.

CORNICE LENGTH

Cornice finished length and proportion is determined similarly to any other valance treatment. Care must be taken to be sure things like doors and heads will clear the long points of the cornice design. Use the following rules in finding the approximate finished length for the cornice.

Ceiling mounted

Overall finished length of the window treatment (including under treatments) ÷ 5 + 2".
This will equal the recommended cornice finished length.

Example: 108 ÷ 5 = 21.6 (round up) = 22 + 2 = 24".
        This is the recommended finished length of the cornice.

Above the window

Overall finished length of the window treatment (including under treatments) ÷ 6, + 2".
This will equal the recommended cornice finished length.

Example: 84 ÷ 6 = 16.8 (round up) = 17 + 2 = 19".
        This is the recommended finished length of the cornice.

Take a tape measure and place it where the top of the cornice would be if made to the recommended measurement, and recheck the length with the client for approval. Adjust the finished length as needed. Also, make sure it is proportionate to the room. If the cornice has a shaped bottom, the finished length may need to be longer to ensure that the short point covers everything it needs to.

> In situations where the project is in the planning stages and only blueprints are available, a scale drawing of the treatment is recommended to check that the cornice is of the correct proportion.

> The cornice should be mounted a minimum of 1" above any drapery or other under treatment. This allows for the thickness of the top board ¾" plus ¼" play.

CORNICE PROJECTIONS

Cornices should be ordered large enough to allow the inside of the box to clear any trim or under treatments, plus about 1"-1½", with the minimum being 3½". Because cornice faces are solid and will not flex or fold like fabric treatments, they need to be made with enough projection to allow installers to reach behind and up to the top to mount them.

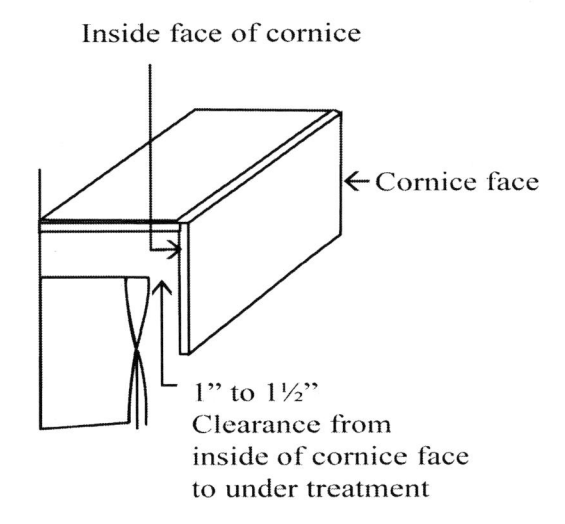

Inside face of cornice

← Cornice face

1" to 1½" Clearance from inside of cornice face to under treatment

CORNICE RETURNS

Cornices are built like a box without a back or bottom, and they are sometimes called cornice boxes for this reason. The front of the box is called the face because it faces the room. The top is called the "header" or dust cap. The sides are called "returns".

Sometimes it is necessary to build the cornice frame so that it will fit inside window openings, and over or around wood trims. In these cases it is sometimes necessary to order the returns and/or header board with cut-outs or "reduced" header boards or "reduced" returns.

Cornices

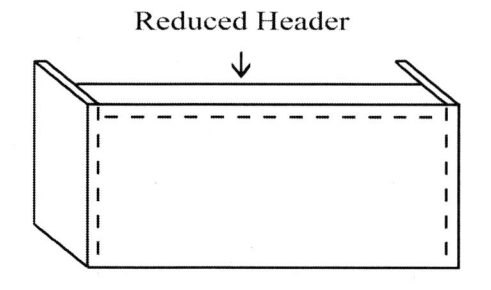

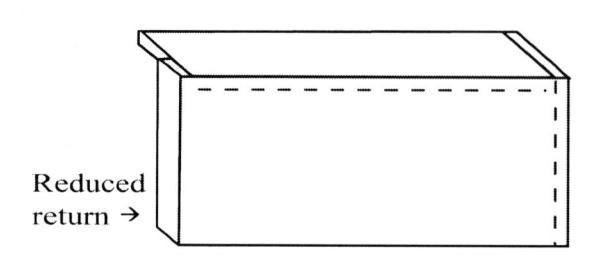

> If the cornice will be visible from above such as in a stairwell, instruct the workroom to cover the dust cap with the same fabric as the face. Check with the workroom for additional yardage requirements.

WELT APPLICATION ON CORNICES

Welt cord is usually applied to cornices in one of three ways. Each of these methods serves to give the cornice a better fit and a nice, finished appearance, yet they serve different purposes in different situations. It is a good idea to become familiar with each method and its purpose in order to inform clients regarding what type of construction they can expect in certain situations.

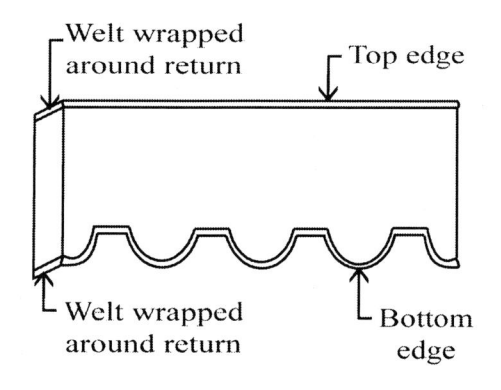

Standard cord application
This is where the welt wraps around the returns. Cord is applied at the top and/or bottom edges and continues around the return, ending at the wall. This method is best used when the return ends of the cornice will be clearly visible and the appearance of the returns is important to the look of the cornice.

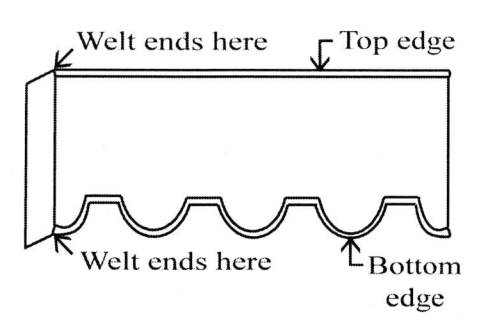

Top and/or bottom only application
In this situation, the cord is applied along the top and/or bottom edges only, ending at the outside edge of the cornice face before the return. In these cases the cornice still has a return board and padding, but the welt does not continue around the corners. This method is used in tight fit situations, where the welt cord pushing against the walls at the sides would cause a bad fit by compacting the padding between the wall and the cornice board. This is most commonly seen when using a contrast color, jumbo size, or shirred welt.

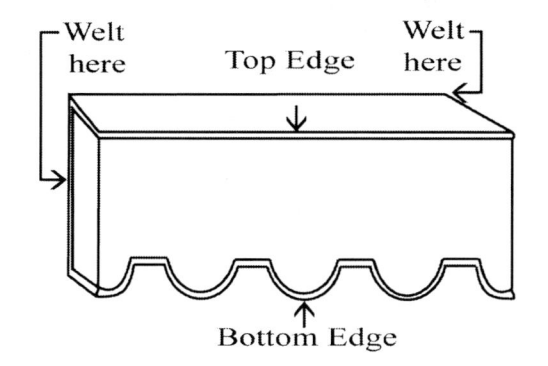

Top, bottom, and side application

With this method, the cord is applied along the top and bottom, and continues up the sides, meeting at the top corners. This application is usually used in situations when there is not a return or end board, such as for wall to wall fits or similar applications. It can also be used when the welt cord is being used to "frame" the cornice face. When this is done, remember to consider the appearance of the return ends if they will be clearly visible.

> This method works well in tight fit situations, as the welt on the outer edges will help to cover gaps that may occur due to the deductions that must be made for ease of installation in such situations.

SPECIAL WINDOW SHAPES

In the course of design work with windows, it is likely that windows with shapes other than the basic rectangle will be encountered, and in fact, odd shapes and configurations are now common. Draperies are probably the most versatile type of covering used to fit these situations. A thorough understanding of the rules governing drapery design and construction makes fitting drapery to odd-shaped windows a fun and satisfying part of the designer's task.

French doors

Many cornice styles can be configured to fit on French doors. Check to see which direction the door swings when opened. If the door swings outward it is safe to have the cornice long point drop below the door opening, however if the door swings inward be sure the cornice mounts above the opening high enough to allow the door to clear the cornice long point when opened. Since a cornice structure is hard, always check for adequate head clearance, especially when mounting over door openings.

Elements of Soft Treatments

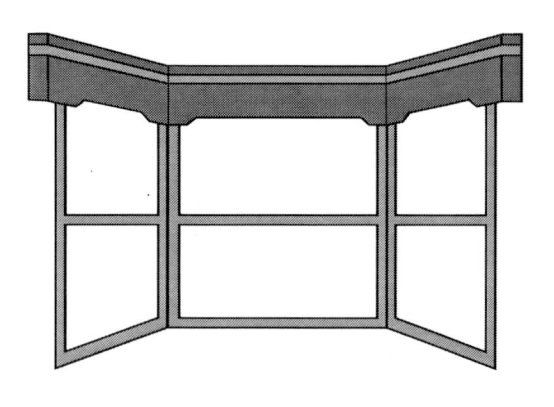

Corners, Bows, and Bays

Cornices mounting inside a bay window will require angle cuts being made at the workroom to allow the cornice to follow the contour of the bay. Clear specifications need to be provided to the workroom regarding whether the cornice should be made in one piece, or multiple pieces. If made in pieces the cornice will be assembled into its bay shape when installed. Because cornices are flat, the mitering in the corner must be exact or there could be gaps that will look very unattractive allowing light to leak through or patterns to not match up. Because of this, wall, window, and angle measurements must be extremely accurate.

Sometimes this problem with gaps can be minimized by designing the cornice so the joints are covered by cascades, jabots, or cording. If the cornice is made in one piece, it may become quite large and transporting it to the installation site may be a problem. One piece cornices also require very accurate measurements or they will not fit when taken to be installed.

Arched windows

A cornice can be an ideal solution for windows with arched tops. The cornice can be built in an arch shape that parallels the shape of the window arch. By doing this, it allows you to place a draw drapery behind the cornice to provide light control and privacy while retaining the architectural intention of the arch shape. This works well in bedrooms where privacy and light control may be of critical importance. Arched cornices will require a template or computer drafted pattern. There are companies who specialize in providing this service to help create a perfect template.

GENERAL INFORMATION

- Dust caps of cornices are typically constructed of ¾" pine board.
- Dust caps are covered in lining unless otherwise specified.
- Face of cornice is typically constructed of plywood or particle board.
- Face of cornice uses a padding of some type.
- Inside of cornices are covered in lining.
- Communicate closely with the workroom regarding measurements.
- If the cornice is inside mounted, specify cording application method on the work order.
- Remember to add both returns to face width when figuring width for labor and yardage.

PRICING

- Cornice labor is usually priced per linear foot.
- Linear foot pricing includes face width plus returns.
- There is typically a minimum per foot charge.
- Face width + both returns ÷ 12, round up = number of linear feet and also is the billable footage (e.g. 100 + (3.5 × 2 =7) = 107 ÷ 12 = 8.91 round to 9').
- Add-on items such as banding, cording, cascades, bows, rosettes, etc., are billed as separate items, usually per linear foot or per each.

RECOMMENDED FABRICS

- Most fabrics work well for cornices.
- With silks, sheers, laces, or any delicate fabric, a layer of lining between the batting and the face fabric is recommended, and is called underlining.
- Underlining will stabilize the fabric and prevent any batting being visible through the fabric in the finished cornice. There is a surcharge for this, so check with the workroom for the surcharge details.

TIPS WHEN MEASURING

- Measure to mount above the window approximately 6".
- Cornices are hard treatments with little or no flexibility. Measure and make allowances accordingly.

Elements of Soft Treatments

Review

1) In what situations would you include both inside width and face width dimensions. Give your reasons.

2) A client is considering a cornice in a library. The window is surrounded by floor to ceiling bookcases, and there are side hang draperies with a sheer panel. Would you recommend a cornice? Why or why not?

3) Outline the benefits of a hard cornice versus a soft cornice.

4) Describe the benefits of applying a welt to a cornice design.

5) A client wants a cornice mounted over draperies covering a 24' wall of windows that are located on the 17th floor of a downtown loft building. What difficulties may arise, and how might those problems be solved?

6) Can cornices be placed on slanted or cathedral windows?

7) When would a reduced header be specified?

TRADITIONAL AND OPEN SWAGS

The swag is a classic window covering that has been used to decorate homes for hundreds of years. It has evolved from a plain and simple window dressing to something ornate and heavily trimmed. Despite this, the basic swag remains the same and adds a timeless elegance to any window, and it will likely always be in some form or another, a window dressing staple.

A swag can be the most stunning of all window treatments, and a thorough understanding of the principles of swag construction go a long way to helping to create these beautiful designs. Open or traditional swags are a kind of valance treatment. They are normally mounted above the window and can be used alone or layered over other treatments. Swags can be specified as traditional board mount, or open throat. A traditional swag is characterized by it being board mounted. The open swag is found mounted onto a pole, small blocks of wood, or sometimes attached by tabs. Most of the time, a complete swag treatment will have some combination of panels, cascades, or jabots added to make it complete.

When a swag is specified, the business rule says the treatment will be cut from a pattern. Both traditional and open swags are constructed, meaning the fabric is cut from a pattern, folded, and formed into the swag shape. One complete swag unit comprises a combination of swags and selected add-on items. Swags can be fabricated with the pattern being cut on the bias, upright, or railroaded, depending on the look that is desired. There are limitations to consider for each method - the style of the treatment, print direction, or pattern on the fabric can have an impact on how a swag treatment is designed and made.

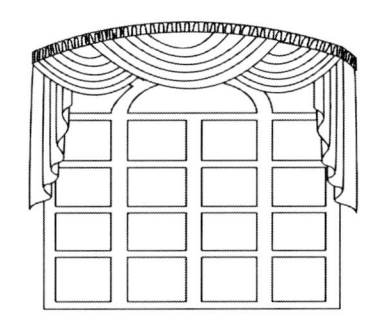

Elements of Soft Treatments

BASIC SWAG STYLES

Almost all swag styles can be made as either traditional board mounted swags or as an open throat style. The exception to the rule is that swags requiring hard returns or any type of structure in order to help the swag hold its shape will not do well as an open throat swag.

Open swags are more labor intensive to manufacture than the traditional swag styles because creating the open throat requires more steps, and the finishing and mounting are considerably more complicated. When swags are ordered, typically the entire swag and all of its components are made and assembled in the work room. The swag is then installed at the job site as a completed unit. Open swag hardware, such as the pole, need to be handled carefully to prevent any damage. If the rod is iron or metal then the swag needs to be more carefully prepared for mounting by means of a hook and loop tape or attachment with pole pockets which must be constructed separately.

Some rods and poles will require splicing in order to achieve the face width specified. When splicing the rod, some planning needs to be done when ordering and cutting the rod so that the splices of the rod will be hidden by the swag overlaps. All of these details add up to this being one of the more difficult treatments to design and manufacture.

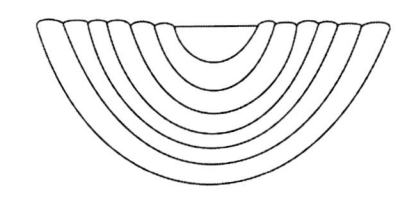

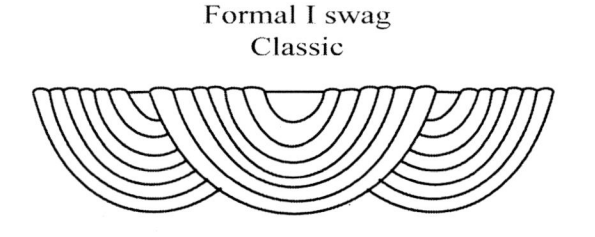

Formal folded swag

The most basic of the swag styles, this swag can be specified as either traditional or open. This swag will have evenly spaced pleats which lay across the top plane of the swag, and are then dressed to cause the swag to fall in evenly spaced folds. This swag style tends to be quite dressy looking and may be used in more formal applications than some of the other swag types. Usually these swags are combined in units with multiple swags and other add-on components

The formal swag fabrication style can be bias, upright (seams), or railroad. However, upright (seams), or railroad will cause the folds of the swags to become pointed and sharp looking. To avoid sharp pointed swags, increase the tip/tip size to help control the arc. It will not remove the points but will help keep them to a minimum. The number of folds per swag will vary depending upon the fullness specified, but most of the time, there are five to six folds.

Formal I swag
Classic

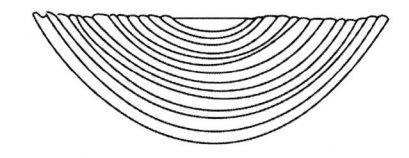

Chapter 7

Gathered I
Left multi swag

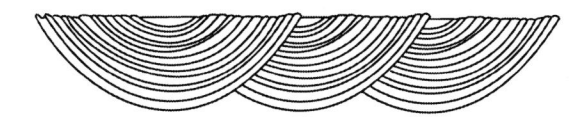

Gathered swag
The gathered swag is far more casual looking. Rather than evenly spaced folds, this style is shirred. The shirring is not uniform in size and has no specific spacing. Depending on length fullness, the gathers will create semi circles of many folds. Gathered swags can be either traditional or open. They are fabricated upright or railroad, and rarely are they bias cut. These swags are also usually combined with multiple swags and other add-on components.

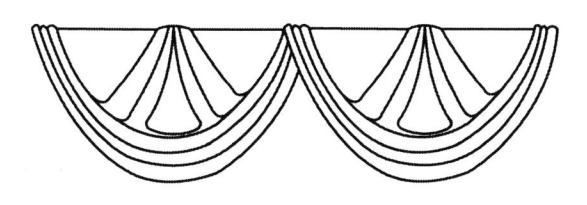

Fan swags
The fan swag style will have some of the swag fullness placed along the top center of the swag. The folds created by this bunching of the fullness in the center will fan out towards the outer edges. These swags may sometimes also have folds along the swag arc or the folds may be simply left to fall out from the center in a semi-circular shape. This style of swag is rarely seen as an open swag style because some form of support for the center and swag tips is required. These swags are fabricated upright or railroad and not bias cut because the swag hangs on the straight grain of the fabric. Fan swags can be fabricated either folded or gathered.

Gathered

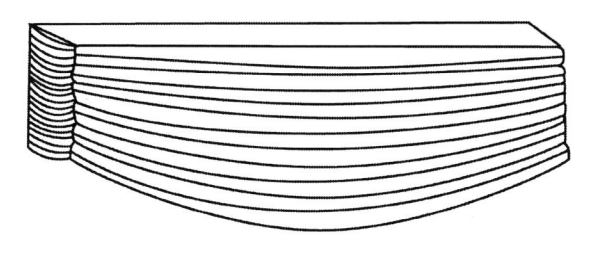

Boxed swag
The boxed swag is made with a hard return and typically there will only be one swag per unit and they may or may not have other add-on components attached. The return board is required in order to give the swag support in the creation of its shape because the folds run along the vertical planes of the sides rather than across the top. This style cannot be done as an open swag unless overlaid as an add-on to a cornice treatment.

This swag style has limitations to the width that can be done using one swag (about 108"). If a swag's face width gets too wide, the folds have a tendency to fall downward and the folds will separate causing spaces between them. The same treatment on different size windows in the same room will not look uniform.

Elements of Soft Treatments

Traditional and Open Swags

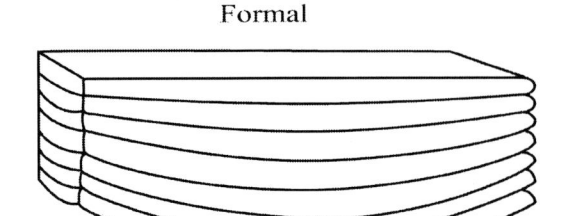

Formal

Georgian
(Formal)

The boxed swag can be specified formal with folds or gathered with shirring. The legs of the hard returns are made equal to one half of the finished length. These swags must be fabricated in the railroad style or upright. If upright, the swag will have visible vertical seams.

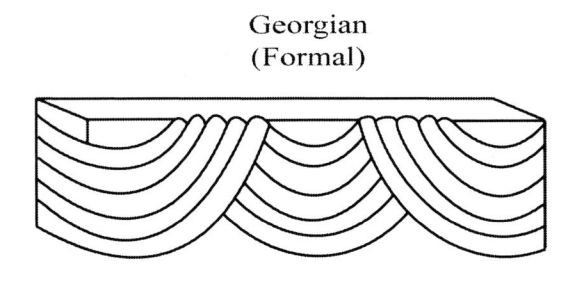

End cap swags
These are similar to the boxed swag in that they are also made with a hard return leg. They differ from the boxed style because they will be made having two or more swags per unit. The fabric will wrap around the returns.

They can be made as a formal folded style or they can be a more casual gathered swag. Depending on the configuration of the swags, short points and long points can sometimes be difficult to control and scale drawings are recommended in situations where these points are critical.

This swag style can not be made as an open swag unless it is used as an overlay on a cornice because it must have the hard return to maintain its structure. These swags can be done as bias cut, upright, or railroad but sometimes on larger widths it may be necessary to have seams. Check with the workroom if there is a concern regarding seaming.

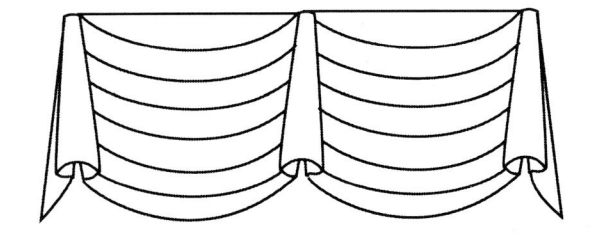

Traditional Kingston

Kingston swag
The Kingston style of swag is very similar to the Empire, with the single distinction being the placement of the pleats. The pleats that form the folds on the Kingston will be placed vertically and they are sewn in place at the back of the horn. The horns are approximately 3"-4" shorter than the finished length of the swag.

The swag sections on these styles will be lined with a drapery lining, and they will also have a strip of fabric approximately 4"-5" wide along the hem on the reverse side (lining side). This is called a facing, and it will prevent any of the lining from showing on the front as the horns open out at the bottom.

Open Kingston

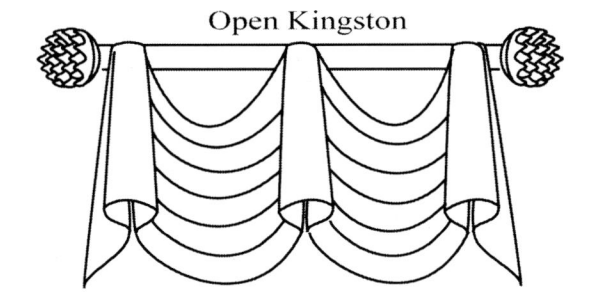

Traditional Empire

Open Empire

Horns, returns, and tails on these styles will need to be contrast or self-lined if not faced because the lined portions are partially exposed from the front view when the swag is assembled. Kingston swags can be made with or without tails.

> The Empire and Kingston styles lend themselves well to the attachment of trims and banding along the lower edge because it is actually straight before the swag is folded and formed.

Empire swag

The Empire swag will have a cone shaped decoration at the corners and between each swag section. These cones are called horns and they are attached to the swag. They are not made as a separate add-on item.

The Empire has pleats that form the folds which are attached at the top plane of the swag. These swags can be made traditional or open style but they are typically folded and rarely, if ever, gathered. The swags can be formal or sophisticated-casual, with the style being largely determined by the choice of fabrics.

These swags must also be specified with or without "tails". The tails are also sewn to and are part of the construction of the swag. If a tail is not specified, the swag unit will have a shorter version of the tail that will form the return. The Empire is fabricated in either the upright or railroad method.

Traditional Bell
(Gathered)

Open Bell
(Formal)

Pick-up swag

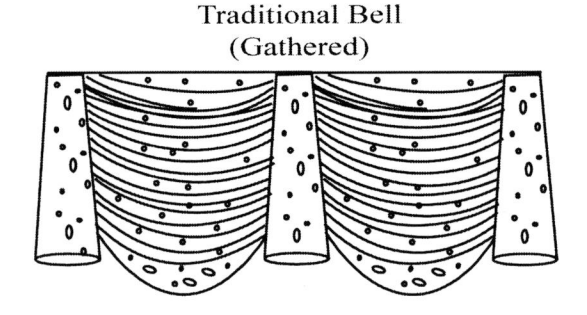

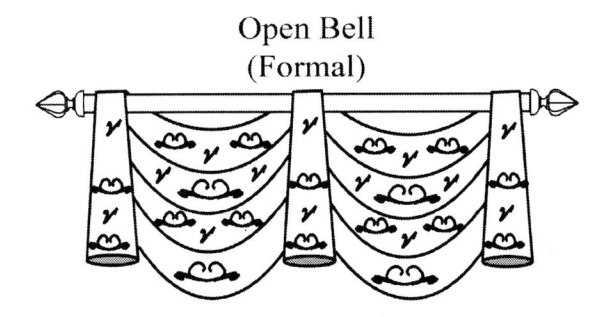

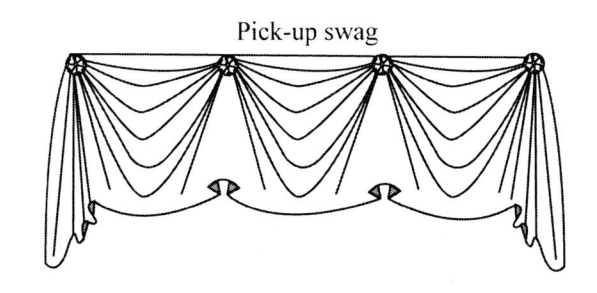

Bell swags

The bell swag also has a similar appearance to the Kingston and Empire styles, however this swag has horizontal pleats and they can be either folded or gathered for a softer look. The body of the swag treatment will be one continuous piece, and the swags are separated by "bells" (jabots), rather than "horns". The bells are made separately and attached as an add-on item (see "Jabots" in Chapter 14). Because the bells are add-ons, sometimes other types of jabots can be substituted for the traditional bell.

This style can be made as either a traditional or open style. With the traditional version of the bell swag, there will usually be a hard return. When made as an open swag, the returns have either a small swag or the bell is modified to allow for a return. The bell swag can be made bias cut, upright, or railroad.

> Because the bottom of the bell swag is curved slightly, it is difficult to add bottom banding. However, the style lends itself well to the addition of cording or trim.

> Remember, the face width of a tradition bell swag will be 1½" smaller due to the thickness of the hard returns.

Pick-up swags

The pick-up swag is also known as a pick-up valance, being that it is not a true swag but something of a cross between a scarf and an Empire or Kingston swag. Since this valance can mimic the Empire and Kingston swag styles, it is often confused with them. This valance style has a lot of interesting and possible variations, such as cuffed tops and alternating colors with the horns.

The pick-up is made from a continuous length of fabric, and the "horns" are formed from the fabric being pulled up behind them, or in the flatter versions, allowing the fabric to sag between them. It is more difficult to control finished size with this style and if exact dimensions are called for, the Kingston or Empire should be chosen instead. The pick-up should always be thought of as a casual and playful alternative to a true swag. It is included here because it can be made as either traditional or open style much as other swags can.

This style should always be made railroaded, because if it is done upright, there will be seams which will be fairly obvious behind the "horn". This may or may not be acceptable, but must be discussed with the client.

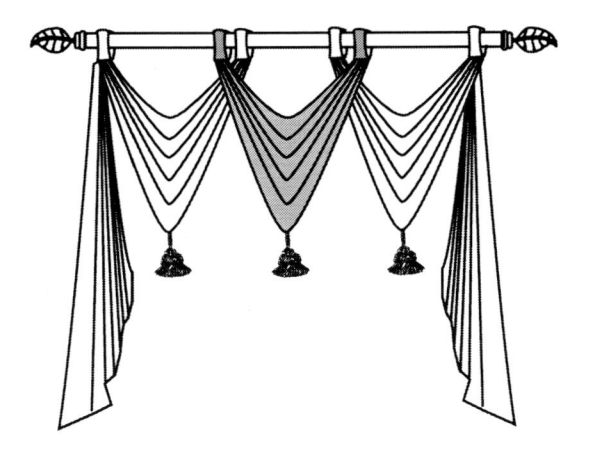

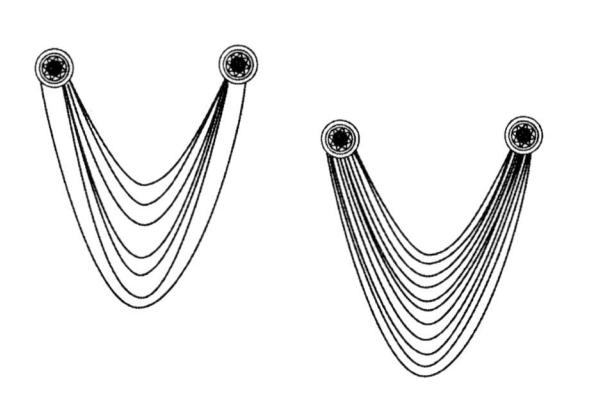

Necklace swags

Necklace swags are also known as point to point swags, tip to tip swags, or drapery swags. They are sometimes called drapery swags because they are often used as an add-on item to a drapery panel to create something of a self valance.

Necklace swags are frequently confused with window scarfs because a number of them hung together can appear as a scarf. They are in fact cut from a swag pattern and each one is made, formed, and hung individually, and they are not created from a continuous piece of fabric like a scarf. The pleats are stacked on top of one another like an accordion rather than spread across a vertical or horizontal plane like the other swag styles.

The necklace swag will always have an open throat and must be supported at its tips by attachment to another treatment like a drapery, or hung by tabs or rings from a rod. These swags can be made bias cut, seamed, or railroad.

SWAGS AND ADD-ON ITEMS

Very few swag treatments are complete without the addition of some kind of add-on item. A list and description of many available add-ons is located in Chapter 14.

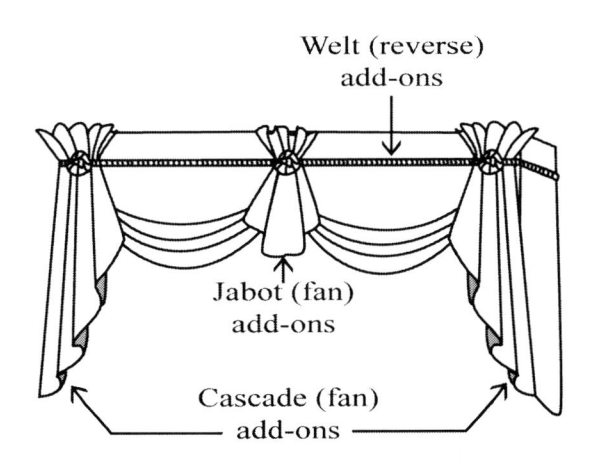

Many add-ons can be incorporated into a swag unit to make unique treatments. At the very minimum, some sort of cascade, tail, or jabot will be added to make the swag a complete unit. This is not to say that swags can never be used alone, but they are commonly paired with add-ons.

Welt (reverse) add-ons
Jabot (fan) add-ons
Cascade (fan) add-ons

Elements of Soft Treatments

Traditional and Open Swags

SWAG STYLE VARIATION

For the most part, a swag is a style unto itself, and the treatment is varied by creating combinations of swags with other add-on items and configuring them to fit the window. The end result then becomes a swag unit. There are an endless number of combinations, and therefore every swag unit created is essentially a variation unto itself. This is most likely the reason the swag has been so popular throughout the ages, and continues to be popular today.

DESIGNING A SWAG TREATMENT

When putting together a swag treatment there are many things that must be considered in creating a functional design. The style of the treatment and customer taste and preferences must also be incorporated into the plan. Keeping all of these things in mind through each step in the process will result in the successful creation of a complete treatment.

When designing a swag treatment, a scale drawing is vital to ensure that all of the short points, long points, widths, and lengths are appropriate and provide sufficient coverage of all of the window elements. If a certain motif in the fabric design is to be centered on every swag, make certain to specify this on the work order since it will affect the yardage and labor price. This is known as pattern placement and can be communicated to the workroom with the work order by tracing around the pattern that is to be centered on a photocopy of the fabric pattern.

Anatomy of a swag

To begin understanding how to go about designing a complete and functional swag unit, let us first learn the associated terminology and its components. Knowing the names of these parts will help immensely in communicating with the workroom about specific dimensions. Shown below are two diagrams of a typical traditional and open swag unit and a table describing the parts and their names, and a brief description of each.

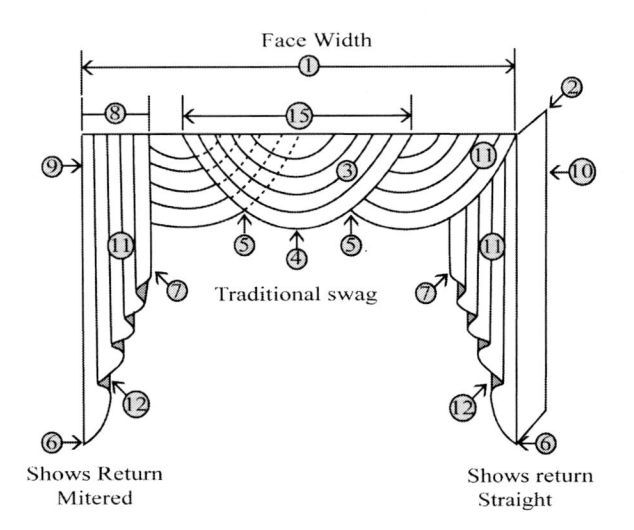

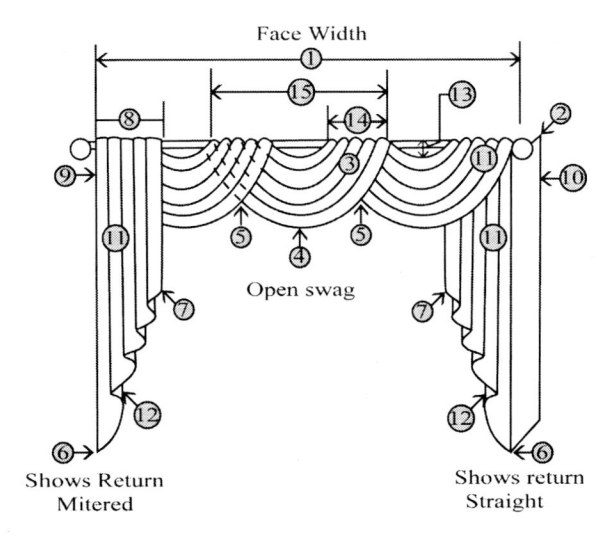

1	Face width	Width of treatment
2	Return	Projection from wall to front edge of treatment, minimum 1½" for straight windows. Corner, bays, or curves 2½"
3	Number of swags	The number of swags across the face width
4	Swag long point	Finished length of the swag
5	Swag short point	The shortest point of where the 2 swags overlap each other
6	Cascade long point	Longest length of the cascade
7	*Cascade short point	Shortest point of the leading edge of cascade
8	Cascade width	Face width of cascade
9	Cascade over swag	Cascade is placed over the swag for a more traditional look
10	Cascade under swag	Cascade is placed under the swag exposing all the swags
11	Face fabric	Main fabric for the swag and cascade
12	Lining fabric	Lining of the cascade in which can be seen from the front of the swag
13	Open throat	The distance from the top of the pole to the top of the swag
14	Swag overlap	The overlapping of swags
15	Tip/Tip	The distance from the left leading edge to the right leading edge of the same swag

*The ratio between long and short point of the cascade is ideally 2:1 or 3:1. This means that for every 2"-3" of length on the long point side of the cascade, there will be a corresponding 1" of length on the short point side of the cascade. For example, if the cascade long point were 60", the ideal short point would be 20"-30". One would need to look at the window and determine at what point between 20" and 30" the short point would best suited. See Add-ons

Overall width of the treatment

As with any other treatment, thorough and accurate measurements need to be taken and the overall width of the swag treatment should be determined. Allow the same clearances for under treatments as would be allowed for any other type of valance, about 2" wider than the opening, trim, or under treatment. Once the overall treatment width has been determined, the next step is to decide how many swags will be used.

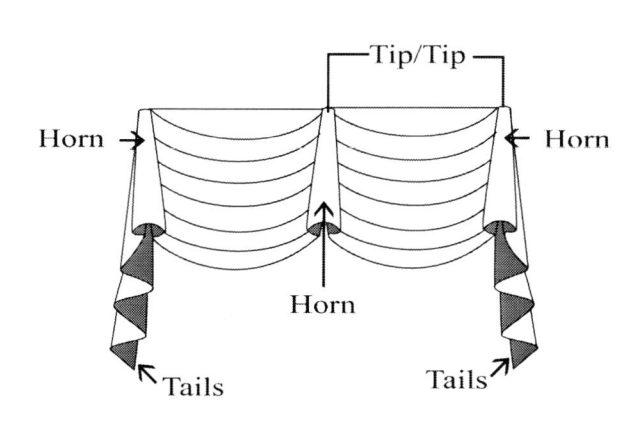

Tip to tip measurement

All swag types use what is called the tip to tip measurement. Tip to tip is simply the finished width of each of the individual swags.

It is necessary to determine the approximate tip to tip dimension that will be used on the treatment in order to determine how many swags will be needed to cover the area being decorated with the swag treatment. In addition, the tip to tip dimension will affect the style of the swag somewhat, as smaller tip to tip dimensions will produce longer and thinner swags, and wider tip to tip dimensions will produce swags which appear shorter and more rounded. Choose a tip

Traditional and Open Swags

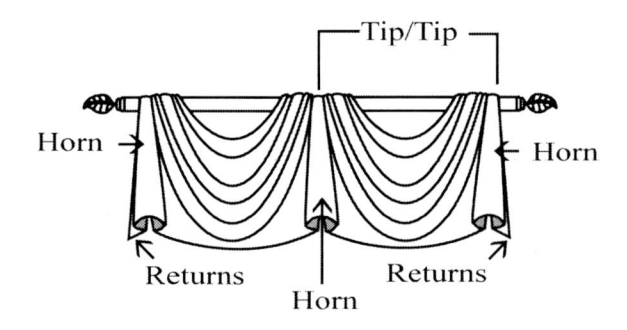

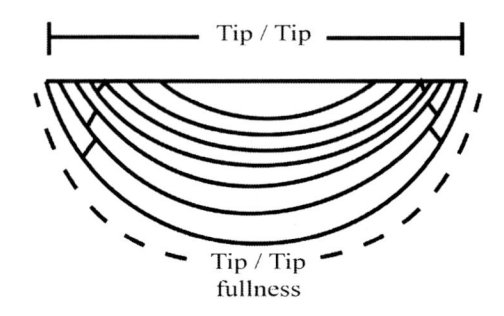

to tip dimension that will adequately cover the overall width and also reflect the style that is to be achieved.

Also, beyond certain dimensions, seams in the swags will be required which may affect how one would plan to arrange the swags in order to conceal the seams. The charts in Appendix B can be used as a guide to help decide how many swags will be needed to cover the treatment width, as well as suggesting maximum tip to tip dimensions for a swag that needs to be made without any seams.

Each style uses a different formula to find the tip/tip. Knowing what tip to tip dimensions to use will also help determine the fabrication method to use: bias, upright, or railroaded. Keep in mind while making these decisions, the kind of fabric that will be used, along with style and client preference.

The diagrams on the next page illustrate how the tip to tip measurement will affect the look of the finished swag, and how the relationship between the tip to tip measurement and swag finished length affects the way the swag will look when complete. The wider the tip/tip, the more rounded the swag will be at the bottom.

To help visualize the finished swag, draw to scale the tip/tip width, then draw the finished length from the center of the tip/tip, connect the three points, A, B, then C. This is approximately what the swag will look like.

A narrow tip/tip look on a traditional swag

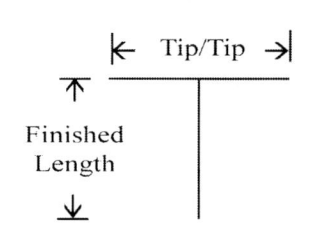

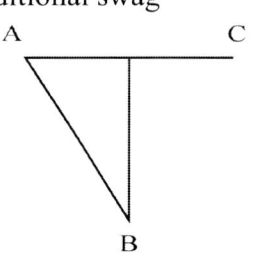

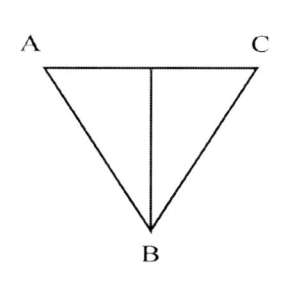

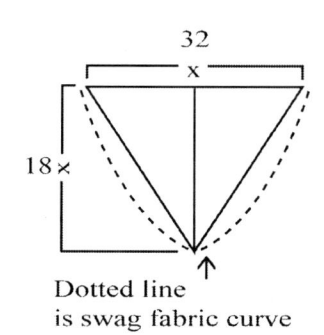

A wider tip/tip look on a traditional swag

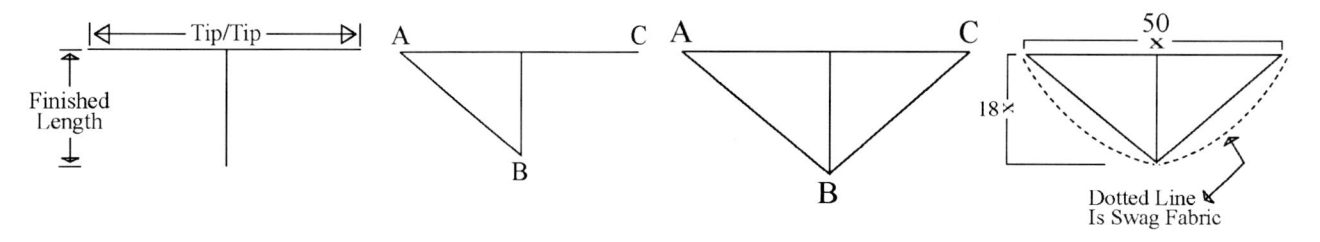

86

Chapter 7

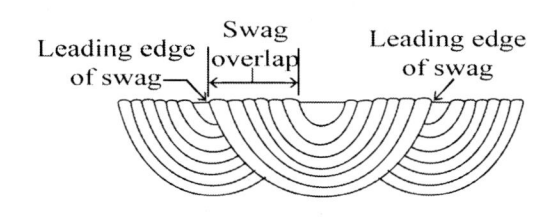

Swag overlapping options
After deciding on an appropriate tip to tip size and number of swags to be used, the next step is to determine how the swags will be placed and choose an overlapping pattern. The overlap is the amount that one swag overlaps another from leading edge to leading edge. The amount of overlap will depend on the swag tip to tip measurements and the number of swags being used. The swag overlapping patterns are shown below.

Traditional swags
Traditional swags can be overlapped in six basic ways: the center swag under, also known as the "Georgian" configuration, the center swag over, known as the "Classic" configuration, multiple swags overlapping left, which places the top swag on the left side of the configuration, multiple swags overlapping right, which places the swag on the right on the top of the configuration, and alternating, which places one swag over, the next under, and so on alternating across the length of the treatment. Sets of swags with even numbers can not be made as a Georgian or classic configuration and multi-left or multi-right must be chosen. Alternating sets will always require an odd number of swags.

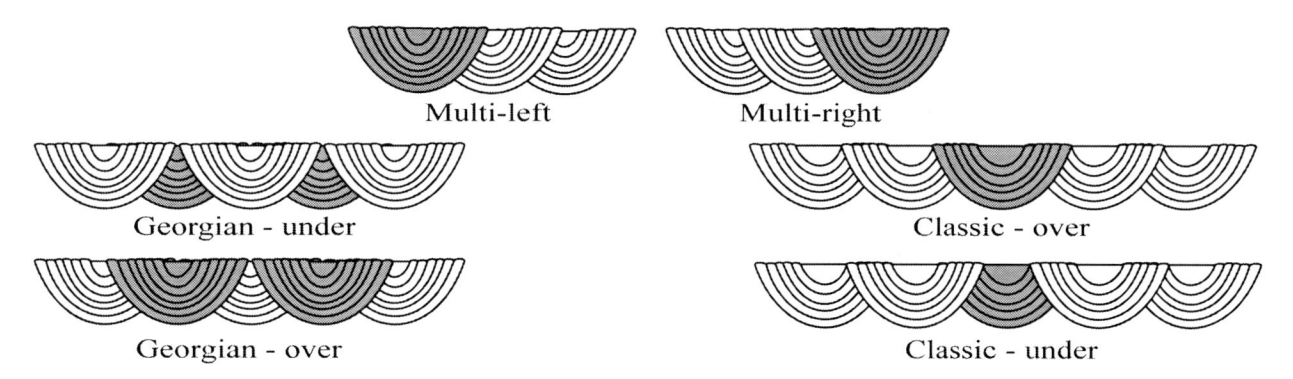

Multi-left

Multi-right

Georgian - under

Classic - over

Georgian - over

Classic - under

Open swags
Open swags are slightly different, because in addition to specifying the overlapping pattern of the swags themselves, the overlapping pattern of the pole should also be considered. This becomes particularly critical with the addition of a cascade and how it will overlap the swags (see Add-on section for cascade overlapping information), or in corner or bay situations where two sets of overlapping swags are joined together. Some examples of how these configurations will look are shown below. In situations where complicated overlapping patterns must be described, a diagram or scale drawing is the best method to communicate the desired outcome.

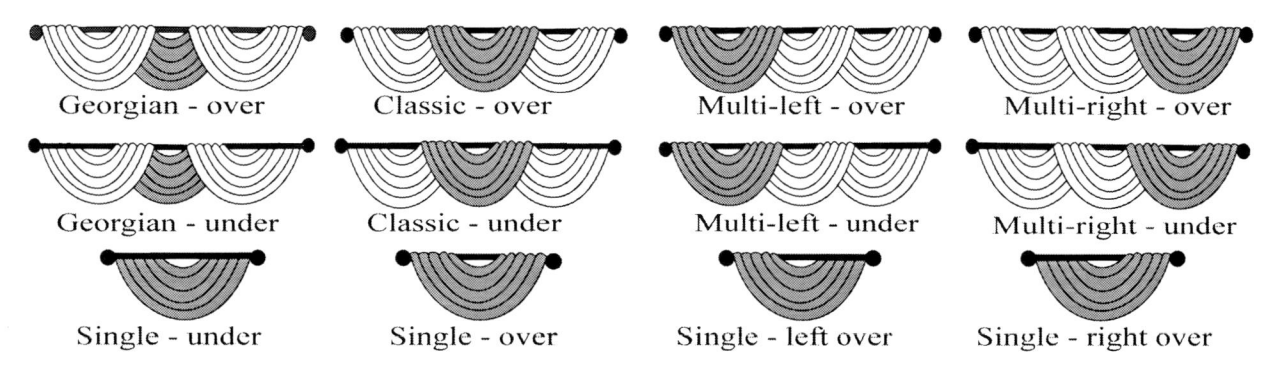

Georgian - over

Classic - over

Multi-left - over

Multi-right - over

Georgian - under

Classic - under

Multi-left - under

Multi-right - under

Single - under

Single - over

Single - left over

Single - right over

Elements of Soft Treatments

Traditional Formal I

Leading edges line
up with center swags
↓   ↓

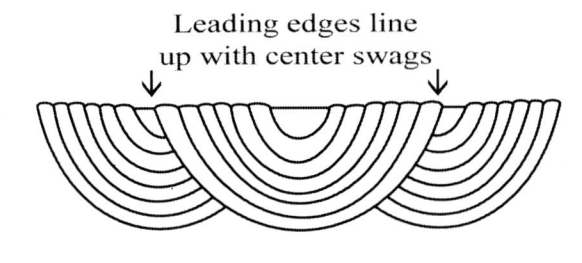

Gathered I

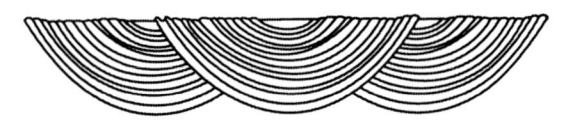

Traditional Formal II

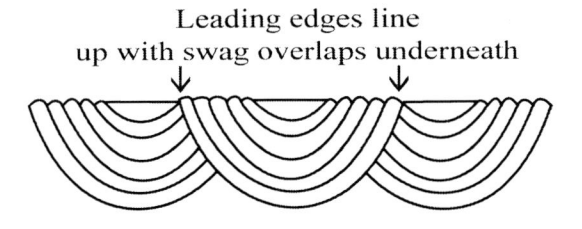

Leading edges line
up with swag overlaps underneath
↓   ↓

Leading edges line
up with swag overlaps underneath
↓   ↓

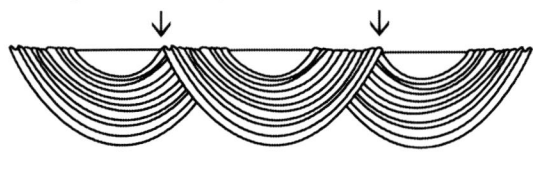

Open swag II

Leading edges line
up with swag overlaps underneath
↓   ↓

Formal and gathered I swags
This style is usually found on traditional swags. There are four different ways to achieve swag overlapping. The swags are mounted in such a way that each swag's tip to tip overlaps just the swag overlap area of the other swag. The leading edge of the swag unit is in the center of the other swag unit. If this style was placed on a pole, the swags' overlap would cover the rod, and would take away from a wrapped swag effect.

This style works well on straight, bowed, arch, slanted, corner, or angled bays.

Formal and gathered II swags
Both of these styles are available for either a traditional or open swag. Traditional swags have up to four different ways to set up the overlapping styles and for open swags there are up to twelve different variations.

The style is set the up the same way as for board or pole mounted swags. They are mounted in such away that each swag unit overlaps each other by the swag overlap setting. This is sometimes determined by the cascade width to simulate the wrap look. The size of the overlap can be approximately 6"-12", depending on the type of window and number of swag units used. See Appendix B for help in calculating swag overlaps.

This style works well on straight, bowed, arch, slanted, corner, or angled bays. Open swags on a bowed or arched window will require a custom rod.

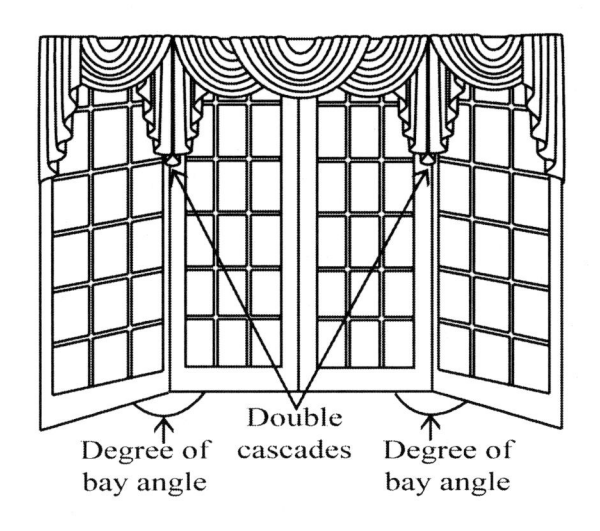

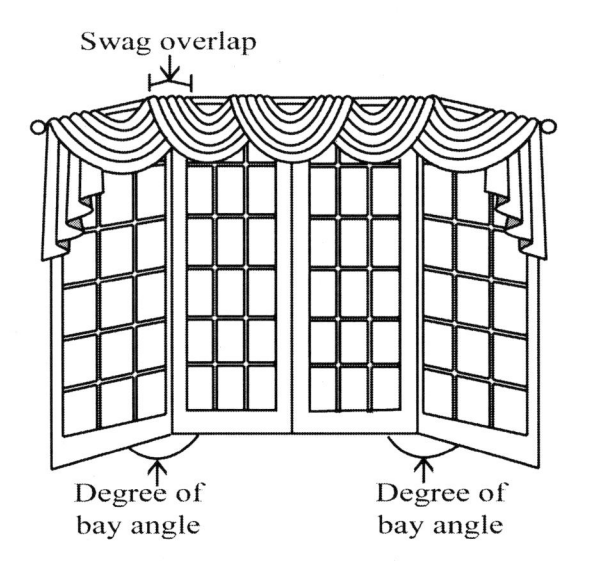

Bay swag overlapping options

For bay windows with the bay degree greater than 165°, it is recommend that a "double cascade" be placed on each of the degree angles of the window, or switch the swag style to Formal II swags. Be careful as the end swags may become more pointed due to the narrow width of side windows.

It helps to break down each section of the bay window to find the overall face width, and then calculate the tip/tip. This will give the approximate back wall face width. If the returns are greater than 3½", it is vital to figure the front board calculation (Appendix B).

For corner or bay windows, a horn, jabot, or double cascade must be placed on the angle of the bay. This allows the board or pole and the double cascade to bend at the angles of the bay.

For open swags on a bay window with an angle degree greater then 164°, the swag overlap cannot overlap the angle any more than 6" each side of the angle of the bay.

MEASURING FOR SWAGS

An estimate of the required swag length can be obtained by using the following formulas.

To find the finished length for ceiling mounted swags:

Measure from floor to ceiling ÷ 5, + 2". This will equal the recommended swag finished length.
Example: 108 ÷ 5 = 21.6 (round up) = 21.75 + 2 = 23.75".
This is the recommended finished length of the swag treatment.

Traditional and Open Swags

To find the finished length for above the window:

Measure the overall finished length of the window treatment (including under treatments) ÷ 6, + 2". This will equal the recommended swag finished length.

Example: 84 ÷ 6 = 16.8 (round up) = 17 + 2 = 19".
This is the recommended finished length of the swag treatment.

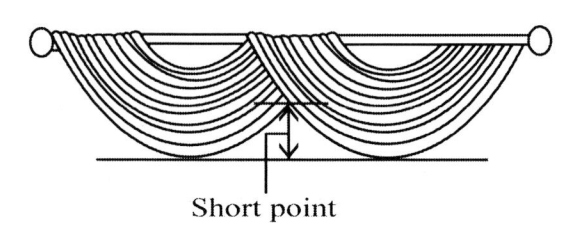

Short points
Swag short points will occur naturally as a result of the tip to tip, swag length, and overlap being combined. Sometimes these dimensions may need to be adjusted slightly in order to raise or lower the short point of the swag when coverage of under treatments or architectural features is necessary. This is another area where a scale drawing of the treatment is most useful.

To lower the short point, use a slightly wider tip to tip dimension and overlap the swags more. To raise the short point, use less overlap and a narrower tip to tip size.

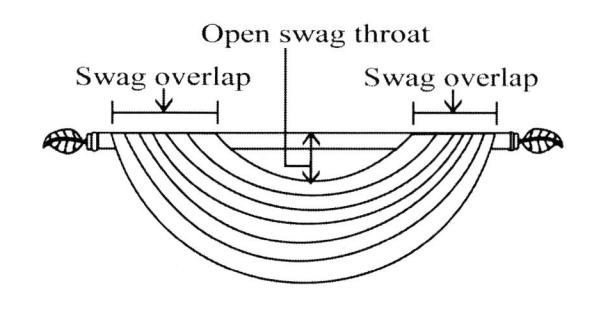

Open swag throat
When designing an open swag treatment, the gap or opening in the center of the swag must be carefully planned. If not, some undesirable results can occur, including light from the window shining through, and unsightly trim, moldings, or even rods of under treatments showing. Plan the height placement of the swag treatment in such a way as to ensure the opening in the swag throat exposes only what one wants to see. Specify the exact depth of the opening and plan swag lengths, tip to tip measurements, and overlaps to allow for the appropriate throat opening.

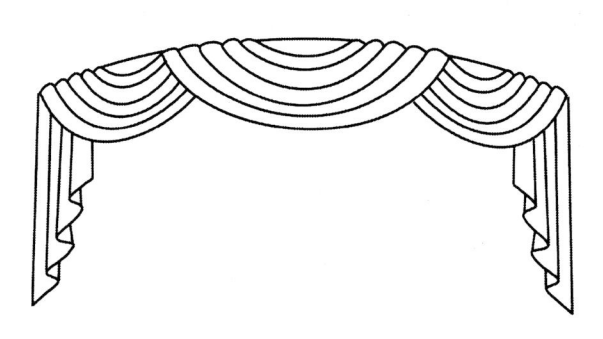

Varying swag sizes
When planning the swag treatment do not be overly concerned with steadfast rules, since there really is no right or wrong way to design these treatments. It is possible to use different sized swags, tip to tip sizes, and swag lengths all within the same treatment. The main goal is to create a functional treatment that will decorate the window in the style the customer wants.

The treatment must be functional in the sense that no odd looking spaces are created, seams are minimized or hidden, and all things that must be covered, such as window trims, moldings, and under treatments, get fully covered.

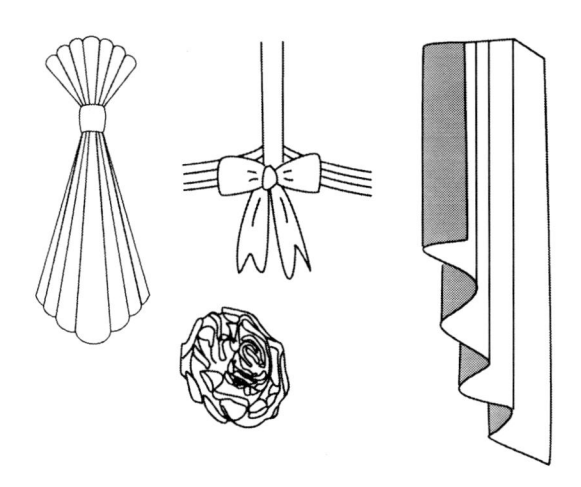

Adding decorations

Add-on items such as trims, ruffles, rosettes, buttons, and banding can also play a major role in creating a specific kind of style. Swaging cord and tassels over the fabric can add drama; a ruffle added to the hem of a swag can add a romantic effect; fringe trims might be sophisticated or playful. Often times it is the case that certain windows, because of their size and configuration, will dictate how the swag treatment must be arranged in order to function well. In these cases, the style must be added solely through fabric choice and decorations.

Filling spaces

Sometimes when designing a treatment, in order for some of the necessary coverage to be obtained odd spaces may be created. These spaces should be filled with add-on items such as cascades, double cascades, jabots, or panels. Sometimes, eliminating some swags and replacing them with a cascade or jabot can completely change the feel of a treatment and shift an odd look into a balanced one. In these cases, put pencil to paper to flesh out ideas.

Elements of Soft Treatments

SWAG RETURNS AND PROJECTION

Swag treatments, like most kinds of valances will have a return. Some swag styles have built in returns, in that the swag will wrap around the return, such as the boxed swag and end cap swag. These types of swags typically will have a hard return. Make the same allowances for swags with hard returns as would be made for any other valance with a hard return. Swags like the Kingston, Empire, and pick-ups have attached tails of some description which usually incorporate a return allowance. Plain, folded, or gathered swags will require the addition of a cascade or panel, and the return will be incorporated as a part of the add-on item.

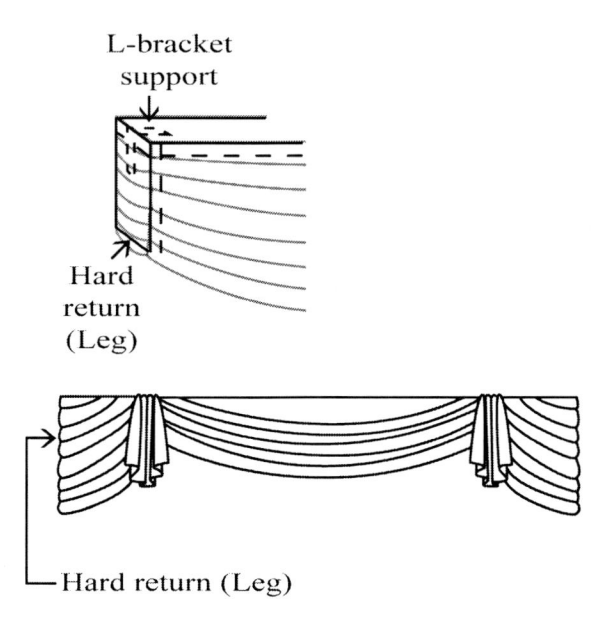

Hard returns

A hard return allows the fabric to wrap around the returns and remain in place. There is a side board that is the same width as the top board. Inside the corner of the hard return there is an L-bracket or other device used to help secure the hard return. The face width inside will be 1½" smaller in width due to the thickness of the hard returns.

> Some traditional swag styles use a hard return, so be careful with these styles, as the inside face width will be 1½" smaller in the width.

Projection

Swag projection allowances are the same as for other valances. Because swags have depth when folded, allow a little more space for clearance over working under treatments, such as vertical blinds and traversing draperies.

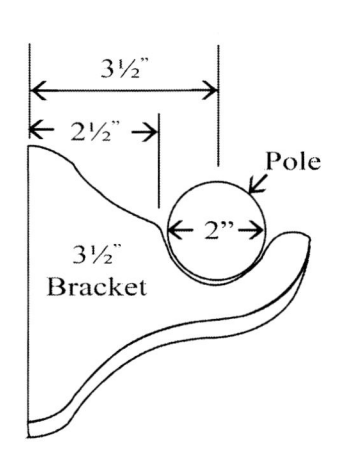

Ordering brackets

When ordering brackets from a manufacturer, the stated returns are calculated from the center of the rod, so if using a 2" pole and a 3½" bracket is ordered, the back of the rod will be 2½" from the wall. A return bracket one size larger may be required to obtain adequate projection for the swag treatment (see drawing).

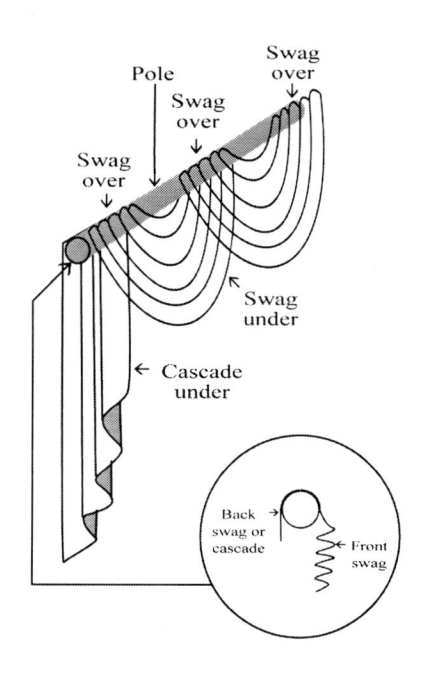

Chapter 7

Open swag projections
When open swags are mounted over draw draperies, increase the projection 1"-1½", because when pole swags are assembled, the swags mount to the front and the back of pole, which can cause the drapery to drag on the swags if there is not enough projection allowance.

> Open swag projections mounted on rods or poles will be limited by the size of available return brackets provided. It is best to order the bracket with the projection closest to what is needed. Send all of the rod parts, including mounting brackets, to the workroom so that they can determine the correct return size needed for the swag or any add-on items, such as cascades and panels.

SEAMING SWAGS

The seaming of swags should be avoided whenever possible. This can often be accomplished by carefully choosing tip to tip dimensions and fabrication method which will get the most swag out of one cut of fabric. Occasionally though, seaming will be unavoidable, usually because the fabric has a pattern which will demand a certain fabrication method or treatment dimensions simply can not be altered.

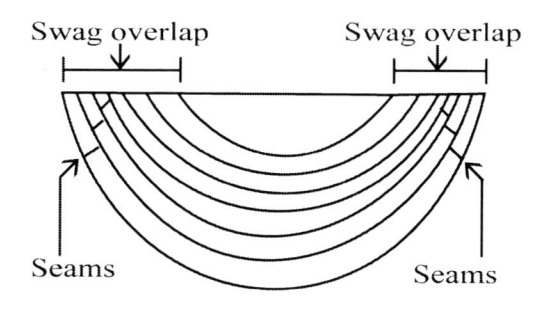

Upright (seams)
When seams are used, they are balanced on each side of the center of the swag. The seams will appear at a slant due to the folding of the swags. The fabrication method used, the number of swags, and the overall treatment width will determine whether or not there will be seams.

When designing the overlapping pattern of the treatment, every effort should be made to hide the seams. They can be placed behind other swags or covered by cascades and jabots (Appendix A).

Elements of Soft Treatments

Traditional and Open Swags

FINISHING AND MOUNTING METHODS

Swags are mounted three ways.

First method

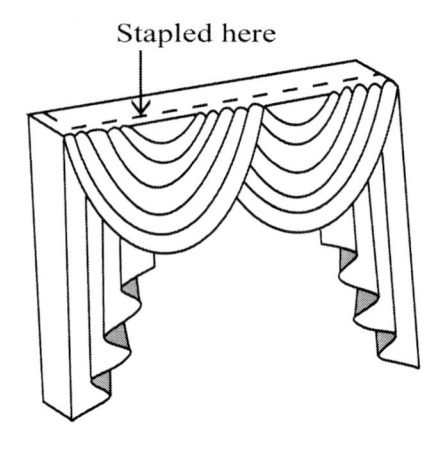

Second method

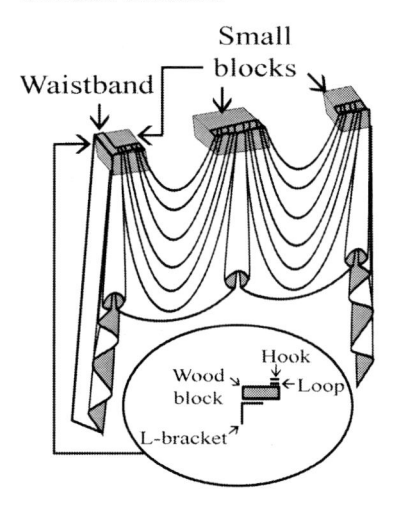

Third method

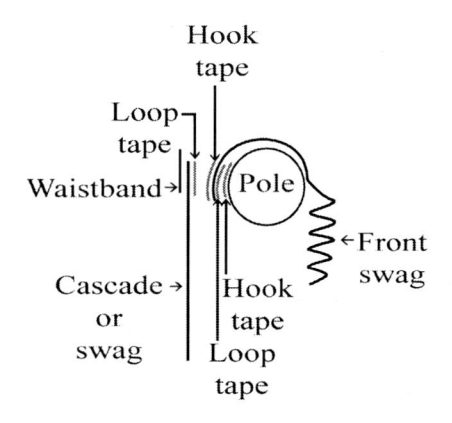

The first and most common method of mounting has swags which are permanently and directly mounted onto the board or pole using staples. In this mounting method, the swag is stapled onto the board or pole at the drapery workroom location. If the swag treatment will be mounted where the mounting will be visible from above, such as in a two story family room, request that the board be covered with the same fabric as the swags.

The second method of mounting is to attach the swag onto the board or pole using hook and loop tape. Very often the swag pieces will have a band of fabric sewn to the top, which will then have loop tape sewn to it. The fabric band along the top is called a "waistband" and it gives the swag a nice, custom finished appearance. Open swags on small wood blocks are installed with L-brackets or angle irons.

If pole mounting, the rod or pole will be wrapped with the hook tape and the swags placed in an overlapping pattern so the hook tape will be concealed toward the back of the rod. The entire preparation of the pole and swags is done at the drapery workroom. This mounting method may be chosen if the customer wishes to remove the swags for frequent cleaning, or if the swags are being attached to an iron pole which can not be stapled.

> Since this method is intended for removal and reattachment of the swag/s, be aware that they can come loose unintentionally. Advise the client that they may have to occasionally re-dress the treatment if the swags come loose.

The third method the swags are made with hook and loop sewn on but they are not attached to a rod or board. The swags are shipped directly to the installer, designer, or customer's location. In this case, the board or pole would be supplied by the installer, designer, or customer.

The board should be covered with lining, fabric, or painted. The installer, designer, or customer then attaches the swags at the job site. This method of mounting is a less custom approach but is sometimes requested as a cost saving method. This is a good option if ordering swag treatments where the product will need to be shipped to the job site, since boards and poles due to their length can sometimes be a problem to ship.

With this method, the wrinkles can be a problem as the swags are not dressed at the workroom. Steaming will need to be done and the design or arrangement of the swag pieces may need some extra communication between designer, installer and customer at the time of installation. Some fabrics do not steam well and the finished appearance of an un-mounted treatment could be disappointing.

STRIPED FABRICS AND SWAGS

Swags using striped fabrics will have unique characteristics, depending on the fabrication method used, and when the folds are set into place the stripes will lay in different direction. This is caused by how the swag pattern is placed on the fabric grain. Understanding what the stripe pattern will look like once fabricated is a useful tool in the designing of swag treatments. Clever use of this knowledge can result in looks which may not otherwise be obtained with a non-striped fabric. Overlap patterns may need to be more carefully planned if the fabric is a stripe.

If the stripe runs vertically on the fabric and it is to run vertically on the swag, the upright fabrication method must be used. The stripes will still have something of a fan effect as they are folded but this may be a desirable look. The same fabric railroad and bias cut will have a completely different appearance. Specifying which manufacturing method is to be used is critical, since if this is not done there could be an unpleasant surprise. The illustrations below give an idea of what a striped swag will look like depending on the fabrication method used. The bias swag can be made to have the grain running to the left or right. Use striped fabrics for a creative and fun treatment.

Traditional swag with stripes

Swag cut on bias | Swag with stripe vertical  | Swag with stripe horizontal

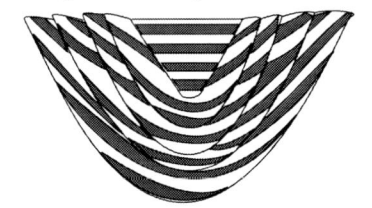

Open swag with stripes

Swag cut on bias | Swag with stripe vertical  | Swag with stripe horizontal

Elements of Soft Treatments

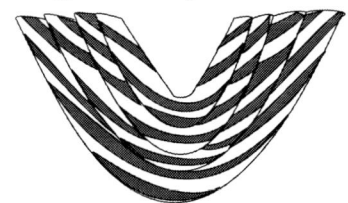

Traditional and Open Swags

LININGS FOR SWAG TREATMENTS

All swags should be lined except sheers, laces, and fabrics which are being used specifically for their transparent qualities. Transparent swags will have a small shirt tail hem if not lined and will need to be made in the railroad or upright method, as a bias cut will not hem neatly. If the swag is being lined and the fabric is lightweight, such as some silks, an interlining can be added to give the fabric more body and keep light from passing through the swags and spoiling the appearance of the treatment. Too much light can erase the overlapping pattern of a swag treatment and cause an undesirable look, so be aware of amount of light coming into the room. There is usually a labor up-charge for adding interlining (plus the cost of the interlining), so check with the workroom about their policies on this.

SPECIAL WINDOW SHAPES

Swag treatments can be adapted to almost any window shape. Because of their "modular" make up, the swag components can almost always be combined in some fashion to fit almost any situation. Bay and corner widows are a window configuration in which swags are particularly adaptable. Extra wall spaces can easily be filled with cascades or panels and a balanced look can be obtained for windows which can be awkward to treat with other designs.

Corner window set-ups

When designing a swag treatment to cover a corner window or bay, it is helpful to imagine the window on a flat plane first. Design the treatment as a single unit and then "fold" it at the corner. After folding the design, a few adjustments in hardware and component placement will be needed, but this method will almost always result in a functional swag unit. The corner image pictured, would work equally as well if the window configuration was on the same plane.

Arched windows

Swag patterns over time have been altered to allow for the treatments to arc and cover windows with arch shapes. When designing a swag for an arched window, gravity will always pull the drape of the swag straight down in a vertical direction. This will cause some swags placed on extreme angles to hang less straight. This is a normal feature of creating an arched or angled top swag treatment, and working with gravity, will result in natural, beautiful designs.

Arched and corner windows

Swag treatments can be used on windows with combinations of odd shapes such as this arched and corner combination. By applying the same principles as mentioned above, first designing the treatment as a single flat unit and "folding" it around the corners, an attractive solution can be achieved. The same principle will work with bay windows.

Traditional and Open Swags

GENERAL INFORMATION

- State on the work order if the swag is wall to wall mounted.
- If the top of a traditional swag is corded, state to make allowances for cord when wall to wall mounted.
- Choosing a fabrication method is part of the swag design.
- Specifying lining and/or interlining is part of the swag design.
- Swag configuration, overlapping pattern, and add-on specification is the designer's responsibility.

PRICING

- Swags are priced per swag or per linear foot. Check with the workroom to find out what pricing method is used.
- If pricing is per foot, there will be a minimum per foot charge.
- Traditional swags: face width + both returns ÷ 12, round up = number of linear feet, and is the billable footage
- Open swags: face width ÷ 12, round up = number of linear feet, and is the billable footage

RECOMMENDED FABRICS

- Use soft fabrics that will drape.
- Add interlining to swags - it helps add body and uniformity in the folds, eliminate light diffusions when overlapped, reduces color bleed through with contrast fabric, eliminate seam bleed through when seams are on swag face, helps folds relax when fabric is not cut on the bias.
- Use caution when using striped fabrics. When cut on the bias, the stripes will not be vertical.
- If using light blocking lining, request ultra soft 100% cotton blackout as the drape of this lining is better for swag drape.

TIPS WHEN MEASURING

- Plan to mount above the window a minimum of 6" (watch for swag short point).
- Watch for treatments that require hard returns. Be sure allowances are made for the thickness the hard return will take up.
- Allow face width to extend 1½"-2" on each side of the under treatment.
- For traditional swags, allow for the projection of the swag to extend 1½"-2½" to clear the under treatment, and more for working draperies or verticals, as swags have depth and tend to rock backward when hanging.

- For open swags, allow for the projection of the swag to extend further as the return is calculated from the center of the rod. Add in ½ of the rod diameter to 1½"-2½" to clear the under treatment, and more for working draperies or verticals as swags have depth and tend to rock backward when hanging.
- Check to be sure the swag short point will cover everything it needs to. Use a scale drawing if necessary.
- Check to be sure the open throat in any open swag does not expose any undesirable elements underneath the swag unit. Use a scale drawing if necessary.
- When mounting above a full working or stationary drapery, go a minimum of 1" above the drapery. This allows for the thickness of the dust cap board. In addition, check the hardware being used to be sure it will fit as planned.
- The swag long point should cover into the glass 3" to 4", and/or should cover the headrail of any blind or shade which are inside mounted.

Review

1) Describe the difference between a traditional and open swag.

2) Why are Empire, Kingston, and pick-ups classified as swags and not as toppers? Explain.

3) Outline how to shorten or lengthen the arc of a swag.

4) A client wants to be able to remove the swag units for cleaning. What mounting method and hardware would you recommend and why?

5) When ordering poles for open swags what should you be cautious of?

6) If a treatment has 3 formal swags, how many overlapping combinations can you come up with? What happens when the treatment has 5 swags?

7) What effect does changing the tip/tip have on a swag? Explain.

Chapter 8

WINDOW SCARFS

Window scarfs are sometimes called "throw swags" or "poor boy swags". Scarfs are just as the term "throw" indicates - they will be irregular given the throw look and considerably less structured than a swag. When installed however, the fabric does have something of a swag effect. When there are multiple swags, they will appear mismatched, as will the tails on the scarf. For clarity, it is best to avoid the use of the word "swag" when referring to this type of treatment.

Scarf valances look similar to open swags, which is why they are often confused. They are manufactured very differently from a structured formal swag: a scarf is made from one long piece of fabric which is usually railroaded, and an open swag is cut from a pattern and constructed in pieces which simulate a wrapped look. Scarfs are installed and formed entirely at the job site, either by the designer or the installer.

The business rule governing the window scarf dictates that when a window scarf is ordered, an informal and unstructured "swag-like" look is desired. There are three sub-categories in this section: pole wraps, scarf holders, and rod pocket wraps. All are made in a similar fashion.

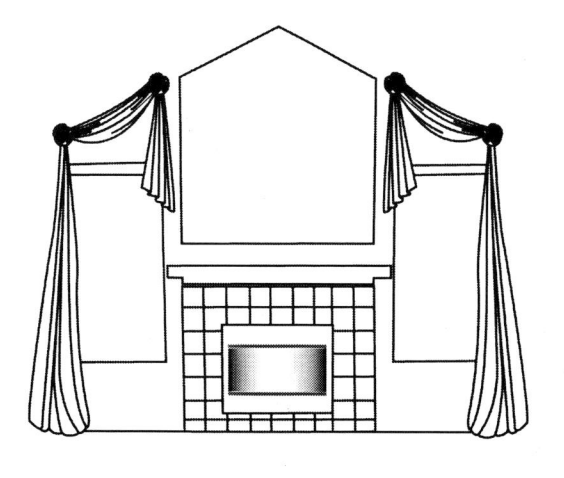

Elements of Soft Treatments

SCARF VALANCE STYLES

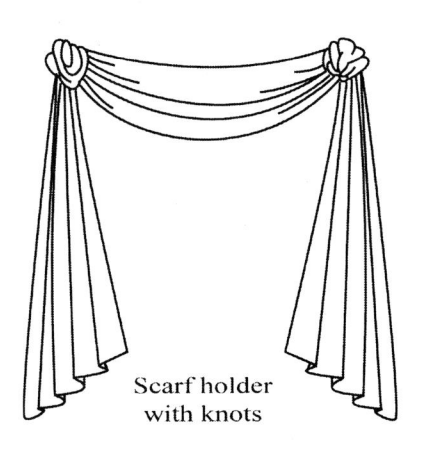

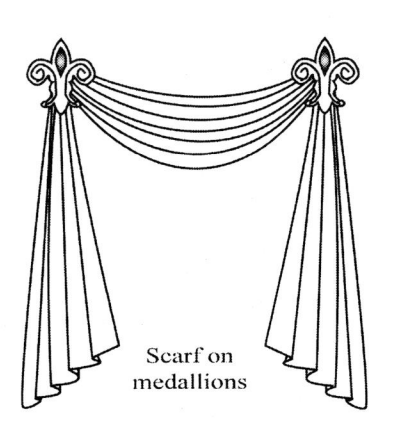

Pole wraps

The fabric is wrapped around a pole or rod of some kind. The fabric should be pillowcased and self-lined, and the ends can be mitered or straight. When the ends are manufactured straight, the tails will miter slightly due to the take up created by the twisting and draping of the fabric when it is wrapped around the pole. If a more dramatic taper is desired on the tails they should be angle cut approximately 15" shorter than the straight edge. This should be done only if the tails are over half the length of the window or the short point on the tail may cause the fabric to be too short to make the wrap around the pole. It is suggested that designers check with the workroom to confirm that the miter will work.

> When the fabric is flipped over the pole, the reverse side will show. For this reason, pole wrapped scarfs should be self lined. Contrast lining can create an interesting two color effect, as every other section will be the contrasting color.

Scarf holders

Depending on the hardware chosen, the fabric can be draped over the holder to expose the hardware, or be knotted to hide the hardware. The tails can either go to the floor, puddle, or can be mitered. With this style, depending on the desired look, the treatment can be either unlined or pillowcased (self lined or contrast lined).

> If the tails are mitered, then the scarf should be pillowcased (self lined or contrast lined), because some of the reverse side will show at the end of each tail.

Scarf holder with knots

Scarf on medallions

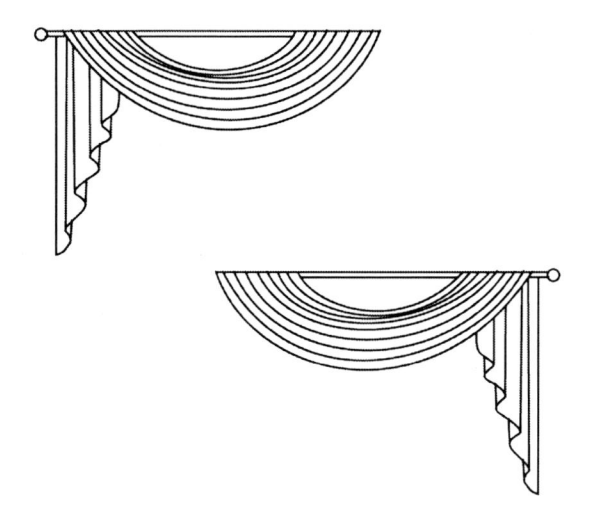

Rod pocket wrap

The fabric has a rod pocket on only one end. The fabric wraps to either the right or left side. It should be pillowcased, self lined, or contrast lined. If rod pocket wraps are unlined, the entire reverse side of the fabric and hems will show when the panel is flipped, causing an undesirable appearance. If the treatment requires more than one wrap around the rod, it should be self-lined, unless a contrast effect is desired.

> If the scarf is contrast lined, every other section will be the color of the lining.

> If the tail becomes a panel to the floor, it must puddle because exact lengths can not be achieved with a scarf.

STYLE VARIATIONS

Since this treatment style is unstructured, many different looks can be obtained depending on how the treatment is dressed. In fact, two scarfs constructed in exactly the same way and hung on the same size rod, should not be expected to look the same. Some of the most popular ways to vary the style of a scarf treatment are to hang them with fewer or more wraps around or over poles. In the case of a scarf with scarf holders or medallions, the medallions can be placed at varying heights giving the windows shape where there might not otherwise be any, or more than one scarf on the same window can create an interesting effect. Also, add-on items such as tied on rosettes can be utilized. Some examples are shown below.

Lifted points

By placing the scarf holders at different heights and varying the length of fabric draped between them, a very plain window can take on an interesting sense of style. Keep in mind that scarf styles typically do not provide complete coverage of window trims and under treatments. If covering these items is important a structured swag may be more appropriate.

Elements of Soft Treatments

Window Scarfs

Multiple scarfs
By varying the heights of scarf holders in combination with the use of multiple scarfs, more coverage can be obtained as well as give the treatment a very full and elegant appearance.

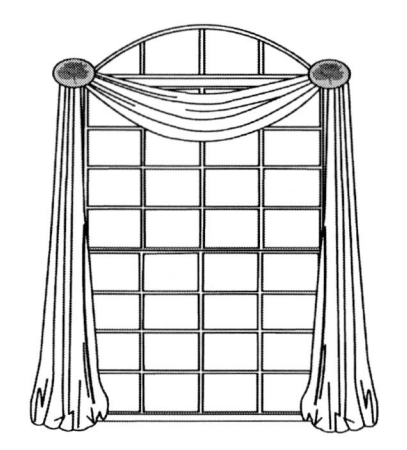

Changing tail lengths
It is possible for tails to be made drapery length. They can puddle on the floor for a dramatic effect, or a bishop sleeve look can be used. Tails can also be asymmetrical with one short and one long. Whenever a scarf is made with a floor length tail, a puddle look is strongly recommended due to the fact that exact lengths can not be obtained with a scarf.

> If cost is a major concern, the length can be reduced. Alternatively, change the drop length of the droops or wraps, as this will reduce the flat width thereby reducing yardage required. Halving the fullness will allow the scarf to be self-lined with one width of fabric folded in half.

MEASURING FOR SCARFS

Since window scarfs are informal and unstructured, measurements are usually more of an educated estimate than an exact measurement. Finished lengths are approximated and are only used for estimating the yardage and labor. Due to the complexity of the wrapping on a pole or scarf device, the length is estimated as it can not be specifically determined, which is why a scarf treatment should only be used in situations where exact fit is not critical.

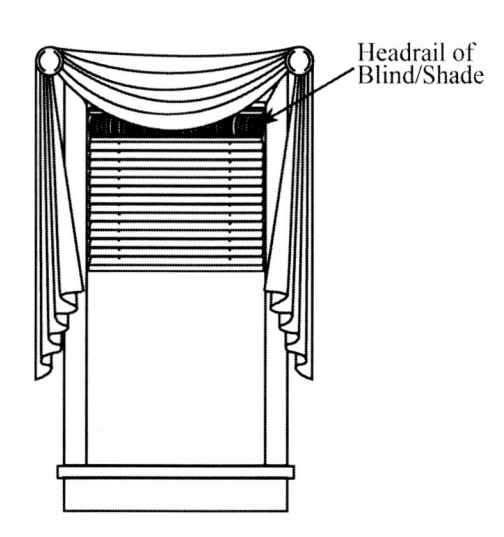

Headrail of Blind/Shade

Scarf holders
Scarfs installed on scarf holders are the easiest to measure. First, determine the placement of the scarf holders, measure between them, and add the length of each tail. The sum of these dimensions will be the scarf long side and this is the finished scarf length when there is only one drop.

When determining the placement of the scarf holders, a few basic rules should be observed. Holders need to be at least 2" above the opening if the hardware will allow it. When this is the case, a significant amount of the fabric drooped in between will cover the glass. Raising the holders will help resolve this in part, but more of the trim or headrails of shades or blinds underneath will be exposed in the short points. This is a characteristic of this kind of treatment and a design choice will need to be made. Discuss the differences with the client and choose the scarf holder placement accordingly.

Scarf holders also need to be placed close to the right and left sides of the opening, hugging the trim edges. If this is not done, tails and side panels will sit too far away from the window and look awkward. When placing a scarf over an inside mounted soft shade or blind, assume that some of the headrail will be exposed once the scarf is installed. If this is not acceptable, choose a structured swag instead.

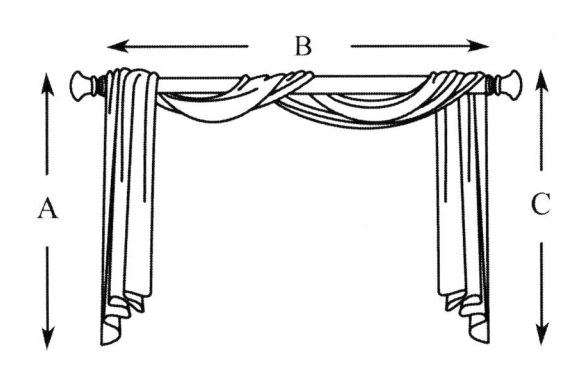

Pole wraps and rod pocket wraps
Measuring for a pole wrap scarf requires determining the rod width and tail length. Rod widths also need to be kept narrow so that tails hug the sides of the window. Place the rod according to client preferences, but at least 6" above the opening if possible. Tail lengths should be a minimum of one third of the window length or longer to help keep them from slipping off the pole once installed.

To estimate the scarf finished length, add the rod width, tail lengths, plus approximately 18" per swag for each wrap around the pole. The sum of these dimensions is the approximate finished scarf length.

> It is wise to remember that short points and long points are hard to control when using a scarf treatment, so be sure the client is aware that window trim will be left showing in places, and/or that glass will be covered.

Manufactured finished length
To help find the manufactured finished length, the string method can be used. If the scarf will be installed on scarf holders, simply drape the string across the holders leaving the desired droop in between. Measure the string length between holders and add the drop lengths. To calculate the length of a wrapped scarf, take a piece of string and wrap it around the pole in the fashion in which the finished scarf will hang, and then measure the string length. This will be equal to the scarf finished length when manufactured.

Elements of Soft Treatments

Alternatively, computer design software can be used to draw the design to scale, and then the computer can make the necessary calculations to determine finished scarf length. Most of the time the workroom can do the conversion from estimated length to manufactured length, but there is usually an additional labor charge to do this (check with the workroom regarding their individual policy).

SPECIAL FABRIC CONSIDERATIONS

The best fabric for this type of treatment is light to medium weight. Thick upholstery fabrics are not recommended because they will not drape softly enough. Sheer fabrics should be self lined. When lining with a contrast fabric, watch for bleed through on these types of treatments. For example, using a dark fabric as the lining, and having a light color fabric on the face will cause the face fabric to appear a different color.

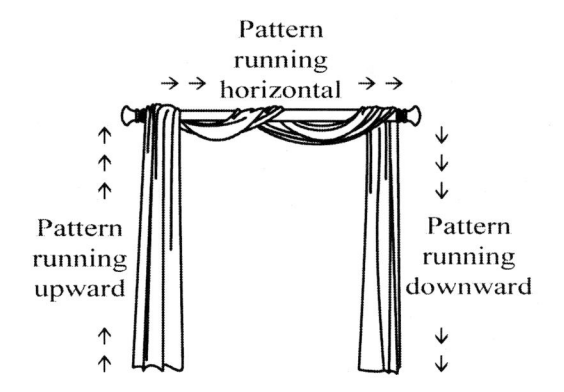

With printed patterns, be careful with the up direction on the print. When the fabric is draped over the pole, the fabric direction changes, thus up can become down. As an example, if you start the swag from the left, the pattern is running up on the left cascade or tail; when running across the top where the swags are, the pattern will be running horizontal; and when it comes down on the right cascade or tail, the pattern will be running down. For this reason, obvious one way patterns are not recommended.

Sometimes it is necessary to have the direction on the print be the same on both cascades. In these cases, there is a very labor intensive process which involves the workroom determining where the seam should be placed to be hidden when it is either wrapped on the pole or on the knot, depending on which style is being used. This is also known as "removing the dart" on some styles. Check with the workroom, as there is usually a detail charge for this work, and additional yardage might be needed to fabricate the swag.

CONTRUCTION METHODS

Below are descriptions of some of the different methods used in manufacturing window scarfs. As mentioned earlier, scarfs are basically one large, flat, continuous piece of fabric which is formed and dressed at installation, and depending on the final expected appearance, some methods may work better than others.

It is best to always self-line or contrast line a scarf, since both sides of the fabric will be exposed, especially when twisted around poles.

Pillowcasing is the method of manufacture used when a scarf is lined. When pillowcased, the lining and face fabrics are sewn together and turned with a knife edge so there is no hem. With treatments that wrap around a pole or are knotted, self lining is recommended unless alternating colors are desired, and then contrast lining will create the alternating color effect.

Unlined is when no lining is used on the reverse. The sides and bottom have a rolled hem which varies from ½"-1½". Be careful with this option, as the rolled hem can be seen as it is dressed on the window. This method should not be used for pole wraps, as when the fabric is twisted on the pole, the side hems will be exposed. Also, be sure that the fabric that is used looks good from the wrong side, as the back of the fabric will be seen when the scarf is hanging.

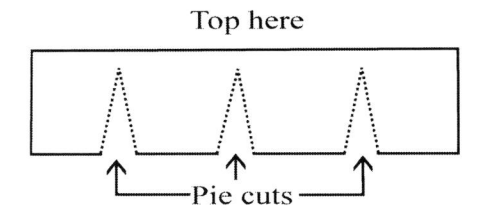

Pie cut scarf

This is used for a scarf which will be hung from scarf holders and there will be more than one droop of fabric. It is sometimes desirable to cut out pie shaped wedges in the scarf to prevent the fabric from becoming too biased when the scarf is hung. Too much bias will cause the tails to hang improperly, or cause the droops to be too shallow. The workroom can calculate the location and depth of the pie cuts, but be aware that there is usually an additional charge for doing this.

SPECIAL WINDOW SHAPES

Most of the time scarfs can be used on a window with an odd shape or configuration, and fabrication and mounting methods will be similar. However, some concerns may arise where it will be necessary to design carefully.

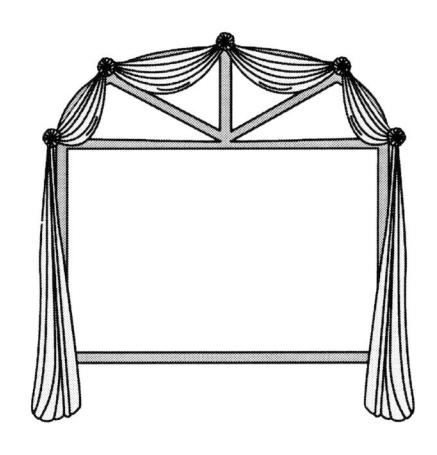

Arched shapes

The scarf treatment is often a good way to soften the look of an arched window without creating a complicated treatment. Drape the fabric softly over scarf holders placed in an arch shape around the window. This simple type of treatment solution can be very pleasing to the eye and it is also a less expensive solution for a client whose budget will not permit a more complicated and labor intensive treatment.

Elements of Soft Treatments

Window Scarfs

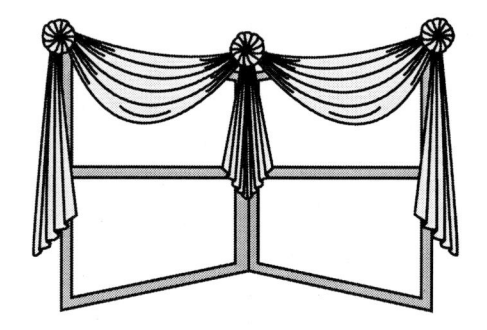

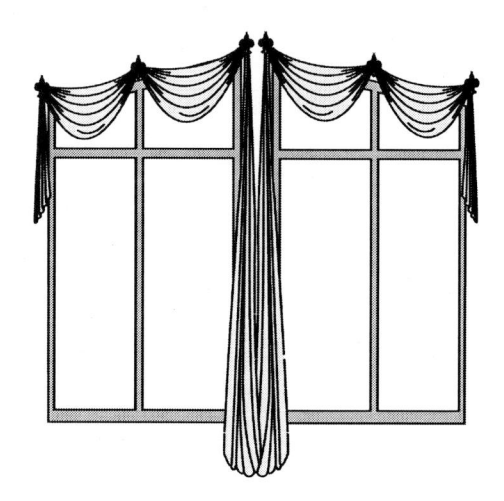

Corner windows

A scarf can be adapted to fit in a corner or bay window configuration with only a few minor changes. Hardware used may need some alteration in order to fit in the corner. Poles should be miter cut or a pole elbow should be used to turn the corner. In the case of a scarf holder, the installer may need to create a wedge for mounting the scarf holder so that it will face outward into the room. Sometimes a small scarf made separately may be needed to drape in the corner to fill the empty space or to hide the pole elbow.

Slanted top windows

In much the same way as an arch, a slant top window can be easily softened with a softly draped scarf and clever placement of scarf holders.

GENERAL INFORMATION

- Window scarfs do not work well over any type of outside mounted under treatments because the scarf can not wrap around the return and this causes the return of the under treatment to be exposed when looking at it from the side. Also, most scarf hardware will not allow enough projection for an under treatment to operate properly.
- Exact drop lengths of droop and tails can not be achieved with a scarf.
- Do not place the hardware point of the scarf too far past the edge of the window. When the fabric is draped over the hardware, it will cause the tails to hang too far away from the window edge.
- Fabric is usually railroaded and is manufactured in one length.
- Exact drop and length measurements of wraps, droops, and tails or panels cannot be guaranteed.
- Scarfs are installed either by the designer or installer at the job site.
- Identical window scarf treatments will never look the same, since these treatments are casual and unstructured.

PRICING

- Window scarfs are priced by the linear foot.
- Expect additional charges for calculating finished lengths, dart placement, or making pie cuts.
- Add-on items such as banding, trim, rosettes and the like will be charged separately.
- There is usually a minimum charge per scarf.
- Linear foot is equal to the total flat length or total finished length of the scarf, divided by 12, plus surcharges.

RECOMMENDED FABRICS

- The best fabric for this type of treatment is light to medium weight.
- Thick upholstery fabrics are not recommended.
- Sheer fabrics should be self lined.

TIPS WHEN MEASURING

- When mounting close to the ceiling, place the hardware to allow for the bulk of the fabric when wrapped or draped.
- Scale drawings can be very helpful in determining hardware placement, short points, and long points. If coverage is critical, a scale drawing is recommended.

Window Scarfs

Review

1) What are the 3 different types of window scarfs? Describe their characteristics.

2) Describe what lining option would be used to achieve a contrasting effect.

3) In which situation/s would you instruct the workroom to remove the dart? Explain your answer in full.

4) Outline the two methods of measuring for window scarfs

5) If it is important that the headrail of a blind be covered, what kind of scarf would be the best to use? Explain.

FABRIC SHADES

Fabric shades are similar to roller shades, but instead of rolling onto a tube, they hang from a board and are made from fabric. Fabric shades are mounted with L-brackets.

Sometimes a fabric shade can be made as a "bottom up-top down", and when this is done the shade stacks downwards and draws up when it is closed. The drawback to this type of shade is that there are guide wires or cords to hold the shade up. The spacing of these guide cords should be approximately 18"-24" apart, and will align vertically, causing the cords to be exposed when looking out the window. Very often the visibility of these guide cords is undesirable, but weighed against the benefit of the top down capability; purchasers will often choose this option despite the cords being exposed.

Fabric shades can also be fitted with motors, allowing the raising and lowering of the shade to be done by electrical switch, remote control, or attached to a home automation system. This technology is evolving quickly with the constant addition of new types of motors and controls. Motorization of window treatments is becoming more popular and affordable.

There are business rules for fabric shades just like the other categories. When you use the term "fabric shade", you are instructing the workroom that it will be some kind of board mounted fabric shade and that it will be strung by some type of a cord system to raise and lower it.

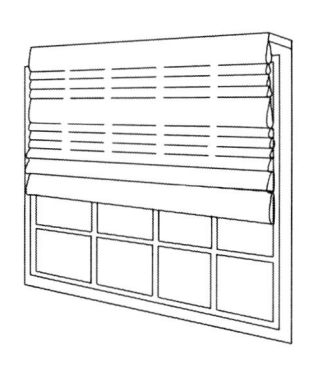

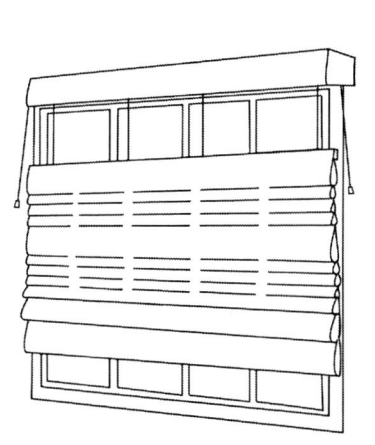

Elements of Soft Treatments

FABIC SHADE STYLES

There are three basic types of fabric shades. They are the Austrian, balloon, and Roman.

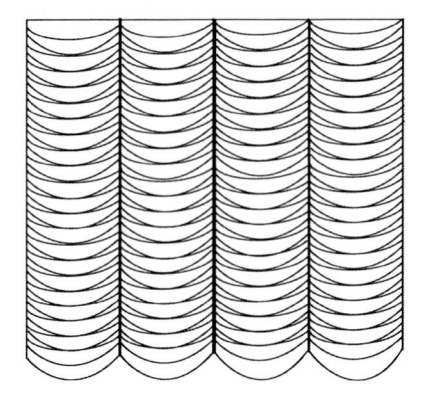

Austrian
This shade has fullness in width and length. The fullness added to the width is very small compared to the fullness in the length. The fullness to the length is achieved by shirring the fabric vertically, usually by some type of shirring tape. Shirring tapes will be visible from the reverse side. This shade style is usually very formal looking and often unlined because of its bulk when stacked.

Austrian shades often have a tendency to bow inward toward the middle of the shade on the sides due to the shirring, and this phenomenon is often referred to as "hour glassing". It will be the most noticeable on an inside mount, and sometimes if the problem is extreme, the hour glassing can be minimized with the addition of several dowel rods on the back.

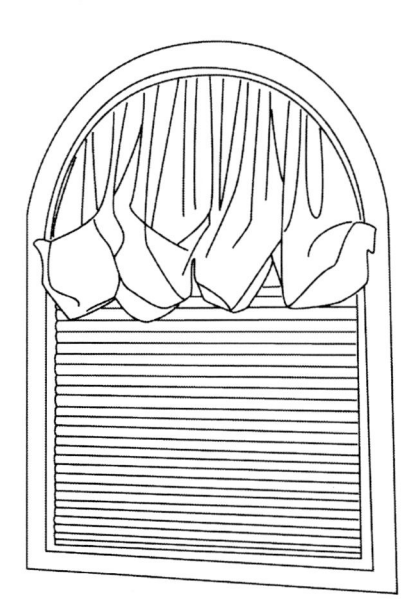

Balloon
This shade has fullness in width and length. It is different from the Austrian style because its fullness is greater in the width than it is in the length. Balloons are usually puffier looking and the stack of this shade is also quite bulky. Its finished appearance is very soft and usually considered formal or feminine. Wrapping around larger board projections will create a tail at each side of the shade.

When measuring for the finished length of balloon shades, remember there is a short and long point. Check with the workroom to see which measurement is used to determine the finished length and be sure there will be enough coverage if the shade is installed inside the window casing.

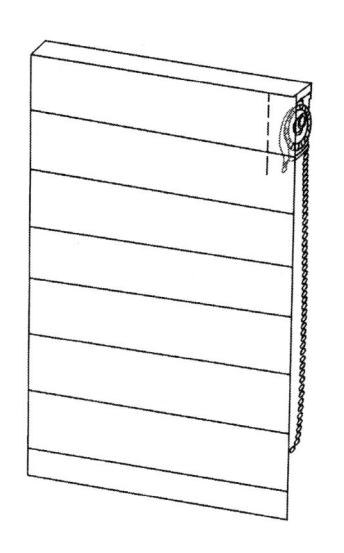

Roman

This shade has more of a flat appearance. The most basic Roman style is completely flat, but because of the absence of structure, a completely flat Roman shade often has operating issues. They tend to bunch when raised rather than fold neatly. This can mean that the folds have to be hand dressed each time the shade is raised and they can appear wrinkled when down. In order to avoid this problem, some fullness is usually added in the length only. The fullness, and therefore control of the stacking is added by means of some type of horizontal tuck.

STYLE VARIATIONS

The basic fabric shade styles can be changed by varying some part of their construction. Putting in additional folds, using more or less fullness, and changing pleat or fold spacing are some of the ways to alter the look. Some examples of these variations are shown below. Add-on items such as banding and trims are also frequently added to fabric shades to make them more interesting.

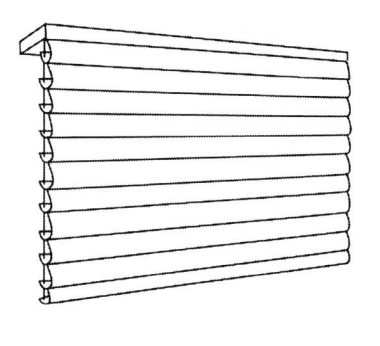

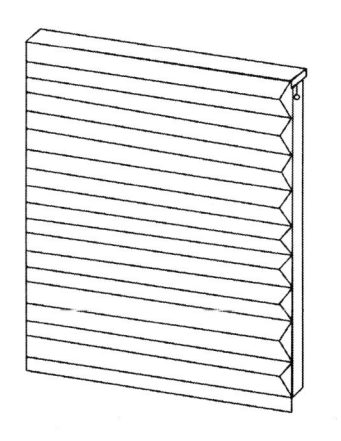

Hobbled

This variation is created by adding fullness to the length of a Roman style. The fullness is held up into soft folds through the use of flat tapes on the back. This style is very popular for use as a motorized shade, as it has a soft appearance and still holds its shape.

Accordion

This is also a variation of the Roman shade. In this case, not as much fullness is added to the length as in the hobbled shade. The folds crease into an accordion pattern, looking much like some manufactured hard shades. Fabrics used for this shade should be stable, tight weaves with a lot of body otherwise the look is more like a wave than an accordion.

Elements of Soft Treatments

Fabric Shades

Waterfall

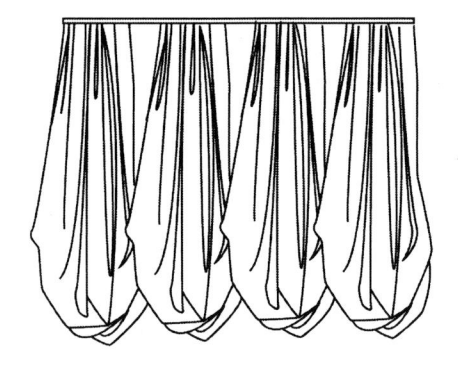

This variation is created by varying the fullness in the gathered section and not using any kind of shirring tape or pocket on a balloon shade. This creates a "waterfall" look.

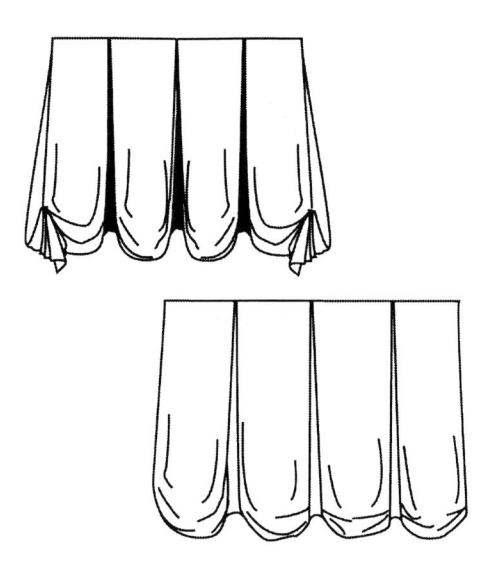

Box pleat

The balloon is also sometimes made flatter in appearance with box style pleats. When this is done, the shade takes on a more formal look than a gathered style. To add even more interest to this variation, add a contrasting fabric inside the pleats to pick up another color or fabric in the room. The contrast color inset is considered an add-on item, so expect that there will be additional workroom charges for this.

London

Another variation of the balloon style, this shade is flat with only two box pleats, each set in about 10"-12" from the side. This is an example of how varied sizes and spacing of pleats can change the look of a shade. The London style tends to be a more formal and stylish look.

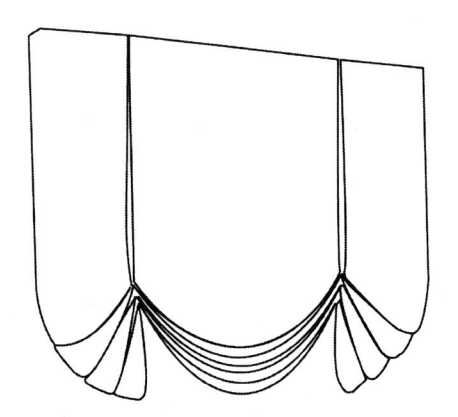

Chapter 9

ANATOMY OF A ROMAN SHADE

Shown below is some of the basic terminology used when talking about the components that make up a typical Roman shade. Knowing the names of the parts and their meaning will make communicating with the client and the workroom easier.

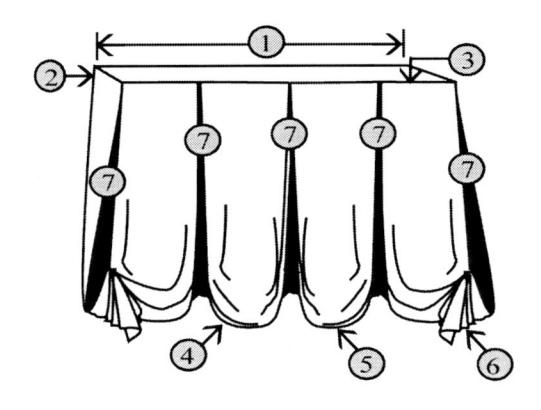

1	Face width	Width of treatment.
2	Return	Projection from wall to front of board.
3	Headrail	Mounting board to which lifting cords are attached
4	Poufs	Spaces between pleats on a balloon style shade
5	Finished length	Dimension from top of shade to its longest point
6	Tails	Free hanging tails
7	Contrast pleats	Different color fabric inset in the pleats

INSTALLATION AND MEASURING METHODS

Measuring for fabric shades is very similar to the other categories of drapery. The face width, finished length, and the shade projection will all need to be determined.

When measuring for fabric shades and giving specifications to the workroom, always state the width first and then the length. This order is a long standing industry protocol and must always be followed unless otherwise specified. If not specified, width first, length second is assumed. Fabric shades will have a 1½" projection unless otherwise specified.

First, determine the type of shade installation planned. There are four methods used for installing fabric shades.

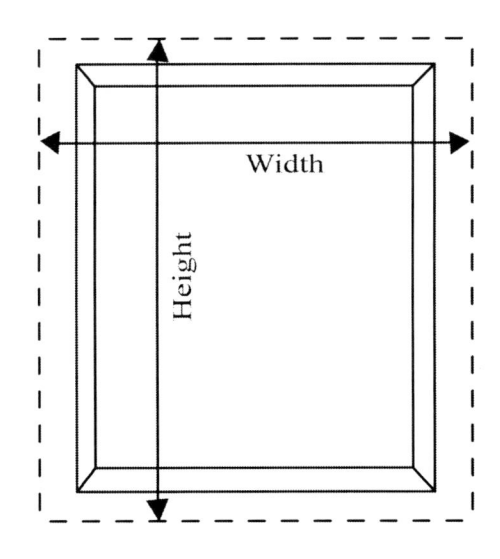

Outside Mount (OSM)

This means the shade will be mounted to the wall outside the window opening. Measure above the window a minimum of 2" and add (see fabric shade stacking formula below) to allow for stacking if the shade is to clear most of the opening when raised. Measure to allow the shade to extend 2"-3" below the window when closed. If there is a window sill or apron, it works best to cover these when outside mounting.

Elements of Soft Treatments

The width of the shade should be a minimum of 3" wider than the opening (1½" each side). If there is window trim, the shade should be a minimum of 2" wider than the trim (1" each side). If, for some reason the architecture of the window requires a projection larger than the 1½" standard, the shade width should be wider to accommodate coverage of the visual gap the larger projection/return will create.

Order the shade a little longer if the window is high because the visual perspective of looking up will cause the shade to look short. Order the shade wider in situations where maximum light blockage is desired as more light will pass behind the shade and into the room when a shade is outside mounted. This is often referred to as "light gap".

The benefits of this shade mount are that they are easy to operate, with an accessible cord. It also offers maximum light control. The biggest advantage is that measurements can be a little less accurate.

The disadvantages of these shades are that they can be caught on window cranks, and light gaps can be a problem. Additionally, end caps or a return wrap will be required.

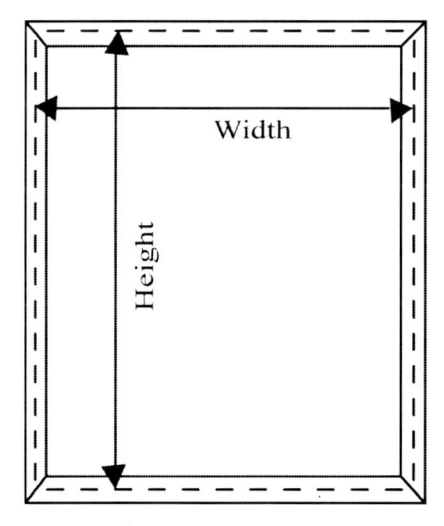

Picture Frame Mount (PFM)
This means the shade will be mounted onto the trim and a small border of the trim will be left showing on all four sides, creating a frame around the shade. Measure the width and length of the window including the wood trim. Measure the face width of the trim and subtract that dimension from the width and length. This will leave half of the width of the wood showing on all sides, creating the "frame" of trim. This mounting requires a ¾" projection (flat mount).

The advantage of this type of mount is that it gives the shade a neat, framed look.

The drawbacks include the need for precise measurements, and if the wood trim is out of square, a shade will make this defect more noticeable, and also potentially create light gaps. Shades using this type of mount require a flat mount.

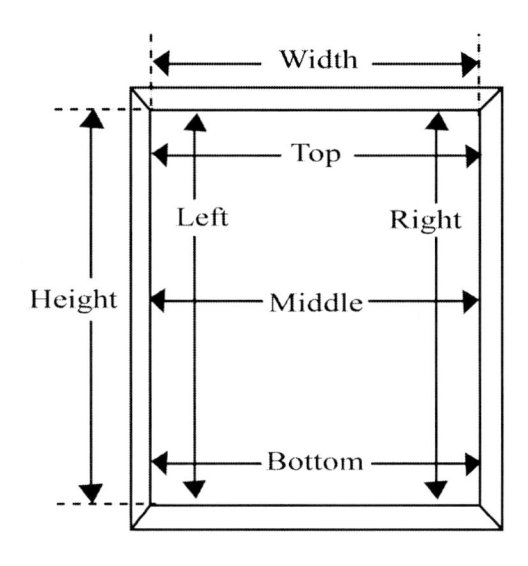

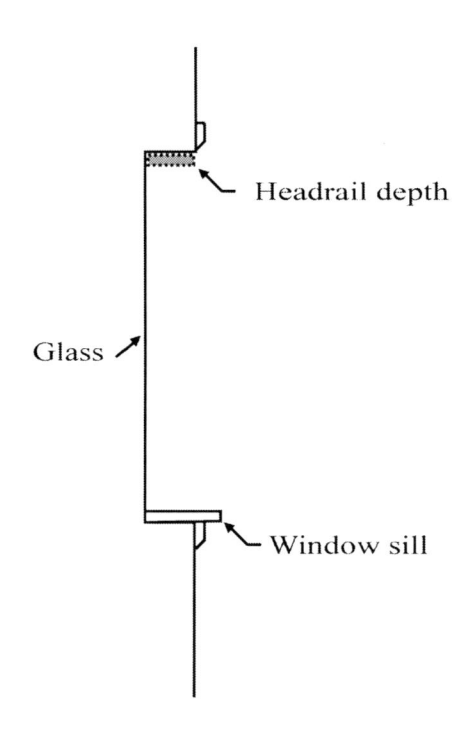

Inside Mount (ISM)
This shade is mounted inside the window casing. The person ordering the shade must make a deduction from the inside casing measurement to allow for the shade to raise and lower smoothly without getting caught on the window framing. It is the designer's responsibility to determine how much the deduction should be. Typically ¼" to ⅜" per side is deducted from the inside casing measurement. The finished length of the shade will be ordered to the exact length of the inside casing measurement. On the shade work order, advise the workroom that "deductions have been taken".

When measuring the inside width, measure in three places: top, middle, and bottom and use the smallest measurement. When measuring the length, measure in two places, left and right, and select the longest measurement. This only applies if it is an inside mount. Be careful with this if the window is out of square, as it will cause problems when the shade is mounted. For inside mount shades, make sure the headrail depth will fit into the window casing. Sometimes the window is not deep enough to allow for the full headrail to fit into the casing.

The benefits of this mounting method are that any wood trim will be shown off, and installation is flush to the wall.

This type of mount has a number of issues, including the shade being caught on window cranks, and with the shade stacking inside the opening, some of the light and view are blocked. Light gaps can be present on the sides of the shade, therefore requiring some side panels to deal with this dilemma. Some shade styles will cause a bow effect on the sides, and this will require additional attention.

Fabric of shade — Headrail

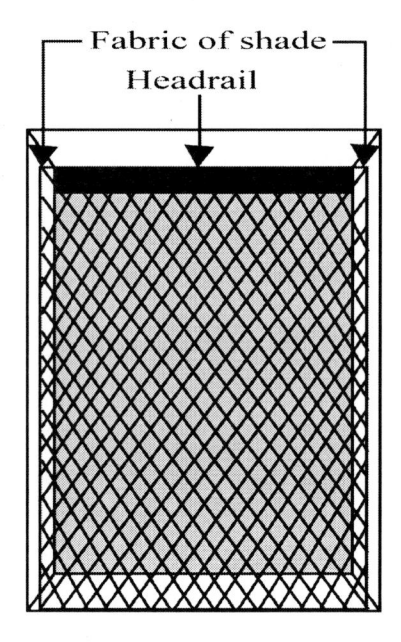

Hybrid Mount (HBM)
This is where the shade is mounted onto a board known as a 1×2, which is actually ¾"×1½". It combines an inside mount and an outside mount feature. The headrail or mounting board is inside the window casing, but the fabric of the shade will extend beyond the ends of the board to allow the fabric to be outside the opening. Small pieces of hook and loop tape are used to attach the extended pieces of fabric to the trim or wall.

Order the shade width as you would for an outside mount, but order the mounting board the width as you would for an inside mount. The shade length would be the same as for an inside mounted shade.

Since it can be cumbersome to open/close the shade as the cords are behind the fabric shade, a reverse mount with self valance and returns is recommended.

The benefits of this type of mount are that there are minimal light gaps, and insulating shades can be magnetically attached to the trim or wall.

The drawbacks to hybrid mounts are that the shade will stack inside the opening, and any shade cords can catch on window cranks and locks.

> The shade width cannot exceed more than 2" of the inside headrail face width.

FABRIC SHADE RETURNS

Fabric shades generally do not have any type of return because the wrapping of the fabric around the corners would interfere with the operation of the shade. Some styles however, will allow for the fabric to wrap around the mounting board to cover the projection of the board, but the expectation that the return of the fabric could be maintained throughout the raising and lowering operation is unrealistic. The typical projection of the shade mounting board is 1½". Larger projections can be specified, however, return wrapping if the style allows it, or an end cap to cover the end of the board and the shade operating mechanisms, would be needed.

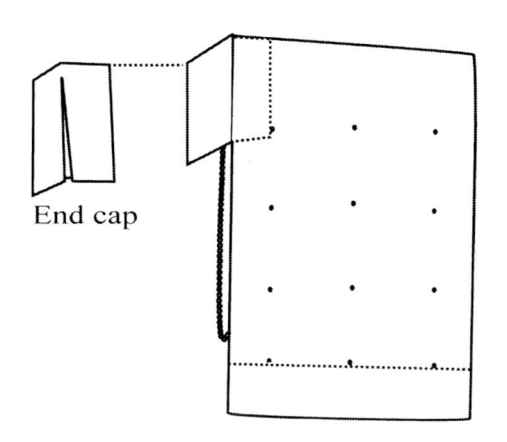

Using an end cap

An end cap is simply a flat, rectangular piece of fabric wide enough to cover the gap between the wall and the face of the shade, and long enough to cover the shade's operating mechanisms. There is usually an additional workroom charge for adding end caps to a shade.

HEADRAIL MOUNTING METHODS

There are three methods by which a fabric shade can be mounted to its headboard. The examples below are pictured with a cleat setup (see Mechanisms).

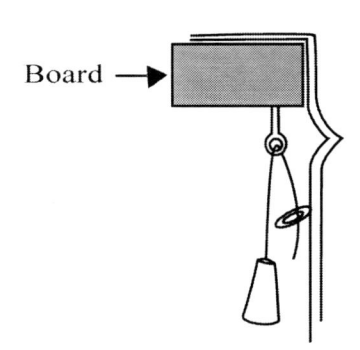

Standard mount

This is where the shade is mounted onto a board known as a 1×2. The shade projection is 1½".

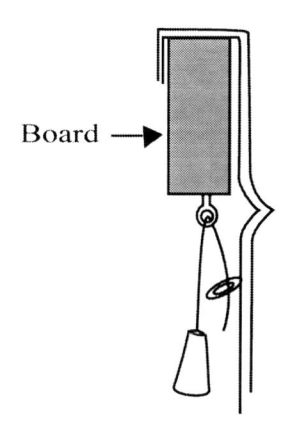

Flat mount

The shade is mounted onto the same type of board as a standard mount (1×2), except that the board is now laid flat. The shade has a small projection. Only cleats or cord locks work with this type of mount.

> This is a good method if mounting directly onto a door frame.

Elements of Soft Treatments

Fabric Shades

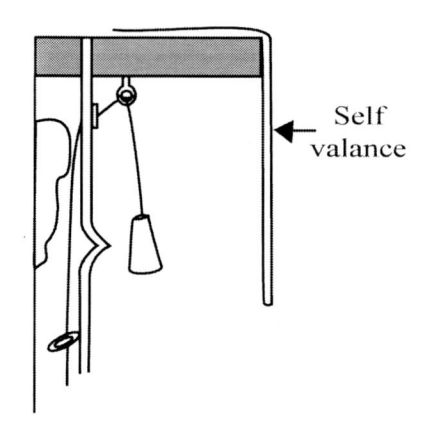

Reverse mount
Here, the shade is mounted onto two boards - the back board is 1"×¾", and the shade is mounted to this board. The other board, which is 1×2, has a valance mounted onto it. The cords are now in front of the shade, making them more accessible. A self valance will need to be ordered, and this will hang in front of the shade to hide the mechanism. This is generally considered to be the best mounting method, and it is usually the most expensive, so additional workroom charges should be expected if this is ordered.

Self valance

> This works well if the shade is an inside mount and the client wants to raise and lower the shade easily.

TYPES OF SHADE MECHANISMS

There are four different types of mechanisms available to raise and lower the shade: cleat, cord lock, mechanical, and motorized.

Cleat
A cord cleat is plastic or metal hardware piece that is mounted to the wall or wood trim. The shade is strung with cording which wraps around the cleat to keep it in a raised position. When a shade is operated, these kinds of mechanisms can be unattractive.

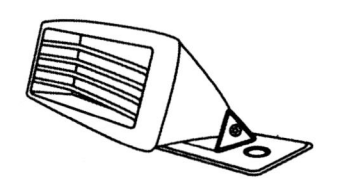

Cord lock
This device is mounted to the underside of the shade headrail, which the cords run though. By pulling to the left or right, the shade will raise or lower. When cord locks are used, the cord can become frayed over time and will need to be replaced. This device can pose a child safety issue if a cord cleat is not also used.

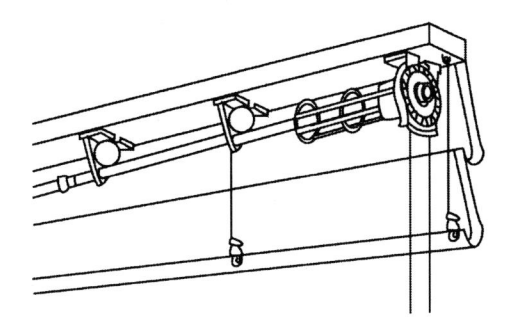

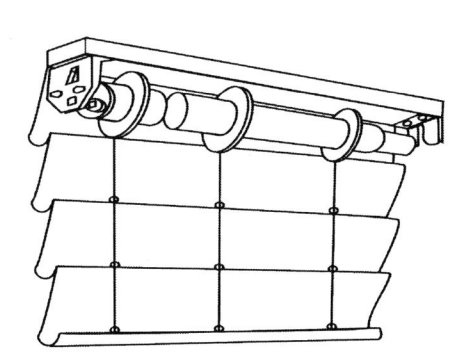

Mechanical

A mechanical system raises and lowers a shade by lift cords that wrap around a shaft. The shade is raised or lowered by operating the loop chain. Shades stay level, adjacent treatments are easily set to matching levels, and heavy shades feel light. There are no tangles of cords. An end cap will be needed to cover the mecansim. If the shade is 15 pounds or less, a mechanical mounting can be done on a 1x2, otherwise a larger projection headrail will need to be used, usually a 1x3 or 1x4, depending on the workroom.

Motorization

When a shade is motorized, the shade is still strung with cords, or sometimes small tapes are used, but they wrap around a tubular type motor which connects to an electrical control system. The control can be through the use of an electrical wall switch, remote control, or home automation system. Motorized lift systems allow very large window openings to be covered with one shade, instead of breaking up the window into smaller sections. They are also practical for use on very high windows that can not be reached.

Electrical motors require a source of power to be at or near the window opening. Hard wiring will allow the use of motors that can lift more weight, but there are some battery operated types of lift systems available for smaller shades. A motorized shade currently requires a mounting board projection with a minimum of 4" to accommodate the motor, and an end cap to cover the mechanism. The Roman style shade, because of its structure, lends itself to motorization better than an Austrian or balloon style.

> If using a cleat or cord lock, it is recommended for child safety purposes that the cords of the fabric shade are braided when the shade is in its down position.

Elements of Soft Treatments

FABRIC SHADE STACKING

It is necessary for window treatment designers to learn the formula for shade stacking, because in many cases shade stack is critical in determining if it is possible to use a shade in a given situation. Some styles of shade will have a very deep stack and because of this, shades may not be the best covering solution, or additional coverings may be required to hide the stack of a fabric shade. Fabric stacking is never an exact science and the formulas given are a way of estimating stack in order to make designing the treatment easier. In a situation where shade stacking is critical (such as above a door), design the treatment with this fact in mind.

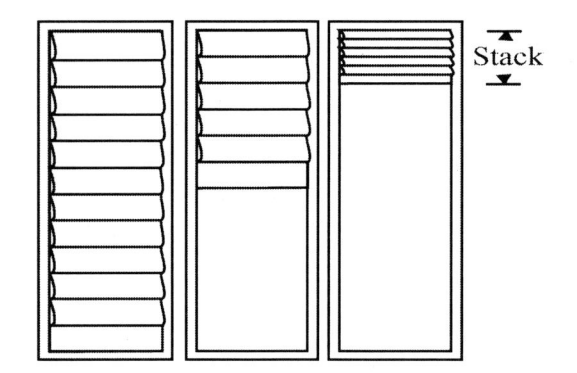

The stacking area on fabric shades is from the top of the headrail to the bottom of the shade when raised (see drawing). There are two formulas for calculating the stacking area. One is for Roman shades and the other is for balloon shades. They will vary according to shade style, fabric, and lining used. The following formulas are based on a medium weight fabric and lined shade.

Roman shades

Length of shade (in inches) × .130 = estimated stack area

Example: 84" finished length. × .130 = 10.92", which rounds up to 11"

Balloons

Length of shade (in inches) x .25 = estimated stack area

Example: 84" finished length. × .25 = 21"

SPECIAL WINDOW SHAPES

Most of the time, a fabric shade can be used on a window with an odd shape or configuration, and fabrication and mounting methods will be similar. However, some areas may arise where it will be necessary to design carefully.

Doors

If the fabric shade is to cover a door opening, figure the stack and design the treatment to install high enough to allow an average sized person to walk under it without stooping when it is raised. Check to be sure there is enough wall space above the door to accommodate the stack. Fabric shades over doors will have to be completely raised in order to go in and out of the door, and in the case of sliding doors, this may defeat the convenient use of the door.

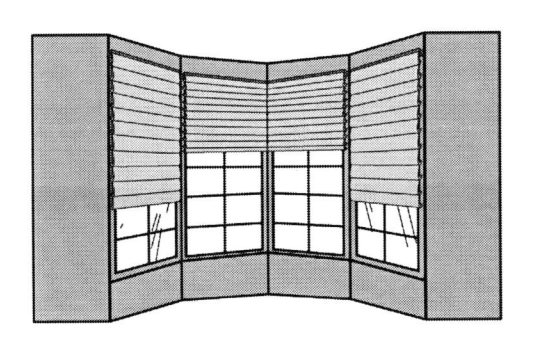

Corner and bay windows

Roman shades can be used for these types of windows, however fabric shades will protrude several inches in front of their headrail when stacked. Be sure there is enough wall space between the windows to accommodate this and make the shades narrow enough that they by-pass each other without hitting when operated.

Arched top windows

Roman shades can have arched or slanted tops, but the shade will only be operable to the base of the arch or lowest point of the slant.

GENERAL INFORMATION

- All shades use a weighted bar at the bottom.
- All shades are board mounted onto a pine board head rail.
- Shades over 15 lbs should have mechanized lift systems to handle additional weight.
- The face fabric on balloon shades will wrap around the end of the board and cover the return.
- Austrian and Roman shades do not wrap around the return.
- Balloon shades wrap around the returns
- Some Roman shade styles may bow, "hourglass", or droop unless horizontal dowels or edge wires are added.

PRICING

- Fabric shades are usually priced by the finished square foot.
- There is usually a minimum square foot charge per shade.
- To determine the square footage: take the finished length × the finished width ÷ 144, round up = billable square feet. (E.g. 60 × 54 = 3240 ÷144 =22.5 round up to 23).
- Fabric shade add-ons such as headrail upgrades, banding, fringe trim, ruffles, etc. are billed as a separate charge, usually by linear foot or per item.

RECOMMENDED FABRICS

- Soft-handed satins, polyesters, laces, and sateen weaves work the best for balloon shades.
- Stiff chintz, harsh linens, or crisp cottons will need to be dressed when raised or lowered on balloon shades.
- Use crisper fabrics for Roman shades.
- Use light-weight fabrics for Austrians.
- Because fabric shades are operable, select fabrics or styles that minimize wrinkles.
- Casements are too bulky and unstable for most shade styles.
- If using light blocking lining, fabric shades will usually have some pin holes or light leaks because of the stitching. Show the client a sewn sample.

FULLNESS RECOMMENDATIONS

- Ask the workroom for specific information by style.
- Ask to see sewn samples of any shade style if there is any doubt.

TIPS WHEN MEASURING

- Balloon and Austrian shades require more stack compared to Roman shades.
- Be careful with windows out of square since this can cause problems when the shade is mounted, by preventing proper operation of the shade.
- When measuring for the finished length of balloon shades, remember there is a short and long point. Check with the workroom to see which measurement they use to determine finished length.
- Specify on the work order if allowances have been taken for inside mounted shades.
- For inside mounts, watch for window cranks, screens, latches, and other obstructions that shades could catch on.
- T-cranks can be purchased to replace window crank handles. These are smaller and can help shades work better when inside mounted.
- Remember: fabric shades will stack in front of the headrail to some degree. Be sure there is room for this in corners, bay windows, and pockets.

Fabric Shades

Review

1) If blocking light is the main concern, what choice of mount would you select and why?

2) If only 2" of space is available above the window for stacking, which mount would you select and why?

3) Your client's room has an 8 foot ceiling and a pair of 7 foot high French doors that open into the room. What treatment would you recommend and what factors should be considered?

4) Which of the three basic shade styles is the best to use if the shade will be motorized and explain your answer.

5) How much room would be needed to stack a balloon shade that is 80" long? Show your working.

6) Your client wants to use a bottom up-top down shade. Which of the basic styles do you recommend and why?

SUNBURSTS

A sunburst is a decorative fabric window covering used for many types of odd shaped windows. The window shapes which particularly lend themselves to a sunburst are round, oval, semi-circular, triangular, or some portion of these shapes. The sunburst is not an operable type of covering but rather is used as a decorative way to filter or block light from an opening which may not otherwise be coverable due to its shape.

The fabric is fixed to a frame made of wood or a curtain rod designed for a sunburst shape. The fabric is often shirred around a half circle shape and then gathered into a tight knot at the bottom center of the half circle, creating a pattern in the fabric that looks similar to rays of light coming from behind a setting or rising sun. Today, the sunburst can be found in many shapes, and is either shirred or pleated.

Sunbursts are made both lined and unlined, and sometimes the frame may be covered with light blocking lining to cut the light coming through rather than filter it. Solar screening material is also occasionally used to cover the back of the frame to cut ultra violet rays and heat in some openings. When ordering a sunburst from the workroom, the term implies that the treatment will be an inoperable covering fixed to a frame or rod.

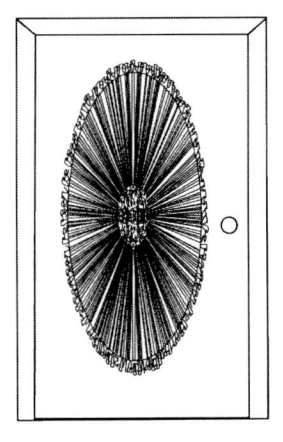

Elements of Soft Treatments

Sunbursts

SUNBURST FRAMES

The fabric is applied to a frame vertically, horizontally, or in a sunburst shape. The three main types of frame styles are the hidden wood frame, padded or painted picture frame, or a rod pocket frame.

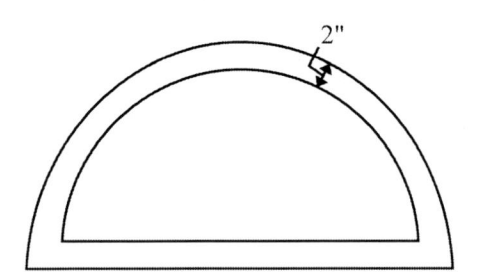

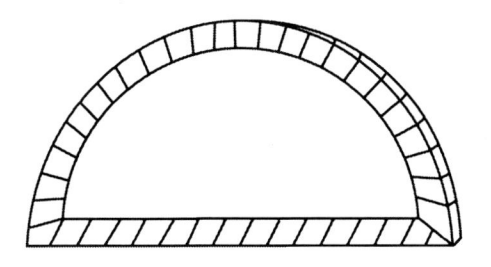

Hidden wood frame

This is the most common way the custom sunburst is made. The frame is cut out of ¾" plywood and is made to the same shape as the window. The frame is approximately 1¼"-2" wide, and the center is cut out.

The frame can be mounted inside the window casing or outside mounted onto the window trim or wall.

There are three ways the wood frame can be covered.

Wrapped frames are covered with small strips of lining, contrast lining or face fabric approximately 3" wide that are wrapped around the frame in a candy cane fashion. This is done prior to attaching the decorative fabric to the face of the frame so that the bare wood will not be exposed from the back, or visible from the front through sheer fabrics. In this method the wrapping will be visible from the outside when looking in toward the house. Use this method when the appearance of the back of the sunburst won't be an issue.

Upholstered frames are made by using one complete piece of fabric or lining which covers the entire frame. When looking in from the street side, it is a much cleaner look, because there is no wrapping effect. Use this method if the window faces the entrance of the home or is located where the back side of the sunburst needs to look as neat as the front.

> When a light blocking effect is desired, order the frame to be upholstered with a blackout lining rather than the sunburst. This will allow the decorative cover to be unlined which is less bulky and then it will have tighter shirring or crisper folds.

Painted frames can be used in place of a wrapped or upholstered frame in order to reduce the cost. Check with the workroom to see if this method is available.

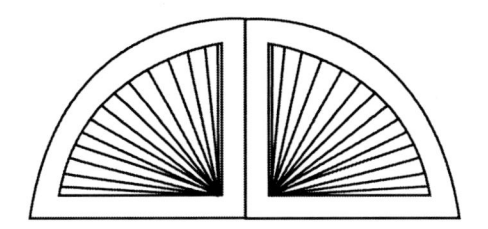

Padded or painted picture frame

When the sunburst is made with this type of frame, an additional frame of wood is added. The added frame is either upholstered with fabric, or painted or stained to enhance the sunburst. The frame that mounts over the sunburst frame is usually about 4" wide but it can vary and have many types of detailing, depending on what is available from the individual workroom. This type of frame usually works only if there is no wood molding around the window, and is in fact often used to create such an effect when the architecture does not provide any.

There are two methods for attaching the sunburst to this type of frame. If the sunburst is an inside mount, the padded or painted frame is attached directly to the sunburst frame. The padded or painted frame is actually on the outside of the wall with the sunburst frame just inside the window casing. The thickness of the padded or painted frame is approximately ¾". In this scenario, there are two frames - the sunburst frame and the padded or painted frame.

If the sunburst is an outside mount, the padded or painted frame has a rabbit cut out on the back inside edge to allow for the thickness of the fabric. This allows the padded or painted frame to sit flush to the wall. The sunburst fabric is then attached directly to the padded or painted frame. The thickness of the frame is approximately ¾".

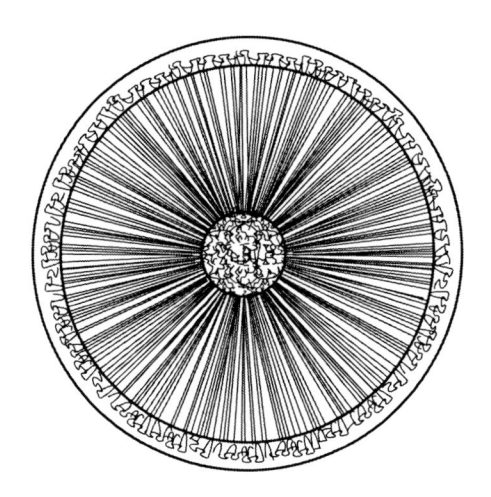

Rod pocket

The rod pocket sunburst is constructed by using a special type of flexible rod in place of a wooden frame. This type of sunburst is only appropriate for certain sizes of windows, usually fairly small ones, and only certain shapes such as small arches, circles, elliptical arches, octagons, or ovals. Because there are a number of limitations with these types of rods, be sure it will work for the size and shape of the window before making a final choice.

Because the rods can not support as much tension as a wooden frame, the fabric should be light weight and shirr easily. The sunburst will be made with pockets or casings to fit the rod, and it will then be assembled and shirred onto the rod by the installer. The rod is then attached to the frame of the window by using clips. The fabric is pulled together in the direction of a rosette, and is held in place with cable ties. This treatment type does not produce a look that is as controlled as the hidden frame or picture frame styles, and because the rods will not support as much tension as the frames, the fabric may loosen and sag.

Elements of Soft Treatments

SUNBURST STYLE VARIATIONS

Sunbursts can be made in one of two styles, shirred or pleated, but the look of the sunburst can be changed in many ways whilst allowing their basic function to remain the same. These treatments are intended to cover openings to control light and are not operable. With this function in mind, there are many interesting ways to change the look of the sunburst. Shirring, pleating, varying spacing and fabric direction, clever use of add-on items such as banding, ruffles, buttons and rosettes are just a few examples. Some illustrations are shown below.

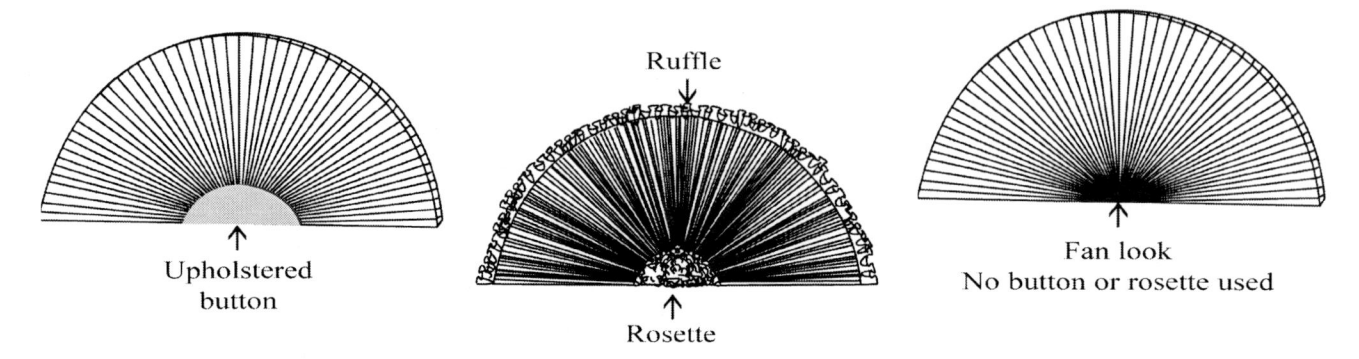

Upholstered button

Ruffle

Rosette

Fan look
No button or rosette used

ANATOMY OF A SUNBURST

The basic sunburst is made up of a frame which is wrapped, upholstered, or painted. The frame is covered with a decorative fabric. Any add-on items such as ruffles, cording, rosettes, or buttons are then added. The height and width of the frame will be the finished width and length of the ordered treatment.

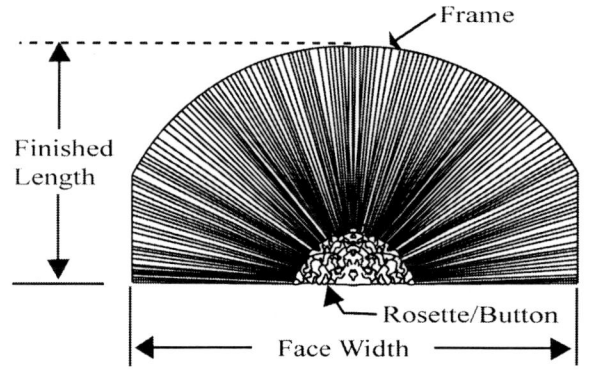

Frame

Finished Length

Rosette/Button

Face Width

COMMON WINDOW TYPES FOR SUNBURSTS

Below are some examples of odd shaped windows that are excellent candidates for a sunburst treatment. These shapes can often be enhanced greatly with the addition of a light filtering covering such as a sunburst.

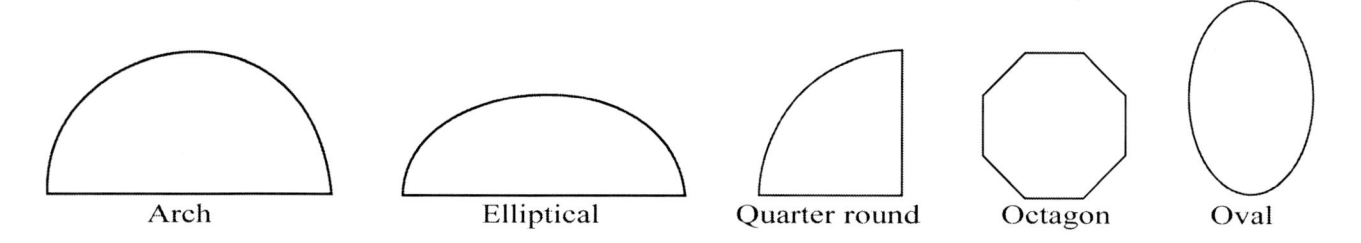

Arch

Elliptical

Quarter round

Octagon

Oval

Triangle   Trapezoid   Round   Square

SUNBURST INSTALLATION

Sunbursts are installed either as an outside mount (OSM) or inside mount (ISM). In both cases, a template of the exact window shape will be required in order to construct the frame or to fabricate the sunburst if it is a rod pocket style.

The sunburst is usually attached to the wall or window casing through the use of some type of L-bracket or finishing nails hidden under the fabric of the treatment. When designing the sunburst, be sure that there will be a way to hide the L-bracket or access the back side when mounting, such as hiding the brackets behind a ruffle or in the folds of the sunburst.

Outside Mount (OSM)
When using an outside mount application, the sunburst will be made larger than the window opening and will be mounted outside the window casing directly onto the wall. This method is preferred because all light gaps will be hidden by the frame against the wall.

Inside Mount (ISM)
When a sunburst is inside mounted it is installed inside the window casing, and as a result there will be a greater chance of light coming in around the outside edges. To minimize this, add a self welt or self ruffle along the outside edges of the frame.

MEASURE FOR SUNBURSTS

Measuring for a sunburst is straightforward.

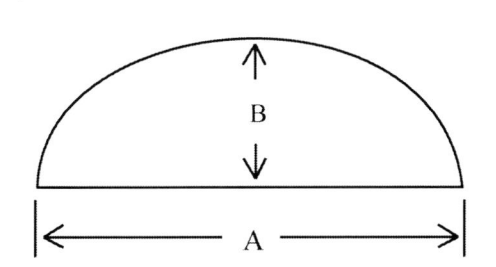

First, determine the type of sunburst frame and shape required. Second, decide which will be the most appropriate method of mounting the sunburst. Next, determine the widest part of the sunburst, (A). This will be the face width. Finally, determine the measurement of (B). This will be the finished length.

If the sunburst is an outside mount, add at least 2" around the perimeters of the window edge or frame to ensure that there is complete coverage of the opening and to close any potential light gaps. If the sunburst will be inside mounted, make a template of the opening or have the installer make a template.

Elements of Soft Treatments

For some outside mounted applications, there are companies that can create a template using drafting programs. They require complete specifications and measurements, which they will then convert into a full pattern for the workroom. The templates are then mailed to the designer or the workroom. Keep in mind that these services are not suitable for an inside mounted sunburst.

> When a sunburst is inside mounted, have the installer "dry fit" the frame before it is covered with the decorative fabric. A dry fit is when the cut, but not upholstered, frame is taken to the job site and the fit is "tested" prior to covering.

SPECIAL WINDOW SHAPES

The sunburst is a treatment that was designed specifically to address the problem of special shaped windows. Some examples of these special applications are shown below.

Eyebrow shape windows
Eyebrow arches can sometimes be difficult to cover with other treatments and a sunburst installed in the shaped part of the opening will allow the lower portion of the opening to be dressed with a more standard treatment. This sunburst is shown with a button or medallion type add-on in the center.

Multi window set-up
Multiple window configurations can also be covered in an attractive way using sunbursts. By treating the odd shapes this way, it leaves the lower windows in a rectangular configuration which can then be addressed with more traditional coverings.

Rectangular windows

Simply because the sunburst was invented for odd shaped openings does not exclude its use in a rectangular opening. A sunburst can be adapted to fit a rectangular opening if such a design is appropriate. The sunburst will not be operable, even in a situation where it is rectangular.

GENERAL INFORMATION

- When frame mounted, the frame is cut from ¾" plywood to the same shape as the window.
- The frame is covered either by wrapping, painting, or upholstering.
- Some shapes will require an add-on rosette or padded button.

PRICING

- Sunbursts are priced by the finished square foot.
- There is minimum square foot charge per each sunburst.
- To determine the square footage, multiply the finished width × finished length ÷ by 144, round up, = square feet.
- Add-on items such as banding, ruffles, buttons are charged separately.

RECOMMENDED FABRICS

- Sheer or light weight fabrics work best with 3x fullness.
- Most cottons will work, and fullness should be reduced to 2.5x.

TIPS WHEN MEASURING

Inside Mount
- A template of the exact inside of the window is required.
- There is a greater chance of light coming in along the outside edges. To reduce this, add a self welt or self ruffle along the outside edges of the frame.

Outside Mount
- When ordering, extend the frame at least 2" past the window edge or trim.
- To ensure a correct fit always supply a template.
- To further reduce any light gaps add a self welt along the back edge of the frame.

Review

1) When would a rod pocket frame be the most suitable frame choice?

2) A lined sunburst frame serves what purpose?

3) In what types of situations would an inside mounted sunburst be a better choice than an outside mount?

4) When is a template of the window required when ordering a sunburst?

5) A client has an elliptical arched window which faces west. What sunburst style and mounting would you recommend and why?

Sunbursts

BEDDING

In design today, the bed is no longer considered just a functional piece of furniture. It has become what is often the focal point of the room. Elaborate bed treatments are now the norm rather than just warm coverings. The current trend is to dress the bed in layers of luxurious fabrics to create a welcoming feeling of comfort and relaxation.

The business rule regarding bedding dictates that when you order a bedding item the product is one that will be used exclusively on the bed. Pre-manufactured items such as blankets, sheets, mattress protectors, and the like will not be covered here as the focus of this book is custom made bedding products used primarily for home decoration and design. These decorative items are primarily bed top covers such as bedspreads, coverlets, comforters, duvet covers, and bed skirts.

BASIC BEDDING STYLES

In recent years there has been a great deal of research into the science of sleep, and the result of this is that beds are no longer made up of a simple box spring and mattress. They have evolved into "sleep systems". This has caused changes in bed size in terms of the variety of bed bases and mattress heights which can now be found. Ready made bedding manufacturers are scrambling to figure out how to supply bed skirts and bedspreads to fit these new configurations and the demand for custom bedding products has grown significantly. The basic bedding styles remain much the same, but because of the new bed heights, more creative combinations of these styles must be utilized to keep the bed looking balanced.

Bed skirts

Once only an occasional accent item, bed skirts are now almost a necessity for any bed. With new bed drop lengths from the top of the mattress to the floor approaching three feet, a bedspread will quickly overpower the bed if the covering goes all the way to the floor without a break and a bed skirt.

The two basic bed skirt styles are tailored and gathered. A quality custom bed skirt will always have a platform, usually made from lining; that covers the box spring or bed base, and then a skirt drop going to the floor. Around the platform there will be a border made from the same fabric as the skirt. This border will prevent the platform lining from showing should the skirt slip or shift slightly while on the bed. This border is sometimes called "deck banding".

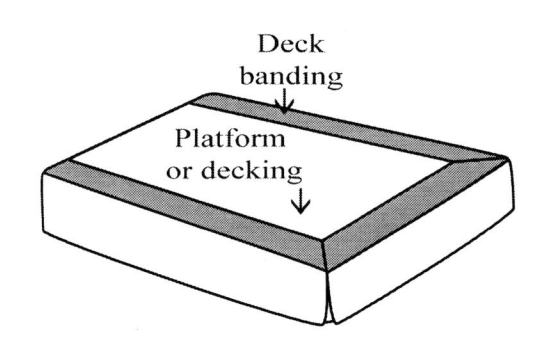

Tailored

These skirts are the simplest and most basic of styles. They are plain and flat, usually with an inverted pleat at the corners to allow a little bit of give in the fabric going around the corner. These skirts can be lined or unlined. A tailored skirt is typically used when a more modern, masculine, or contemporary style is wanted.

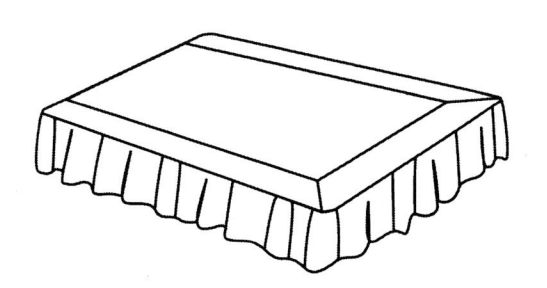

Gathered

These skirts generally have a softer and sometimes more feminine appearance than a tailored bed skirt, and are used to create a feeling that is more traditional or romantic. The skirting fabric is shirred onto the platform at a fullness of 2x to 3x depending on the fabric used. These skirts can be lined or unlined.

Chapter 11

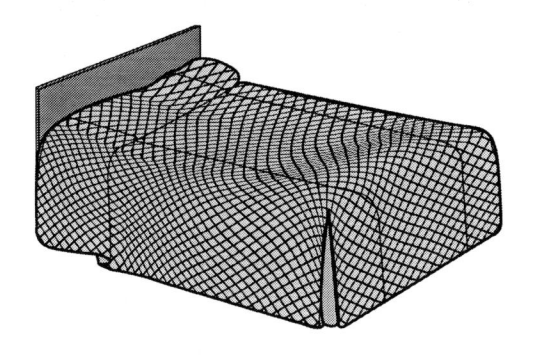

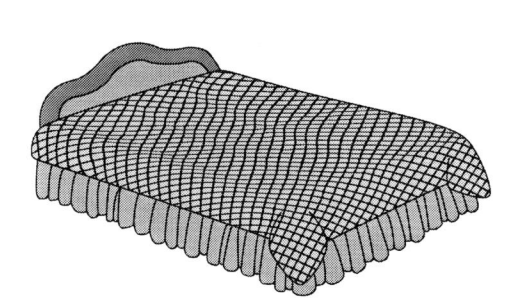

Bedspreads and Coverlets
The bedspread is a bedding layer that covers the mattress and has sides which drop all the way to the floor. They can be made without a pillow tuck, but traditionally the bedspread has some sort of pillow tuck or attached pillow sham. These coverings have a definite right and wrong side, along with hemmed edges.

Bedspreads are quilted before they are cut and hemmed. For the extra high bed/mattress combinations sometimes found today, the traditional spread may have a 3' drop length. This can make the bed look out of scale. Bedspreads with traditional drop lengths of around 2' are still being used, except bed skirts are added to break the line of the extremely long drop

In doing this, the bedspread technically becomes a coverlet, since a coverlet is defined as a shortened bedspread used with a bed skirt. A coverlet traditionally does not have a pillow tuck or attached sham but is occasionally made with one.

The basic styles for bedspreads and coverlets are the plain throw and fitted styles.

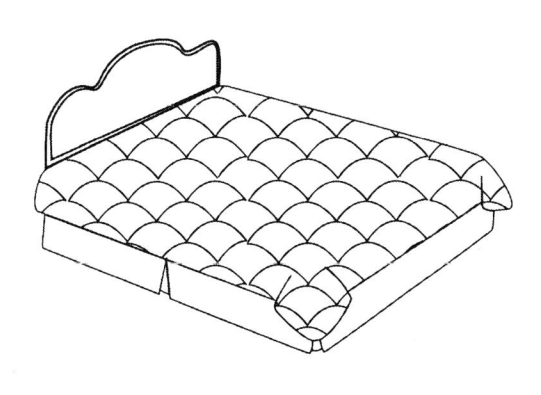

Plain throw
Usually quilted, this style is basically a rectangular shaped piece of fabric which, when placed on the bed creates a cone shaped corner, and is made with or without pillow tucks. If the throw is made short and used with a bed skirt, it is considered a throw style coverlet.

Elements of Soft Treatments

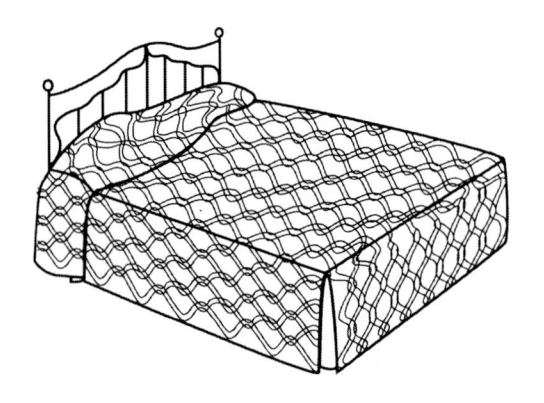

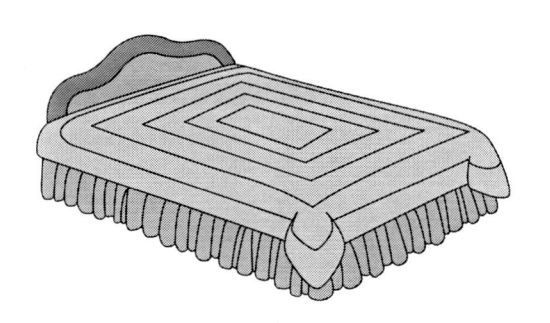

Fitted

This bedspread style will have seams at the edges of the mattress with the drop or skirt being attached as a separate piece of fabric. The fitted style spread gives the bed a tailored, more formal look than the throw style. It is more labor intensive to make and therefore more expensive. The typical fitted style will also have tailored corners, and can be made with or without a pillow tuck. The short version of this spread, without a pillow tuck is typically referred to as a fitted style coverlet.

Comforters

These are short coverings which do not go all the way to the floor. Comforters differ from a coverlet in that they will never be made with a pillow tuck, and they lie loosely on top of the bed, sometimes folded at the foot of the bed. They usually have a fill which is fluffier, or has more "loft", than the fill which is used on a bedspread or coverlet. Comforters are completely assembled before they are quilted, and the quilting on a comforter is usually a pattern within itself, which is simple and looser than quilting found on bedspreads and coverlets. Comforters will have a decorative fabric on both sides and are reversible. They are often used in conjunction with a bedspread or coverlet to add a decorative element to the bed treatment. They might also be used to provide additional cover or warmth when sleeping.

Duvet covers

Similar in function to a comforter, a duvet is an unquilted covering which is made from decorative fabrics. The basic duvet cover is a rectangular removable sack. The closures can vary from zippers to snaps and buttons. They are made to be seen from both sides as they are frequently laid on the bed folded. A duvet insert is placed inside, and it is usually made from a sturdy down proof or down resistant cover of high thread count bleached muslin. To keep the insert from moving or shifting, snaps or ties are placed inside the duvet cover to fasten it to the insert.

Chapter 11

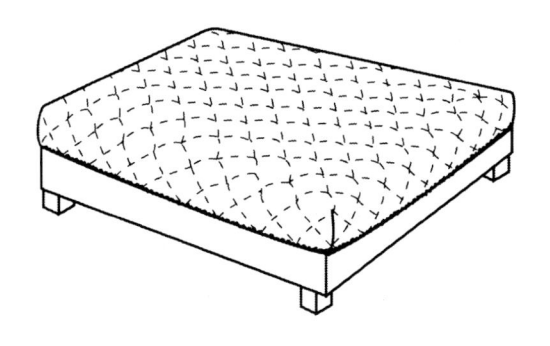

Bed cap
A recently evolved form of bed covering, the bed cap is made to fit tightly around the mattress form, much like a mattress pad. It has elasticized and fitted corners for a clean and tight fit around the mattress. These covers are frequently used for a tailored, modern look, and are commonly found on "space age" memory foam type beds currently being sold, along with the traditional water bed, day bed, and futon.

STYLE VARIATIONS

The look of the basic bedding styles mentioned can be changed in many ways, primarily through the use of add-on items such as banding, cording, ruffles, and so forth, but also some style variation is possible. Varying spacing, corner and pillow cover styles, and adding scallops or edge designs are a few of these variations.

Bed skirts
Styles are most commonly changed by varying the spacing of the pleats or gathers to create a different look. Additional layers of fabric can add a degree of interest to a basic bed skirt, as in the double layer gathered style.

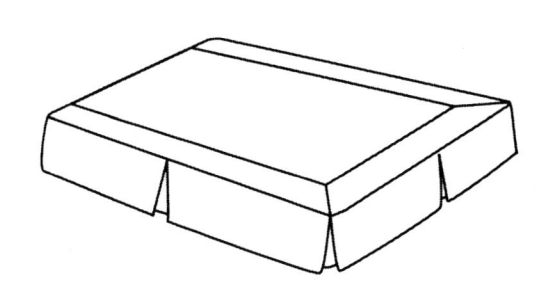

Tailored box pleat
This is made with an inverted box pleat in the center of each of the three sides and corners of the box spring

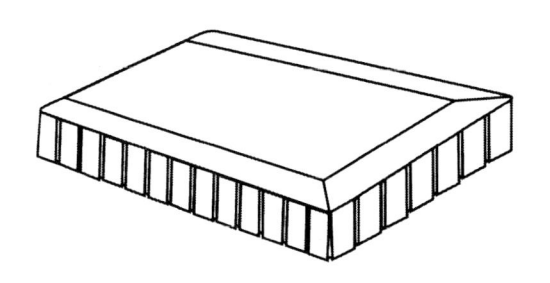

4"–6" box pleat
This style is made with inverted box pleats that are spaced approximately 4"-6" apart, depending on the size of the box spring.

Elements of Soft Treatments

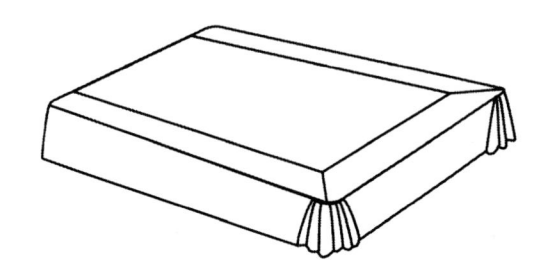

Gathered Corners

This variation is a combination of a tailored and gathered skirt. Small groups of gathers are placed at each corner to soften the look of a tailored skirt.

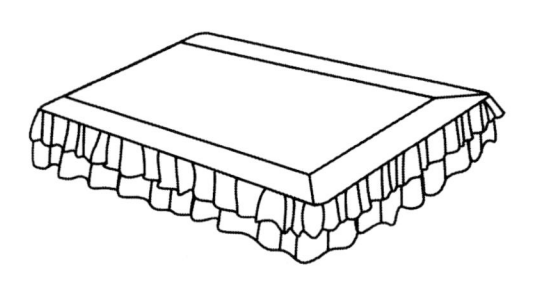

Double layer gathered

This is a combination of two layers of gathered fabric. Both lengths must be specified on work orders.

Bedspreads, Coverlets, Comforters and Duvets

These coverings can have hem edge cut outs or scallops to vary the basic look. Also, changing the skirt on a fitted bedspread will cause it to look quite different.

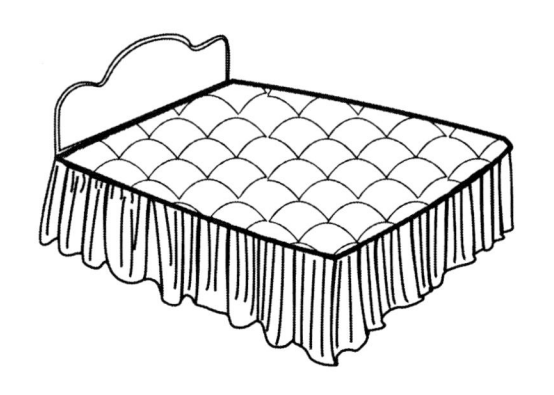

Quilted with gathered drop

With this variation, the fitted bedspread is constructed with the top part being quilted and the drops being gathered. Here, contrasting top fabrics may be paired with the gathered drop. To add more interest, add a top welt around the mattress or make the skirt from a sheer or lace fabric.

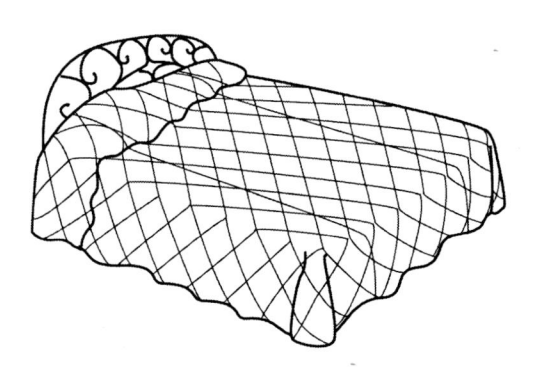

Scalloped bottom with matching reverse sham

By adding some shaping to the lower hem, the covering will take on a fun or formal look, depending on the shape. A reverse sham on a bedspread can also be shaped in the same style as the bedspread bottom. This pairing of styles will give the bedspread a well groomed and formal look

Chapter 11

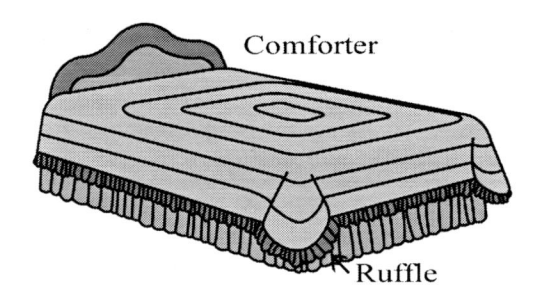

Comforters and Duvet covers

These are usually changed through the use of add-on items such as color banding, ruffles, trims, buttons, ties, and so on.

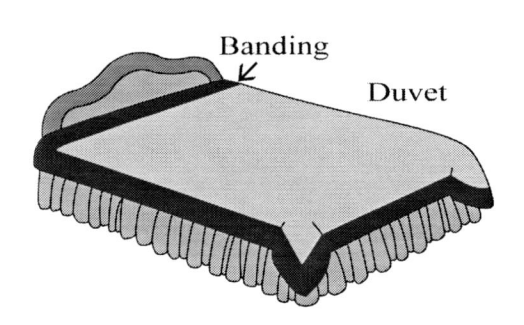

HOW TO MEASURE FOR BEDDING

With the current rate of evolution in bed styles today, it is wise to measure the bed before ordering any bed covering. A chart of generally accepted "standard" bed sizes and coverings is included (Appendix B), however these dimensions should be used only as a guide for estimating size and yardage. Most beds today will vary slightly from the standard dimensions in some way, and these deviances can easily cause an ill fit and unattractive product.

Measuring for a bed skirt

This can be a challenging exercise because the mattress will be sitting on top of the base or box spring. In order to accurately measure, the mattress will need to be lifted or moved to get precise measurements. Difficult as this might be, doing so will be worth the effort with the final fit and appearance of the finished skirt.

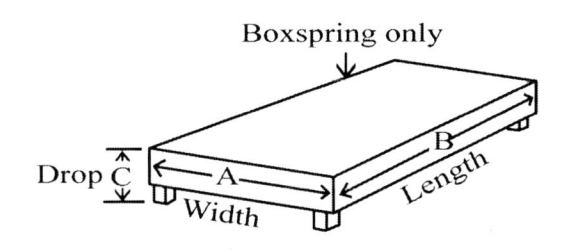

Before ordering and manufacturing the bed skirt, accurately measure the width, length, and drop of the bed base, since these are the dimensions that will be required by the workroom to create the finished skirt. The width and length measurement will usually be box spring only measurements from edge to edge, including cording if there is any. The drop length should be measured from the top edge of the base or box spring to the floor.

Elements of Soft Treatments

143

Bedding

> If the bed has a frame that the base sits inside and the skirt will cover that frame, measure out and around the frame including it in the drop measurement.

> When ordering finished drop length, make a ½" deduction for floor clearance if the bed skirt is to clear the floor without touching.

Measuring for bedspreads and coverlets

These should be taken with the bed fully made. Mattress pads, feather beds, sheets, blankets, quilts, and any other items that are normally used on the bed should be in place while measuring. These items can sometimes add several inches to the bed size and cause an ill fitting finished product if added after measurements are taken.

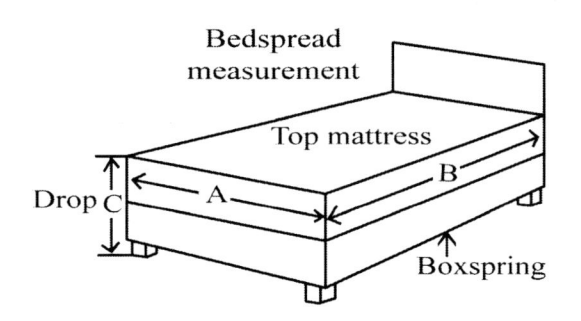

Bedspreads
Measure the bed width, length, and drop from the top of the made up bed to the floor.

Coverlet
Measure the bed in the same manner as for a bedspread for the width and length. For the drop length, measure from the top of the bed to the top of the box spring base then add 2"-3". This will be the appropriate drop length for the coverlet.

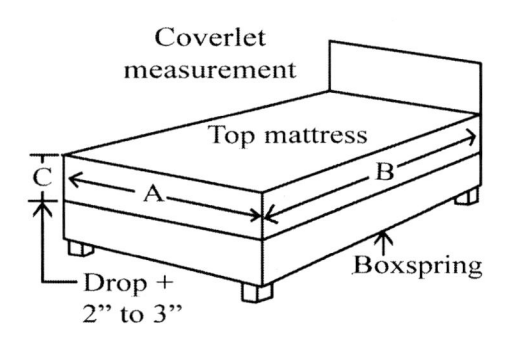

> If finding the mattress edges is difficult with the bedding in place, estimate the location of the corners and place dressmaker's pins in those locations. Measure from pin to pin. The drop lengths will need to be the same on both sides.

> If a coverlet or bedspread will have a shaped or scalloped hem, remember to take the short and long point of the shape into consideration when deciding on the ordered finished length.

Measuring for comforters, duvet covers and bed caps

This is carried out in the same manner that would be done for a coverlet, with a few exceptions.

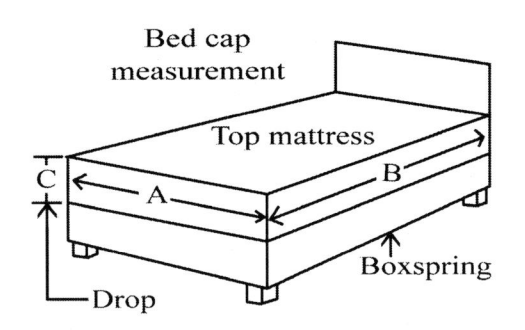

Bed cap
The bed cap drop will be equal to the distance from the top of the mattress to the base of the box spring.

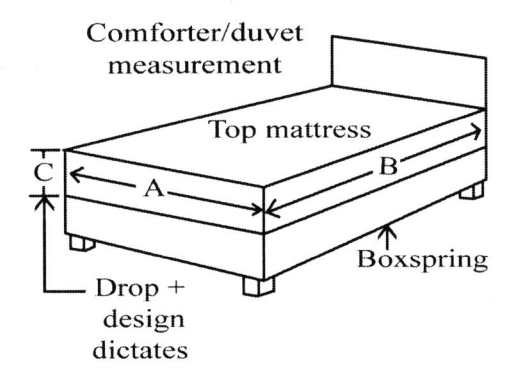

Comforter or Duvet
A comforter or duvet drop length can be made as short or long as the design dictates, or it can be to customer preference. Typically, a minimum comforter drop will be at least to the top of the bed base or box spring.

Duvet covers
These must be made to fit the duvet insert rather than the bed. When ordering these, measure the bed as would be done for a comforter, choose a duvet insert with an appropriate allowance for drop, and have the cover manufactured to fit the duvet ordered.

> Whenever possible, send the duvet to the workroom so that the fit will be accurate. The workroom can then insert the duvet into the cover before delivery and also be sure ties and/or attachments are appropriate and in the proper places.

PILLOW TUCKS

Bedspreads are almost always ordered with some sort of a pillow tuck, or pillow covering, and coverlets may or may not be ordered with these. The two most common types are the "standard" pillow tuck and a reverse sham.

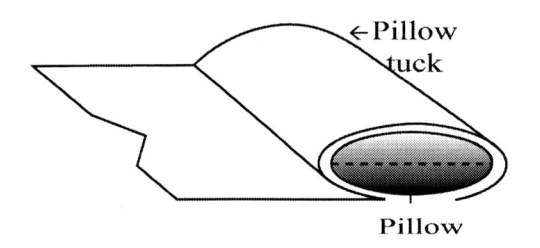

Pillow tuck

This is a continuation of the fabric beyond the headboard which is tucked up and around the pillows. The pillow tuck is the simplest way to cover pillows, the easiest to manufacture, and usually the least expensive. This method of covering pillows is often referred to as a "standard" pillow tuck because it is the most commonly used.

A standard pillow tuck typically adds 25"-30 inches to the overall length of the bedspread. It is wise to always measure around the pillows and specify the desired number of inches that will be used for the pillow tuck, as sometimes clients will want to cover more than one pillow.

> If covering extra large or multiple pillows stacked upon one another, add additional inches to the ordered length of the pillow tuck to ensure complete coverage of the pillows. This is known as an "oversized" pillow tuck.

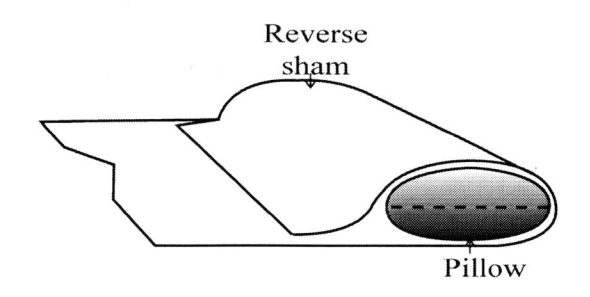

Reverse sham

This can be added to a coverlet, but they are most commonly found on bedspreads. When manufacturing these, the fabric is cut off, reversed and seamed back on so that the fabric can be flipped over the pillows. This will then expose the top edge of the bedspread. Creative banding or border effects can be used for design impact.

A reverse sham allowance is typically 36"-45" depending on whether the sham will have a scalloped or decorative edge. Always measure and specify how many inches will be needed for the reverse sham to ensure that there will be enough coverage.

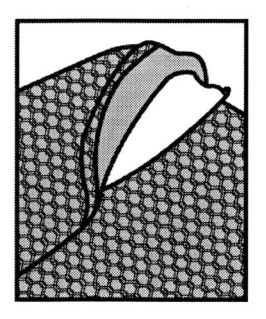

> The reverse sham does make it more difficult to make up the bed because placement of the bedspread needs to be exact in order to achieve the proper appearance of the sham. Discuss this with the client to see if this will cause any issues for them.

CORNER STYLES

Sometimes the style of corner used for a particular bed covering is strictly a matter of design choice. More often a specific corner style must be used in order to fit a covering in and around certain styles of bed frames. The two most commonly used corner styles are the throw drop corner and the split corner with a gusset.

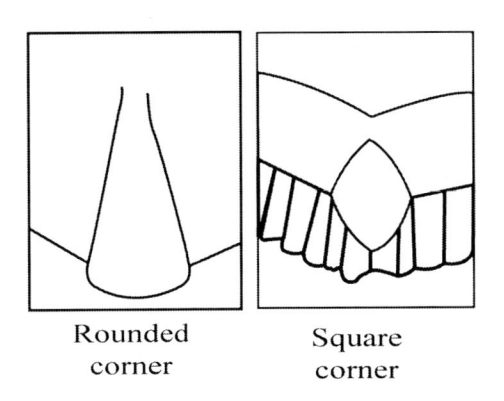

Rounded corner   Square corner

Throw style corner
This is a cone shaped corner, and it appears when a rectangular bedspread is placed on the bed and allowed to drape around the corners. The cut of the corner can be rounded or square. A rounded corner must be specified if the bedspread drop is floor length or the corner will drag on the floor. The square corner is usually seen on coverlets, comforters, and duvets.

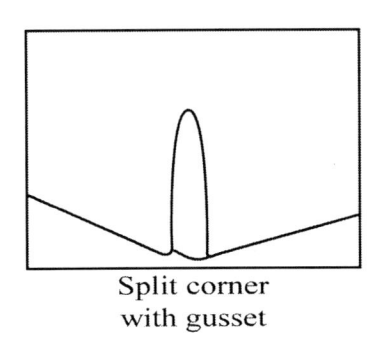

Split corner
These are typically found on a fitted style bedspread or coverlet. They can also be used on a throw style if the corner needs to be split to fit around a bed frame as in the case of a bed with bed posts at the foot. Most of the time there will be a "gusset" inserted at the corner behind the split to prevent any under coverings from showing through the split.

Split corner with gusset

> The gusset can be made with a shorter drop length than the body of the bedspread if needed in order to clear a bed rail.

QUILTING

When layers of fabric, fill, and lining are stitched together in some kind of pattern it is said to be quilted. The two main components to creating a quilted product are the combination of the fill and quilt pattern being used.

Fill
This is the padding, or "batting", which will be stitched between the front and back layers of fabric to create the fluffiness of a quilted effect. Batting can be made from 100% cotton, wool, polyester, or polyester and cotton blends, each having their own characteristics, advantages, and disadvantages. The batting choice will typically be one which is most compatible with the style of quilting that will be done, coupled with the intended use of the covering. Some battings are more appropriate for hand

Elements of Soft Treatments

quilting or hand tying, while others work better with machine quilted products. Some fills wash and wear better than others.

The fill typically used in custom bedspreads, coverlets, and comforters today is a polyester or polyester/cotton blend batting because those tend to work best for machine quilting and most of the quilted bed coverings today are machine quilted. Cotton fill is breathable and will likely be more comfortable for sleeping if the item will be used for that purpose. If a client has concerns about allergies to certain types of fill, a hypo-allergenic synthetic batting should be ordered.

The batting can be supplied in various weights with different levels of "loft". Loft is basically the fluffiness of the fill, and is usually referred to as low, medium, or high loft, or some variation thereof. Generally speaking, fill choices can be 2 ounces, 4 ounces, 6 ounces, 9 ounces, or 12 ounces. Some even get as high as 24 ounces, and these are usually used in model homes. Fill choices can vary from one workroom to another, so it is best to ask them about the batting they use and have them supply samples that the customer can choose from.

The quilt pattern is the design that is stitched on the layers of fabric to fasten them together. Many quilting options are now available, thanks to computerized sewing machines, and many unique designs can be digitized and transformed into a quilting pattern, although the more traditional methods of quilting are still the most frequently used. The traditional methods of quilting are hand tying, loom quilting, hand guided quilting, and computer quilting.

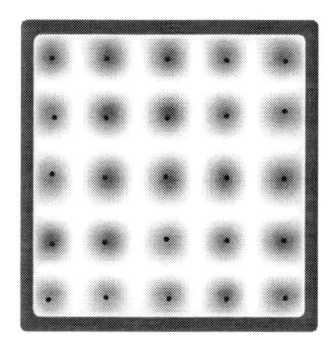

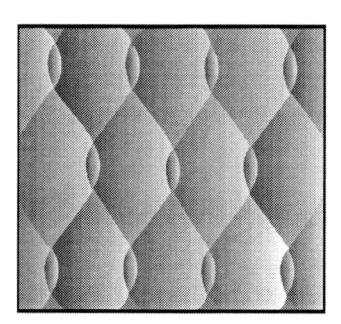

Hand tied
With this quilting method, the layers will be stitched together in patterned intervals throughout the covering, creating a loosely tufted appearance. Usually this is done with yarn, thread, or ribbon which is then hand tied into bows or knots.

Loom quilted
Patterns are made by semi-automated quilting machines. The layers of fabric, fill, and lining are threaded onto a loom which is wide enough to accommodate the manufactured fabric width of 48" or 54". The layers of materials then pass through a series of many needles which simultaneously stitch in the pattern and re-roll the finished quilted fabric. Since the quilting looms are made to quilt the fabric in rolls, loom quilted fabrics only come in set fabric widths. This means that in a large quilted product such as a bedspread the seams will be more visible since the seaming to create the spread width will be done after the fabric is quilted.

Chapter 11

This distinction is important to remember for two reasons: first, a loom quilted product will have a visible seam on the reverse, and second, when loom quilted, the fabric pattern OR the quilting pattern can be matched at the seam but it is not possible to match them both.

Hand guided quilting

This is done with a quilting machine which sews a single line of quilting and is hand guided by an person following a pattern of some kind. These patterns can be printed versions with an appearance similar to a loom quilting pattern, or the operator can follow or outline a pattern in the fabric, such as a flower or other design. Due to the hand crafted nature of hand guided patterns, they can have some quilting imperfections. These are considered part of the beauty and are accepted as part of the nature of a hand made product.

These products are seamed before they are quilted, which results in seams that are less visible and patterns which are matched across the entire width of the large quilted pieces.

> When outline quilting, the pattern will be determined by the quilter unless a specific diagram is supplied. Supply a photocopy of the fabric with the desired outline done in marker if the pattern outline matters in the design.

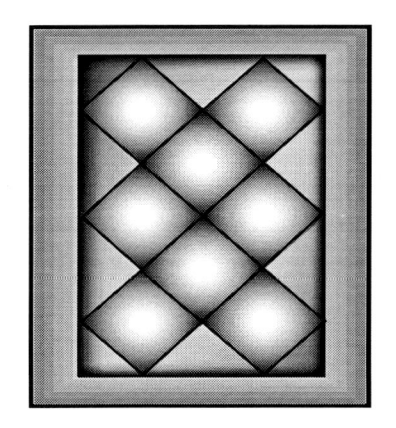

Computer quilting

This is most typically done on comforters. In this process, the fabric layers are assembled, turned right sides out, and fastened to a large frame. The quilting machine is guided around the inside of the frame by a computer which is programmed to follow a digitized pattern. Computer generated patterns are usually one large pattern unto itself, unlike loom and hand guided patterns which are repeats of the same pattern.

Elements of Soft Treatments

Quilting shrinkage

This is a phenomenon that naturally occurs when fabric and batting layers are quilted together. Due to the take up or puffiness that is created by the stitching, the fabric will become shorter and narrower. The amount of shrinkage that will occur in a given fabric depends on the weight and loftiness of the fill, and the quilt pattern being used. Heavy, lofty fill and tightly quilted patterns will shrink more than loosely quilted, light weight, thin filled products.

Estimating shrinkage can be a tricky process, but a good bedding workroom can supply a formula for making an educated guess in each given situation. This shrinkage factor is most important in calculations of yardage required to make bedding products, so have the bedding workroom calculate yardages and they will generally compensate for shrinkage in the manufacturing process.

> Design comforters to be a little large to compensate for shrinkage, since this is the most difficult element to compensate for. Comforter size will rarely be exact, so do not use a comforter in exact measurement situations. Discuss this with the client.

DUVET CLOSURES

When ordering a duvet cover it will be necessary to tell the workroom what type of closure should be used. The closure on a duvet cover can be incorporated into part of the cover design, or it can be specified to be a functional part of the cover. Since a duvet cover is a sack into which a duvet is inserted with the intention of it being occasionally removed, it needs to open and close with some ease. Two common closures used on duvet covers are the envelope style and the plain closure.

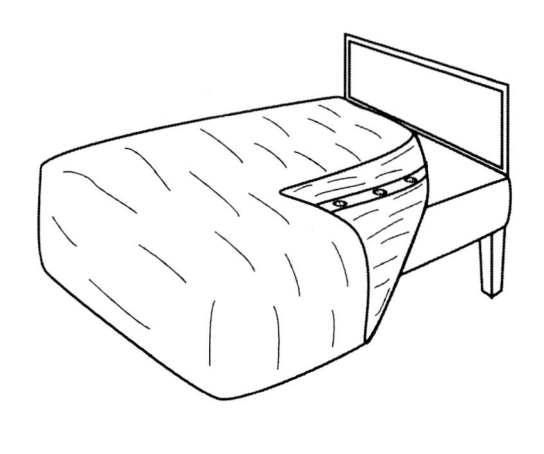

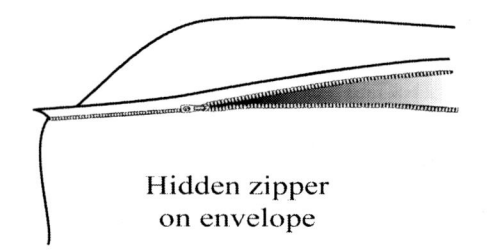

Envelope style

This closure places the opening about 15"-18" inches from either the top or bottom end of the cover. These can also be specified to be on the front or the back, depending on how the duvet will be folded and used on the bed. The duvet is then inserted into the cover like a letter into an envelope and the opening is held shut by means of a zipper, hook and loop tape, snap tape, or buttons.

Zippers on envelope closures are hidden under a small flap of the fabric in a style known as a lap, or hidden zipper application. The small flap of fabric is sewn so the zipper is covered by the fabric and is not visible.

Hook and loop fastener and snap tapes can be used in the same fashion but are considered less desirable if used on the front, as stitching may be visible and they may ripple and pucker more than a zipper.

Hidden zipper on envelope

Buttons may leave gaps, so if a buttoned appearance is desired, one might order a zipper fastener with the buttons sewn on in such a fashion that they appear to button.

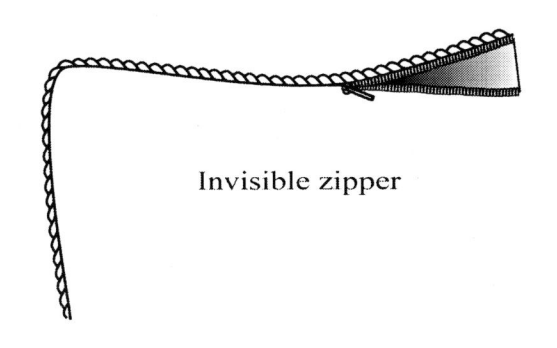

Plain style

These closures will be placed at the top or the bottom of the cover, at or in the seam where the front and back are joined together. Usually placement is on the bottom if the duvet will be used when sleeping as the fasteners can be disturbing, and on the top if the duvet is to be decorative and will lay folded on the bed. Zippers, hook and loop fastener, snap tape, and buttons are all appropriate fasteners on a plain style closure.

When zippers are used, an invisible zipper can make the cover appear much like a comforter, and will be completely reversible with the fastener being strictly functional.

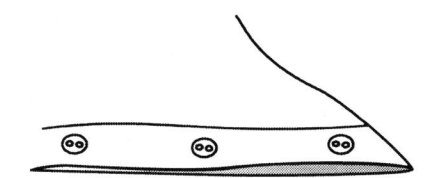

Invisible zipper

Hook and loop, snap tape, or buttons will require a small flange for attachment. These can be decorative and incorporated into the cover design. Zippers can be applied with a flange as well if a zipper is the fastener of choice and a decorative flange is desired. Buttons can come unfastened and leave gaps, so be sure to discuss these choices with the client.

Buttons on plain closure

GENERAL INFORMATION

- Pillows and pillow shams are usually part of a bedding ensemble (see pillow chapter).
- A daybed is simply a twin size bed turned sideways. Always tell the workroom if the covering is for a daybed as seams and patterns will need to run the opposite direction from a regular covering.
- See Appendix B for the chart on common mattress and bedding sizes along with common pillow sizes.

PRICING

- Bedding items are priced per each and are dependent on the bed size.
- Add-on items such as banding, cording, ruffles, buttons, and so on, are priced separately by the linear foot or per each.

RECOMMENDED FABRICS

- Most fabrics are suitable for use as bedding. Heavy or upholstery weights may be too heavy if the item will be used to sleep under.
- Sheer fabrics will require interlinings to prevent fill from showing.
- Crisp or stiff fabrics that retain wrinkles should be avoided.

Review

1) Why is a pillow sham not considered to be a bedding item?

2) When would the use of a bed skirt not be appropriate?

3) A client has a four poster bed with iron posts and a decorative rail between the posts at the foot of the bed. What type of bedspread would you suggest, and why?

4) A client wants a throw bedspread and does not want the corner to drag. What must you specify

5) How does quilting shrinkage affect the yardage that will be needed?

6) How does loft affect shrinkage?

Bedding

PILLOWS AND PILLOW SHAMS

Pillows used in interior design are made to perform the function of adding softness, color, or pattern to a room. They enhance the overall design and create a mood of comfort. The pillow originated as a padded fabric sack which was used to lay ones head on while sleeping, or to prop or pad body parts while resting. Because this is a function associated with comfort, the role of the pillow in interior design has evolved from something purely functional into a decorative and mood creating feature. Although decorative, these items are still a working part of daily life and therefore, when designing the decorative pillow it is good to keep in mind this dual purpose. If too fussy, they may lose some of their appeal over time with use.

The business rule differentiating the decorative pillow from the pillow sham is that a pillow is a decorative fabric casing which is stuffed and sewn closed. A pillow sham will be a decorative fabric casing which has a separate non-decorative pillow inserted inside it, and is made with some type of a constructed closure which allows it to be opened and the insert removed. A pillow sham can be removed for ease of cleaning or to replace the pillow insert should it deteriorate over time with use.

According to this rule, when a pillow is ordered, a decorative or non-decorative non-removable cover is provided. When a pillow sham is ordered, the decorative cover will be removable and an inner, non-decorative pillow insert will be provided, or a pillow sham can be ordered with no insert and the consumer can provide one of their own choosing.

Elements of Soft Treatments

Pillows ans Pillow Shams

BASIC PILLOW STYLES

Pillows and pillow shams can be made in many different shapes and styles, and any of the designs can be ordered as either a pillow or as a pillow sham. There are five basic pillow styles which are the base for most types of decorative pillow.

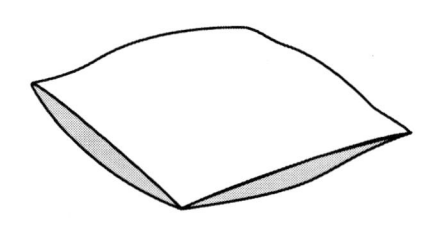

Knife edge

This is the most basic pillow style, and is typically used with a pillow insert, in its most basic form. It is simply a front and back sewn together with a plain edge. The basic knife edge pillow will have no cording or trim but these items are frequently added to the knife edge as add-on items when it is used as the decorative covering.

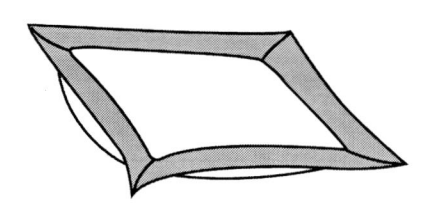

Flanged

A flanged pillow will be made with a border around the outside edges, the flange is not stuffed. The flange can be narrow to make a decorative statement, or it can be large and floppy. Flanged pillows can have a structured and tailored appearance, or they can be soft and romantic depending on the flange size and style specified.

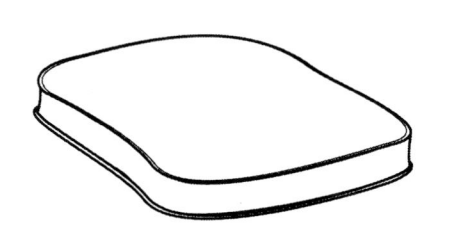

Boxed

This pillow is made with a top, bottom, and side sections, or gusset, which gives the pillow a third dimension by adding thickness. A boxed pillow usually has a more tailored appearance than some other pillow styles.

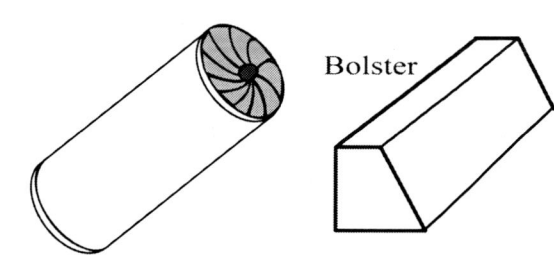

Neck roll/bolster

This style of pillow is made in a cylindrical shape. The smaller versions are called a neck roll because they are small enough to tuck behind ones neck to provide support if lying down. The bolster is larger than the neck roll and is used to tuck into corners of furniture more for supporting or "bolstering" larger body parts. Bolsters are also sometimes made in triangular wedge shapes if the look desired is a more tailored one, or if a wedge shape would be more practical for its use.

Chapter 12

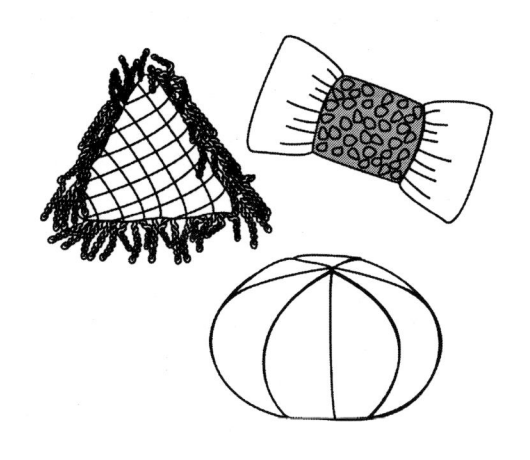

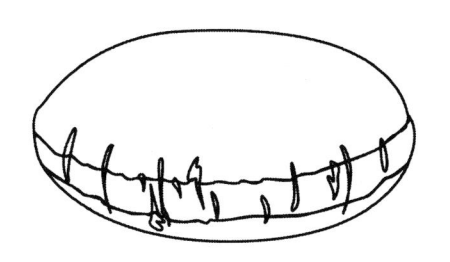

Specialty
Pillows styles in this category are ones that come in various shapes other than squares or rectangles. There are the common shapes such as round and triangular, and there are some more exotic types like heart shapes and round balls. These can all have characteristics of the knife edge, flanged, or boxed pillow, as well as their own unique shape or size. These pillows are very decorative and are frequently used to make specific design statements.

Floor pillows
These are very large and densely stuffed pillows that are used as cushions on the floor for sitting and lounging. Floor pillows can be large knife edge styles, boxed cushions, or lounge cushions made especially for reading, leaning, or television viewing. Because these are large and often "stored" in the room in plain view they can be a very classy decorative element if incorporated properly into the design scheme.

PILLOW STYLE VARIATIONS

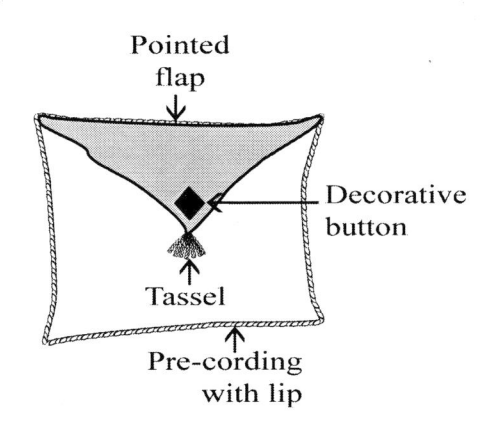

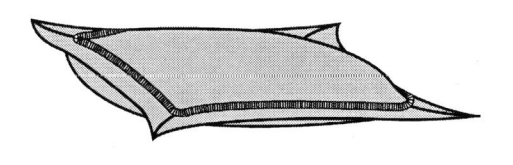

Add-ons
Through the use of add-on items, there are an infinite number of pillow variations. Cording can, and usually is, added to almost any style. Ruffles, overlays, banding, trims, buttons, appliqués, patchwork, embroidery, and many more of these kinds of embellishments can be added to a decorative pillow to make a design statement, add color or pattern, or add interest to a design scheme.

Shams
Almost any pillow style can be ordered as a sham. A sham is most appropriately ordered in any situation where the pillow may be subject to heavy use and require frequent laundering or cleaning, such as bedding or sofa pillows. Sometimes the workroom

Elements of Soft Treatments

157

Knife edge sham

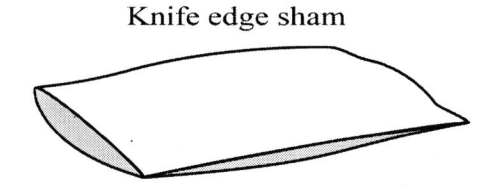

may prefer to make pillows as shams for ease in stuffing them, or because some fabrics are difficult to close by machine or hand to get a neat, good quality, durable closure. Conversely, some pillow styles are not suitable as shams and should not have removable covers since they can be more expensive to manufacture and the need to remove the cover may never arise. These may be best made with a permanent closure. Discuss concerns regarding the use of the pillow cover with the client and order pillows, or pillow shams, according to their preferences.

> A quality, well constructed pillow sham will have finished edges on all of its inside seams. To judge the quality of a pillow sham, open it, remove the form, and look inside.

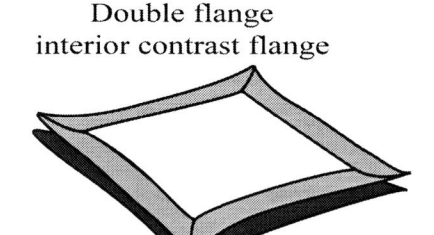

Double flange interior contrast flange

Multiple layers
An interesting way to vary a pillow style is to add multiple layers of ruffles, double layers of flange on flanged pillows, or multiple add-ons.

> The number of items added to a basic pillow makes the design more complex, and a more detailed design, usually translates into more expensive. Be sure not to design beyond the customer's budget as this is very easy to do when designing pillows.

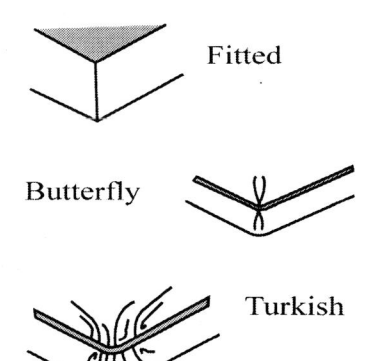

Fitted

Butterfly

Turkish

Corners
There are some variations of the way that pillow corners can be sewn to add interest to a pillow design. Turkish tucked corners are a kind of gathered corner which, when sewn on a knife edge pillow, will give it a much softer appearance. A boxed stitched corner will give a knife edge pillow a third dimension much like a boxed pillow except with a softer appearance than a true boxed style.

Square cut (Dog ears)   Tapered cut

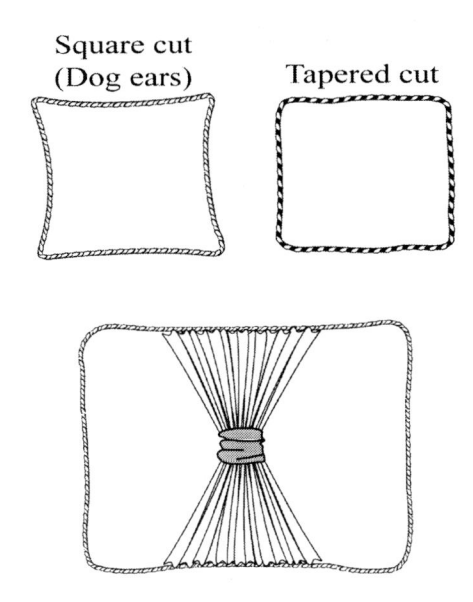

Taper cut corners will give the pillow a more rounded appearance and this method of cutting the pillow will keep the pillow corners from looking "dog eared", or too pointed after the pillow is stuffed.

Overlays

Many kinds of fabric overlays can be added to the basic pillow styles to create special effects. Putting a sheer or lace fabric over a solid color can make lace patterns stand out while adding color at the same time. Sheer fabric can be gathered and over laid on a pillow of a different color or to add softness or to create a romantic styling. Flaps over laid like an envelope flap are another currently popular overlay style.

PILLOW FORMS AND FILL

Pillows can be stuffed with many different fillings from synthetic polyester fiber to buckwheat hulls, all depending on the purpose for which the pillow will be used. Many of the pillow fills that are marketed are intended for sleeping and support pillows. Since sleeping and support are expected to be a limited part of the life of a decorative pillow, they are most commonly stuffed with some type of polyester fiber which tends to be the least expensive of the available choices. For luxury and durability, down and feather/down fill is used to some extent in decorative pillows, and occasionally foam or shredded foam when a firmer or formed shape is needed.

Down and feather/down fills

Down fill is the most expensive of the choices for decorative pillows, but it is the most desirable because down is durable, shapeable, and will regain its loft quickly when fluffed. Because of its cost, down is often blended with some percentage of feathers which allows the fill to be lower in cost and still retain most, or some, of the same properties as pure down. Feather/down blended fills are usually sold as some percentage of down to feathers. For example, 10% down and 90% feather is a 10/90 fill and 25/75 is 25% down and 75% feathers. White goose down (WGD) is the finest purest down, grey duck (GD), and grey goose (GG), are also sometimes substituted for white goose down to help control cost.

Some people will want to avoid feather/down fill because down can cause severe allergic reactions. Be sure to check with the client regarding any allergies to down before ordering down filled pillows. Some purified and hypoallergenic down fills are available at a greater cost.

Polyester cluster fiber

This is a synthetic fill made from polyester micro fibers which are spun in such a way that they perform similarly to down when used as pillow filler. It is white like white goose down, shapeable, and fluff-able. The polyester is usually hypo-allergenic and less expensive than down, thereby making it a popular alternative to down. The disadvantage to cluster fiber fill is that it will lose its loft with use and time and, it will periodically need to be replaced in order for the pillow to retain its original appearance.

Pillows ans Pillow Shams

> When ordering pillows with cluster fiber fill, order the pillow as a sham with an insert so that the covering can easily be removed and the insert periodically replaced.

Polyester batting
Sometimes called polyester fiber fill, this fill is also a synthetic, but it is not as lofty as the cluster fiber and tends to be a bit denser. Plain polyester fill is an excellent choice for a pillow that is small and strictly decorative such as a specialty pillow.

Foam fill and shredded foam
Foam fills will be used when a very firm pillow is required, such as in the case of a floor pillow, cube, or cushion which is expected to support weight, be sat upon, or if the pillow has a specific shape which needs to be retained, such as a cube.

PILLOW SIZES AND THEIR PURPOSE

Pillow forms will come pre-manufactured in a number of sizes, and a good custom workroom can make pillow forms in virtually any custom size or shape (see Appendix B for standard sizes). Pre-made pillow form sizes used for decorative pillows found on sofas, chairs, and beds are approximate and will vary depending on the manufacturer. They are typically squares in even number sizes from 12"x12" to 24"x24".

Larger sizes are currently more popular and pillow squares from 16" to 22" are being combined to create groupings in common sitting areas. These groupings may also contain some specialty shaped pillows if the intent of the design is as an accent.

> Insert sizes are sometimes not exact to their stated size when purchased, so when ordering a decorative covering for a pillow insert that will not be provided by the workroom, send the insert to the workroom along with the order so they can custom fit the cover to the insert.

> When ordering pillow inserts, always use an insert one size larger than the finished pillow size, and this will make the finished pillow nice and full.

Larger pillow squares from 26"x26" to 30"x30" are known as Euro size because the larger size pillow concept originated in Europe. These Euro pillows will typically have removable shams and are used with one on a twin bed, two on a queen, and three on a king size. Of course other combinations are acceptable, depending on the design. Euro shams are often ordered to go with a coverlet that does not have a pillow tuck to create a backdrop for a grouping of other pillows, in order to create the feel of an inviting bed.

A 20"x26" rectangular pillow is a sleeping pillow for a twin or queen size bed, with one for a twin, two for a queen. Some rectangular sleeping pillows can also be found in a 20"x30" size, for use on a queen or twin bed. A rectangle 20"x36" is a sleeping pillow for a king size bed, and two are typically used. These sleeping pillows will sometimes be covered with decorative removable shams which will actually be removed nightly, and the pillow will be used without its cover for sleeping and replaced daily when the bed is made.

Huge rectangles can be custom made in sizes that will be as wide as the bed and then only one, very large covering will be used. These types of pillows are also often ordered to be used with a coverlet that does not have a pillow tuck but are also being seen as decorative pillows in some contemporary bedroom design schemes. Smaller rectangles of 12"x16", 14"x18", and 16"x20" are used as accent pillows in pillow groupings on beds and sofas, and these are also sometimes called boudoir or kidney pillows because they are stuck in the back of chairs and sofas to give extra lumbar support while sitting.

PILLOW AND PILLOW SHAM CLOSURES

Pillows
By definition, pillows will always be permanently stitched closed and can be reversed because the front and back will not be determined by the closure. The closure on a pillow can be stitched either by machine or by hand.

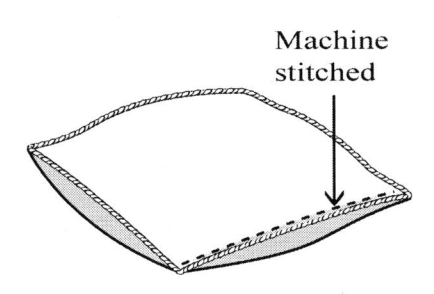

Machine stitched

A machine stitched closure is usually a top stitch along the bottom edge of the pillow, and this closure is less desirable since it can be quite visible, especially on some types of fabrics. It is, however, a faster and less expensive way to close the pillow after stuffing. A machine stitched closure on a pillow would be most appropriately used on an insert where it will ultimately be covered up or in situations where the pillow would receive heavy use, as machine closures are more durable than a hand closure.

The hand stitched closure is the preferred method of closing a decorative pillow and should be specified unless the client has another preference.

Pillow shams
Pillow shams can be closed with three different types of closures, some of which are more appropriate in given situations depending on use. Sometimes the client will have a personal preference and the method of closing the sham should always be discussed.

The three basic types of sham closures are overlapping, button, and zippers.

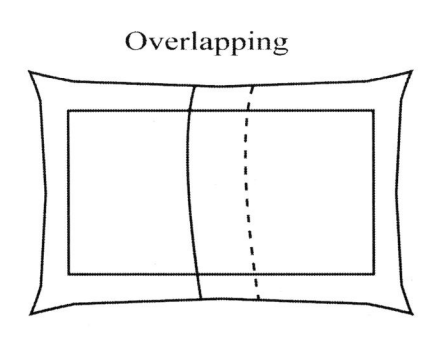

Overlapping

Overlapping
Usually the least expensive type of closure for a pillow sham, an overlapping closure is placed on the back of the sham. The backside will have two pieces which overlap each other allowing the pillow insert to be slid in between them. Shams with overlapping closures will have a definite front and back and they can not be reversed.

Elements of Soft Treatments

These closures should not be used when the sham cover will be frequently removed as they can be delicate and tear the cover if the insert is not removed and re-inserted carefully. The overlapping closure can also cause the sham to gap open in the back if the insert is stuffed very fully. This gapping can be minimized by overlapping the pieces by several inches, but this can make the sham more susceptible to tearing when the insert is taken in and out. The gap can be eliminated with the addition of a hook and loop tape to each side of the closure, however the hook and loop tape can be stiff an unappealing, so discuss use and preferences with the client before ordering.

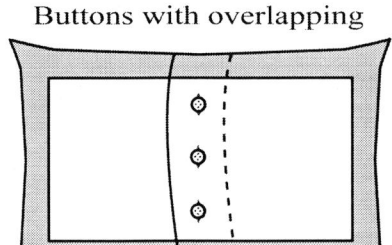

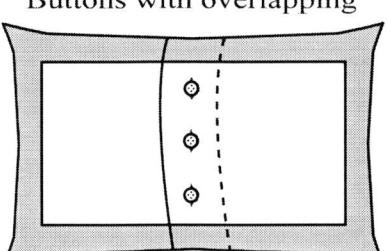

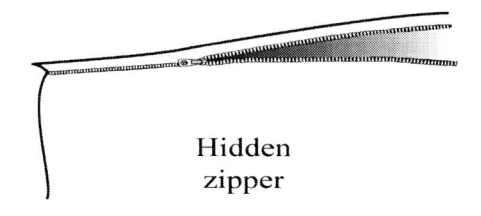

Buttons with overlapping

Button

A button closure is similar to the overlapping closure, except the pieces of the sham back are held closed with buttons and button holes. These closures can be an attractive accent and are sometimes even moved around to the front of the sham just for the decorative effect. The buttons and button holes do however add to the cost of manufacturing the sham, and while these closures do make the insert easier to get in and out, they can still gap open between the buttons. Again, client preference should be the guide in choosing this sham closure.

Hidden zipper

Zippers

These are the preferred method for closing a pillow sham, and are slightly more expensive than an overlapping closure but comparable in cost to a button closure. Zippers make inserting and removing the insert easy, they are durable, and they hold the sham closed firmly without any gaps.

Zippers can be applied either as a hidden zipper or as an invisible zipper. A hidden zipper is usually inserted along the bottom edge of the sham and it will have a small flap of fabric which covers the zipper. Pillows with hidden zippers will have a definite front and back and should not be displayed with the zipper side to the room.

An invisible zipper is a different type of zipper which is made so that the zipper teeth turn inward when zipped closed and it gives the appearance of a stitched seam resulting in an almost invisible closure, with only the zipper pull visible if properly applied.

Invisible zipper

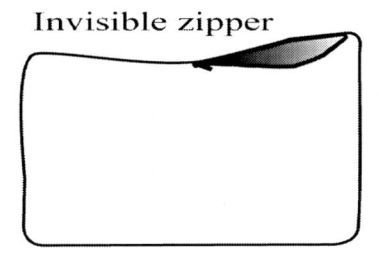

Shams with these closures can be used with either side as the face as they will not have a definite back side.

Occasionally, the detailing of the sham design will prohibit the insertion of an invisible zipper, such as in the case of heavy bullion fringe, bulky edges with ruffles and cord, or eyelash trim which can easily get caught in the zipper. If there is any doubt as to whether this closure will work on a given design, check with the workroom before ordering, as they may wish to make samples to see how well it will work.

> Most flange pillows do not have zippers, however they can be made this way. They are quite expensive to put in place. The preferred closure is envelope or machine stitched.

GENERAL INFORAMTION

- Manufactured pillow sizes are measured seam to seam before stuffing.
- Flanges, ruffles, and similar add-ons are added to the ordered finished size.
- Pillow tolerances are within ½" overall, as fabric will shrink when stitched.

PRICING

- Pillows are priced per each for a basic style. Different workrooms may have different items included or not included in their basic styles, so ask for detailed pictures or samples to be sure of what is considered the basic style pricing.
- Add-on items are priced separately and are usually priced per each or per pillow.

RECOMMENDED FABRICS

- Almost any fabric can be used for a pillow so long as the pillow style is appropriate.
- Since pillows are casings for an insert or stuffing, the fabric used for a pillow should be opaque so the stuffing does not show through.
- Sheer or lace fabrics should be used only over another tightly woven fabric.
- When using a stretchy, delicate, or thin fabric, order the pillow with an under-liner sewn to fabric to help control stretch and prevent insert from being detected through the fabric.

Review

1) Detail the difference between a pillow and a pillow sham and what is the function of each?

2) In what situations would down/feather be a recommended fill for a pillow, illustrating your answer with examples.

3) What is the distinguishing characteristic of European pillows and how are they used?

4) When ordering flanged shams with 3" flanges for a King size bed, how many and what standard size inserts should be ordered?

5) What is loft? Explain how it relates to fills.

Pillows ans Pillow Shams

Chapter 13

SOFT TREATMENT ACCESSORIES

In addition to all of the beauty that window treatments add to an interior design, there are dozens of other soft fabric accessories that can be added. Some are as grand and complicated as a window treatment can be, while others are simple soft accents which can add a personal touch that will make a room's design absolutely divine. Many custom window treatment workrooms will also offer at least some of these items for manufacture in addition to their drapery items, and some of these accessories are entire trades and crafts for which separate workrooms are required.

The category which is most outstanding in this respect is upholstery and the manufacture of upholstered items. Upholstery workrooms and window covering workrooms can and do crossover into the manufacture of many items and it is wise to have associations with both types as work that cannot be done by one, can often be completed by the other. Upholstery is listed here as an accessory but it can be a soft treatment element all on its own.

A soft treatment accessory will be defined here as any item made from or covered with decorative fabrics and made with the intention of enhancing an interior design scheme.

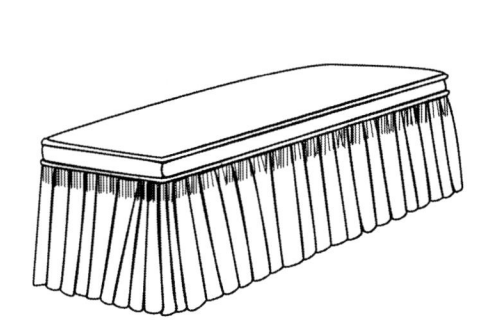

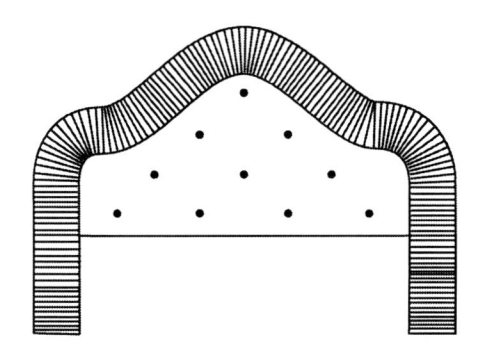

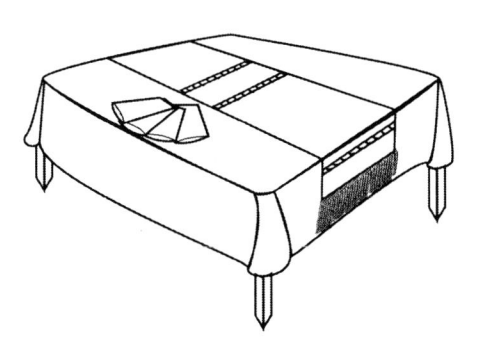

Elements of Soft Treatments

ACCESSORY CATEGORIES

For the purposes of this book, accessories are divided into three groups: bedroom accessories, kitchen accessories, and upholstery items. This division is because the accessories listed are generally found in these areas but many items can be crossed over from one category to another or used in other rooms. They are categorized this way, hopefully to make their descriptions easier to find.

Bedroom accessories

Most accessory items associated with bedrooms will involve the continuation of the theme of making the bed and its environs inviting.

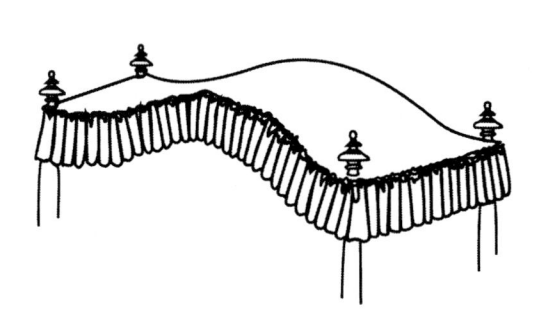

Canopies and coronas

Usually the most intricate accessory treatment for a bedroom will be a bed canopy. The corona is similar to a canopy except that the upper portion is constructed in a circular shape, whereas a canopy is generally a rectangular shape. Originally the bed canopy was a draping consisting of netting which was closed around the bed at night to keep insects such as mosquitoes from disturbing ones sleep. These netting types of canopies are returning again in bedroom designs, but they are now more for the decorative effect, rather than that particular function.

Other current canopy styles can range from simple gathered curtains draped around the bed to grand affairs with upholstered crowns, drape panels, valances, and all kinds of add-on items. The canopy can also be used to change the mood of a very plain bedroom.

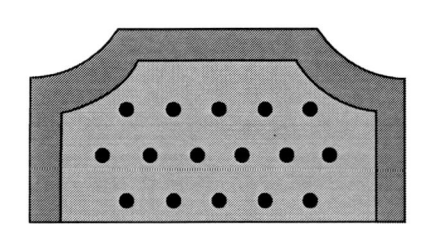

Headboards

Fabric headboards again can be simple fabric covered boards mounted to the wall, or very beautiful upholstered items with rouching, tufting, and many add-on features. These can be excellent ways to incorporate a fabric or texture into a bed treatment, carrying it from a window or other element in the room.

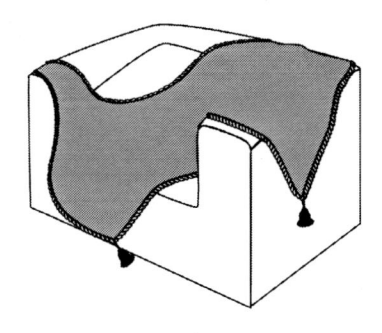

Decorative throws

These are often made to incorporate fabrics in the same manner as headboards, except they can be tossed on the bed, or over a chair or bench to give the room a subtle touch of comfort. They are generally not fussy, as the intention of the throw is to be subtle, but they can have trims added or even be made from a novelty fabric, such as faux fur if a statement is called for. A decorative throw is also an item which can be used in other rooms such as living rooms or family rooms. The throw can be made to be washable and provide the function of protecting the furniture from pet hair, or wear, so throws can have practical uses as well.

Table rounds

These are coverings made to go over small tables, usually placed between chairs or next to the bed in place of a night stand. Table rounds are also used to incorporate multiple fabrics into decor, accentuating a window or bed treatment. These can be used in the same way in living rooms and family rooms. Table rounds can be plain or very fancy, depending on the effect desired.

Table square

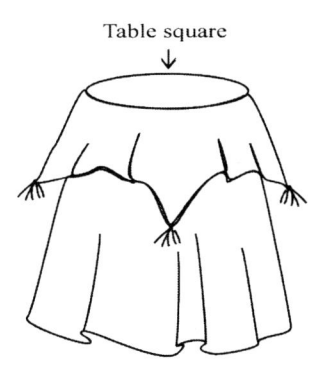

Table squares

These can be large squares which are used to cover tables in the same fashion as a table round or they can be smaller ones used alone. Smaller ones are also used to lay over the top of a table round or square to incorporate yet another fabric in a scheme. They are sometimes made from sheer or lace fabric or they will have fancy trims to add interest.

Kitchen accessories

The following items are generally associated with use in a kitchen or dining room, but can occasionally be found elsewhere in the house as well. Kitchen and dining room accessories tend to be more functional and less decorative but they can still have ornamental elements to them. Some common kitchen accessories are listed below.

Elements of Soft Treatments

Soft Treatment Accessories

Table cloths

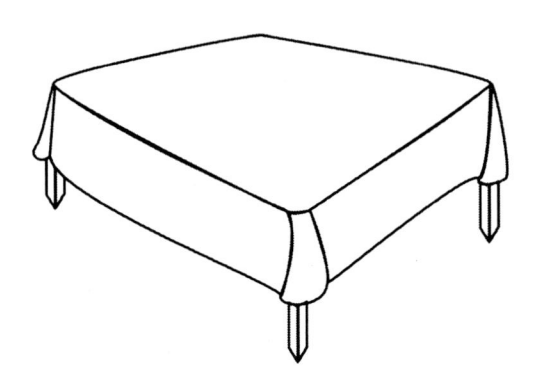

Table cloths are usually functional coverings used to protect the table while dining. Decorative table cloths can be made with the intention of covering the table most of the time. These may be removed while dining and replaced with a functional cloth and then switched back after eating. Tablecloths can be purchased ready made in a variety of standard sizes, however the custom table cloth can be made to any size including extra long and extra wide tables, in addition to being made from virtually any appropriate fabric. This versatility makes the custom made table cloth a very popular accessory item today.

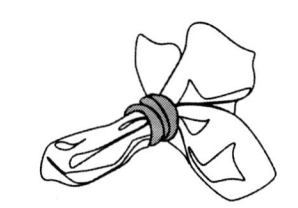

Napkins

Napkins are made to be functional or decorative in the same manner as the table cloth.

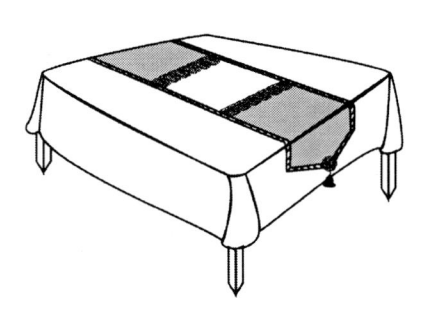

Table runners

These are more of a decorative item. They sit permanently in the center of the table to add a splash of color or pattern to the room. This is also an accessory which can be used to carry a window treatment fabric over into the room to help pull together a theme. Table runners will generally be the length of the table or slightly longer and about 12"-18" inches wide, depending on the width of the table.

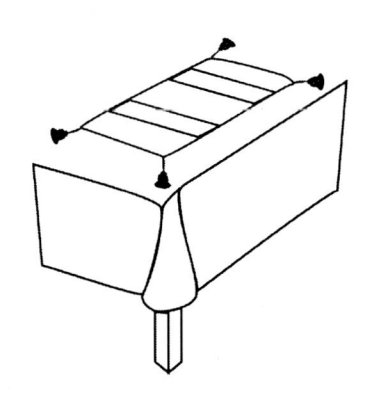

Placemats

Placemats are typically considered to be less formal than a table cloth or table runner, and they are more often found in the kitchen rather than a dining room.

Chapter 13

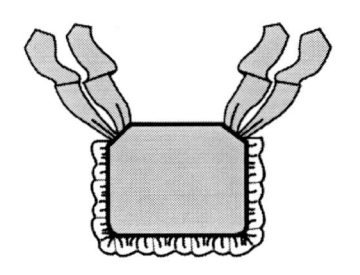

Chair pads
Chair pads are made as decorative items which cover chair seats which are not otherwise upholstered. They can also cushion the chair seat for added comfort. In formal dining rooms, the chair pad becomes more of a chair dressing, resembling a slip cover, and they will sometimes include skirts, bows, and other embellishments.

Upholstered items
This category includes many accessories which can be found in almost any room. While they can be purchased pre-manufactured, they often need to be custom made to suit the overall look of the room.

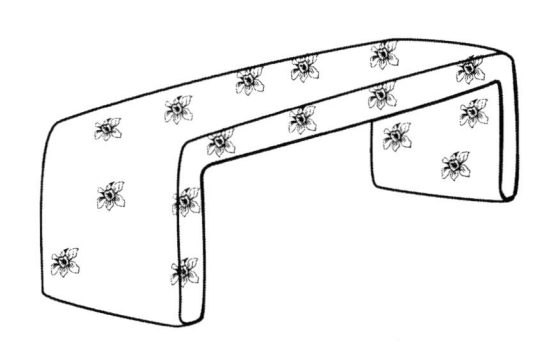

Benches
These come in many sizes and have many uses, from small seats or benches in dressing room sitting areas to large upholstered benches used as seating in bedrooms, kitchens, and family rooms. Bench styles also range from simple to ornate depending on the use and design of the room. They can be purchased pre-manufactured but are often ordered as a decorative accessory, or recovered in order to obtain fabric co-ordination with other room elements.

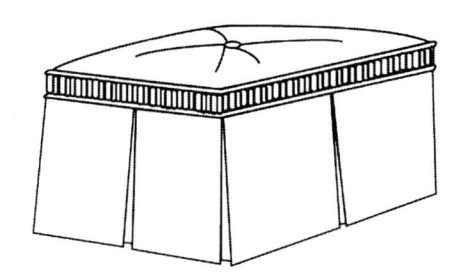

Footstools
Footstools are used for resting ones feet while sitting, and are generally fairly small. Recently though, the traditional footstool has morphed into some large affairs, and are sometimes also used in place of coffee tables in some sitting areas. The larger versions are called ottomans or poufs.

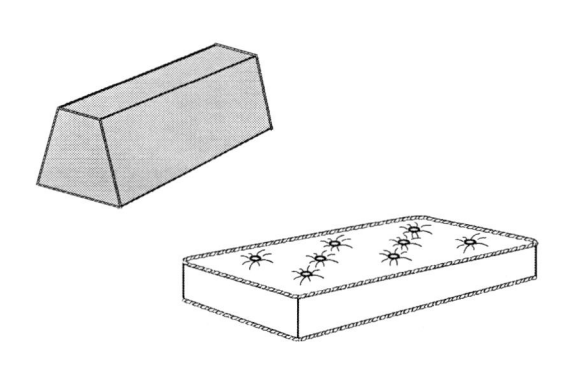

Cushions and bolsters
Cushions are ordered to replace those on pre-manufactured sofas and chairs, and custom manufactured for window seats.

Elements of Soft Treatments

171

Soft Treatment Accessories

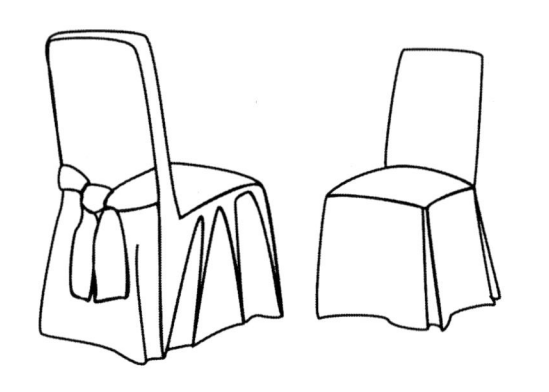

Slip covers

Slip covers are fabric coverings which are made to fit tightly over a sofa or chair and imitate the original upholstery closely. They are usually made so that the cover can be removed and laundered, thus preserving the original upholstery. A properly made slip cover is a very good, if not undetectable imitation of the original upholstery. Slip cover making is another example of one of those crafts which may require a separate workroom for manufacture. Upholstery workrooms will sometimes cross over into the craft of making slip covers and window treatment workrooms can also sometimes manufacture them.

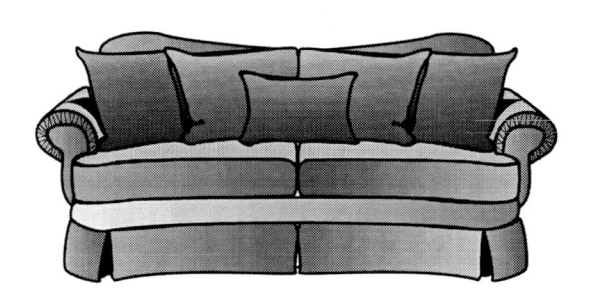

Furniture

Upholsterers can be capable of making most of the above items, and they can be called upon to re-cover antique and heirloom pieces which the client cannot part with. Many master upholstery craft people can custom build upholstered furniture pieces from scratch, and a good upholstery workroom is a valuable part of a designer's set of contacts.

ACCESSORY EMBELLISHMENTS AND VARIATIONS

All of the usual embellishments can be added to accessories to help incorporate them into a room design. Trims such as bullions, cording, fringe, cord, and tassels are common. Buttons, bows, banding, ruffles, and any of these types of add-ons can be used on an accessory item as easily as they can be added to a window covering.

MEASURING FOR ACCESSORIES

Most accessory items have their own set of rules for determining measurements. Some have basic "standard", or near standard sizes, while others must be precisely specified by the designer. If ordering an accessory item that is unfamiliar, work closely with the workroom and they can usually provide some guidance. Providing the workroom with things like scale drawings, photographs, and physical samples whenever possible will garner the most from their expertise.

GENERAL INFORMATION

- Pricing and fabric choices for accessory items have their own set of rules, so work closely with the workroom for guidance.

Review

1) A client is redecorating a girl's bedroom, from a childlike look to one more suited to a teen. Describe 3 accessories you might use in the room to achieve the desired look.

2) A client has a 160" length dining table which comfortably seats 12. What sort of table linen would you recommend for day to day décor and why?

3) Make a list of as many soft treatment accessory items as you can think of. (Hint- it is OK to find things not mentioned in the chapter).

4) Which of the categories would items on your list fit into, or do they require their own category?

5) How many soft treatment workrooms should a designer have a good working relationship with and what kinds of workrooms should they be?

6) When measuring for and ordering accessory items, who are the most important people to consult and why?

Chapter 14

ADD-ONS

Add-ons are items or accessories which are ordered in addition to the basic treatment design. Enhancing a simple treatment with a variety of embellishments allows for customization. Basic treatments are rarely ordered without at least one or two add-on items. Refer to Appendix C for a comprehensive list of thumbnails.

Depending on the workroom chosen, add-ons may be hand or machine sewn, stapled, glued, bonded, or overlaid, and for some applications, only one method or another is possible. Check with the workroom to see which application method they use in given situations.

Add-ons are fabricated either upright, railroaded, or bias cut (Appendix A), and each add-on will have its own set of standard specifications, such as 1"-2" bottom hems, 1½" side hems, etc. This information may either be provided or required by the workroom in order to figure the yardage and to estimate the labor. Refer to the work order form to determine the necessary information.

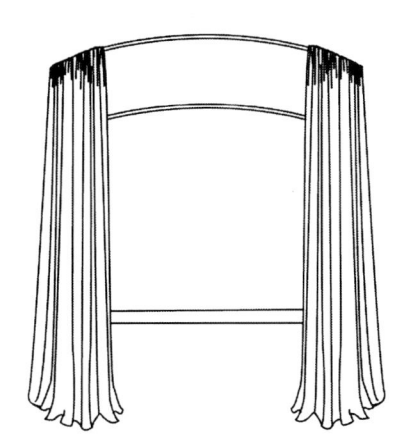

Elements of Soft Treatments

Add Ons

PLACEMENT OF SOME ADD-ONS

Depending on the add-on chosen, codes are used to specify where it should be placed on the treatment. Here are some recommended symbols that describe the placement of banding, trims, fringes, and pre-cording.

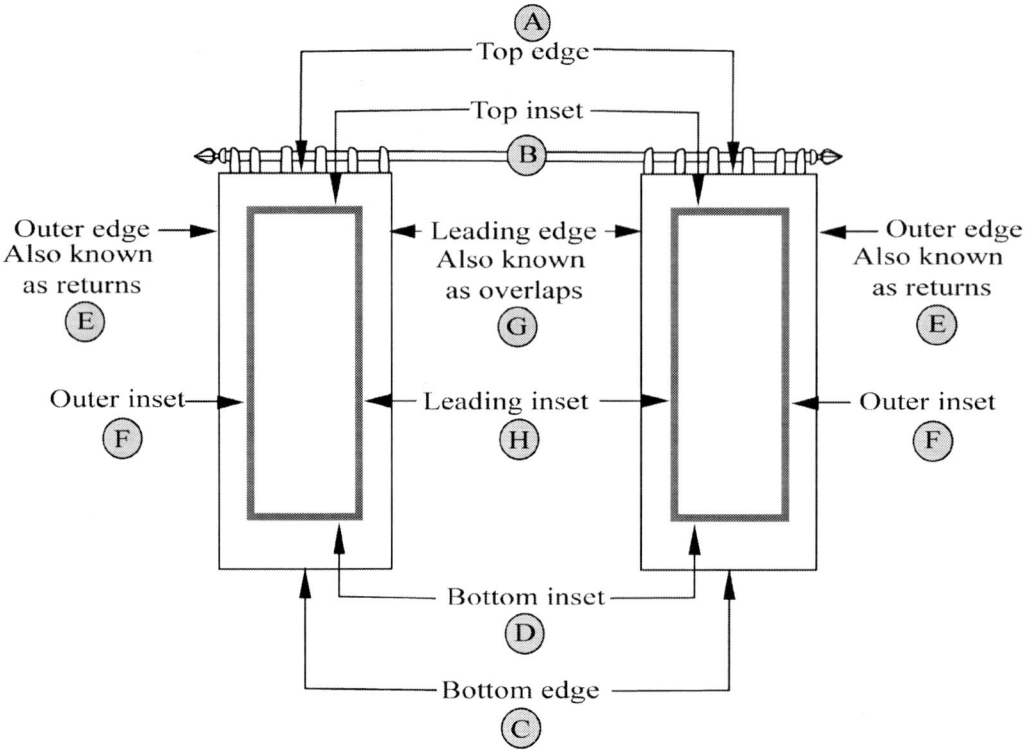

Placement Chart

	Placement Code	Description
A	TopEd	Horizontally placed on top edge
B	TopIn	Horizontally placed down from top edge to given size inset
C	BotEd	Horizontally placed on bottom edge
D	BotIn	Horizontally placed from bottom edge to given size inset
E	OutEd	Vertically placed on outer edge
F	OutIn	Vertically placed and set in from outer edge to size given inset
G	LedEd	Vertically placed on leading edge of treatment
H	LedIn	Vertically placed from leading edge to given size inset

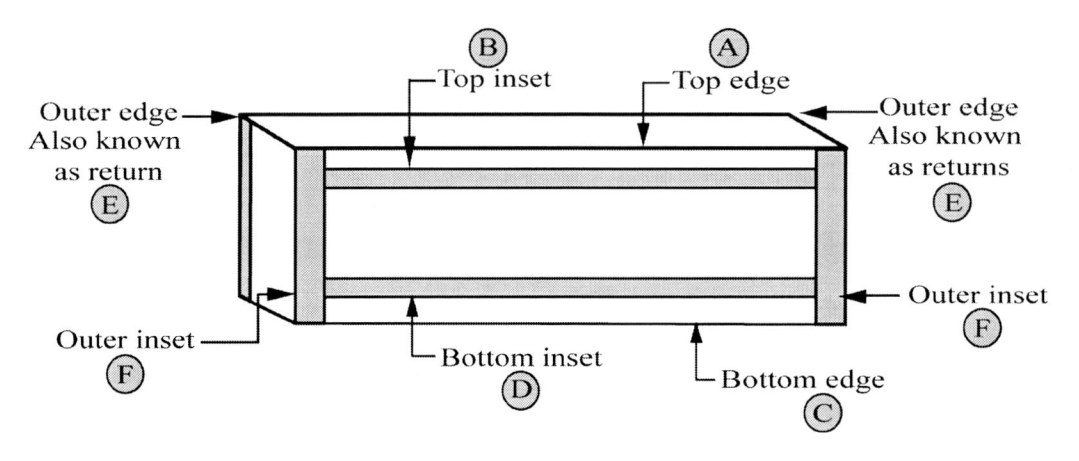

176

Chapter 14

TYPES OF ADD-ONS

The diagrams below show some examples of add-ons and what they are called.

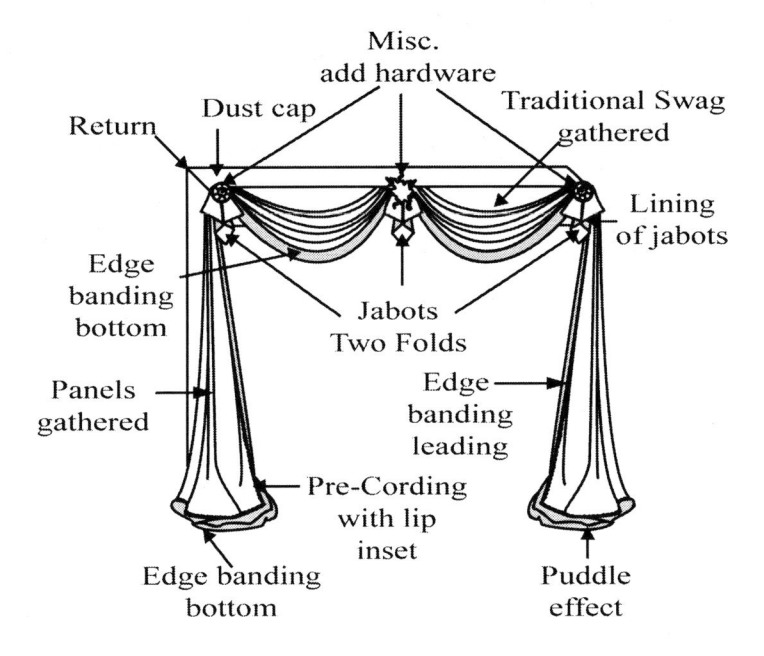

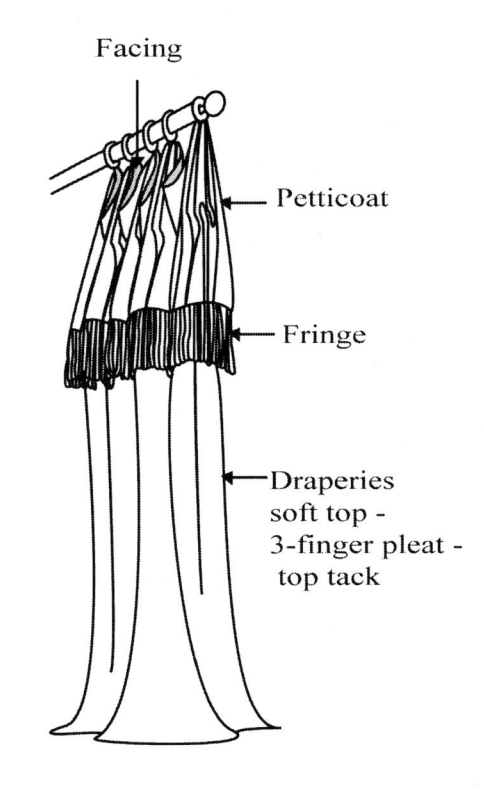

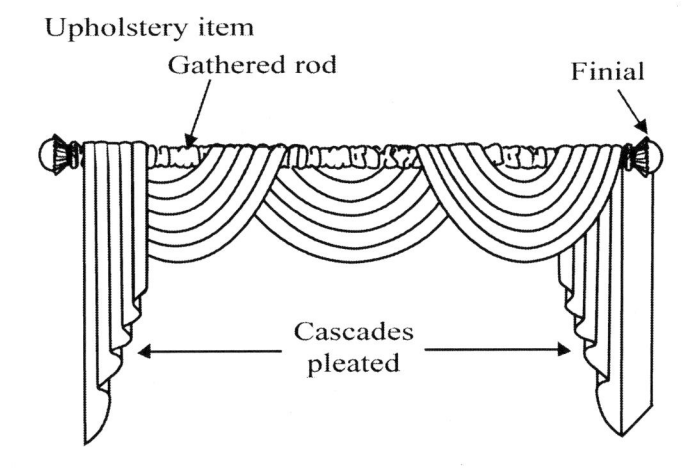

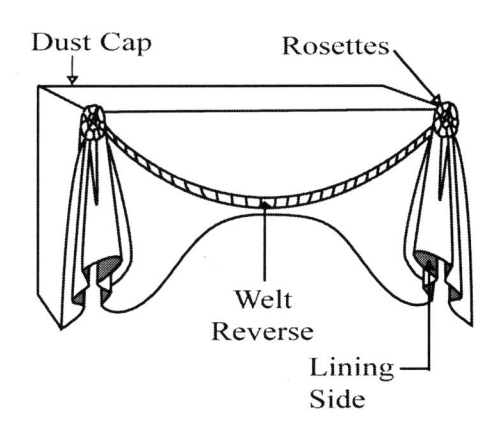

Diagram 1 labels:
- Return
- Dust cap
- Misc. add hardware
- Traditional Swag gathered
- Lining of jabots
- Edge banding bottom
- Jabots Two Folds
- Edge banding leading
- Panels gathered
- Pre-Cording with lip inset
- Edge banding bottom
- Puddle effect

Diagram 2 labels:
- Facing
- Petticoat
- Fringe
- Draperies soft top - 3-finger pleat - top tack

Diagram 3 labels:
- Upholstery item
- Gathered rod
- Finial
- Cascades pleated

Diagram 4 labels:
- Dust Cap
- Rosettes
- Welt Reverse
- Lining Side

Elements of Soft Treatments

177

Add Ons

HOW ADD-ONS ARE PRICED

Add-on items are priced any number of ways: per foot, each, square foot, per pair, or per width. Depending on the workroom, there may also be a minimum charge.

ADD-ON STYLES

Add-on styles are broken down into groups to make them easier to identify.

Banding	Miscellaneous	Swags – Open tops
Build ups	Panels	Swags – Tabs
Buttons, etc.	Pelmets	Swags – Traditional formal
Caps	Petticoats	Swags – Traditional gathered
Cascades	Pre-cording	Tabs
Contrast	Pre-trims	Tiebacks
Facing	Rosettes/Knots/Bows	Ties
Fringe	Ruffles	Upholstery items
Inlays/Overlays	Swags – Draperies	Welts
Jabots	Swags – Medallions	

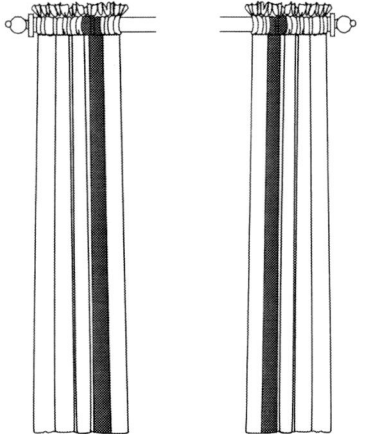

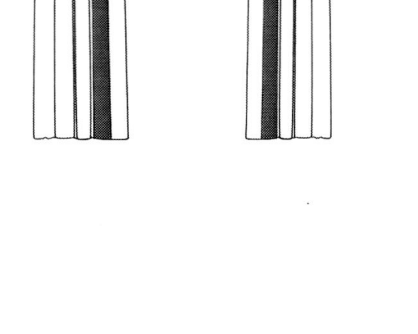

Banding

Banding can be fabricated either upright with seams, railroaded, or bias. The banding is applied to the treatment either by gluing, hand or machine stitching, bonding, or even a combination of these methods. When banding is machine stitched, the banding can sometimes become puckered. If glued, the banding may come off when dry-cleaned or laundered. Fabric bonding is a fast, inexpensive and widely accepted method of applying banding in the modern workroom. Hand-stitching is the most expensive to apply as it is labor intensive. It is still widely used and considered a custom upgrade.

Bias banding is a method used to add interest to certain treatments when applied, such as plaids or checks. When applying banding on the bias, be aware that there will be a lot of wasted fabric due to the bias cut.

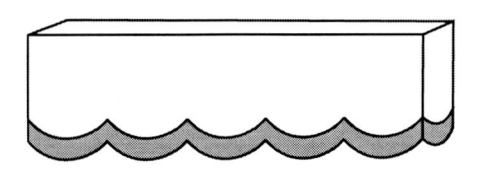

> When using strips cut on the bias, the pattern will become diagonal. To mirror the stripe direction, as on left and right panels, the second strip will need to be cut in the opposite direction, thereby requiring extra yardage.

Chapter 14

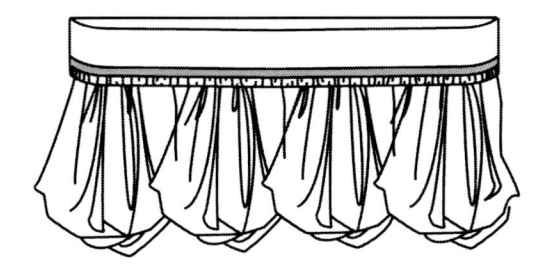

Build ups
These can also be thought of as the combination of two different types of treatments, such as the blending of a cornice and a topper. In a build up, the topper is placed at the bottom inside of the cornice box or headrail of a fabric shade. This makes the treatment look as if it was fabricated as one complete unit. Manufacturing a build up is easier than having the installer assemble it on the job site. By allowing the workroom to assemble it, the workroom can make adjustments easier than the installer, and therefore it will be less expensive, and use less hardware when installed.

Shown here is a cornice with a gathered balloon. The balloon is attached to the back face of the inside of the cornice.

Buttons and similar items
This is where buttons, decorative nail heads, or tassels can be found. They can be applied to a cornice, along the top of toppers, shades, etc.

Caps
These are added to some toppers and a number of types of fabric shades, and are used to hide the ends of the dust cap board or where the ends of the dust caps are exposed (where the fabric does not wrap around the return). They are also used in some cases on traditional swags where there is no cascade, or to hide the headrail or hardware of under treatments. They can be fabricated with either a pleated corner or a wrapped around corner effect. The pleated corner helps hold the shape of the corner better than the wrapped around effect.

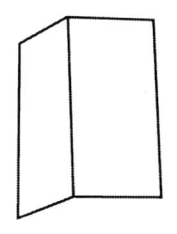

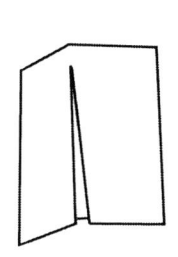

Elements of Soft Treatments

Add Ons

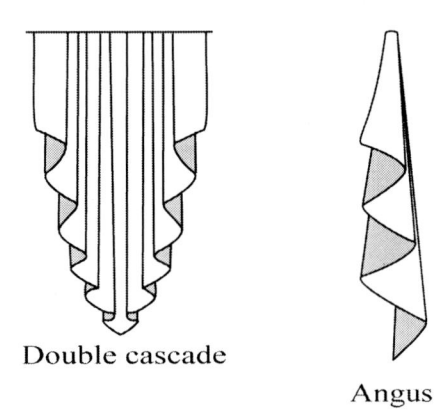

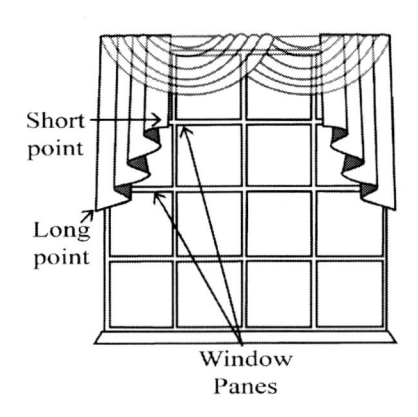

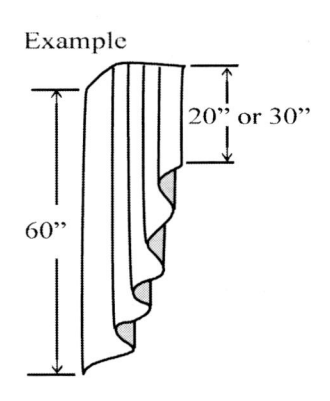

Cascades

These can be used for cornices, open swags, toppers, traditional swags, and rod pocket valances. Calculating the yardage on cascades is similar to figuring the yardage on a drapery with comparable allowances. Most cascades require at least one width of fabric. Double cascades usually require two widths, but check with the workroom to verify this.

Most cascades are self-lined or contrast lined. Be aware of the possibility of bleed through, which is caused by using a dark lining with a light fabric for the front. The dark fabric will change the color of the front fabric. To minimize this effect, add an interlining.

If using a sheer or lace fabric, a ¼" shirt tail hem is used. Be careful with the shirt tail look, as the rolled edge on the bottom front edge of the cascade will be visible.

Cascades can be applied to the treatment either under or over the main treatment.

There are several ways to find the short point of a cascade. One method is to set the length the same as the finished length of the swag. Another way is to take the finished length of the cascade and divide by either two or three. The cascade should fall above or below the center of the window. The short point should always be at least 15" shorter than the long point, otherwise the cascade will have a bottom edge which is too flat and a pleasant cascading appearance will not be obtained. Use the architectural features of the window, such as window panes, as guides to help set the long and short points of the cascade.

Example:
Finished length of cascade 60"

$60 \div 2 = 30$" or $60 \div 3 = 20$"

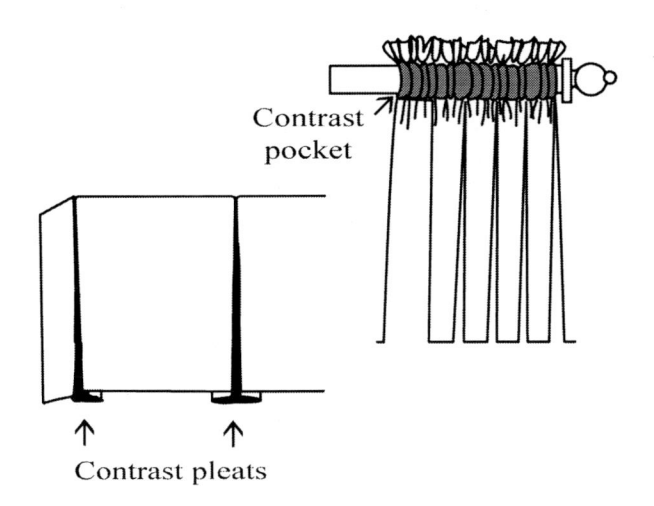

Chapter 14

Contrast
This is used on shades or toppers. A contrast color can also be added to inverted pleats on pleated balloons, toppers, and box pleated valances. Contrast pockets or pocket and headers can also found on rod pocket panels and rod pocket valances.

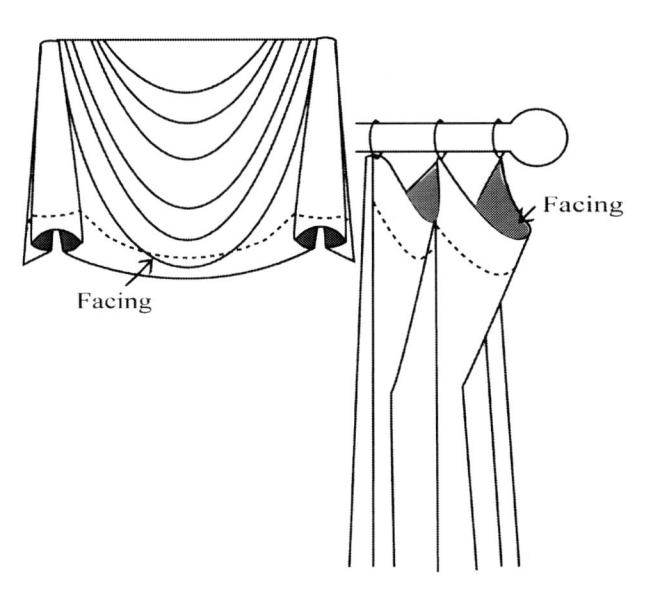

Facings
This is similar to banding, however a strip of contrast fabric is applied to the reverse side (or lining side), along with the lining and can be seen from the front when the treatment is hung. This can be found on the tops of draperies, cascades, the horns/bells of Empire or Kingston swags, and roll-ups.

A facing placed along the edge where it can be seen from the front will cause a banding effect when the light passes through the drapery. It can also cause bleed through depending on the darkness of the fabric. Interlining may minimize this effect.

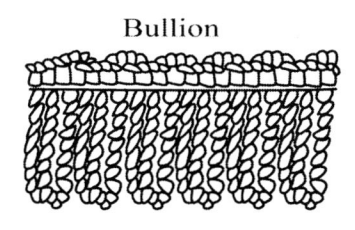

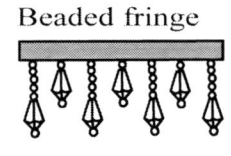

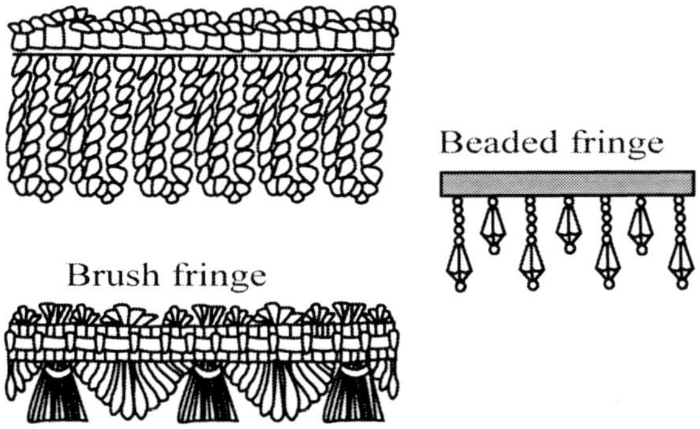

Fringe or bullion
All treatment categories can use fringing, with the exception of sunbursts. Fringe can also be known as bullion, although bullion is much larger and heavier than tassel fringe.

When placing some bullion fringes onto swags, the fringe can be so heavy that it will cause the folds on the swags to separate, thereby causing them to not hang correctly. If there are questions about the weight of the bullion, check with the workroom.

Elements of Soft Treatments

Add Ons

There are two ways fringe can be applied to a treatment.

Applied fringe will be placed onto the face of the treatment and top stitched, glued or bonded. The trims chosen for application should have an attractive edge as they will be clearly visible on the finished product.

Inserted fringe will be pillowcased between the face and the lining of the treatment and will be caught in the stitching when the two fabrics are seamed. The fringe must be pre-manufactured with a lip when inserted in this manner.

Trim may be placed in two ways, flush on the edge or set in. Always specify the preferred location of the trim, and if set-in, specify how far in from the edge of the treatment. Some clients can have very particular preferences regarding trim placement, so be sure of their expectations before placing the order with the workroom.

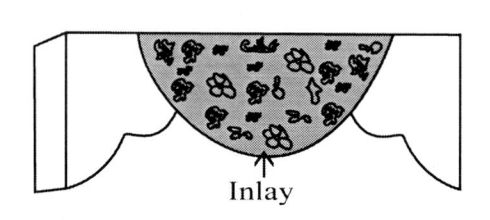

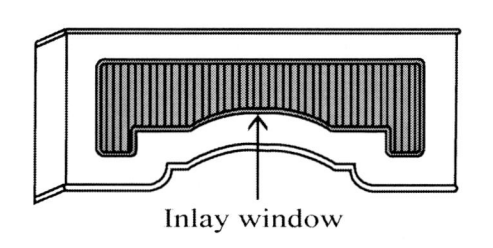

Inlays or Overlays

These are found on some cornice designs where a raised or a window effect is desired. There are four ways they can be applied to the cornice.

Inlays are where the contrast fabric is directly applied to the main cornice design, and either tack strip or ply grip is used to hide the staples from the face.

An **inlay window** is where there is a separate piece of plywood or stiffener which is padded and upholstered and then fastened to the back inside of the cornice. On the main cornice design, there is a window effect cut out of the cornice.

182

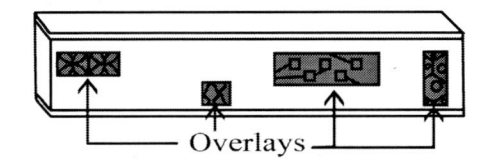

Chapter 14

Overlays are where there is a separate piece of plywood or stiffener. It can be padded and upholstered and then fastened directly on top of the front of the main cornice.

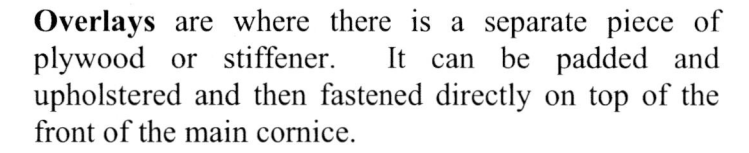

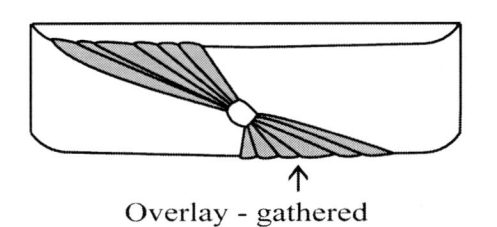

An **overlay gathered** is where the contrast fabric is mounted directly onto the main cornice design

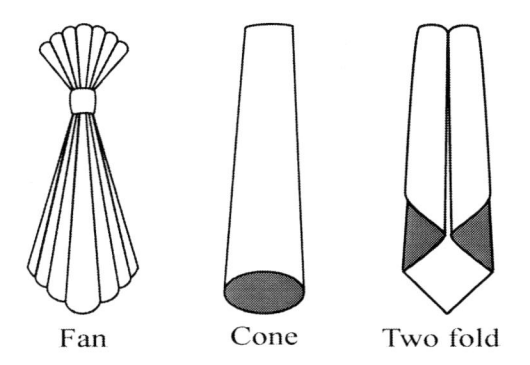

Overlays

Overlay - gathered

Fan   Cone   Two fold

Jabots
These can be used on swags, toppers, and cornices. Jabots are a decorative piece hung over any seams, between swags to fill space, or used for a strictly decorative effect. Jabots can include tie shapes and cone shapes, and may be rounded on the bottom or pointed. Jabots are usually self-lined or contrasted lined. The same rules apply for bleed through.

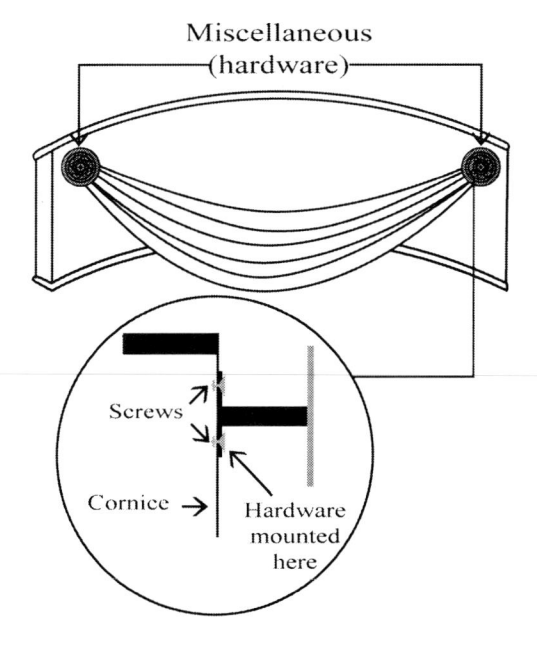

Miscellaneous
(hardware)

Miscellaneous
This is where a variety of miscellaneous items can be found, and they can be applied to all treatment categories. It includes such things as adding hardware, like medallions to a treatment, covering dust cap boards with matching fabric, and putting hook and loop along the edges for treatments for mounting.

Screws

Cornice → Hardware mounted here

Elements of Soft Treatments

Add Ons

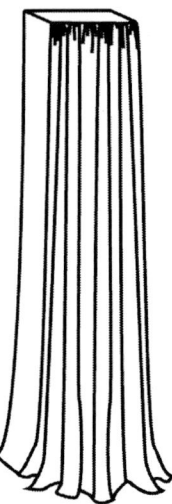

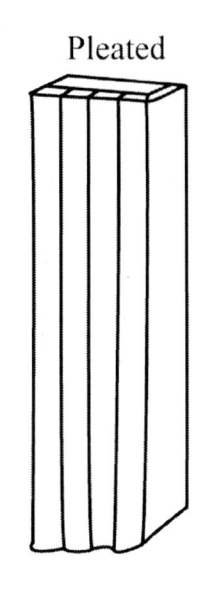

Gathered Pleated

Panels
These are found on traditional swags, open swags, toppers, and cornices. They are mounted onto the same board (dust cap), or pole, as the main treatment. Most of the time, one width of fabric is enough, but it is recommended that the face width of the panel to the fullness width be double checked. Construction is the same as for rod pocket panels, with the exception that they are mounted onto a board.

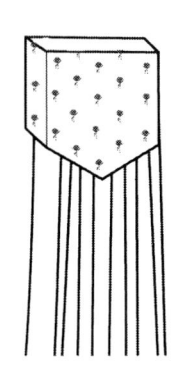

Pelmets
These are found on cornices, rod pocket panels, rod pocket valances, shades, and toppers. They have 1x fullness only, or are flat. Pelmets can be lined or unlined when the bottom is straight. When shaped along the bottom edge, they are either self-lined or contrast lined.

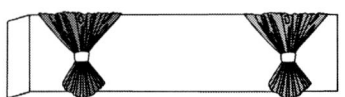

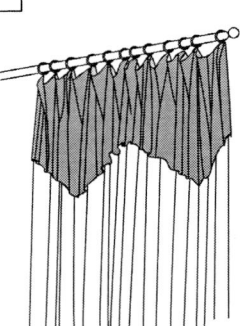

Petticoats
These are found on cornices, draperies, rod pocket panels, and toppers. They require fullness in width and can be straight along the bottom or shaped. If the bottom is straight, they can be lined or unlined. When the bottom is shaped they need to be self-lined or contrast lined. Since petticoats are placed over another fabric, there is a small chance that bleed through will happen if using a dark fabric for the back layer.

Chapter 14

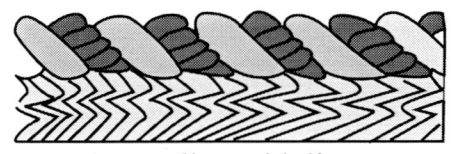

Precording with lip

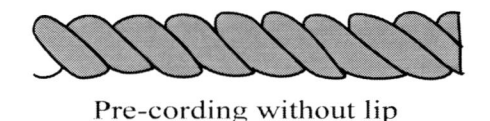

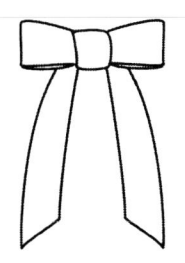

Pre-cording without lip

Pre-cording

Every treatment category can use pre-cording, of which there are two types - cord made with and without a lip. They can be either hand or machine stitched, or glued to the treatment. When the pre-cording has an attached lip, it can be used for pillow casing between the face and lining fabrics, as well as for gluing it to the tops of cornices, toppers, and shades. When the pre-cording has no lip, it is supposed to free hang in front of the treatment. Many strands can be braided to create a thicker looking rope. It can also be knotted in sections to add character.

> There will be a workroom up charge for adding or removing cord lip. Be sure to order the correct one from the manufacturer to save on fabrication expense.

Pre-trims

Every treatment category can use pre-trims. These are trims which lay flat and can have some kind of decoration sewn into it. They can be applied by hand or machine sewn, glued, or bonded directly onto the treatment. Depending on the style and how wide the pre-trim is, it may need to be attached along both edges.

> Keep in mind when selecting trims for shaped curves that some pre-trims do not bend well around curves or sharp turns.

Rosettes, knots, bows

Every treatment category can use rosettes, knots, or bows. They are all individually handmade. After they are assembled, they are either pinned or hand stitched to the treatment.

Elements of Soft Treatments

185

Shirred ruffle

Pleated ruffle

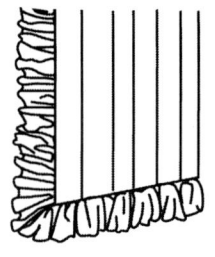

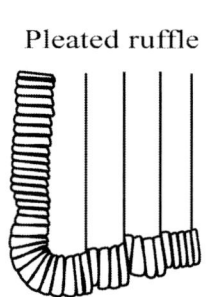

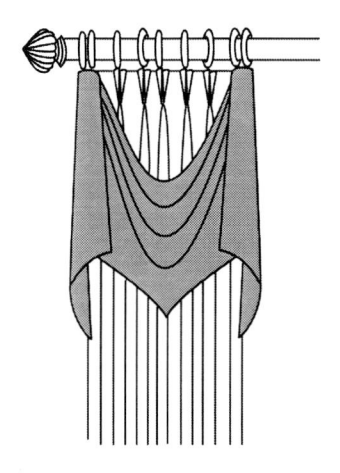

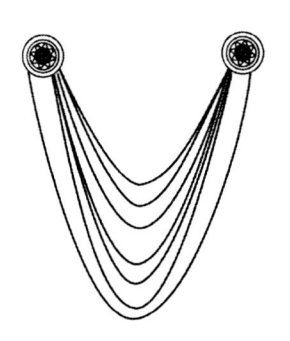

Ruffles

Every treatment category can use ruffles, and there are two types of ruffling.

A **shirred ruffle** is a gathered looking effect.

A **pleated ruffle** has approximately ½"-¾" pleats, which add a crisp look.

Ruffles are usually made using straight cuts. They are self-lined, but can also be made with a ¼" shirt tail hem. Patterns are usually not matched unless specified to do so. Ruffles can be applied, with a "header" or inset in the same way as pre-trims are done. Always specify the client's preference.

Swag - Draperies

These are seen on draperies and rod pocket panels. They are made in individual swag units so that they hang in front of the drapery or rod pocket panel. They use drapery hooks or pins to attach to the main drapery.

Swag - Medallions

These will be found on cornices and toppers. They are made in individual swag units so that they hang in front of the cornice or topper by means of a medallion or finial.

Chapter 14

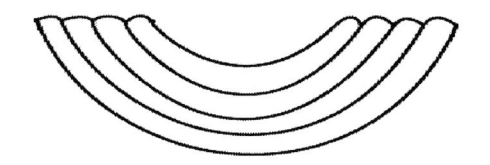

Swag - Open tops
These are found on cornices, toppers, and shades. They are made in individual swag units so that they hang in front of the cornice, topper, or shade. The top gap is open to reveal the main treatment fabric. The gap is approximately 4"-8" deep, depending on the main treatment design. They are stapled to the top of the dust cap or headrail.

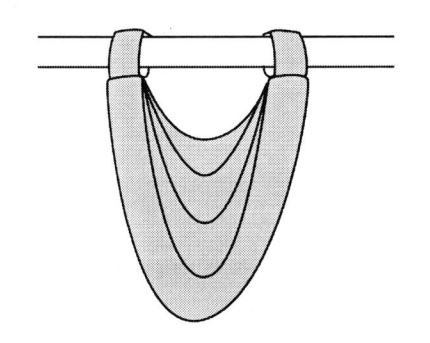

Swag - Tab
These are seen on draperies and rod pocket panels. They are made in individual swag units with a tab, which is sewn to the top of the swag overlap.

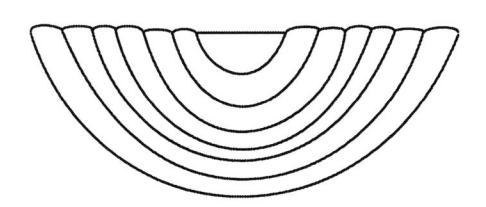

Swag - Traditional formal
These are found on cornices, toppers, and shades. They are made in individual swag units so that they hang in front of the treatment. They are stapled to the top of the dust cap or headrail. They can be cut on the bias, upright, or railroaded.

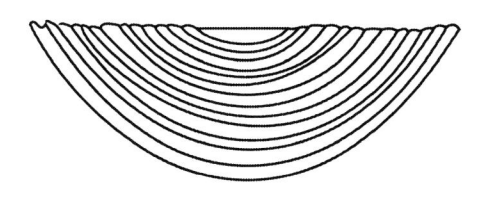

Swag - Traditional gathered
These are made for cornices, toppers, and shades. They are made in individual swag units so that they hang in front of the cornice, topper, or shade. They are stapled to the top of the dust cap or headrail. The fabrication style is either upright (seams) or railroaded.

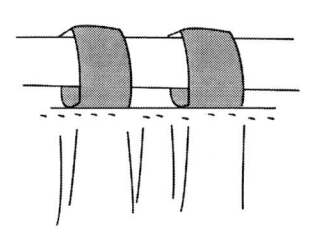

Tabs
These are found on draperies, drapery valances, toppers and cornices and are made in many different styles.

Elements of Soft Treatments   187

Add Ons

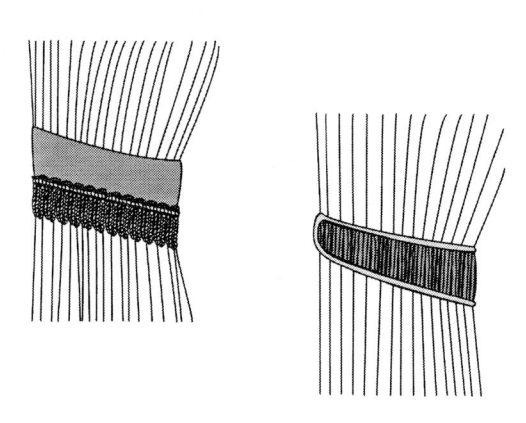

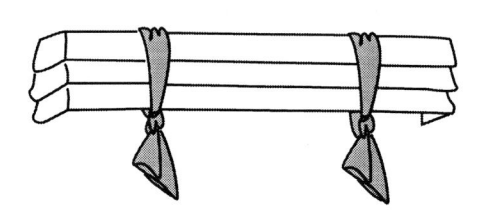

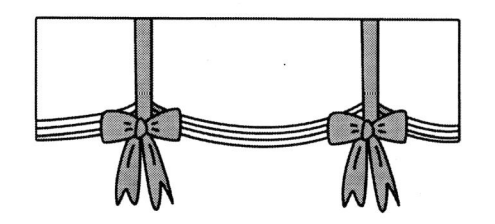

When using tabs, there is take-up involved. This is when the rod goes through the tabs, and the drapery will draw upward due to the roundness on the rod. This can vary from 1½" on a 3" diameter pole to ¾" on a 1⅜" diameter pole. This is based on a throat gap, which is from the bottom of the pole to the top of the drapery (Appendix B).

Tiebacks

These are found on draperies, rod pocket panels, open swags, and traditional swags. They are made in many different styles and are used to hold back side panels in a fixed position. Tiebacks are usually made with a stiffener to give them a crisp look and help them hold their shape. They can also be made from braided cord and there are various shirred versions.

> To give the drapery a clean, straight look when the tieback wraps around towards the wall, use a hidden tieback holder which can be found at a drapery hardware supply house.

Ties

These are found on draperies, drapery valances, scarf swags, shades, toppers, cornices, and traditional swags. They are made in many different styles, and are either used to hold up the treatment design or for decorative purposes. Some pole type treatments can be made up entirely of nothing but ties of various lengths.

Gathered

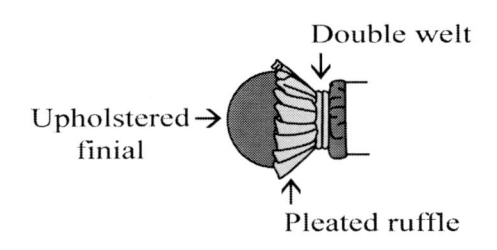

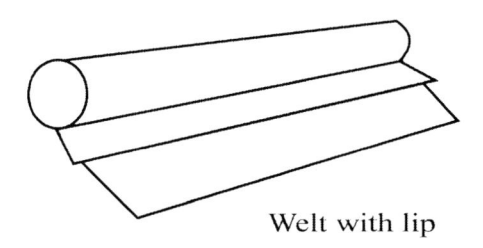

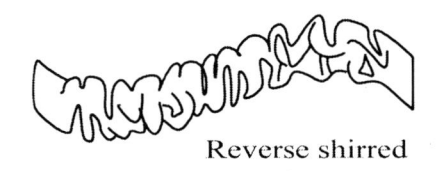

Upholstered finial → [Double welt ↓] [Pleated ruffle ↑]

Welt with lip

Reverse shirred

Reverse welt

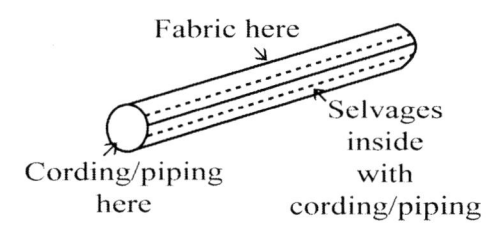

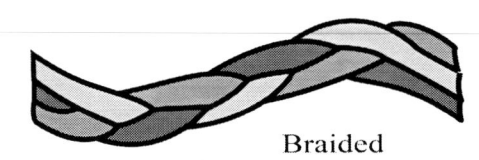

Fabric here ↓ / Selvages inside with cording/piping / Cording/piping here

Braided

Twisted

Upholstery items

These are found on open swags and scarfs. They contain upholstered rods and upholstered finials. Upholstered rods can be manufactured either shirred or with fabric flat on the rod. Upholstered finials are fabric covered finials or finials made entirely from fabric, and can also be very simple fabric wrapped balls, or very elaborate with ruffles, trim and cording added.

Welt cording

Every treatment category can use welt cording, which is also sometimes called piping. Piping is added to a treatment in many different ways, the most basic of which is a welt made from fabric with a lip which allows it to be inserted into a seam. The cording or piping around which the fabric is wrapped can be anywhere between $1/16^{th}$ of an inch in diameter to 2". The smaller sizes are called "micro" welt and the large size is "jumbo" welt. Each type has its own uses and purposes, some practical and some strictly decorative.

Micro cords can also be used to hide difficult to sew pre-trim lips, such as those on beaded trims. Occasionally welt will be made without any piping or cord inserted, and this is called a "flat welt" and can be quite useful for creating a neat finished edge on cascades or box pleats where sharp creasing might be undesirably influenced by the thickness of the cord. They also work well along the edges of draperies or rod pocket panels where a little contrast color is introduced without the thickness of a piping.

> Some workrooms will insert micro cord between the two sides of every knife edge seam.

Fabric can be shirred onto the cord in order to create a soft ruffled effect or the cord can be wrapped without a lip, then twisted, braided, knotted, or draped over items to incorporate multiple colors or add interesting effects.

Elements of Soft Treatments

Add Ons

Review

1) What are the three ways that banding can be cut? Draw an illustration showing the differences between them.

2) What are the eight placement codes and what do they mean?

3) How are cascades measured?

4) What is meant by 'bleed through' and how and when can it be a problem? How can it be minimized?

APPENDIX A
Fabric Direction

Fabrics are manufactured in various widths ranging from 36" to 132" wide. The widths most commonly used for soft treatment fabrication today are the 54" to 132". The smaller widths are generally found in fabrics made for the garment industry or hand loomed materials. 45"-48" goods are being replaced by 54"-55" as older looms are replaced with newer, wider ones. Because the manufactured pieces of cloth will allow soft treatments to be manufactured in various ways, it is important for the soft treatment designer to understand what fabric direction means, the terms for describing direction, and how the different uses will affect a given design.

When fabric is loomed it has threads which run vertically up and down. These threads are called warp threads and are usually stronger and less stretchy than the weft threads which run horizontally across the "woof" or width of the goods. These weft threads are woven across the warp threads and change direction on the right and left side of the loom, creating a finished selvage edge, which also helps to keep the fabric from fraying or unraveling.

Patterns can be woven into the fabric, or they can be printed on after the fabric is woven. Patterns that are printed have traditionally been screen printed which would only allow the pattern to run vertically or horizontally across the goods and changing pattern size was a complicated process involving much re-tooling in the print process. Recently however, computer printing of fabrics is becoming a reality and the printing process is being revolutionized, allowing patterns to be re-sized instantly, printed in any direction, and virtually any design that can be digitized can be printed onto cloth for use in a decorative scheme. While this is an exciting development, it can be an additional complication in the design and manufacture of soft furnishings, making fabric, pattern, and fabrication direction specifications more critical now than ever before.

FABRIC DIRECTION

Fabric directions share the same names as fabrication styles. When referring to a fabrication style, the terms upright, railroad, and bias refer to the direction the treatment will be cut when it is made, or the direction the pattern is printed. The selvages will be the finished edges on the right and left side as the fabric comes off of the roll. The selvages are usually printed with the company's name and color dye lots that were used to print the fabric. When fabricated, the selvage edges are usually cut away during treatment manufacture in order to eliminate puckering and bleed through from the company name and color ways. Sometimes the company name is printed so close to the edge of the printed pattern that not all of it can be removed and it can bleed through and show slightly.

Fabric Direction

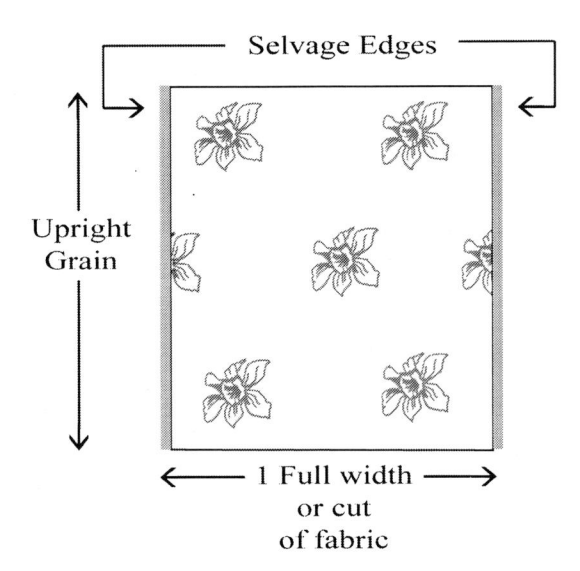

Upright fabrication

With this method of manufacture, the fabric is placed on the upright direction of the fabric grain with the warp threads running vertically. The selvages are on the left and right edges of the fabric width. If the treatment being made is wider than the width of the goods, it will be necessary to seam the fabric together at the selvages to create more width. The seams are either balanced on each side or offset to one side depending on the type of treatment being made.

When using printed goods made for soft furnishing manufacture, it is possible to match the print of the pattern at the seam so that the pattern will be continuous across the width of the item. This is because the printed pattern will typically have a consistent repeat throughout the length of the roll and the fabric can be cut to allow matching at the selvages. When using fabric that is hand printed or hand loomed, the pattern repeat may not run true and pattern matching is less likely to be possible due to the hand crafted nature of these types of goods.

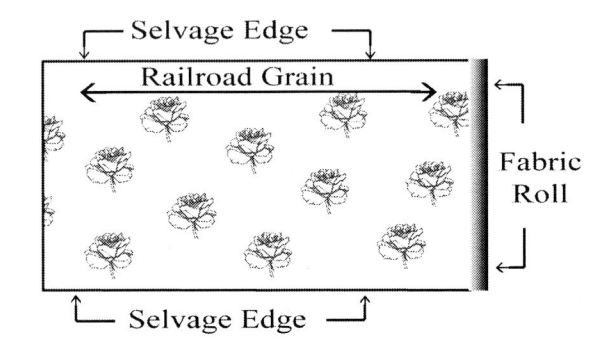

Railroad fabrication

When a treatment is being made railroad, the fabric is placed sideways so the selvages are along the top and bottom, and the treatment is cut with the warp threads running from right to left. Usually there are no seams when an item is made in this way. When using fabric for banding, contrasting inserts, or facing, it is usual to get three to four cut lengths out of one railroad width of the fabric. However pattern matching if required is much less likely to be possible when the railroad method is used, since the item width would have to be longer than the bolt length. When making valances and under treatments from fabric of the same pattern, and one will be made railroad and one will be made upright, the pattern needs to be of a nature that will look appropriate running in any direction.

On some "seamless" fabrics, usually transparent types of goods 118" wide or wider, the product is made railroad allowing the treatment to be made without seams. In these cases the length of the item will be limited by the width of the fabric.

Appendix A

> Whenever possible, try to railroad the fabric on cornices and valances when using non-directional and solid fabrics. This will eliminate seams, which can be noticeable with some fabrics.

> Be especially cautious with velvets and fabrics which have a nap, as changing direction will cause the color to look different.

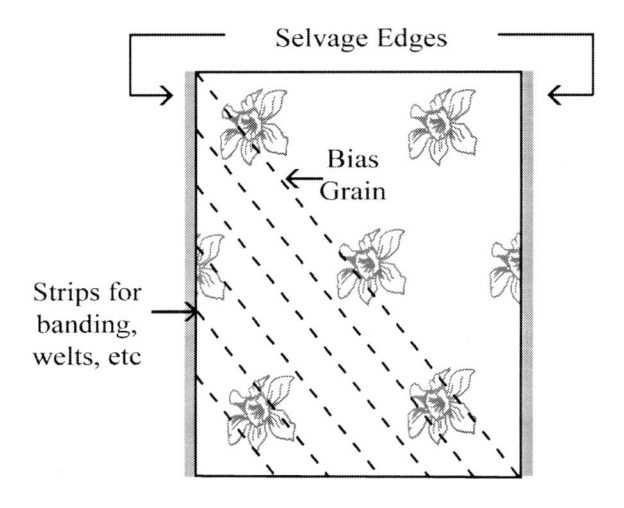

Bias fabrication

When bias fabrication is ordered, the treatment pattern is placed so that it is lying on the diagonal grain of the fabric. Items cut on the bias grain will have a great degree of stretch because the warp and weft threads will be severed allowing them to separate and give. This is useful when making swags or covering cord that will have to be bent or curved, because it allows the fabric to contour to these shapes with fewer kinks, folds, and ripples. Sometimes banding is cut on the bias even though it will be applied straight, and this is usually done to create an interesting effect with a pattern, such as a check or stripe.

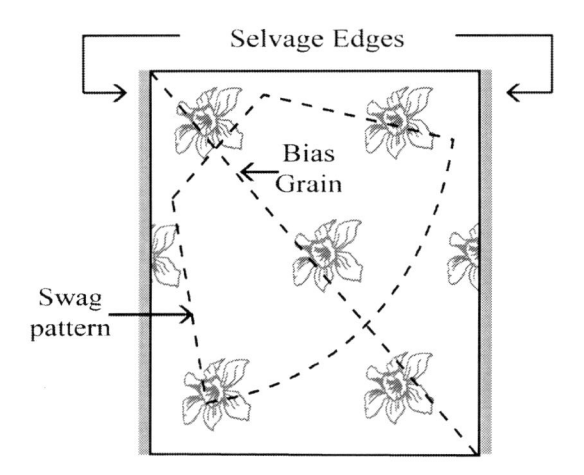

SEAM PLACEMENT

The visibility of seams will always be minimized in the production of a quality product. One way to accomplish this is through proper seam placement. Very often when fabricating soft treatment items, half or partial widths will be required in order for the fabric piece to be wide enough for a given product. Draperies, rod pocket panels, and some add-on items, will use offset partial widths. Valances, toppers, cornices, swags, and fabric shades will generally have balanced seaming for placement of partial widths. These two methods of seam or partial width placement are described below.

Elements of Soft Treatments 193

Fabric Direction

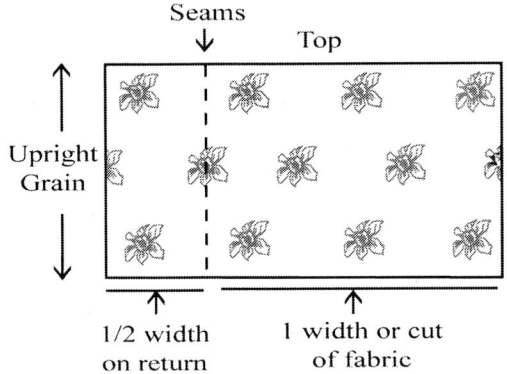

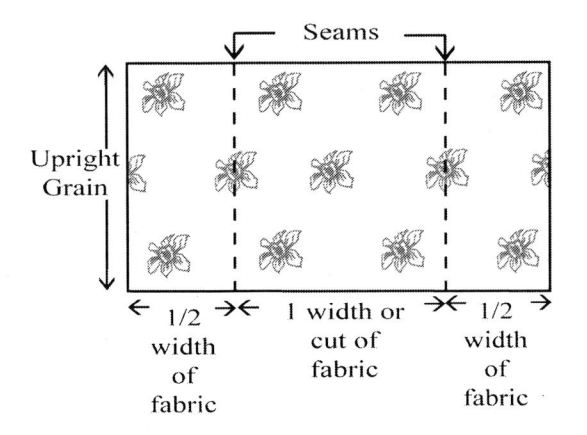

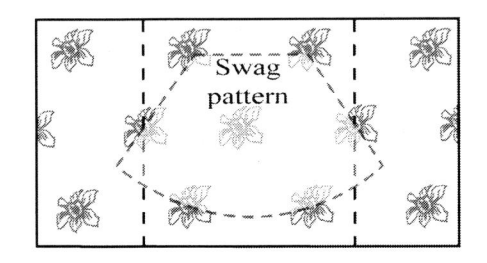

Panels with offset seaming

Industry standards dictate that when half or partial widths are used on draperies and rod pocket panels, the half width always goes on the return side of the drapery. The reason for this is to make the seam less noticeable when the drapery is hanging. For pairs, the half widths are placed on the return side of each half of the pair. For center stacking panels, partial width placement will have to be specified by the designer.

Balanced seaming

The industry standard for seam placement when there is an odd number of widths required for a flat valance, topper, cornice, swag, or fabric shade, is to split the odd width and the partial pieces are to be balanced on either side of the full width, or widths. If the item has an even number of widths, one should be split and the partial pieces placed to the outside edges of the product. This is done to help keep the eye focused on the center width and motif design of the fabric, and locates the seams where they will be less visually prominent. When placing seams in bay and corner windows this rule may need to be broken. Be sure the workroom is aware if different seam or pattern placement will be required.

SEAM VISIBILITY

In addition to proper placement of seams, pleated or folded items should always have the seam hidden in a fold or behind a pleat if at all possible, so that its visibility is minimized. With swags, the seams will be partially vertical when the folds are in place, and if a swag must be seamed, every effort should be made to design the swag treatment so that the seaming will be hidden by another swag or add-on item.

While great effort is taken to construct products with minimal seam visibility, light passing through the treatment will cause the seams to show up as dark shadows due to the extra thickness at the join.

While great effort is taken to construct products with minimal seam visibility, light passing through the treatment will cause the seams to show up as dark shadows due to the extra thickness at the join. This shadowing can be minimized by using interlining. In some cases when the treatment is exposed to direct light, light blocking interlining may be required to eliminate this effect. These measures will add bulk to the treatment and labor costs will increase, however the consideration is often worth the effort in the appearance of the finished product

FABRIC REPEATS

When fabric is printed, the pattern is repeated throughout the bolt. The repeat is the distance between any given point of the motif to where the other point is repeated again. The fabric repeat can be either vertical or horizontal. For some prints and plaids, pattern repeats do not run true and patterns will drift, matching at the top and not at the bottom. This is prevalent in hand printed or hand loomed fabrics. Integrate these "natural" fabric characteristics into the design plan.

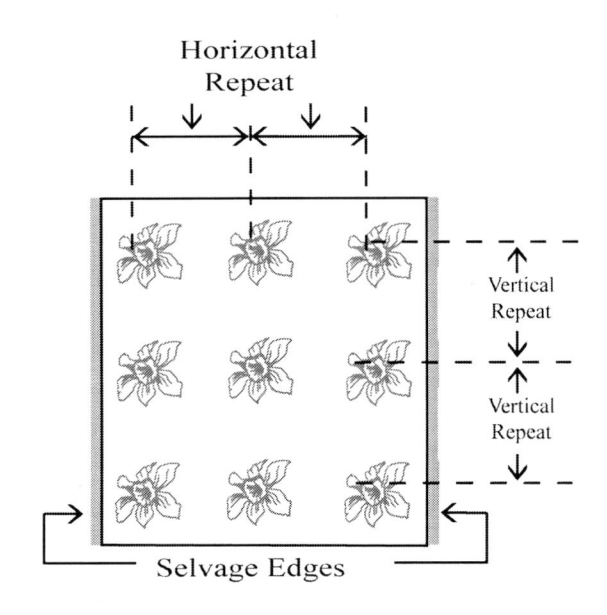

Vertical and horizontal repeats
The vertical repeat is measured vertically going down the length of the fabric. Vertical repeats match horizontally across the width of the goods. The horizontal repeat is measured across the width of the fabric from selvage to selvage.

Drop repeats
It is not uncommon to see vertical drop repeats. In this case, the fabric repeat drops down either a full repeat or a half of a repeat. When this happens, in order for the pattern to be matched when seaming, an additional allowance in yardage needs to be made. To allow for a drop repeat, add one repeat per width to the cut lengths. If the fabric is printed with a half drop repeat, take the full drop repeat and divide it by two. For example, 25 ÷ 2 = 12½, and this is the half drop repeat measurement that needs to be added to the cut lengths. There is usually a lot of waste when using drop repeat fabrics, as can be seen in the diagram below.

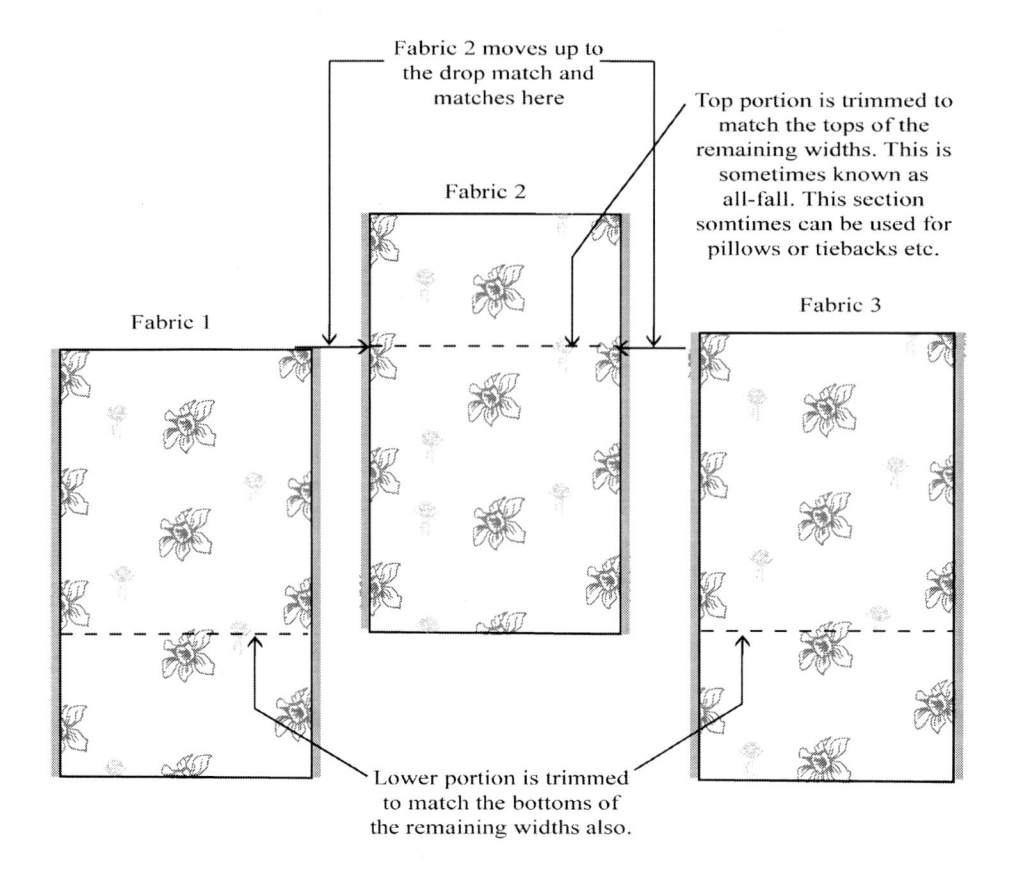

Fabric 2 moves up to the drop match and matches here

Fabric 2

Top portion is trimmed to match the tops of the remaining widths. This is sometimes known as all-fall. This section somtimes can be used for pillows or tiebacks etc.

Fabric 1

Fabric 3

Lower portion is trimmed to match the bottoms of the remaining widths also.

FABRIC PATTERN LAYOUT

When selecting fabric, pay close attention to how the motif is placed on the fabric. The location of the print on the fabric will influence where the treatment pattern is placed on the fabric. This step requires some thought, since some planning will be involved with where the motif will be positioned on the completed treatment. It is the designer's responsibility to tell the workroom which design on the fabric should be centered. This is called pattern placement, and there is usually a workroom charge for this, since additional planning and yardage are required. Usually the information on a swatch will not be sufficient to determine motif placement, and if this will be critical, order a full repeat, full width cutting from the fabric vendor before calculating and ordering yardage.

There are five common ways fabric is printed.

1 point fabric
This is where the main motif is placed down the center of the fabric width.

Appendix A

2 or 4 point fabric

This is where there are two motif designs across the width of fabric. Depending on the vertical repeat, there will either be two or four motifs within the repeat.

This design is good if planning to have the motif centered on a jabot, flat pelmet, pillows etc. With this repeat, two motifs per width or cut of fabric is possible.

3 point fabric

The motif is placed in a stepping stone design. This layout is usually found on a fabric printed with a drop repeat, but not always. This type of motif design is not recommended for fabric shades as the pattern can not be in the center of the shade. It can be worked around, however it requires significantly more fabric and there will be an up-charge from the workroom There could also be seams on smaller shades as the workroom will be off-setting the pattern to get the motif centered.

5 point fabric

This design placement occurs when the pattern has a row with two full motifs printed across the top, the next row has two half motifs and one full centered motif. The two row theme then will repeat itself.

Elements of Soft Treatments

Fabric Direction

APPENDIX B
Technical Specifications

DRAPERY PIN OR HOOK SETTINGS

Drapery hooks are used on draperies and drapery valances in order for them to attach to the ring or drapery slide. When placing the order for draperies or drapery valances it must be specified on the work order the hook setting which goes with the rod chosen. If the wrong setting is given to the workroom it could cause the drapery to be installed incorrectly. If the installer has to re-hook the draperies due to the wrong setting there could be a re-hooking charge from the installer.

Pin Setting Chart

Rod Type	Pin setting from top	Decimal settings
Regular Traverse	1¾"	1.75
Decorative	½"	0.5
Ceiling mount	1¼"	1.25
Wood pole rings	¼"	0.25
Cafés	¼"	0.25
Oval rodding or curtain rods	1"	1
Under draperies	1¼"	1.25
Side panels on oval rod	1"	1

Note: pin setting is from top of drapery to top of drapery hook.

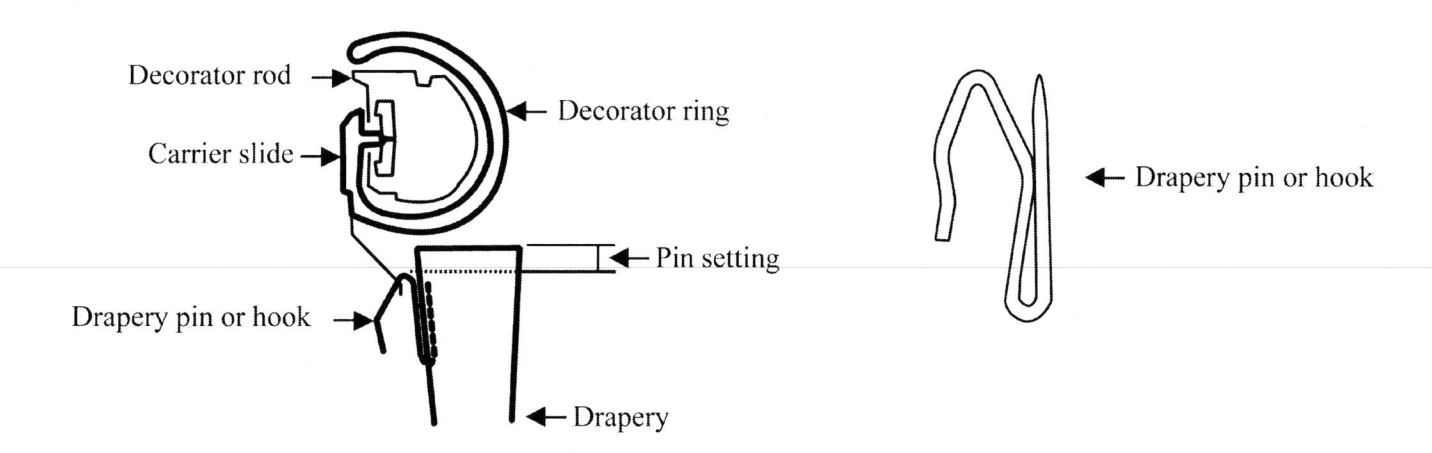

Technical Specifications

TAB TAKE UP

Tab take up occurs when a tab is slipped over a rod or pole. It is caused by the wrap of the fabric compensating for the diameter of the pole, which in turn causes the overall length of the panel or valance to take up, or become shorter. The space between the bottom of the pole and top of the drapery is called the tab throat. This space can be very small or very large depending on style. A short throat length tends to look more tailored and structured while a longer throat appears casual and relaxed.

To figure the tab length take the desired tab throat measurement + diameter of pole + ½ of the pole diameter = tab length. When writing up the work order, always allow for take up in the finished length by adding this dimension to the ordered finished length of the product.

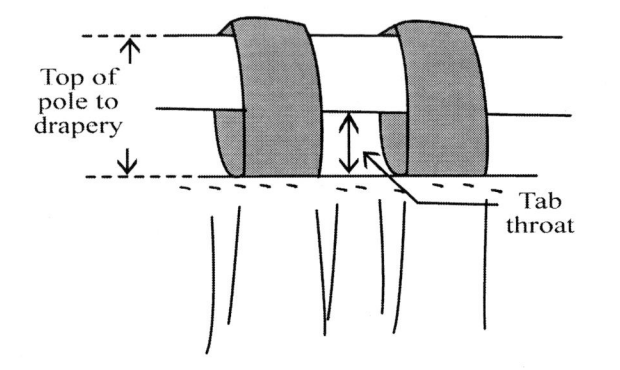

Example:

Tab throat = 3", Diameter of pole = 2", ½ of pole diameter = 1", sum of these is the tab length.

3" + 2" + 1" = 6" is tab length

The examples below are drawn to full scale. Based on the drawings, a good rule of thumb to find the take up is ½ of the diameter of the pole.

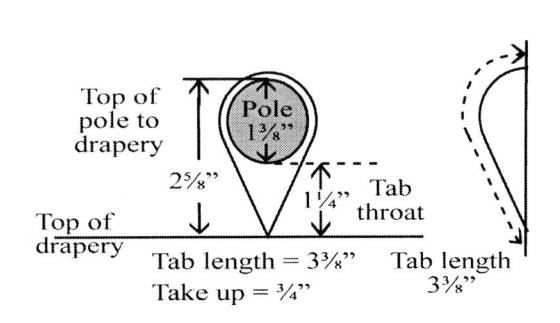

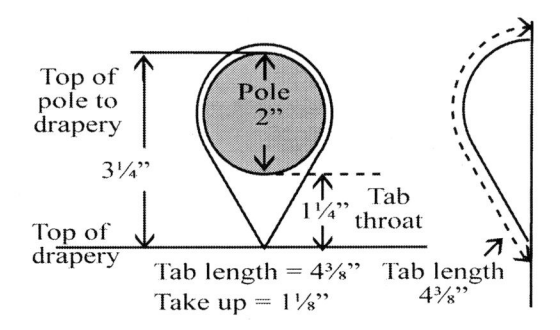

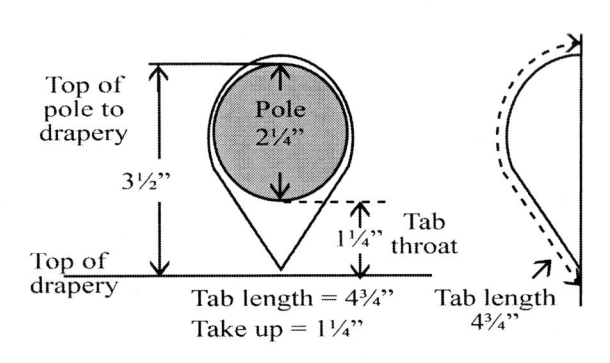

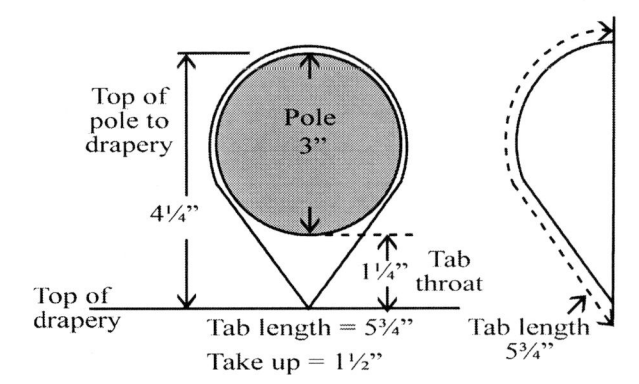

Pole 1⅜"
Top of pole to drapery 2⅝"
Tab throat 1¼"
Tab length = 3⅜"
Take up = ¾"
Tab length 3⅜"

Pole 2"
Top of pole to drapery 3¼"
Tab throat 1¼"
Tab length = 4⅜"
Take up = 1⅛"
Tab length 4⅜"

Pole 2¼"
Top of pole to drapery 3½"
Tab throat 1¼"
Tab length = 4¾"
Take up = 1¼"
Tab length 4¾"

Pole 3"
Top of pole to drapery 4¼"
Tab throat 1¼"
Tab length = 5¾"
Take up = 1½"
Tab length 5¾"

ROD POCKET SIZE CHART AND TAKE-UP

This chart shows the rod pocket size and take-up needed. This chart reflects the fabric take-up based on a single casing on the top only type of set-up. If multiple rod casings are involved in the design, increase the take-up for each rod. Casing size will remain the same. Take-up is based on a lined, medium weight fabric. For thick or upholstery weight fabrics, add ½"-¾" to the pocket size below. However if in doubt, have the workroom test to make sure it is enough.

Rod Pocket Size and Take-up Chart

Type of Rod	Pocket size	Decimal	Take-up
Oval rodding (cut to measure rodding)	1½"	1.50	½
Tiny rod in shutters	½"	.50	⅛
⅜" brass rod	1"	1.0	¼"
1" curtain or tension rod	1½"	1.50	½
¾" round pole	1½"	1.50	¾"
1" round pole	2"	2.0	1"
1¼" round pole	2¾	2.75	1¼"
1⅜" round pole	3"	3.0	1½"
2" round pole	4½"	4.50	2"
3" round pole	6"	6.0	2½"
4½" wide curtain rod	5½"	5.50	½"
2½" wide curtain rod	3½"	3.50	½"

Elements of Soft Treatments

Technical Specifications

DESCRIPTION AND SITUATION RETURN CHART

For wood blinds, the valance that comes with the blind tends to be ½" wider than the projection of the headrail. The return sizes shown above may require the shade or blind valance to be removed.

If the valance is going over a roller shade, the headrail varies approximately 1¾"-3¼". The reason for this is as the fabric rolls onto the tube, the roll expands due to width and length of the shade and the thickness and weight of the fabric. Calling the vendor once the size of the shade has been determined is recommended.

Return and Situation Chart

Description	Situations	Return Size Needed
Curtain rod with clearance of 1½"	For inside mount shades	2"
Curtain rod with clearance of 2"	For inside mount shades	2½"
Curtain rod with clearance of 3"	For partial inside mount roman shade or blind	3½"
To clear projection of headrail of 1¼"	Cellular shade	2" to 2½"
To clear projection of headrail of 1¾"	1" mini blind, 1" wood blind or pleated shades	2¾"
To clear projection of headrail of 2"	2" cellular shade	2"
To clear projection of headrail of 2½"	2" mini blind or 2" wood blind	3½"
To clear projection of headrail of 2¾"	Vertical cell shade	3¾ to 4"
To clear projection of headrail of 3"	Roman blind, shutter blind, or 2½" or 3" wood blinds	4"
To clear projection of headrail of 3½"	3½" headrail of a soft shade blind	4½"
To clear projection of headrail of 4"	4" headrail of a soft shade blind	5"
To clear projection of headrail of 4½"	4½" headrail of a soft shade blind	5½"
To clear projection of headrail of 5"	5" headrail of a soft shade blind	6"
To clear single standard traverse rod	Traversing sheer under rod pocket side panels	5½"
To clear a double traverse rod set-up	Traversing overdrape and sheer under rod pocket side panels	7½"
To clear projection of headrail of 6¼"	Vertical shutter blind (this includes vanes in open position)	7¼"
To clear projection of headrail of 7"	Motorized shade	8"

Appendix B

SWAG TIP/TIP CHARTS

How to use the charts

These charts are used mainly for the bias method of fabrication of swags, however they can be used as a guide for the other fabrication styles. If a swag will exceed the Minimum/Maximum Tip/Tip, it cannot be cut from one width of fabric. It will require extra widths and a seam will be needed.

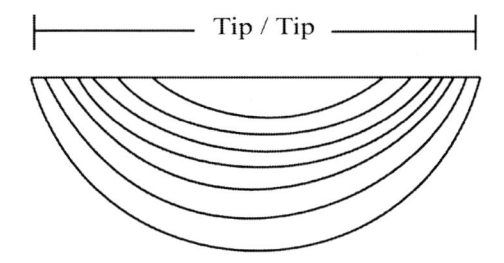

Locate the column that matches the width of the fabric being used and the face width required for the treatment. The number at the top of the column indicates the recommended number of swags to use to avoid seaming. The approximate tip to tip limitations are shown below the face width measurements.

TRADITIONAL AND OPEN SWAG TIP TO TIP

Formal I Swags

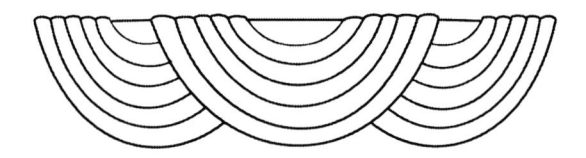

Recommended Sizes, Number of Swags, and Tip/Tip Chart

Max. Finished Length Bias	# of Swags	1	2	3	4	5	6
18"	Face width (48" fabric)	20"-44"	40"-56"	60"-84"	80"-112"	100"-140"	120"-168"
18"	Min/Max. Tip/Tip	20/44	27/38	30/42	32/45	33/47	35/48
21"	Face width (54" fabric)	20"-50"	40"-62"	60"-93"	80"-124"	100"-155"	120"-186"
21"	Min/Max. Tip/Tip	20/50	27/42	30/47	32/50	33/52	35/53

Elements of Soft Treatments

Technical Specifications

Formal II Swags

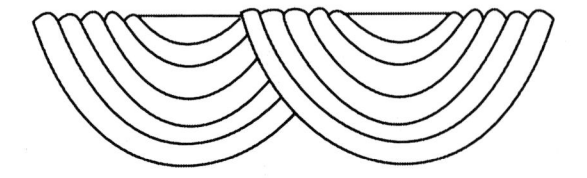

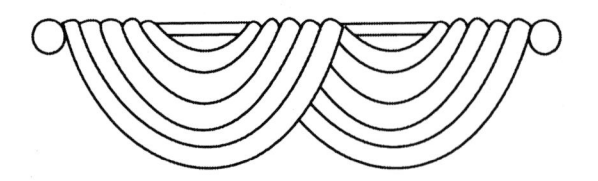

Recommended Sizes, Number of Swags, and Tip/Tip Chart

Max. Finished Length Bias	# of Swags	1	2	3	4	5	6
18"	Face width (48" fabric)	20"-44"	44"-74"	64"-108"	84"-142"	104"-176"	124"-210"
18"	Min/Max. Tip/Tip	20/44	28/41	27/42	27/48	28/42	28/42
21"	Face width (54" fabric)	20"-50"	44"-90"	64"-138"	84"-182"	104"-226"	124"-270"
21"	Min/Max. Tip/Tip	20/50	28/49	27/52	27/52	28/52	28/52

Limitations of each fabrication style (Appendix A):

Bias
    Finished length - approximately 18"-21" (based on 48" or 54" fabrics).
    Tip/Tip - use chart as a guide. If wider, check with workroom.

Upright
    Finished length - limits none.
    Tip/Tip - maximum is approximately 108" (check with workroom).

Railroaded
    Finished length - over 22" could require horizontal seams (based on 48" fabric).
    Tip/Tip - maximum is approximately 108" (check with workroom).

Boxed swags top to tip chart

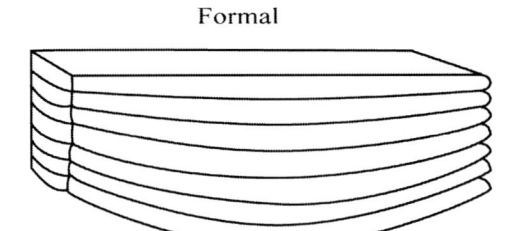

Formal

Number of Swags and Tip/Tip Chart

# of Swags	1
Face width (48" fabric)	36"-108"
Min./Max. Tip/Tip	36/108
Face width (54" fabric)	36"-108"
Min/Max. Tip/Tip	36/108

Limitations of each fabrication style (Appendix A):

Bias
    Usually not available unless fabric is 132" wide (check with workroom).

Upright
    Finished length - limits none
    Tip/Tip - maximum is approximately 108" (check with workroom).

Railroaded
    Finished length - over 22" could require horizontal seams (based on 48" fabric).
    Tip/Tip - maximum is approximately 108" (check with workroom).

Technical Specifications

End cap tip to tip chart

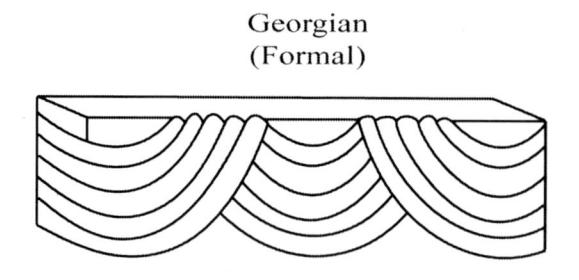

Georgian
(Formal)

Recommended Sizes, Number of Swags, and Tip/Tip Chart

Max Finished Length Bias	# of Swags	3	5	7
18"	Face width (48" fabric)	43"- 88"	68"-152"	92"-219"
	Min./Max. Tip/Tip	26 / 50	23 / 51	22 / 50
21"	Face width (54" fabric)	43"- 88"	68"-152"	92"-219"
	Min./Max. Tip/Tip	27/52	23 / 51	22 / 50

Limitations of each fabrication style (Appendix A):

Bias
    Finished length - approximately 18"-21" (based on 48" or 54" fabrics).
    Tip/Tip - use chart as a guide. If wider, check with workroom.

Upright
    Finished length - limits none.
    Tip/Tip - maximum is approximately 108" (check with workroom).

Railroaded
    Finished length - over 22" could require horizontal seams (based on 48" fabric).
    Tip/Tip - maximum is approximately 108" (check with workroom).

Kingston and Empire tip to tip chart

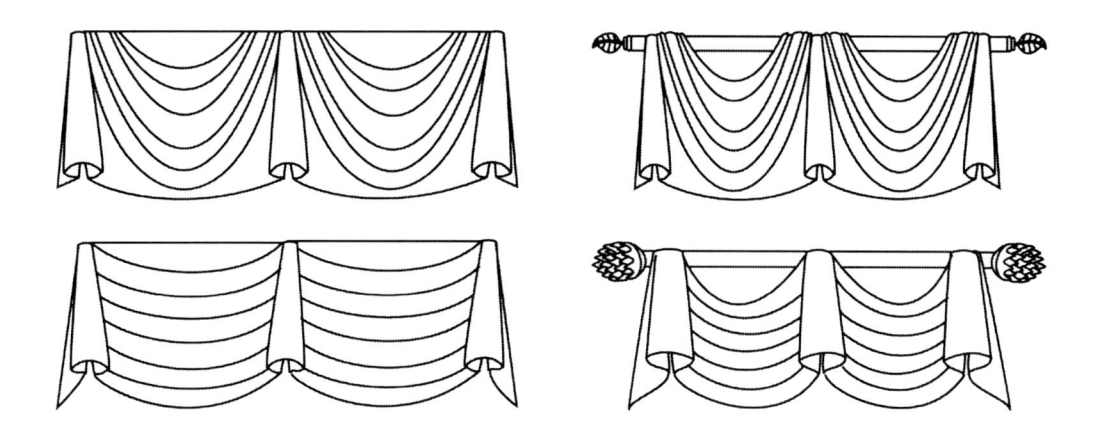

Recommended Sizes, Number of Swags and Tip/Tip Chart

Max Finished Length Bias	# of Swags	1	2	3	4	5	6
20"	Face width (48" fabric)	20"-28"	40"-56"	60"-84"	80"-112"	100"-140"	120"-168"
	Min/Max. Tip/Tip	17/25	19/27	19/27	19/27	19/27	19/27
20"	Face width (54" fabric)	20"-31"	40"-62"	60"-93"	80"-124"	100"-155"	120"-186"
	Min/Max. Tip/Tip	17/28	19/30	19/30	19/30	19/30	19/30

Limitations of each fabrication style (Appendix A):

Bias
  Finished length - approximately 20" (based on 48" or 54" fabrics).
  Tip/Tip - recommend 17"-38" maximum. Check with workroom if wider.

Upright
  Finished length - limits none.
  Tip/Tip – recommend 17"-38" maximum. Check with workroom if wider.

Railroaded
  Finished length - over 24" could require horizontal seams (based on 48" fabric).
  Tip/Tip – recommend 17"-38" maximum. Check with workroom if wider.

Elements of Soft Treatments

Technical Specifications

Bell swags tip to tip chart

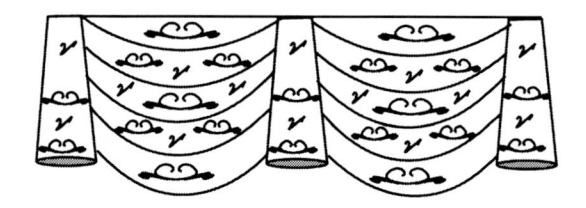

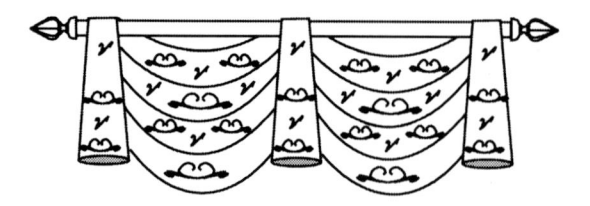

Recommended Sizes, Number of Swags and Tip/Tip Chart

Max Finished Length Bias	# of Swags	1	2	3	4	5	6
21"	Face width (48" fabric)	20"-28"	40"-56"	60"-84"	80"-112"	100"-140"	120"-168"
	Min/Max. Tip/Tip	17/25	19/27	19/27	19/27	19/27	19/27
21"	Face width (54" fabric)	20"-31"	40"-62"	60"-93"	80"-124"	100"-155"	120"-186"
	Min/Max. Tip/Tip	17/28	19/30	19/30	19/30	19/30	19/30

Limitations of each fabrication style (Appendix A):

Bias
    Finished length - approximately 18"-21" (based on 48" or 54" fabrics).
    Tip/Tip - use chart as a guide. If wider, check with workroom.

Upright
    Finished length - limits none.
    Tip/Tip - maximum is approximately 108" (check with workroom).

Railroaded
    Finished length - over 22" could require horizontal seams (based on 48" fabric).
    Tip/Tip - maximum is approximately 108" (check with workroom).

Appendix B

COMMON MATTRESS AND BEDDING SIZES

Common Mattress and Bedding Sizes

Bed Type	Mattress Size	Duvet with 12" drop	Comforter / Coverlet with 16" drop	Coverlet with 16" drop and 25" pillow tuck	Bedspread with 18" drop and 25" pillow tuck
Crib	27-28 X 52	N/A	32 X 54 (no drop)	N/A	N/A
Twin	38-39 X 75	63 X 88	74 X 91	74 X 116	75 X 118
Daybed	75 X 39	99 X 52	107 X 57	107 X 80	111 X 82
XL Twin	38-39 X 80	63 X 92	69 X 98	69 X 123	74 X 123
Full	53-54 X 75	78 X 88	85 X 91	85 X 116	89 X 118
XL Full	53-54 X 80	78 X 92	85 X 96	85 X 121	89 X 123
Queen	60 X 80	84 X 92	92 X 96	92 X 121	96 X 123
Olympic Queen	66 X 79-1/2	90 X 92	98 X 96	98 X 121	102 X 123
King/Eastern King	76-78 X 80	102 X 92	106 X 98	106 X 123	112 X 123
California King	72 X 84	96 X 96	104 X 100	104 X 125	108 X 127

Measure to find the best drop length for each given situation. Due to new mattress models, drop sizes will vary.

BED SKIRTS

Standards drops on bed skirts are 14" / 16" /18". If they exceed these drop lengths, there is an up-charge as they are considered oversized.

COMMON PILLOW SIZES

Common Pillow Sizes

\multicolumn{4}{c}{Pillow fillers should always be ordered 1" larger than finished pillow size if possible.}
Squares	\multicolumn{3}{l}{Available in sizes from 12 X 12 to 36 X 36}
Twin/Full	20 X 26	Travel Pillow	12 X 16
Queen	20 X 30	Boudoir Pillow	12 X 16
King	20 X 36	Jumbo Boudoir	16 x 24
Euro	27 X 27	Neck roll	6 X 15
Jumbo Euro	32 X 32	Jumbo neck roll	9 X 32

Sizes listed are approximate. Manufacturer's sizes will vary. Check with the vendor for exact sizes. Custom sizes and shapes are also available.

Elements of Soft Treatments

Technical Specifications

APPENDIX C
Thumbnails

Here is a collection of thumbnail images of different styles for each treatment category.

Draperies Quick Reference

Pleated Tops

Boxed Pleat	Boxed Pleat Inverted	Cartridge Pleat
Five Finger Pleat	Five Finger Pleat Tack Top	Four Finger Pleat
Four Finger Pleat Top Tack	Goblet Pleat	Tack Roll Pleat
Windsor Pleat	Three Finger Pleat	Three Finger Pleat Top Tack
Two Finger 8" Space	Two Finger 6" Space	Five Finger Pleat Top Tack

Elements of Soft Treatments

Draperies Quick Reference

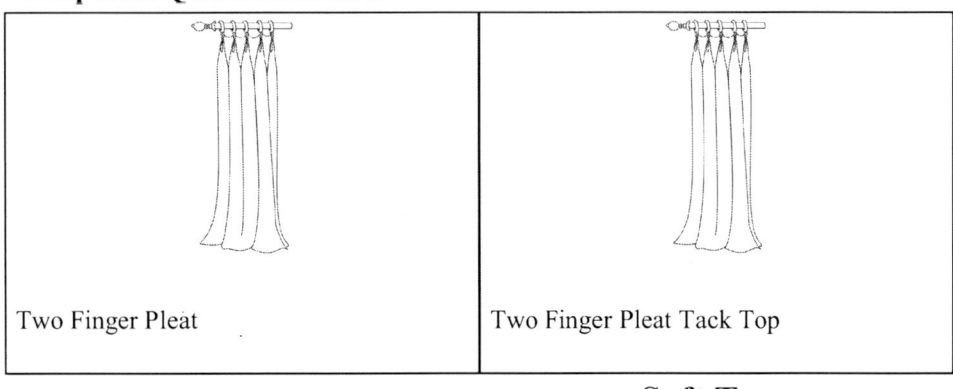

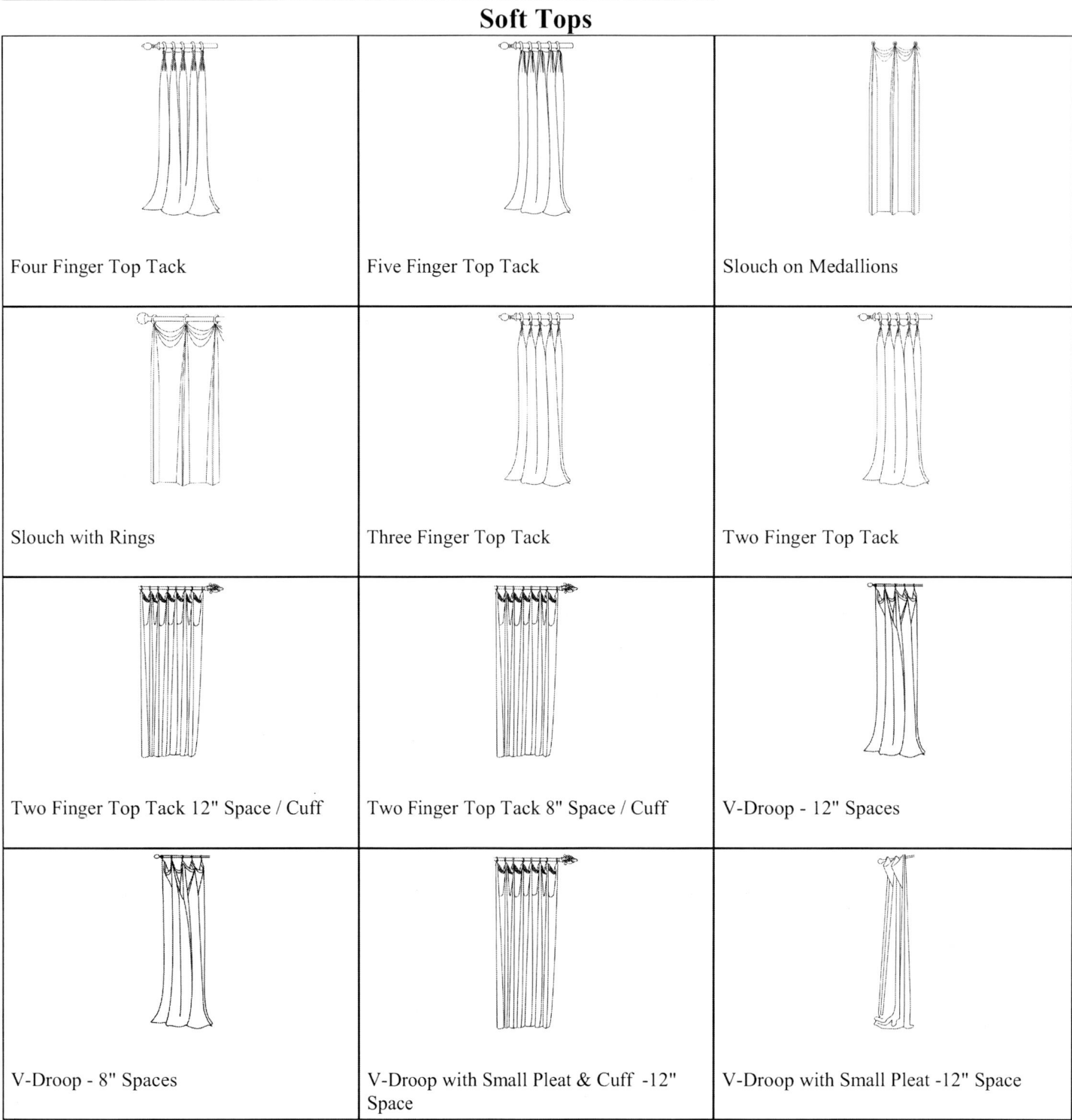

Two Finger Pleat	Two Finger Pleat Tack Top

Soft Tops

Four Finger Top Tack	Five Finger Top Tack	Slouch on Medallions
Slouch with Rings	Three Finger Top Tack	Two Finger Top Tack
Two Finger Top Tack 12" Space / Cuff	Two Finger Top Tack 8" Space / Cuff	V-Droop - 12" Spaces
V-Droop - 8" Spaces	V-Droop with Small Pleat & Cuff -12" Space	V-Droop with Small Pleat -12" Space

214

Draperies Quick Reference

Tab Tops

Scalloped Top	Tab Panel Droop on Medalions	Tab Panel with Base Tab Gathered
Tab Straight Top	Tab with Long Shirt Tail Ties	Tab with Pointed Tip Tab
Tab with Curved Tabs		

Elements of Soft Treatments

Draperies Quick Reference

Unusual Headings

Accordian Pleat Overlap Masters (10" Snaps)	Accordian Pleat Butt Masters (10" Snaps)	Accordian Pleat Overlap Masters (7.5" Snaps)
Accordian Pleat Butt Masters (7.5" Snaps)	Accordian Pleat Overlap Masters (8.5" Snaps)	Accordian Pleat Butt Masters (8.5" Snaps)
Diamond Pleat Tape Single	Gathered Shirr Tape 2-Cord	Gathered Shirr Tape 4-Cord
Pencil Pleat Tape 4-Cord	Grommeted Top (Rod Thru)	Ripplefold® Butt Master
Ripplefold® Overlap Master	Shower Curtian - Grommet	

Draperies Quick Reference

Special Set-ups

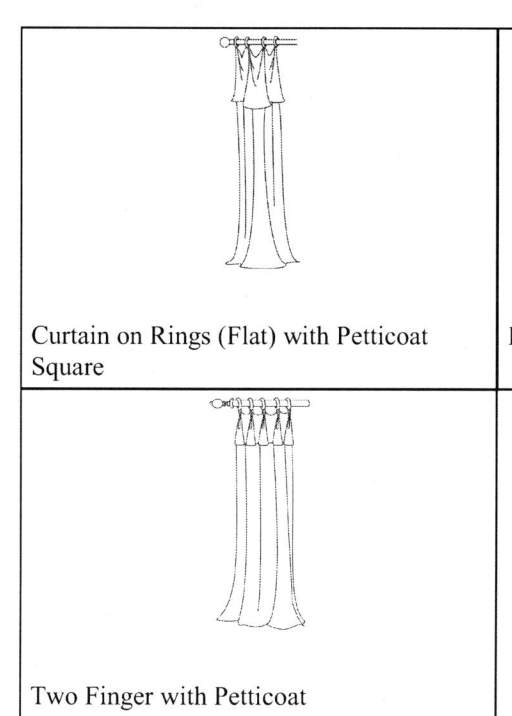

Curtain on Rings (Flat) with Petticoat Square	Flat Curtain with Petticoat Straight	Pinch Pleat 5-Finger with Petticoat
Two Finger with Petticoat		

Elements of Soft Treatments

Rod Pocket Panels Quick Reference

Rod Pocket Top Only

Banding Inset	Banding Leading Inset Left	Banding Leading Inset Right
Banding Leading Right	Banding Leading Left	Banding on Leading & Outer
Banding Top with Top Inset Fringe	Banding Top	Banding Bottom
Bishop Double	Bishop Single	Bishop Triple
Flat Pelmet Straight Bottom	Flat Pelmet Angled Bottom	Petticoat Square Bottom with Tieback

Elements of Soft Treatments

Rod Pocket Panels Quick Reference

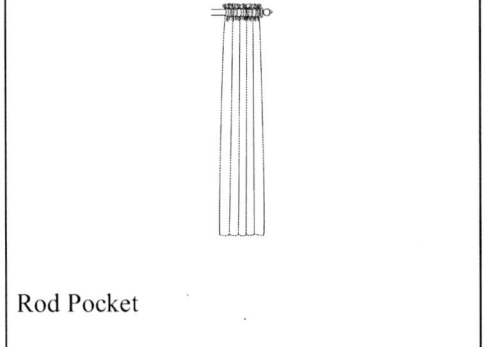

Rod Pocket

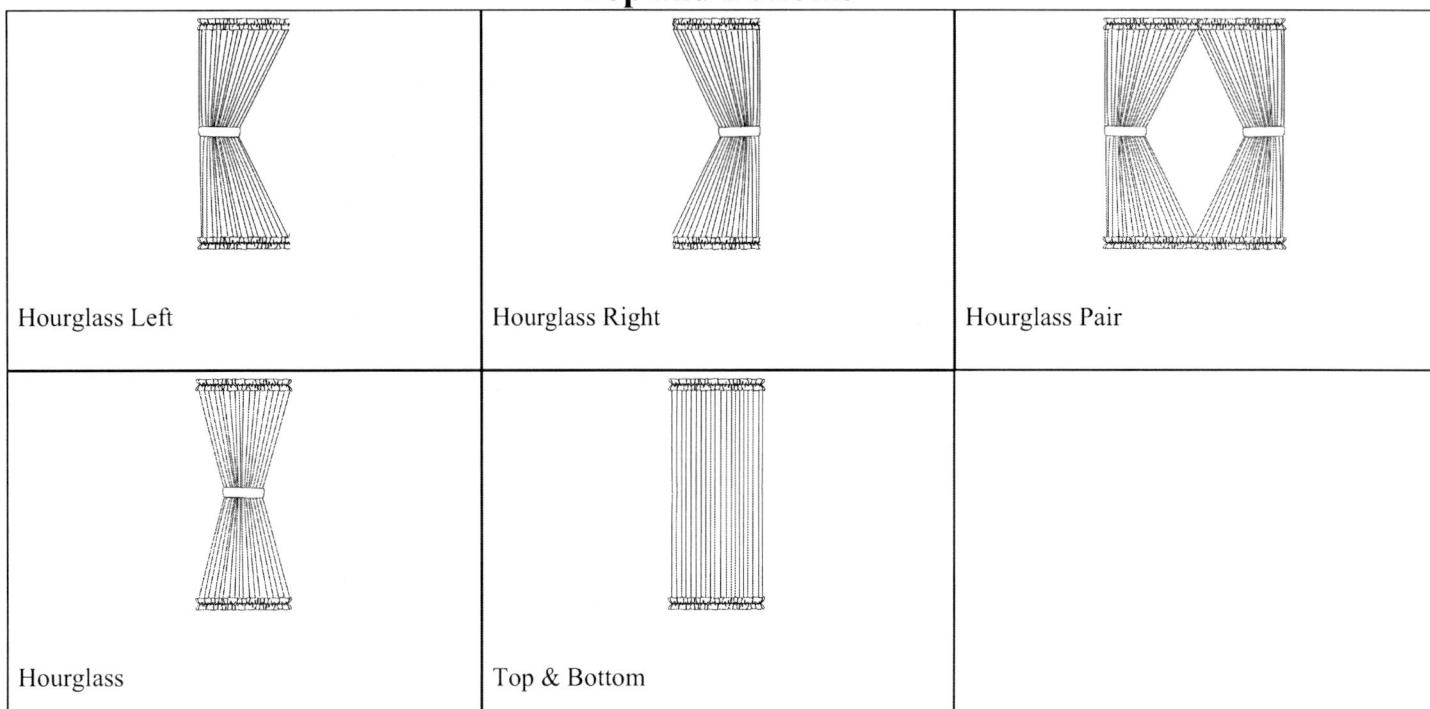

Top and Bottoms

Hourglass Left

Hourglass Right

Hourglass Pair

Hourglass

Top & Bottom

Rod Pocket Panels Quick Reference

Unusual Headings

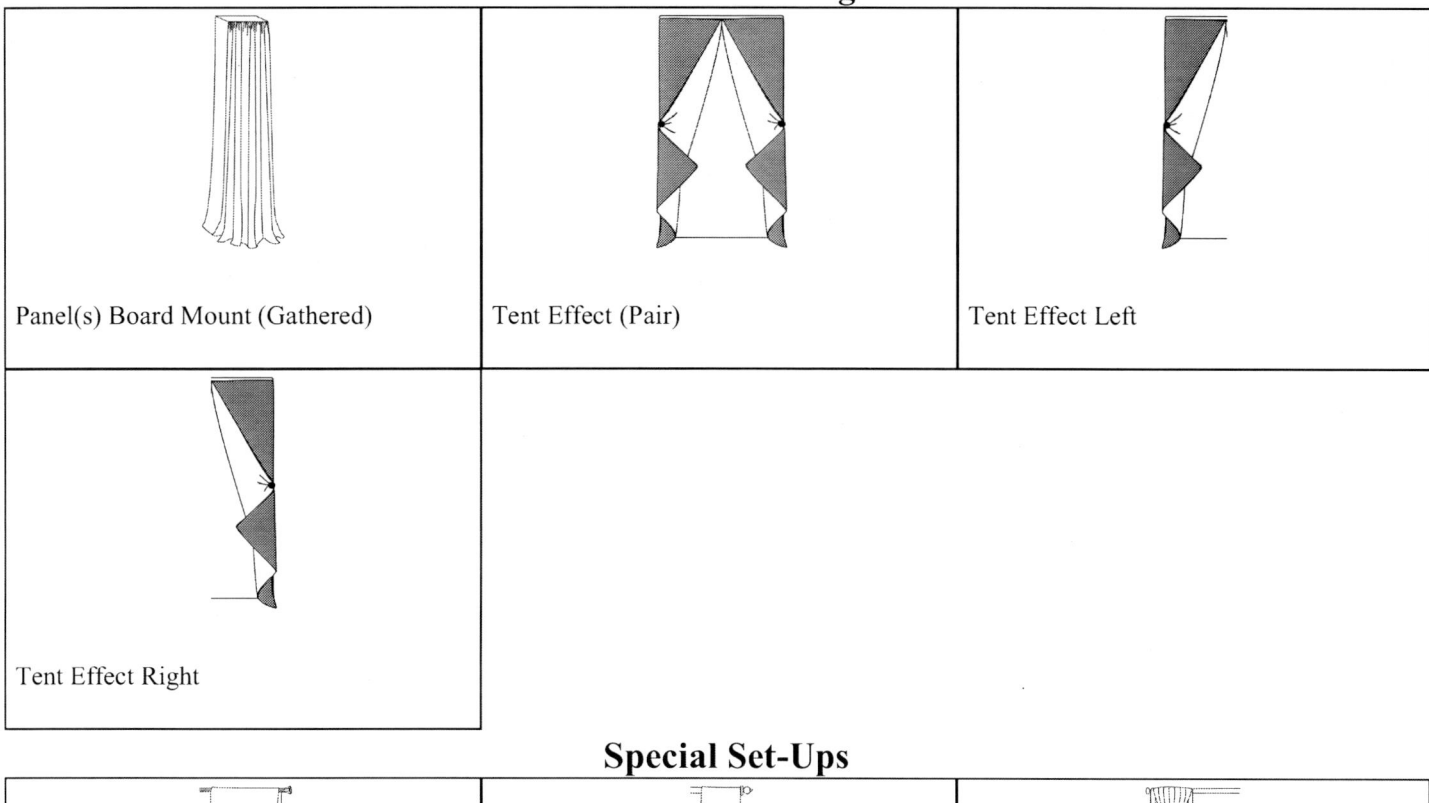

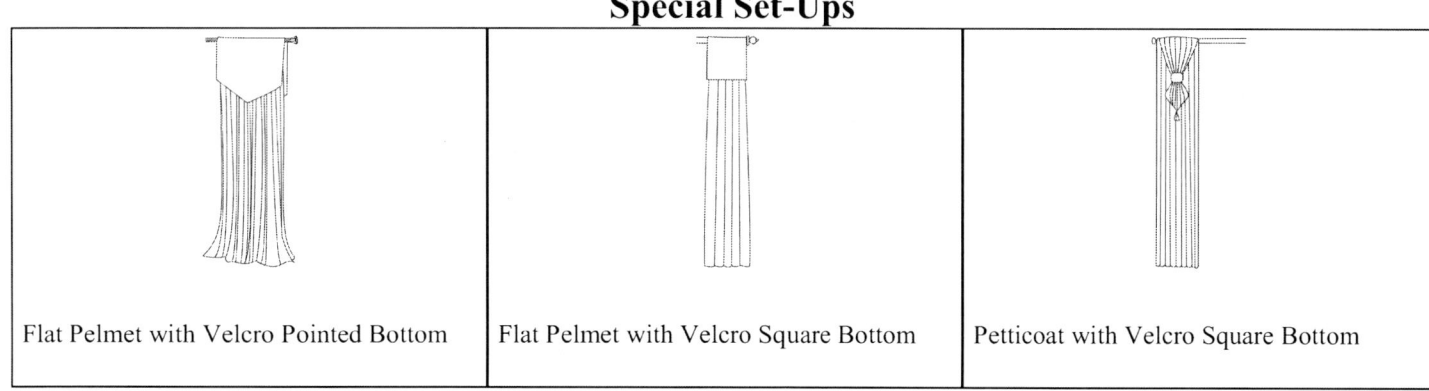

Panel(s) Board Mount (Gathered)	Tent Effect (Pair)	Tent Effect Left
Tent Effect Right		

Special Set-Ups

Flat Pelmet with Velcro Pointed Bottom	Flat Pelmet with Velcro Square Bottom	Petticoat with Velcro Square Bottom

Elements of Soft Treatments

Toppers Quick Reference

Austrians

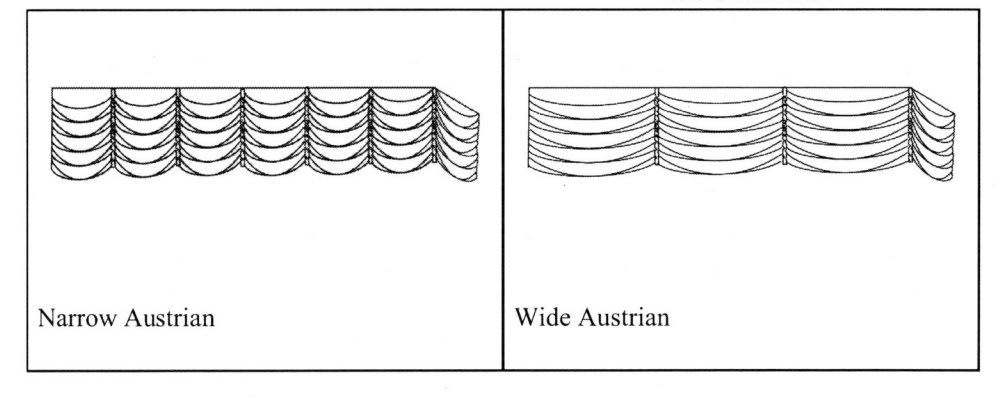

Narrow Austrian

Wide Austrian

Elements of Soft Treatments

Toppers Quick Reference

Balloon

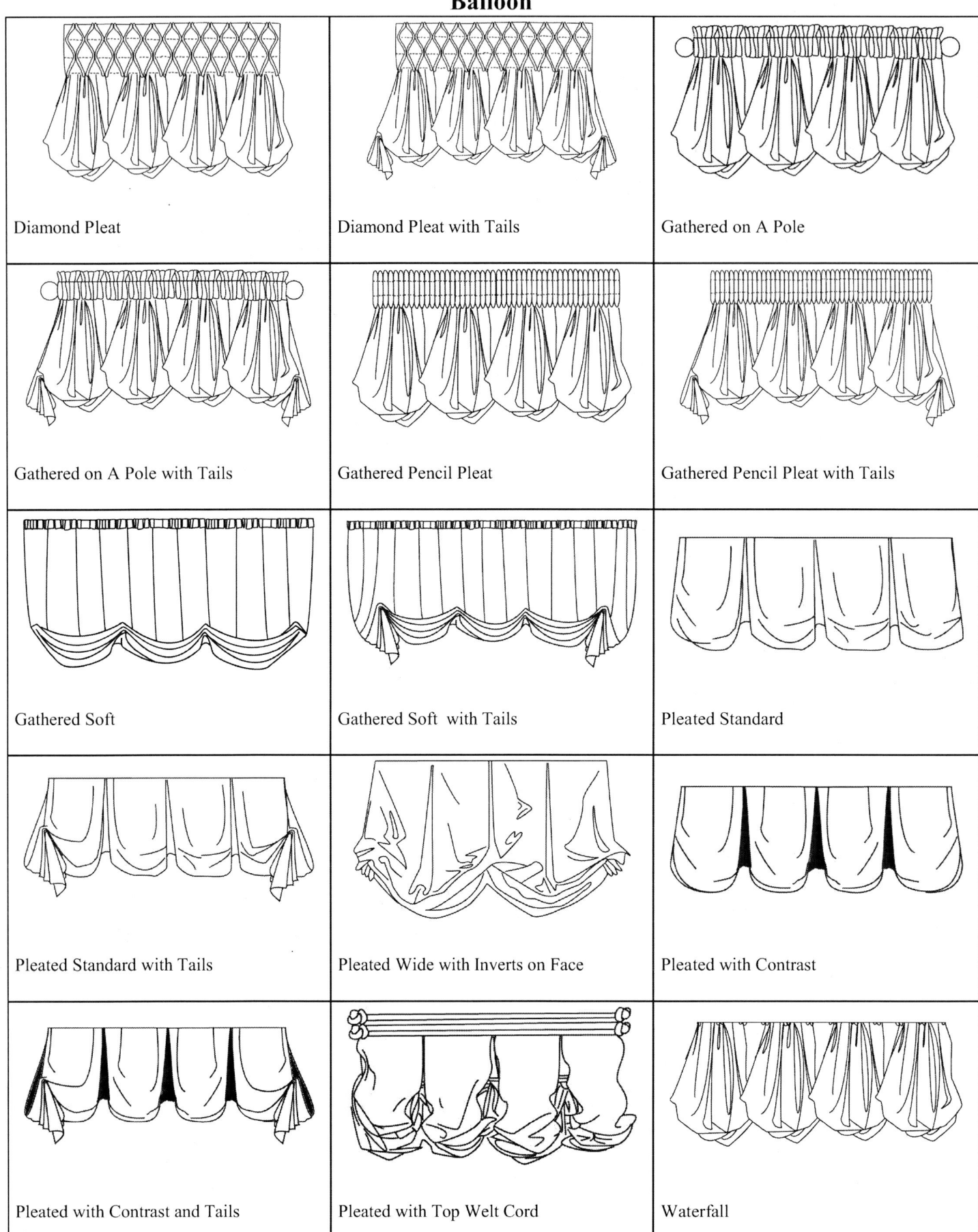

Diamond Pleat	Diamond Pleat with Tails	Gathered on A Pole
Gathered on A Pole with Tails	Gathered Pencil Pleat	Gathered Pencil Pleat with Tails
Gathered Soft	Gathered Soft with Tails	Pleated Standard
Pleated Standard with Tails	Pleated Wide with Inverts on Face	Pleated with Contrast
Pleated with Contrast and Tails	Pleated with Top Welt Cord	Waterfall

Toppers Quick Reference

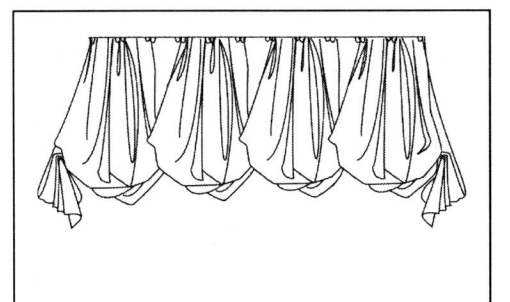

Waterfall with Tails

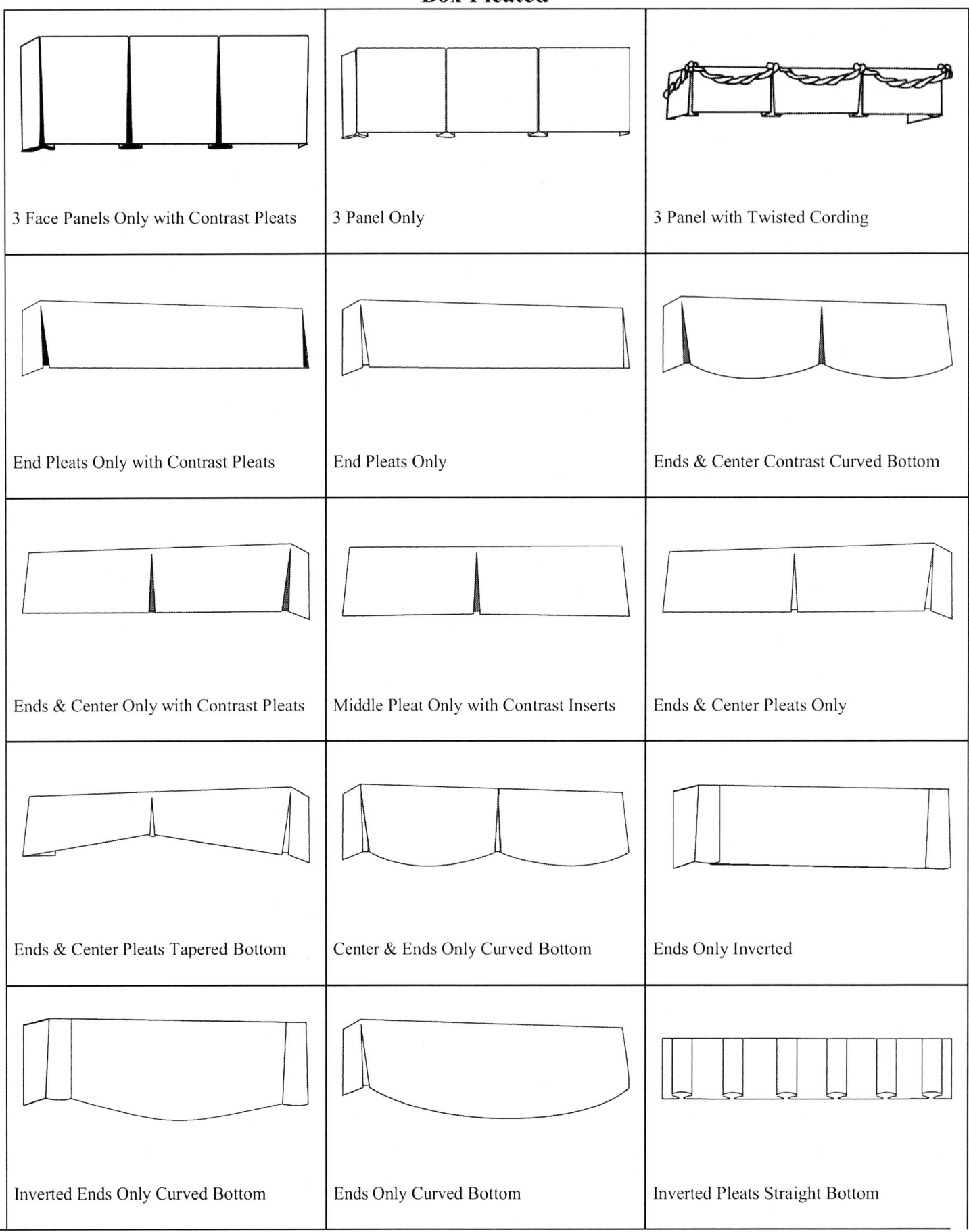

Toppers Quick Reference

Box Pleated

3 Face Panels Only with Contrast Pleats	3 Panel Only	3 Panel with Twisted Cording
End Pleats Only with Contrast Pleats	End Pleats Only	Ends & Center Contrast Curved Bottom
Ends & Center Only with Contrast Pleats	Middle Pleat Only with Contrast Inserts	Ends & Center Pleats Only
Ends & Center Pleats Tapered Bottom	Center & Ends Only Curved Bottom	Ends Only Inverted
Inverted Ends Only Curved Bottom	Ends Only Curved Bottom	Inverted Pleats Straight Bottom

Toppers Quick Reference

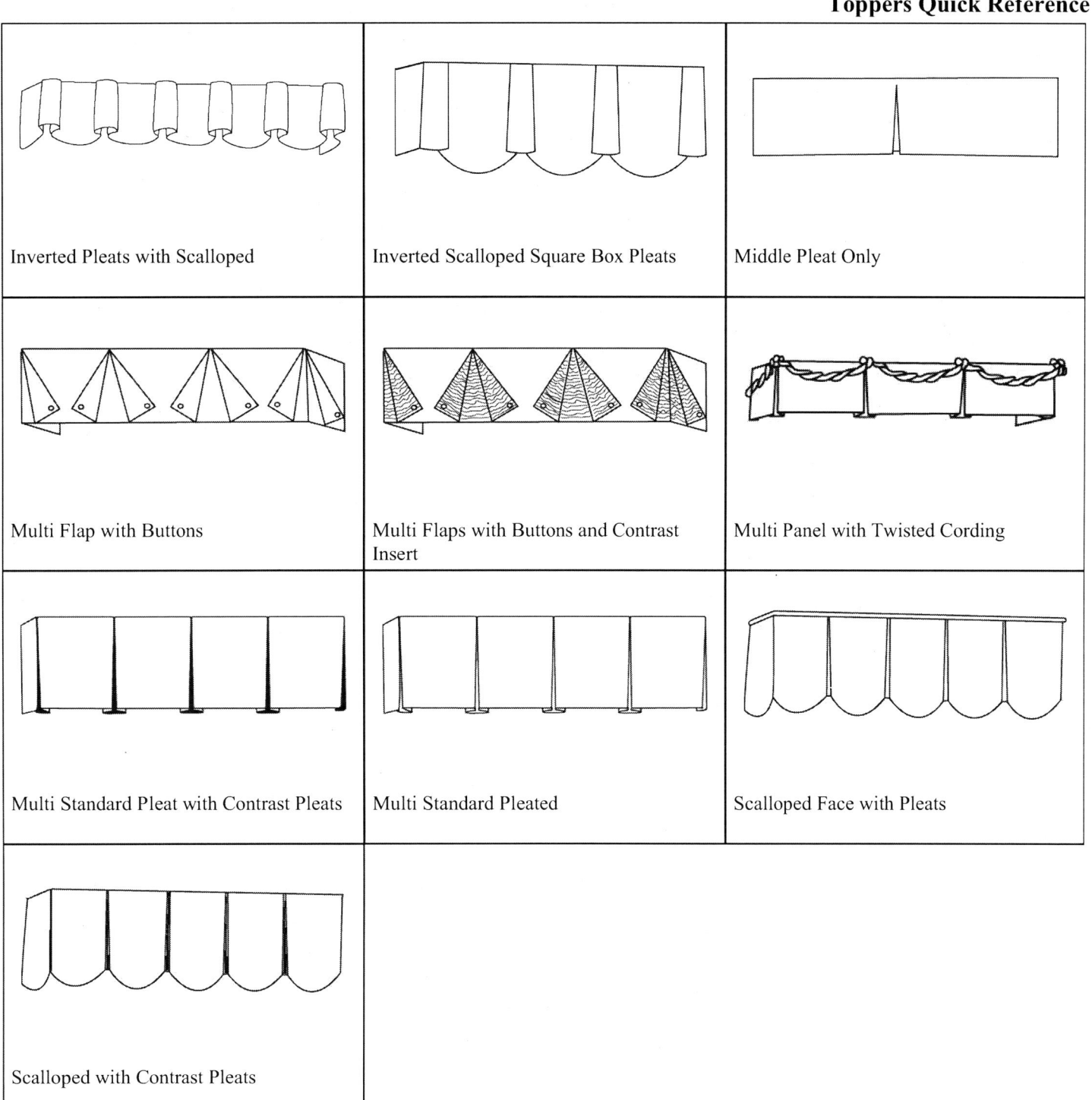

Inverted Pleats with Scalloped	Inverted Scalloped Square Box Pleats	Middle Pleat Only
Multi Flap with Buttons	Multi Flaps with Buttons and Contrast Insert	Multi Panel with Twisted Cording
Multi Standard Pleat with Contrast Pleats	Multi Standard Pleated	Scalloped Face with Pleats
Scalloped with Contrast Pleats		

Elements of Soft Treatments

Toppers Quick Reference

Hobble

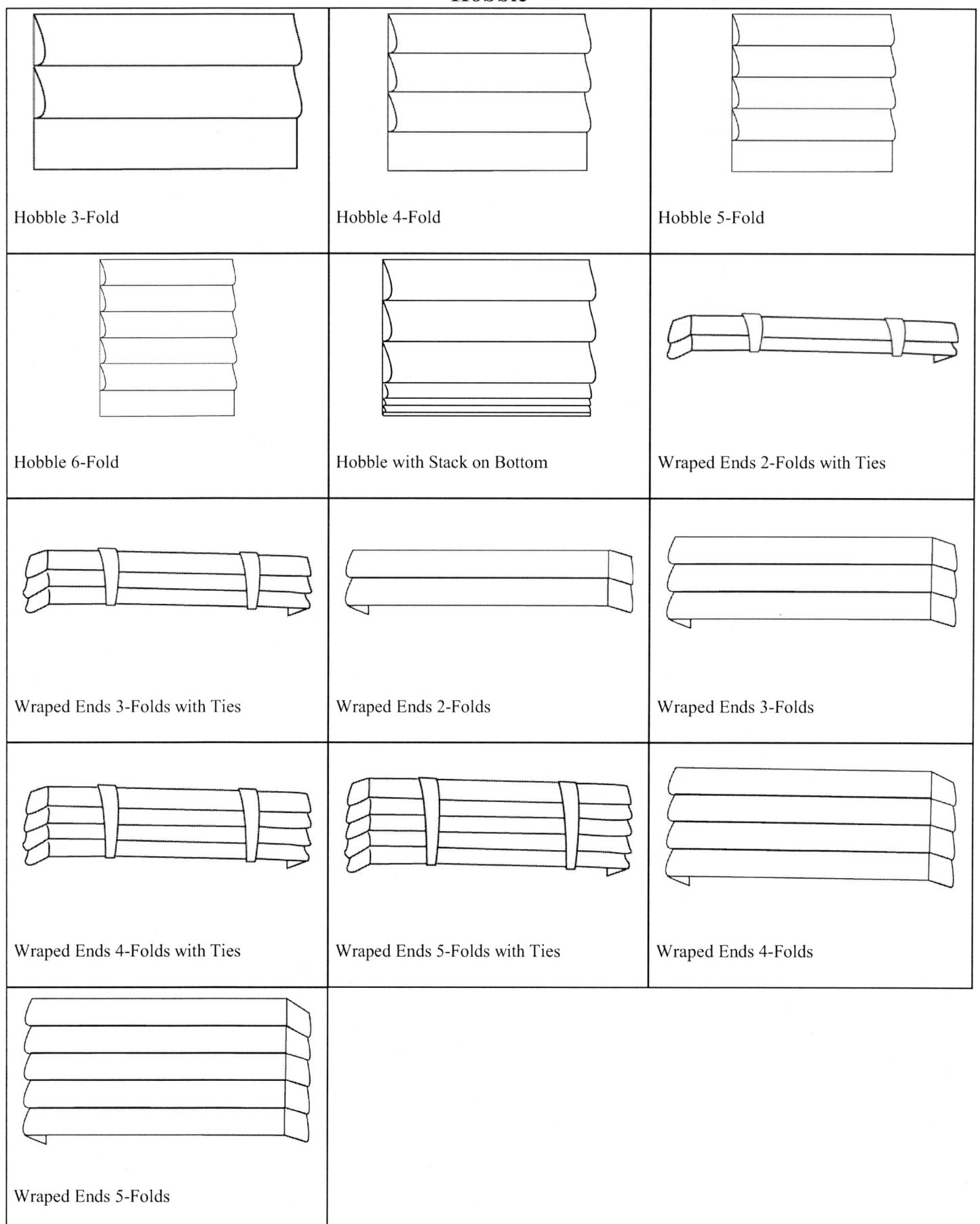

Hobble 3-Fold	Hobble 4-Fold	Hobble 5-Fold
Hobble 6-Fold	Hobble with Stack on Bottom	Wraped Ends 2-Folds with Ties
Wraped Ends 3-Folds with Ties	Wraped Ends 2-Folds	Wraped Ends 3-Folds
Wraped Ends 4-Folds with Ties	Wraped Ends 5-Folds with Ties	Wraped Ends 4-Folds
Wraped Ends 5-Folds		

Toppers Quick Reference

Pull-ups and Roll ups

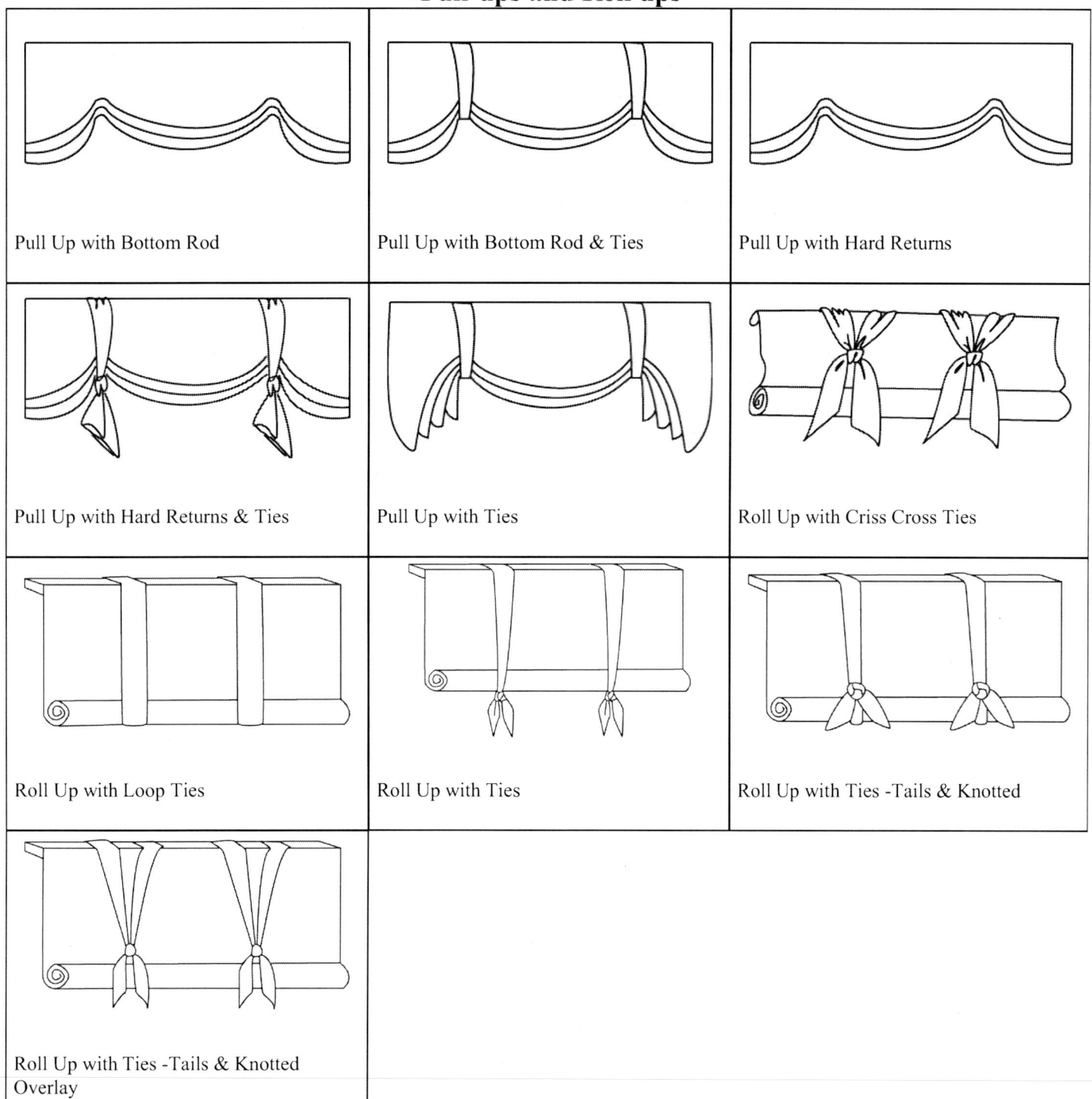

Pull Up with Bottom Rod	Pull Up with Bottom Rod & Ties	Pull Up with Hard Returns
Pull Up with Hard Returns & Ties	Pull Up with Ties	Roll Up with Criss Cross Ties
Roll Up with Loop Ties	Roll Up with Ties	Roll Up with Ties -Tails & Knotted
Roll Up with Ties -Tails & Knotted Overlay		

Elements of Soft Treatments

Toppers Quick Reference

Romans

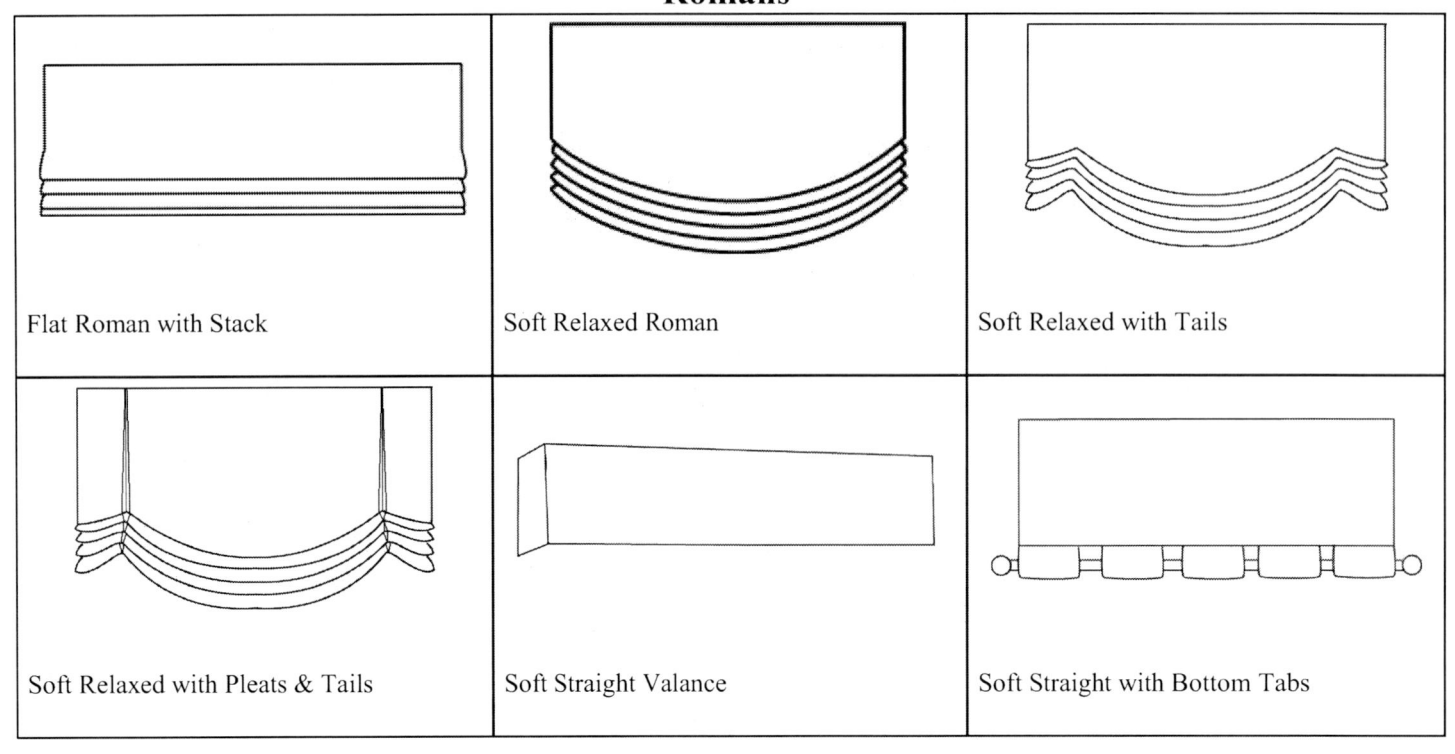

Flat Roman with Stack	Soft Relaxed Roman	Soft Relaxed with Tails
Soft Relaxed with Pleats & Tails	Soft Straight Valance	Soft Straight with Bottom Tabs

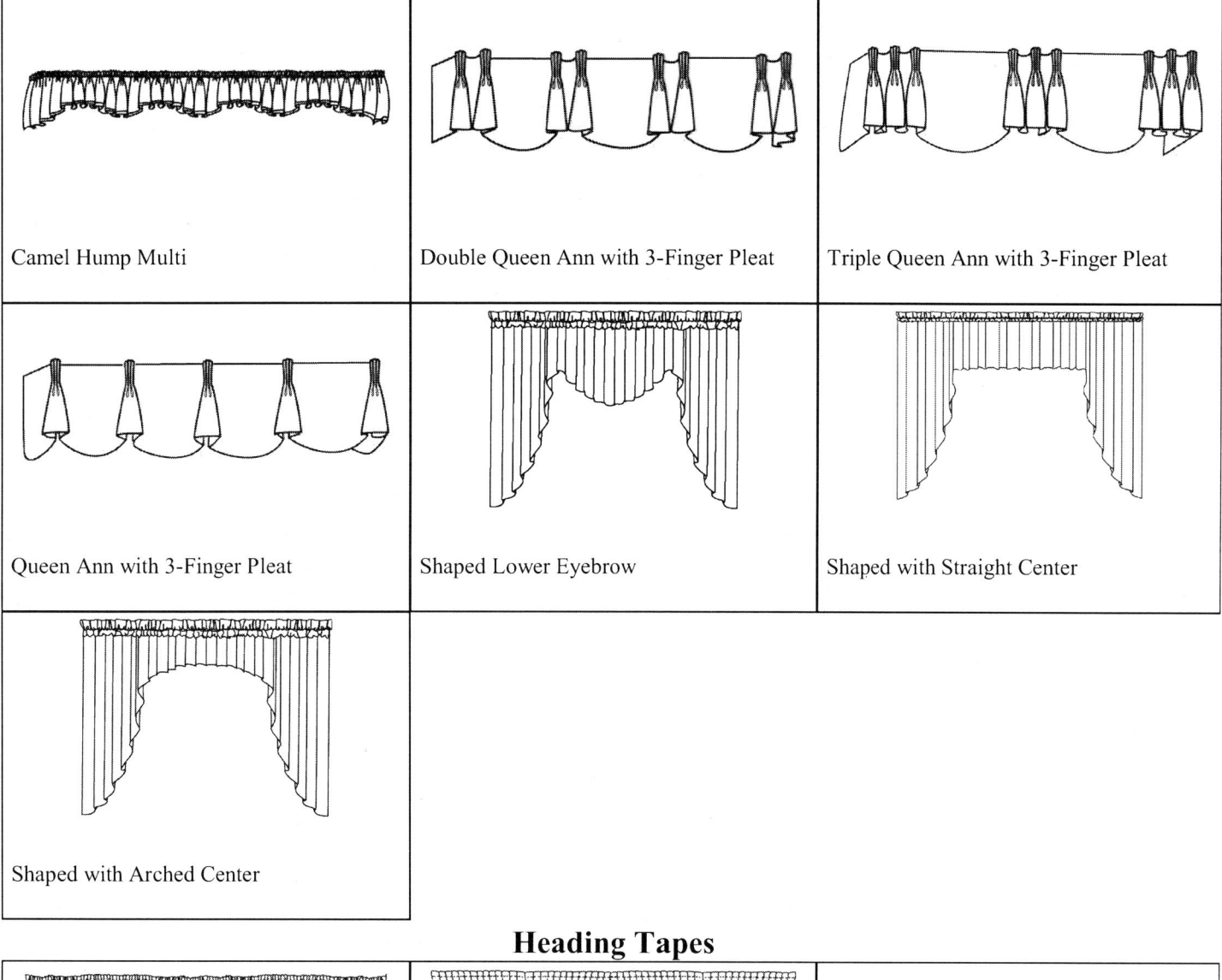

Toppers Quick Reference

Shaped Bottoms

Camel Hump Multi	Double Queen Ann with 3-Finger Pleat	Triple Queen Ann with 3-Finger Pleat
Queen Ann with 3-Finger Pleat	Shaped Lower Eyebrow	Shaped with Straight Center
Shaped with Arched Center		

Heading Tapes

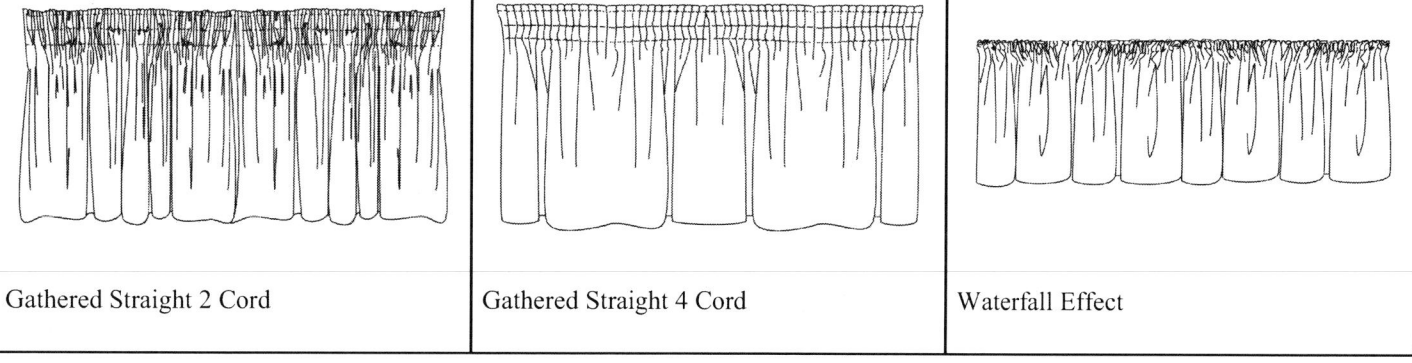

Gathered Straight 2 Cord	Gathered Straight 4 Cord	Waterfall Effect

Elements of Soft Treatments

Toppers Quick Reference

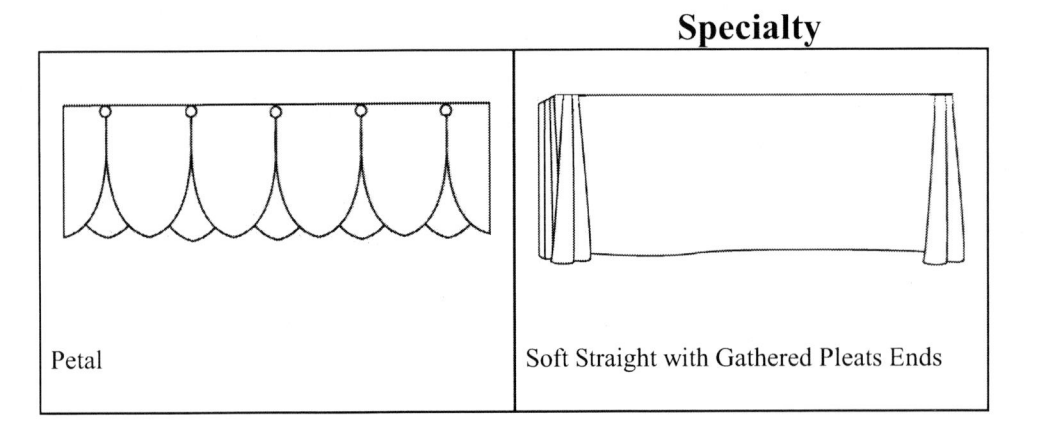

Specialty

Petal

Soft Straight with Gathered Pleats Ends

Drapery Valances Quick Reference

Pleated Tops

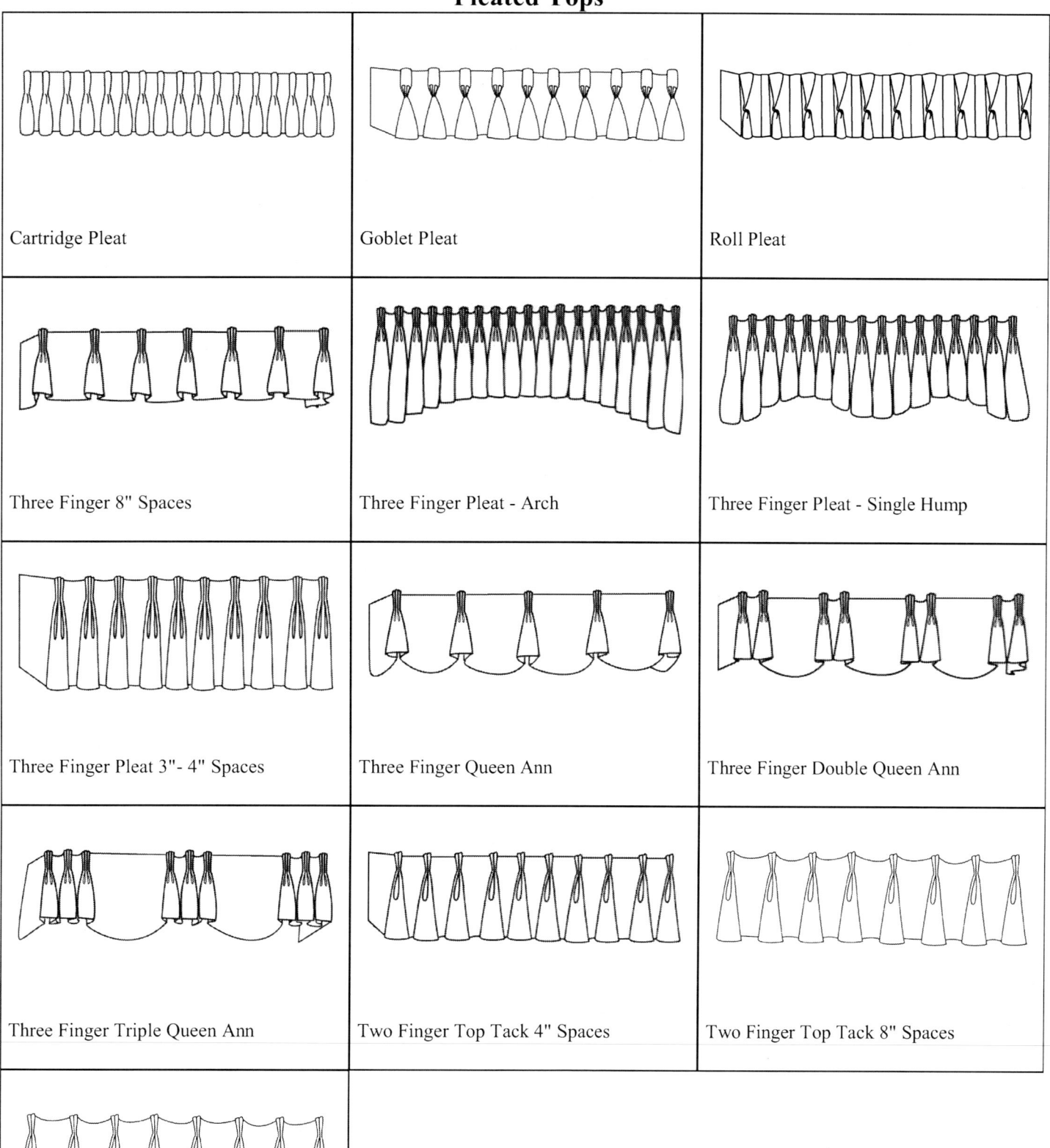

Cartridge Pleat	Goblet Pleat	Roll Pleat
Three Finger 8" Spaces	Three Finger Pleat - Arch	Three Finger Pleat - Single Hump
Three Finger Pleat 3"- 4" Spaces	Three Finger Queen Ann	Three Finger Double Queen Ann
Three Finger Triple Queen Ann	Two Finger Top Tack 4" Spaces	Two Finger Top Tack 8" Spaces
Two Finger Top Tack 6" Space		

Elements of Soft Treatments

Drapery Valances Quick Reference

Soft Tops

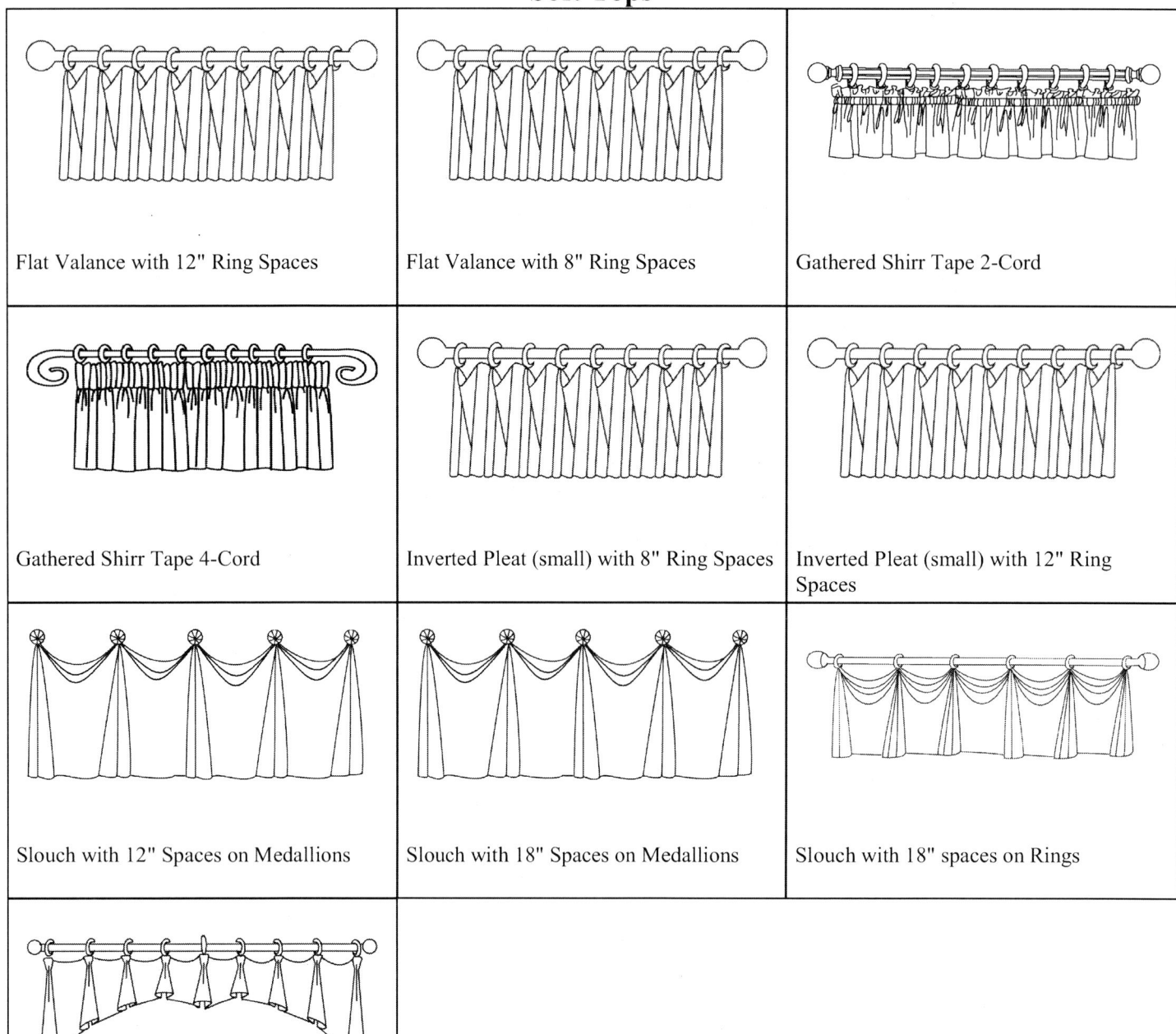

Flat Valance with 12" Ring Spaces	Flat Valance with 8" Ring Spaces	Gathered Shirr Tape 2-Cord
Gathered Shirr Tape 4-Cord	Inverted Pleat (small) with 8" Ring Spaces	Inverted Pleat (small) with 12" Ring Spaces
Slouch with 12" Spaces on Medallions	Slouch with 18" Spaces on Medallions	Slouch with 18" spaces on Rings
Three Finger Pleat - Pointed Middle		

Drapery Valances Quick Reference

Tab Tops

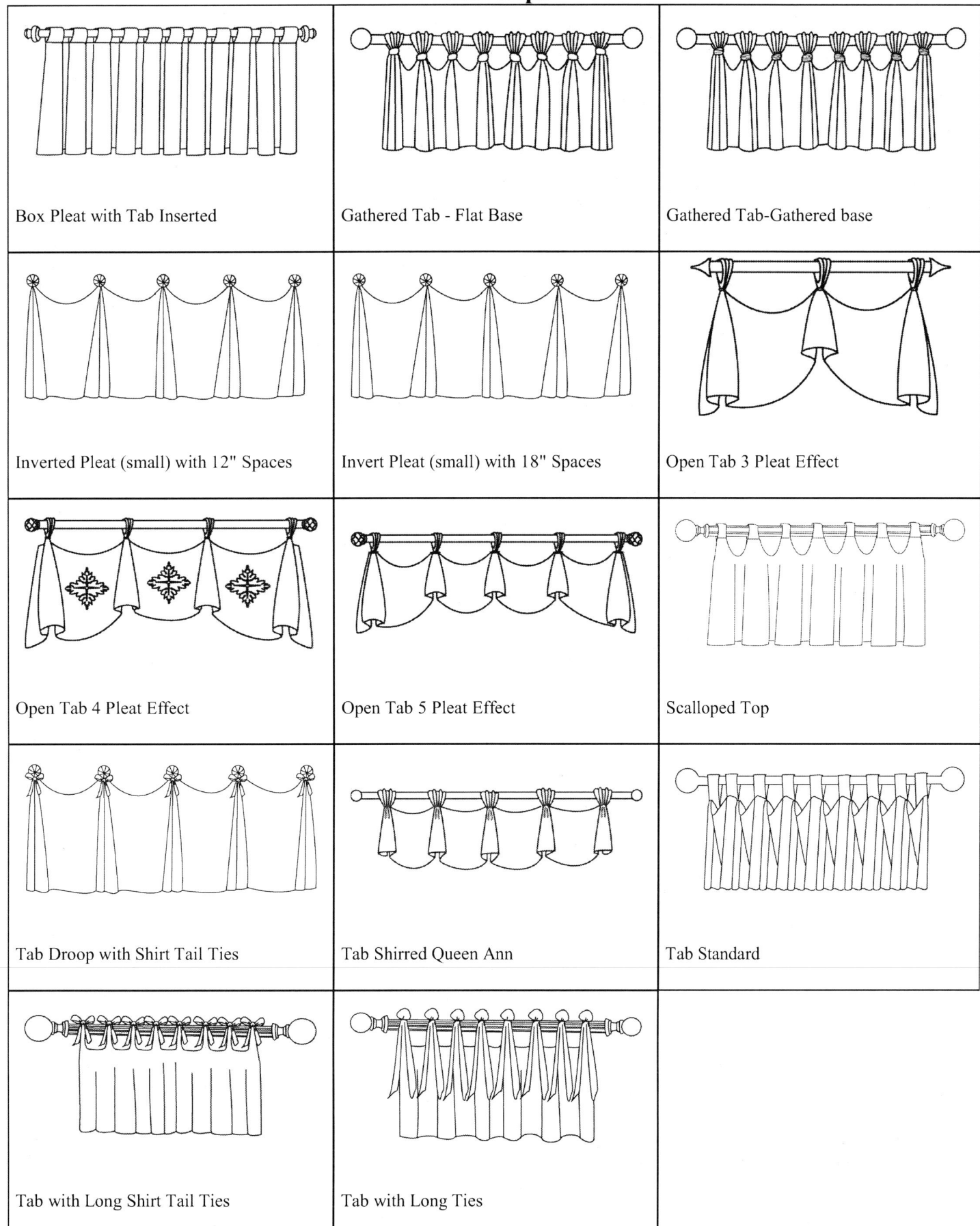

Box Pleat with Tab Inserted	Gathered Tab - Flat Base	Gathered Tab-Gathered base
Inverted Pleat (small) with 12" Spaces	Invert Pleat (small) with 18" Spaces	Open Tab 3 Pleat Effect
Open Tab 4 Pleat Effect	Open Tab 5 Pleat Effect	Scalloped Top
Tab Droop with Shirt Tail Ties	Tab Shirred Queen Ann	Tab Standard
Tab with Long Shirt Tail Ties	Tab with Long Ties	

Elements of Soft Treatments

Drapery Valances Quick Reference

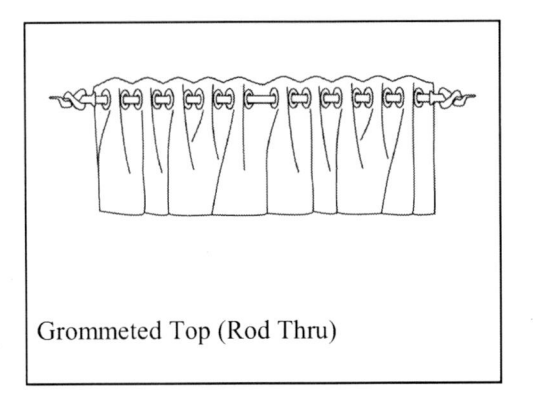

Unusual Headings

Grommeted Top (Rod Thru)

Rod Pocket Valances Quick Reference

Rod/Pole Sleeves

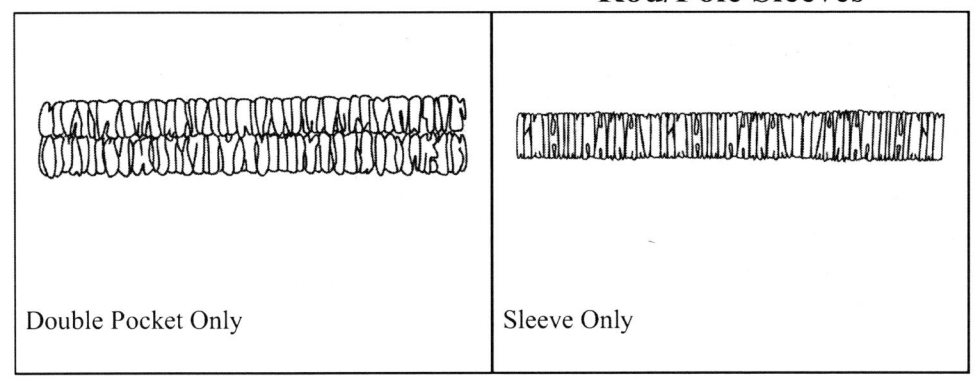

Double Pocket Only	Sleeve Only

Rod Sleeves with Headers

Upper Header Only	Double Pocket Shaped Header Top / Bottom	Double Pocket with Headers
Sleeve with Top & Bottom Header	Triple Casing with Header	

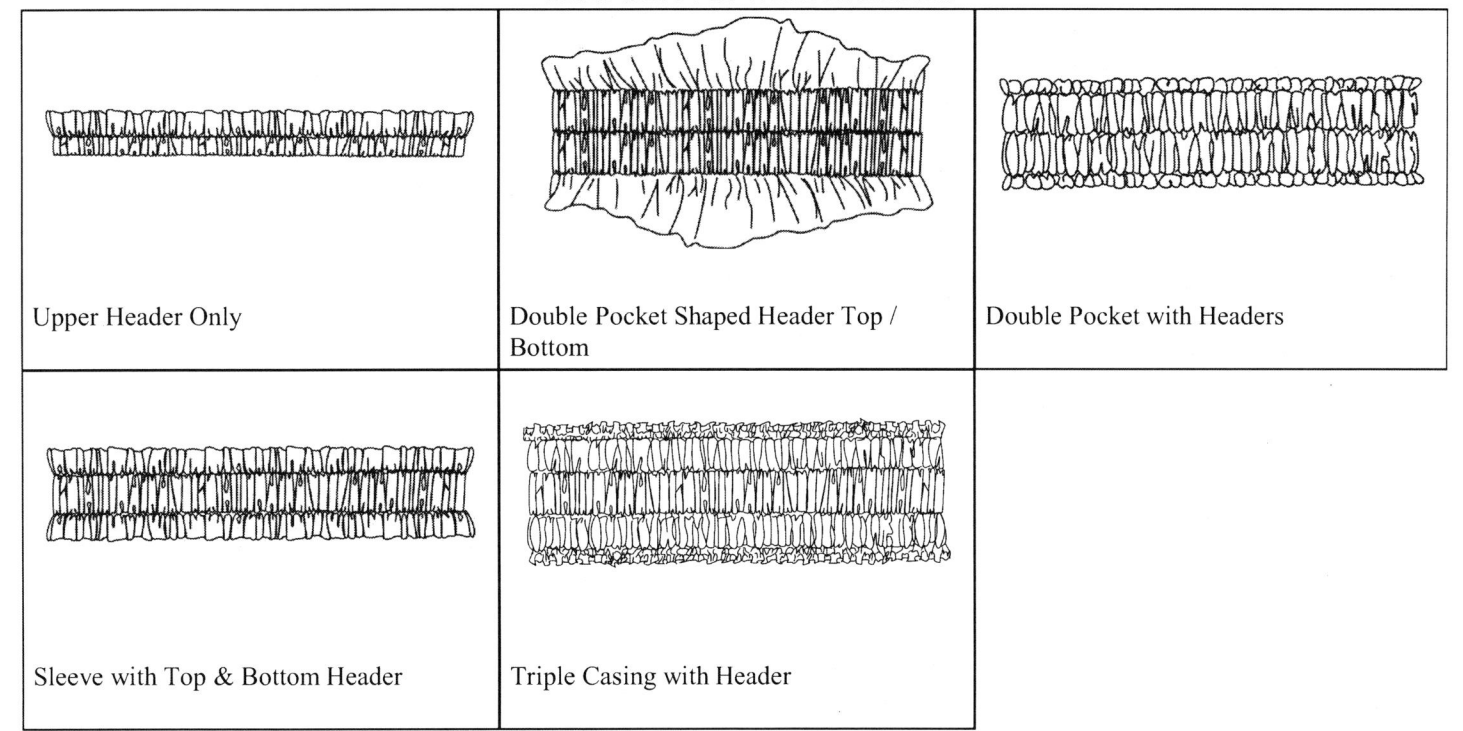

Elements of Soft Treatments

Rod Pocket Valances Quick Reference

Valance with Header and Skirt

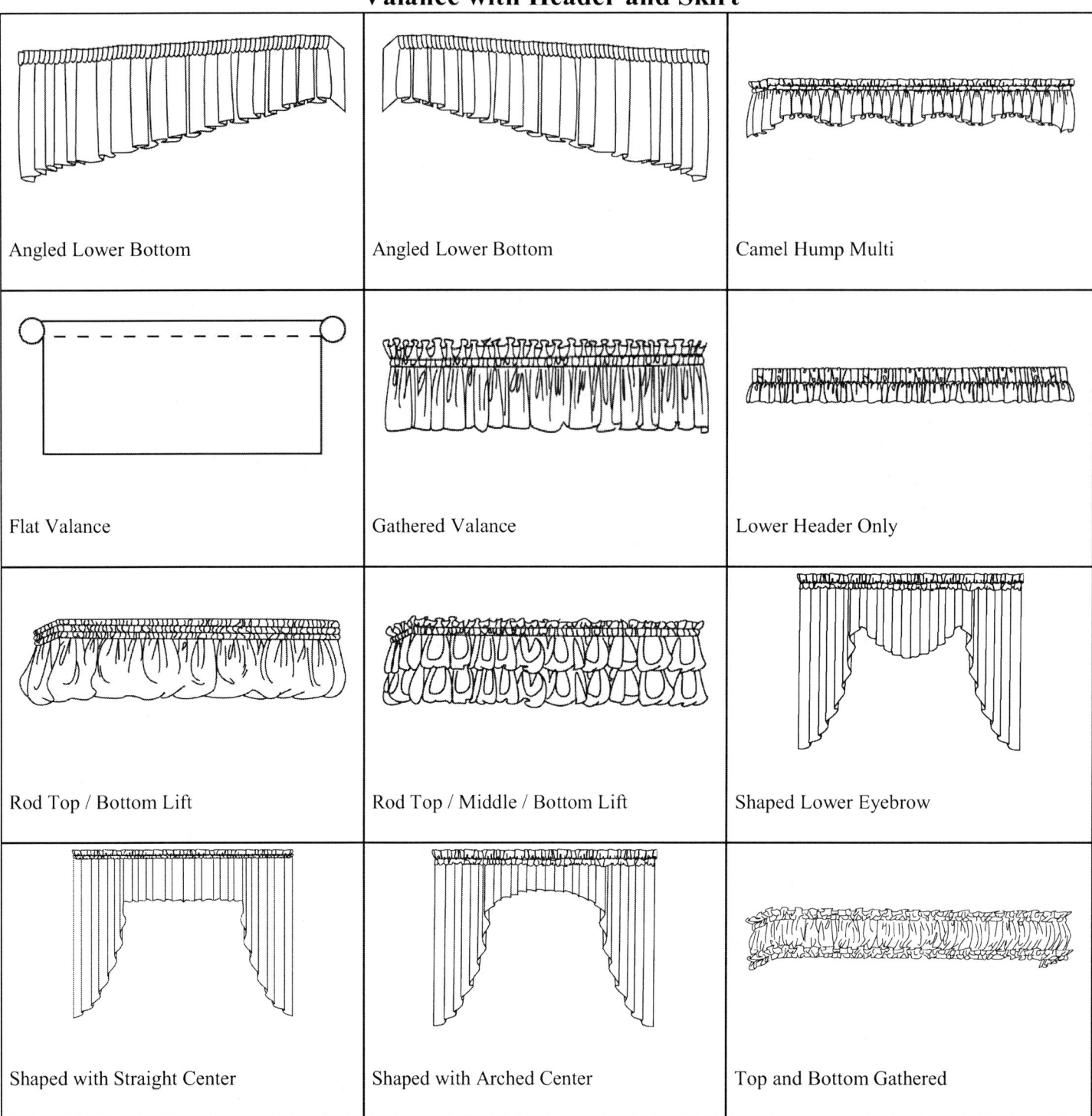

Angled Lower Bottom	Angled Lower Bottom	Camel Hump Multi
Flat Valance	Gathered Valance	Lower Header Only
Rod Top / Bottom Lift	Rod Top / Middle / Bottom Lift	Shaped Lower Eyebrow
Shaped with Straight Center	Shaped with Arched Center	Top and Bottom Gathered

Rod Pocket Valances Quick Reference

Specialty

| Rod Pocket Straight Awning | Rod Pocket Scalloped Awning |

Cornices Quick Reference

Standard Straight

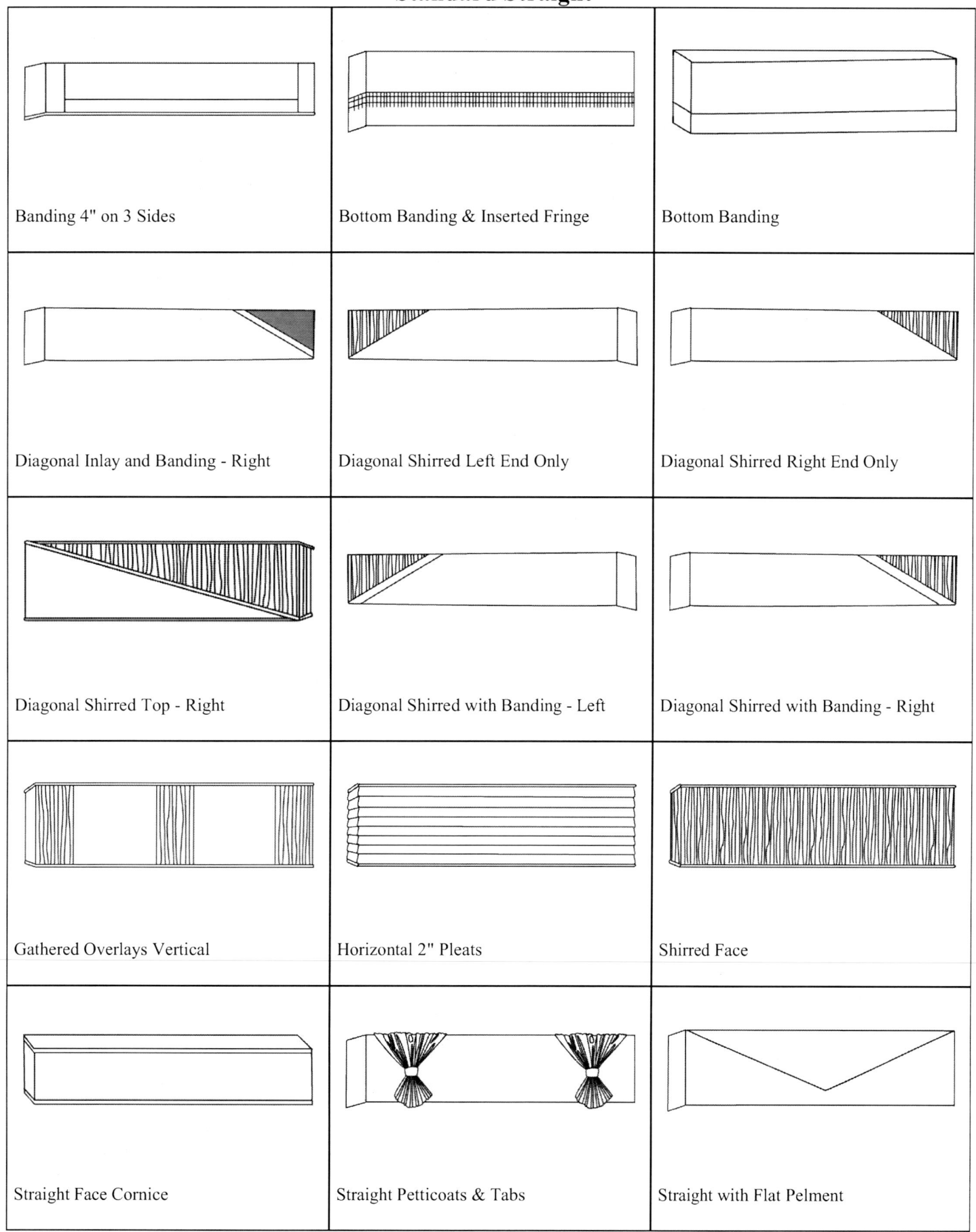

Banding 4" on 3 Sides	Bottom Banding & Inserted Fringe	Bottom Banding
Diagonal Inlay and Banding - Right	Diagonal Shirred Left End Only	Diagonal Shirred Right End Only
Diagonal Shirred Top - Right	Diagonal Shirred with Banding - Left	Diagonal Shirred with Banding - Right
Gathered Overlays Vertical	Horizontal 2" Pleats	Shirred Face
Straight Face Cornice	Straight Petticoats & Tabs	Straight with Flat Pelment

Elements of Soft Treatments

Cornices Quick Reference

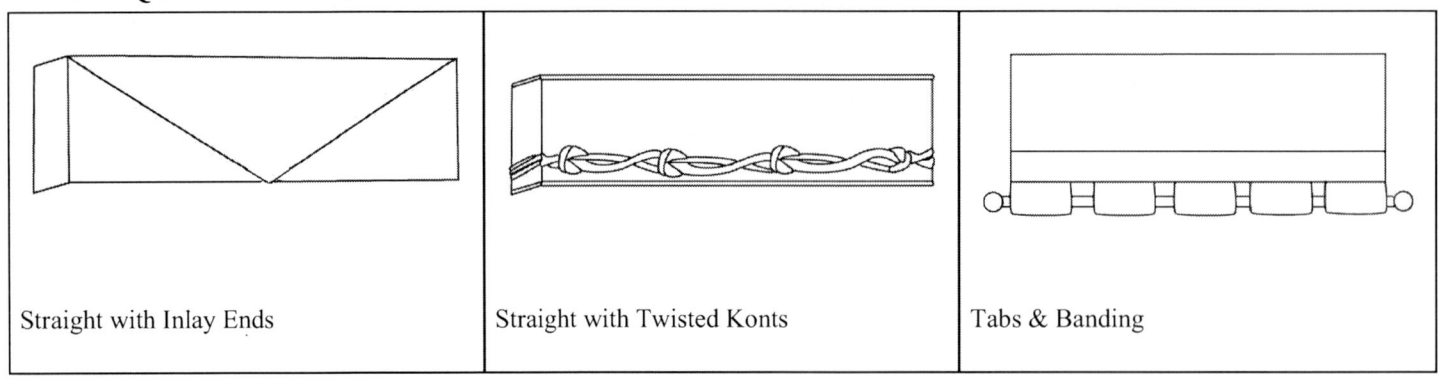

| Straight with Inlay Ends | Straight with Twisted Konts | Tabs & Banding |

Cornices Quick Reference

Shaped Bottom - Repeating Patterns

Cups Multi with Square Space	Narrow Multi Slant Down	Narrow Multi Slant Up
Royal Crown Down	Royal Curved Down	Scalloped Cups with Square Space
Cups with Square Space	Scalloped Cups	Slant Step Up and Down
Straight Step Up and Down	Spaced Upward Points	Spaced Downward Points
Wavy Wide S-Shaped	Wide Cups	Wide Slant Up and Down

Elements of Soft Treatments

Cornices Quick Reference

Shaped Bottom - Proportional Shape

Double Cup Ends with Center Dip	Eyebrow Full Bottom	Eyebrow Set-in on Bottom
Free Formed Curves with Center Dip	Half Set-In Arch Way - Right	Half Set-In Arch Way - Left
Longated Center Curve - Cup Ends	Longated S-shaped - Pointed Center	Longated Center Curve - Radius Ends
Longated S-shaped Narrow Center Cup	Longated Three Step - Right	Longated Three Step - Left
Single Radius Step	Single Radius with Raised Eyebrow	Single Step with Slant Edges

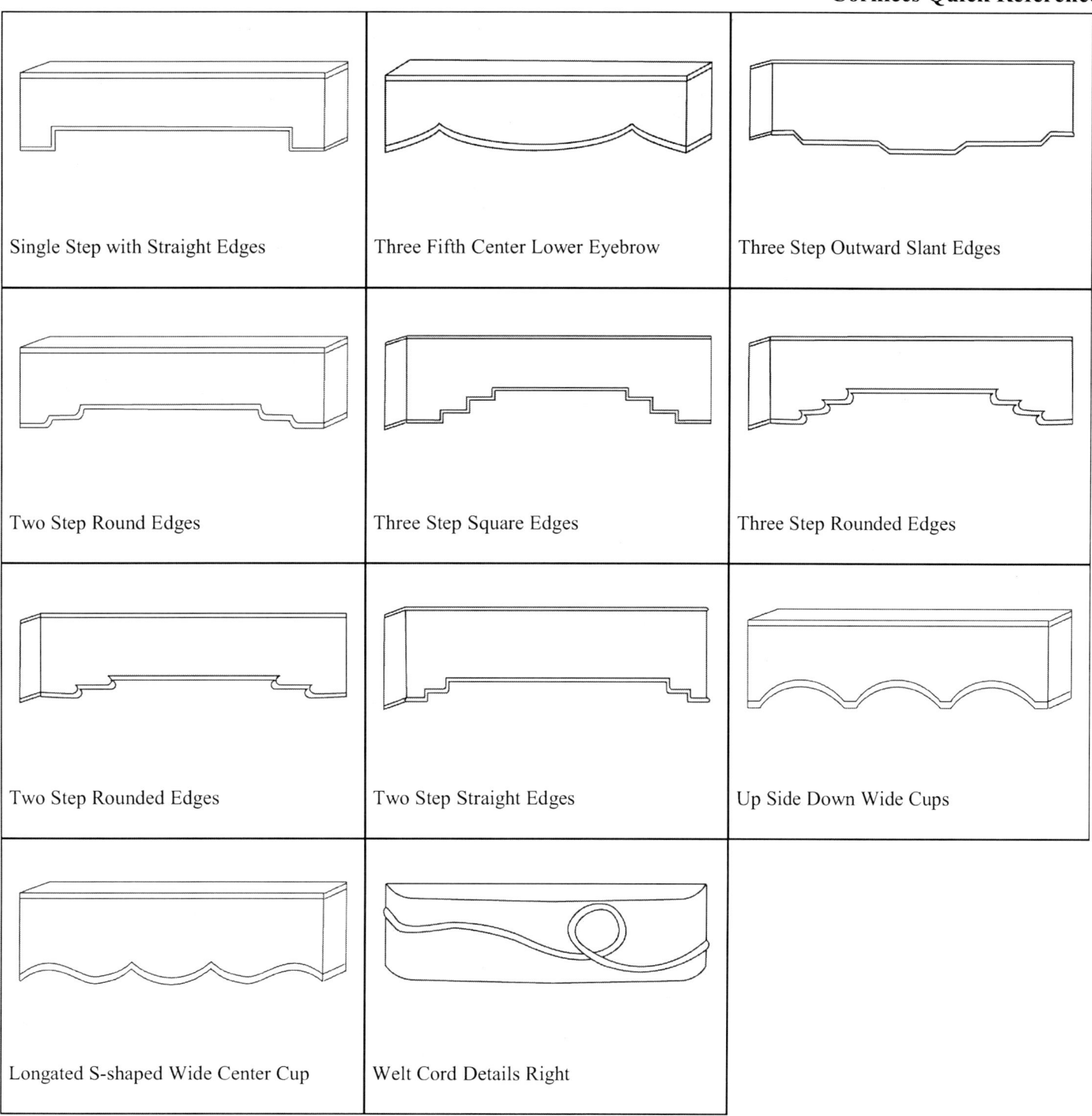

Cornices Quick Reference

Single Step with Straight Edges	Three Fifth Center Lower Eyebrow	Three Step Outward Slant Edges
Two Step Round Edges	Three Step Square Edges	Three Step Rounded Edges
Two Step Rounded Edges	Two Step Straight Edges	Up Side Down Wide Cups
Longated S-shaped Wide Center Cup	Welt Cord Details Right	

Elements of Soft Treatments

Cornices Quick Reference

Shaped Sides

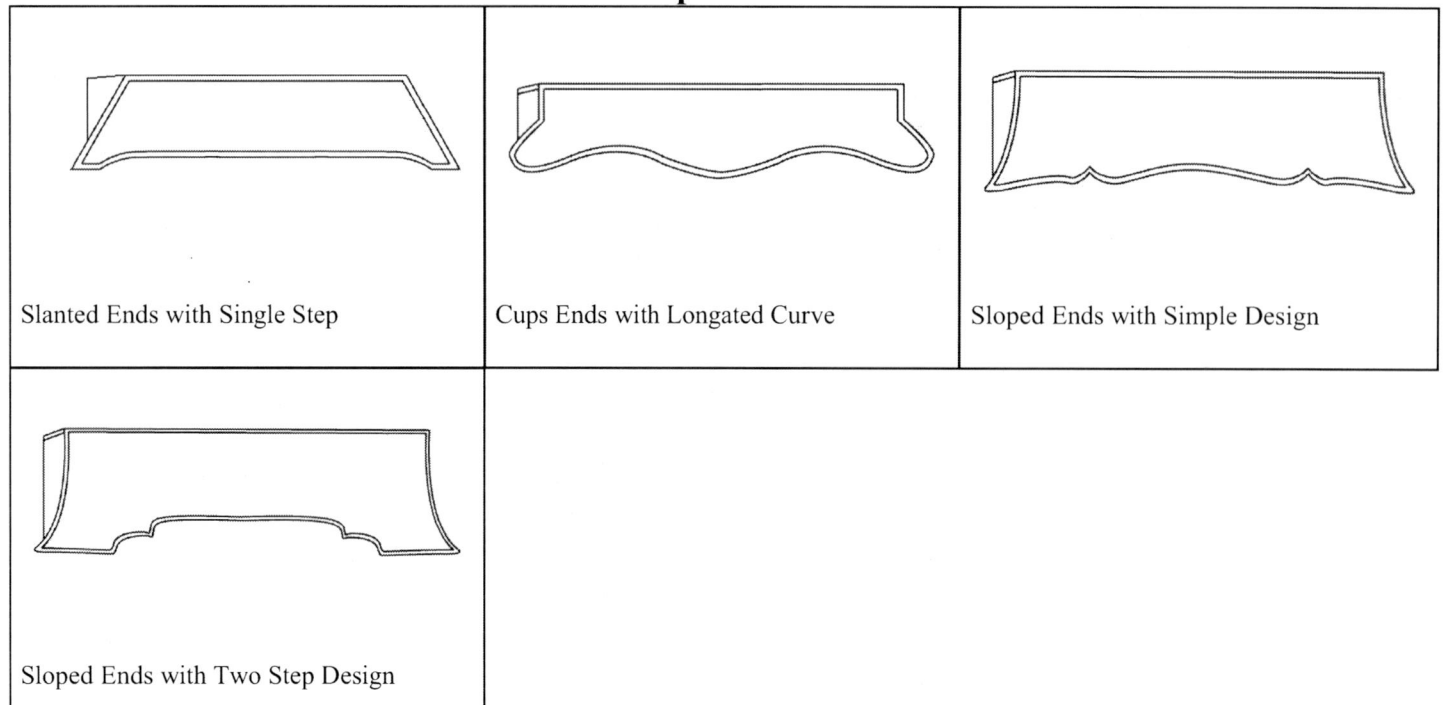

Slanted Ends with Single Step	Cups Ends with Longated Curve	Sloped Ends with Simple Design
Sloped Ends with Two Step Design		

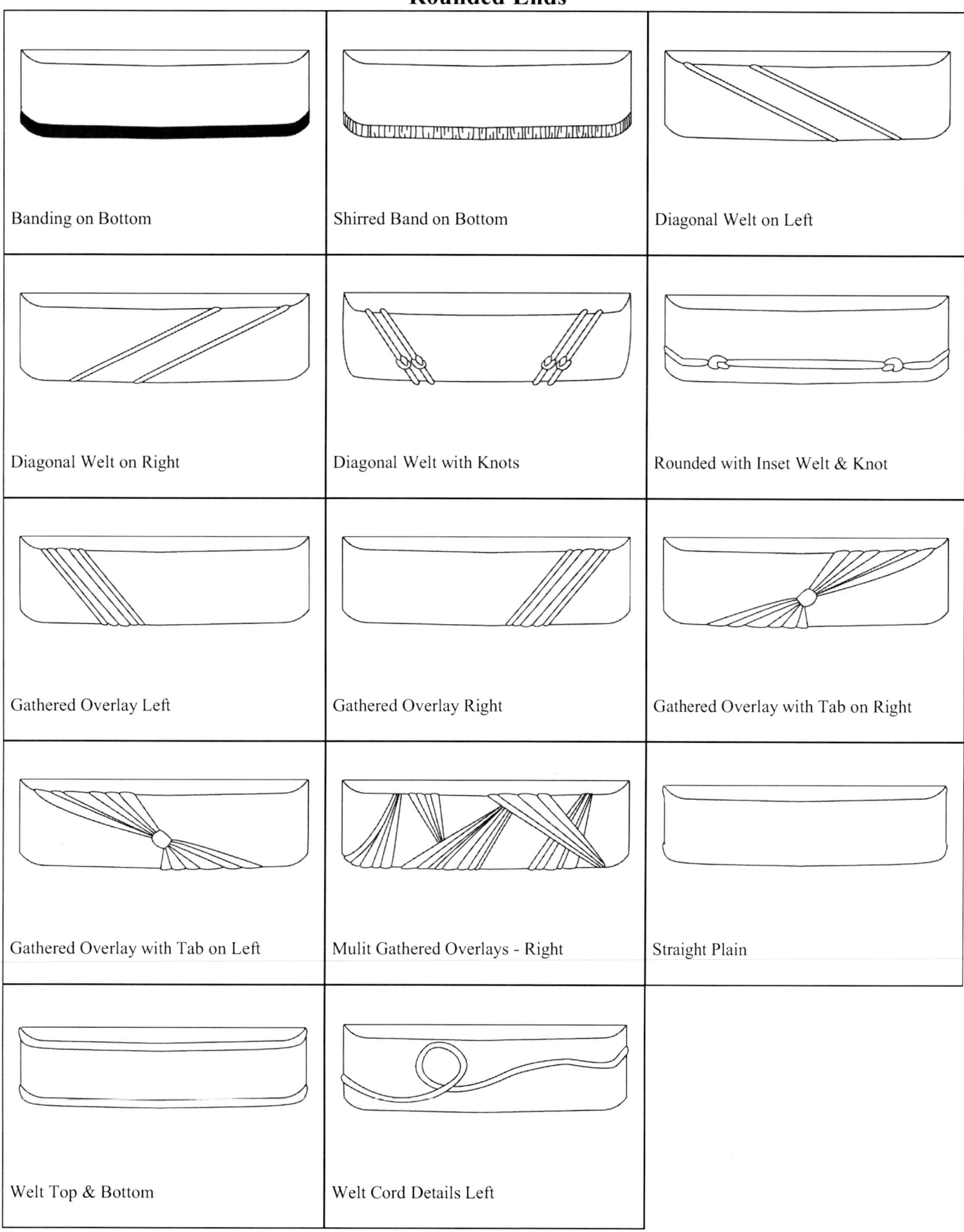

Cornices Quick Reference

Rounded Ends

Banding on Bottom	Shirred Band on Bottom	Diagonal Welt on Left
Diagonal Welt on Right	Diagonal Welt with Knots	Rounded with Inset Welt & Knot
Gathered Overlay Left	Gathered Overlay Right	Gathered Overlay with Tab on Right
Gathered Overlay with Tab on Left	Mulit Gathered Overlays - Right	Straight Plain
Welt Top & Bottom	Welt Cord Details Left	

Elements of Soft Treatments

Cornices Quick Reference

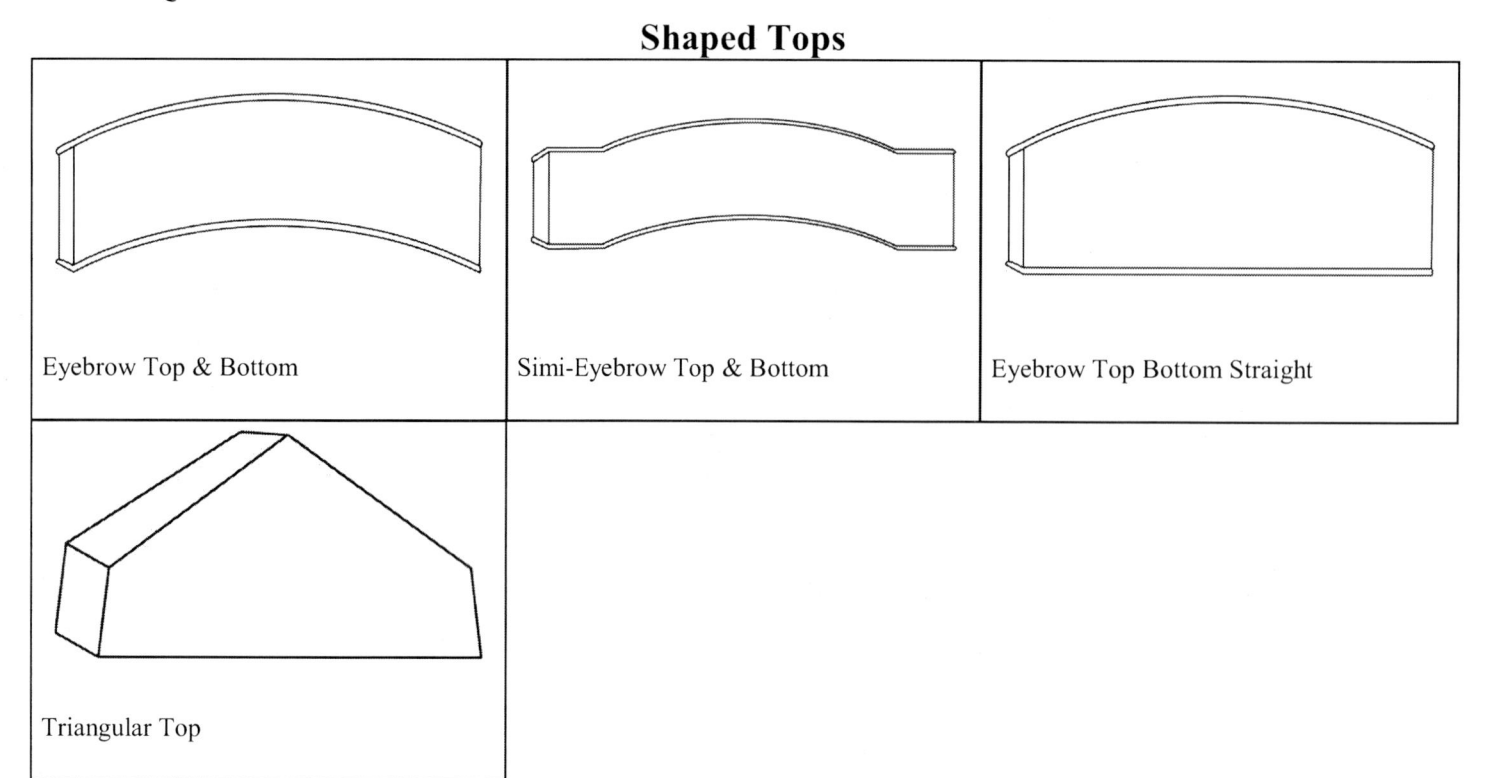

Shaped Tops

Eyebrow Top & Bottom	Simi-Eyebrow Top & Bottom	Eyebrow Top Bottom Straight
Triangular Top		

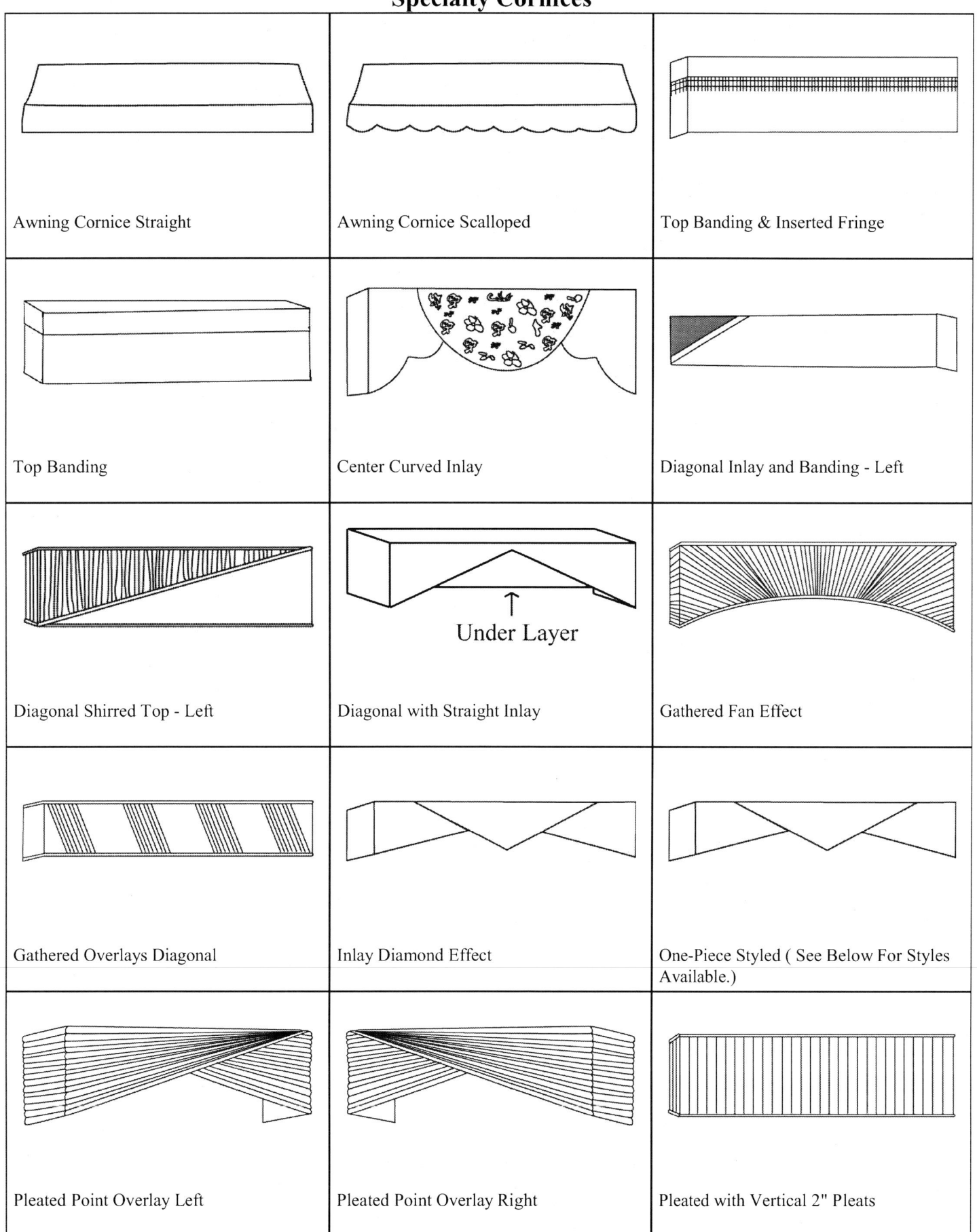

Cornices Quick Reference

Specialty Cornices

Awning Cornice Straight	Awning Cornice Scalloped	Top Banding & Inserted Fringe
Top Banding	Center Curved Inlay	Diagonal Inlay and Banding - Left
Diagonal Shirred Top - Left	Diagonal with Straight Inlay (Under Layer)	Gathered Fan Effect
Gathered Overlays Diagonal	Inlay Diamond Effect	One-Piece Styled (See Below For Styles Available.)
Pleated Point Overlay Left	Pleated Point Overlay Right	Pleated with Vertical 2" Pleats

Elements of Soft Treatments

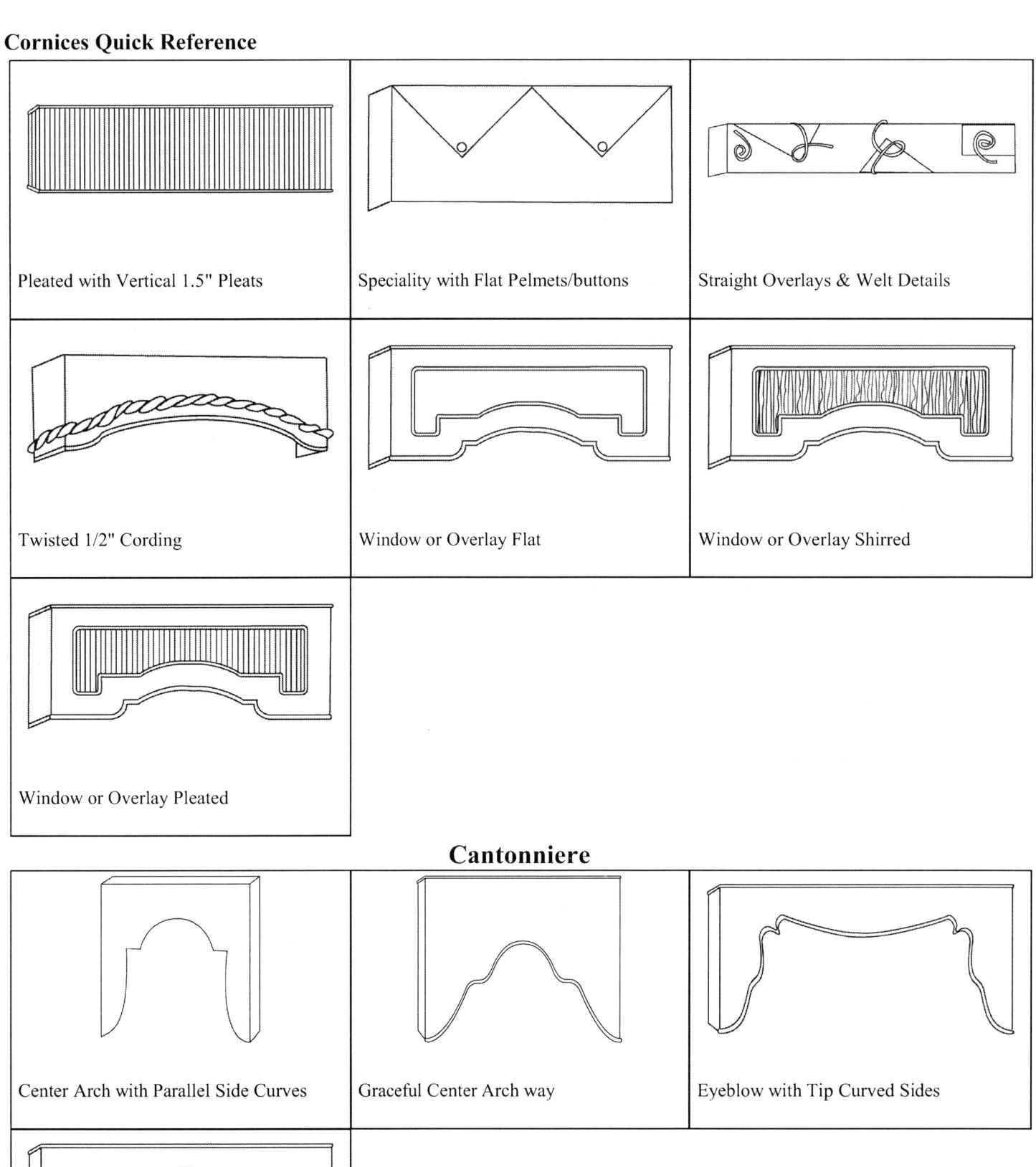

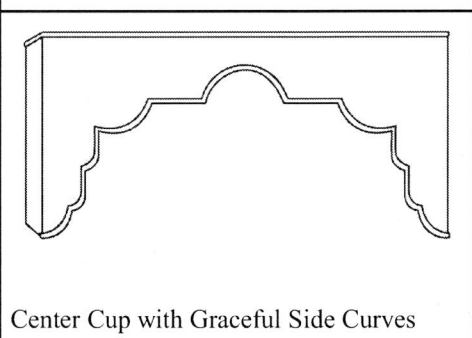

Cornices Quick Reference

Pleated with Vertical 1.5" Pleats	Speciality with Flat Pelmets/buttons	Straight Overlays & Welt Details
Twisted 1/2" Cording	Window or Overlay Flat	Window or Overlay Shirred
Window or Overlay Pleated		

Cantonniere

Center Arch with Parallel Side Curves	Graceful Center Arch way	Eyeblow with Tip Curved Sides
Center Cup with Graceful Side Curves		

Cornices Quick Reference

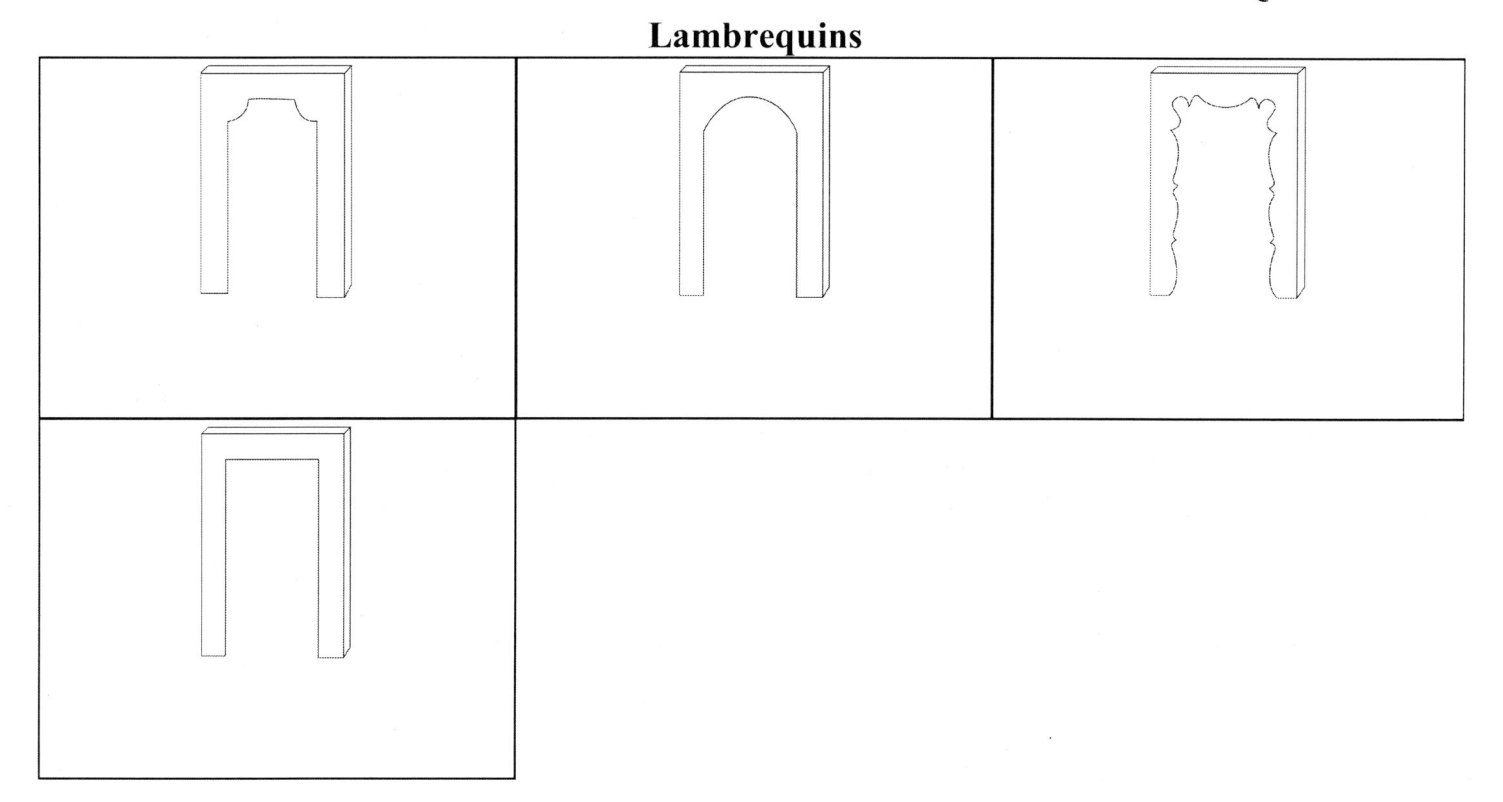

Lambrequins

Elements of Soft Treatments 251

Traditional Swags Quick Reference

Formal I Swags

Classic Formal Swag - 3	Classic Formal Swag - 5	Classic Formal Swag - 7
Georgian Formal Swag - 3	Georgian Formal Swag - 5	Georgian Formal Swag - 7
Left Formal Multi Swag - 2	Left Formal Multi Swag - 3	Left Formal Multi Swag - 4
Left Formal Multi Swag - 5	Left Formal Multi Swag - 6	Left Formal Multi Swag - 7
Right Formal Multi Swag - 2	Right Formal Multi Swag - 3	Right Formal Multi Swag - 4

Elements of Soft Treatments

253

Traditional Swags Quick Reference

Right Formal Multi Swag - 5

Right Formal Multi Swag - 6

Right Formal Multi Swag - 7

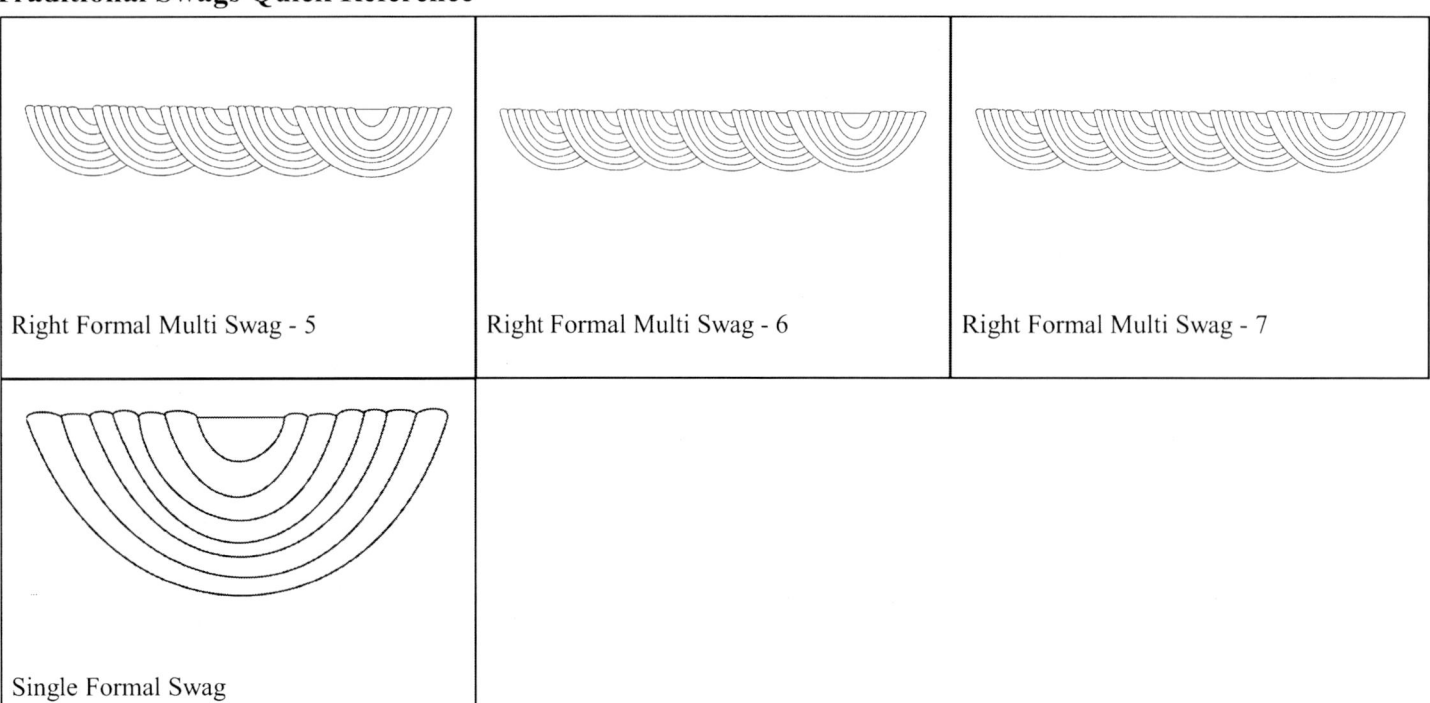

Single Formal Swag

Traditional Swags Quick Reference

Formal II Swags

Classic Formal Swag - 3	Classic Formal Swag - 5	Classic Formal Swag - 7
Georgian Formal Swag - 3	Georgian Formal Swag - 5	Georgian Formal Swag - 7
Left Formal Multi Swag - 2	Left Formal Multi Swag - 3	Left Formal Multi Swag - 4
Left Formal Multi Swag - 5	Left Formal Multi Swag - 6	Left Formal Multi Swag - 7
Right Formal Multi Swag - 2	Right Formal Multi Swag - 3	Right Formal Multi Swag - 4

Elements of Soft Treatments

Traditional Swags Quick Reference

Right Formal Multi Swag - 5

Right Formal Multi Swag - 6

Right Formal Multi Swag - 7

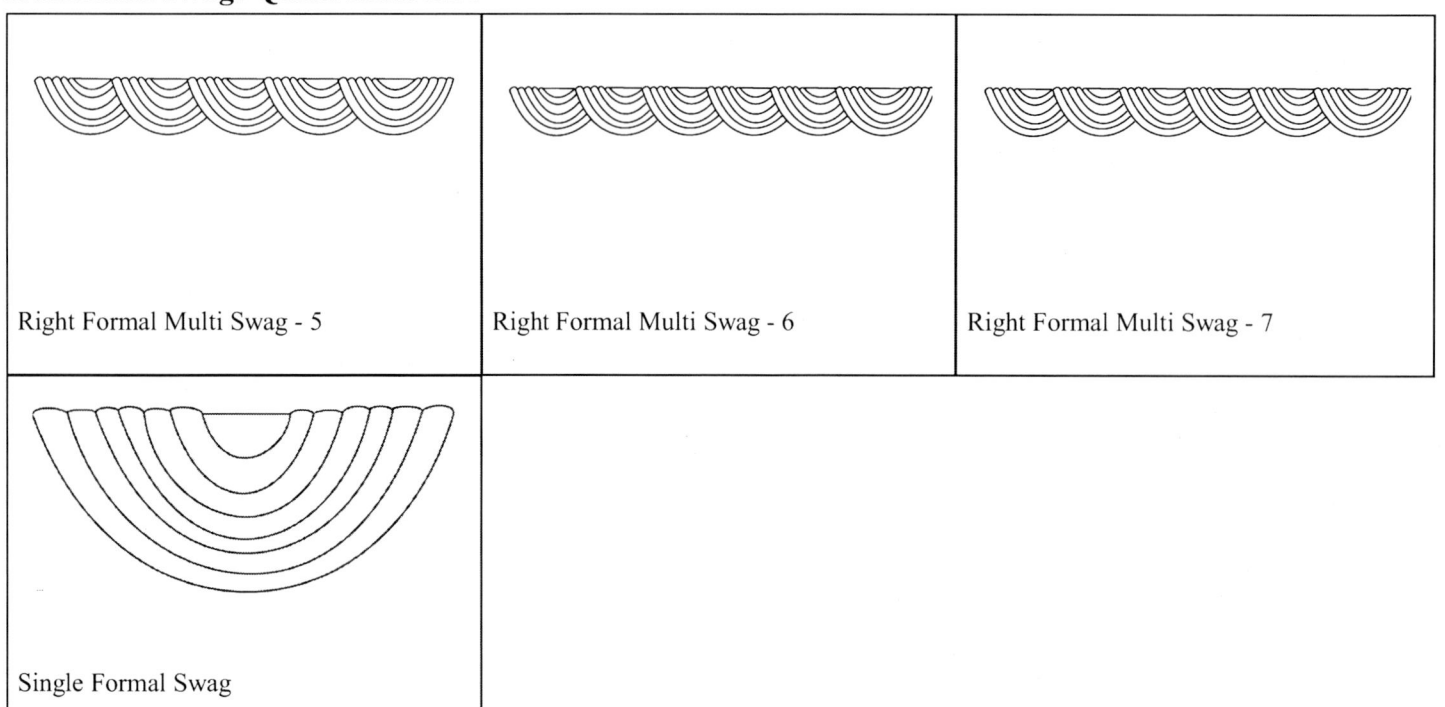

Single Formal Swag

Traditional Swags Quick Reference

Gathered I Swags

Classic Gathered Swag - 3	Classic Gathered Swag - 5	Classic Gathered Swag - 7
Georgian Gathered Swag - 3	Georgian Gathered Swag - 5	Georgian Gathered Swag - 7
Left Gathered Multi Swag - 2	Left Gathered Multi Swag - 3	Left Gathered Multi Swag - 4
Left Gathered Multi Swag - 5	Left Gathered Multi Swag - 6	Left Gathered Multi Swag - 7
Right Gathered Multi Swag - 2	Right Gathered Multi Swag - 3	Right Gathered Multi Swag - 4

Elements of Soft Treatments

Traditional Swags Quick Reference

Right Gathered Multi Swag - 5

Right Gathered Multi Swag - 6

Right Gathered Multi Swag - 7

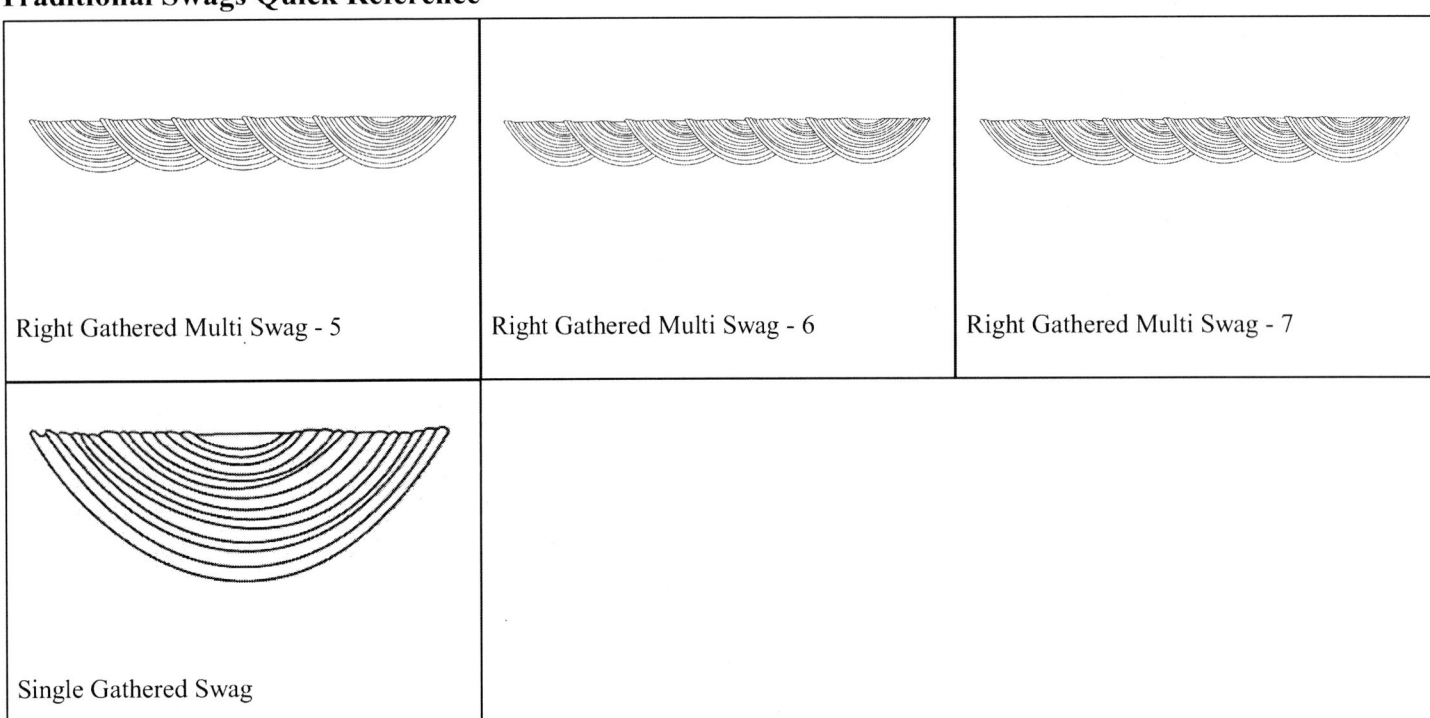

Single Gathered Swag

Traditional Swags Quick Reference

Gathered II Swags

Classic Gathered Swag - 3	Classic Gathered Swag - 5	Classic Gathered Swag - 7
Georgian Gathered Swag - 3	Georgian Gathered Swag - 5	Georgian Gathered Swag - 7
Left Gathered Multi Swag - 2	Left Gathered Multi Swag - 3	Left Gathered Multi Swag - 4
Left Gathered Multi Swag - 5	Left Gathered Multi Swag - 6	Left Gathered Multi Swag - 7
Right Gathered Multi Swag - 2	Right Gathered Multi Swag - 3	Right Gathered Multi Swag - 4

Elements of Soft Treatments

Traditional Swags Quick Reference

Right Gathered Multi Swag - 5	Right Gathered Multi Swag - 6	Right Gathered Multi Swag - 7
Single Gathered Swag		

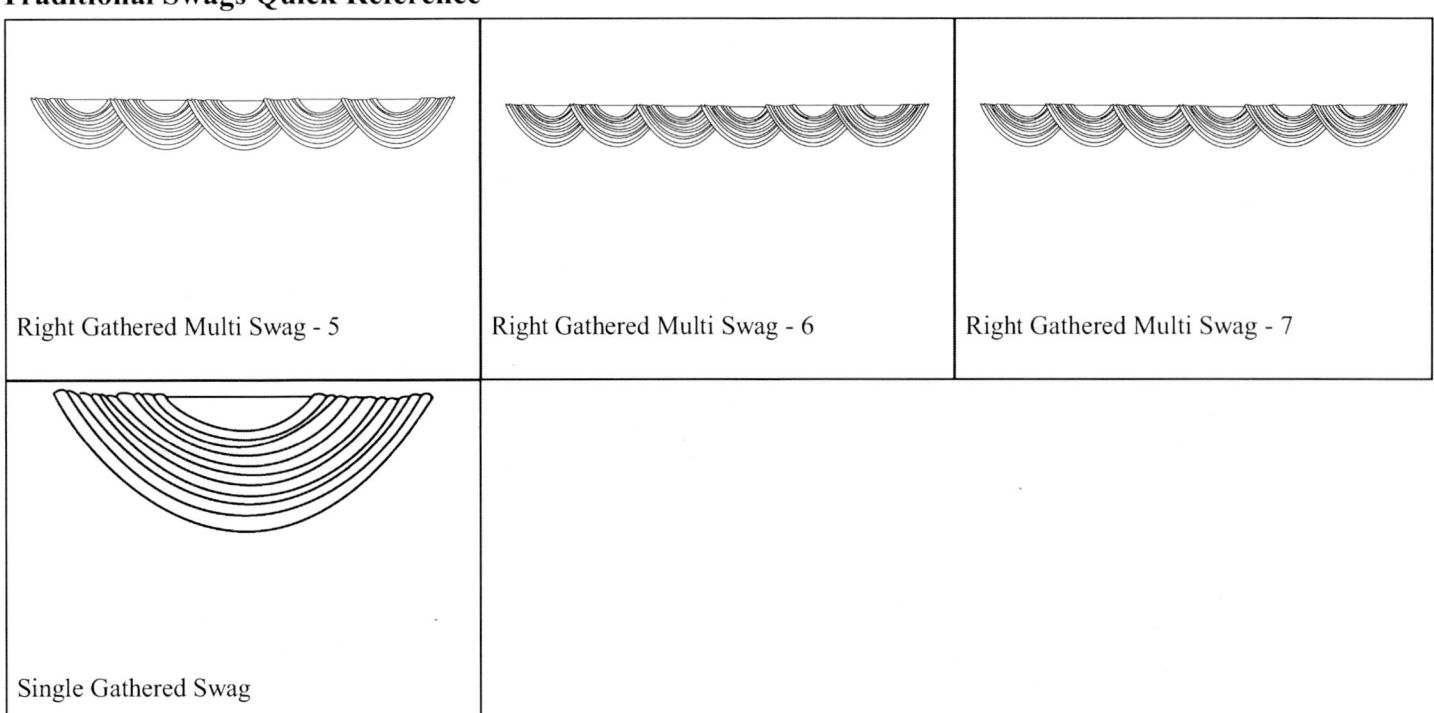

Traditional Swags Quick Reference

End Cap II Swags

Classic End Cap Formal - 3	Classic End Cap Formal - 5	Classic End Cap Formal - 7
Classic End Cap Gathered - 3	Classic End Cap Gathered - 5	Classic End Cap Gathered - 7
Georgian End Cap Formal - 3	Georgian End Cap Formal - 5	Georgian End Cap Formal - 7
Georgian End Cap Gathered - 3	Georgian End Cap Gathered - 5	Georgian End Cap Gathered - 7

Elements of Soft Treatments

Traditional Swags Quick Reference

Box Swags

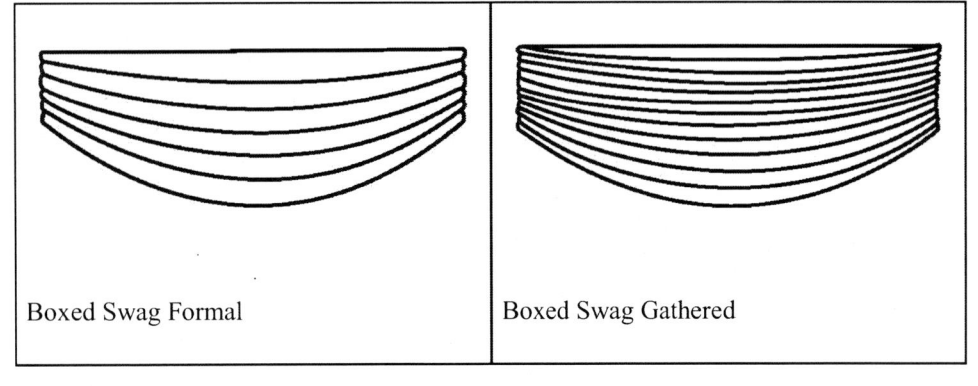

Boxed Swag Formal

Boxed Swag Gathered

Traditional Swags Quick Reference

Empire Swags

Empire with Return - 1	Empire with Returns - 2	Empire with Returns - 3
Empire with Returns - 4	Empire with Returns - 5	Empire with Returns - 6
Empire with Tails - 1	Empire with Tails - 2	Empire with Tails - 3
Empire with Tails - 4	Empire with Tails - 5	Empire with Tails - 6

Elements of Soft Treatments

Traditional Swags Quick Reference

Kingston Swags

Kingston with Returns - 1	Kingston with Returns - 2	Kingston with Returns - 3
Kingston with Returns - 4	Kingston with Returns - 5	Kingston with Returns - 6
Kingston with Tails - 1	Kingston with Tails - 2	Kingston with Tails - 3
Kingston with Tails - 4	Kingston with Tails - 5	Kingston with Tails - 6

Traditional Swags Quick Reference

Bell Swags

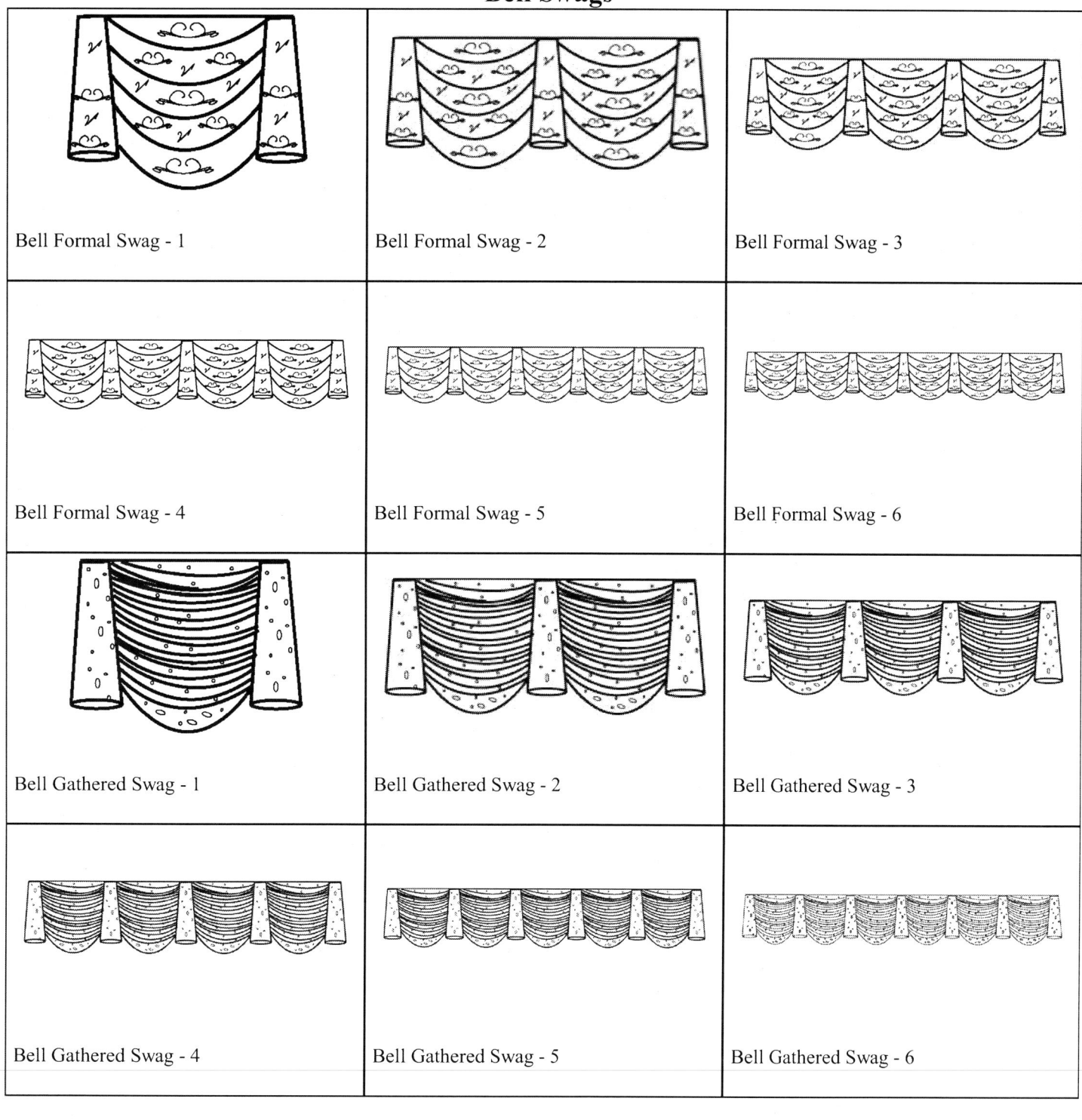

Bell Formal Swag - 1	Bell Formal Swag - 2	Bell Formal Swag - 3
Bell Formal Swag - 4	Bell Formal Swag - 5	Bell Formal Swag - 6
Bell Gathered Swag - 1	Bell Gathered Swag - 2	Bell Gathered Swag - 3
Bell Gathered Swag - 4	Bell Gathered Swag - 5	Bell Gathered Swag - 6

Elements of Soft Treatments

Open Swags Quick Reference

Formal II Swags

Classic Formal Swag Over - 3	Classic Formal Swag Over - 5	Classic Formal Swag Over - 7
Classic Formal Swag Under - 3	Classic Formal Swag Under - 5	Classic Formal Swag Under - 7
Georgian Formal Swag Over - 3	Georgian Formal Swag Over - 5	Georgian Formal Swag Over - 7
Georgian Formal Swag Under - 3	Georgian Formal Swag Under - 5	Georgian Formal Swag Under - 7
Left Formal Swag Over - 2	Left Formal Swag Over - 3	Left Formal Swag Over - 4

Elements of Soft Treatments

Open Swags Quick Reference

Left Formal Swag Over - 5	Left Formal Swag Over - 6	Left Formal Swag Over - 7
Left Formal Swag Under - 2	Left Formal Swag Under - 3	Left Formal Swag Under - 4
Left Formal Swag Under - 5	Left Formal Swag Under - 6	Left Formal Swag Under - 7
Right Formal Swag Over - 2	Right Formal Swag Over - 3	Right Formal Swag Over - 4
Right Formal Swag Over - 5	Right Formal Swag Over - 6	Right Formal Swag Over - 7

Gathered II Swags

Open Swags Quick Reference

Classic Gathered Swag Over - 3	Classic Gathered Swag Over - 5	Classic Gathered Swag Over - 7
Classic Gathered Swag Under - 3	Classic Gathered Swag Under - 5	Classic Gathered Swag Under - 7
Georgian Gathered Swag Over - 3	Georgian Gathered Swag Over - 5	Georgian Gathered Swag Over - 7
Georgian Gathered Swag Under - 3	Georgian Gathered Swag Under - 5	Georgian Gathered Swag Under - 7
Left Gathered Swag Over - 2	Left Gathered Swag Over - 3	Left Gathered Swag Over - 4

Elements of Soft Treatments

Open Swags Quick Reference

Left Gathered Swag Over - 5	Left Gathered Swag Over - 6	Left Gathered Swag Over - 7
Left Gathered Swag Under - 2	Left Gathered Swag Under - 3	Left Gathered Swag Under - 4
Left Gathered Swag Under - 5	Left Gathered Swag Under - 6	Left Gathered Swag Under - 7
Right Gathered Swag Over - 2	Right Gathered Swag Over - 3	Right Gathered Swag Over - 4
Right Gathered Swag Over - 5	Right Gathered Swag Over - 6	Right Gathered Swag Over - 7

Open Swags Quick Reference

Right Gathered Swag Under - 2	Right Gathered Swag Under - 3	Right Gathered Swag Under - 4
Right Gathered Swag Under - 5	Right Gathered Swag Under - 6	Right Gathered Swag Under - 7
Single Gathered Swag Over	Single Gathered Swag Left Under	Single Gathered Swag Right Under
Single Gathered Swag Under		

Open Swags Quick Reference

Kingston Swags

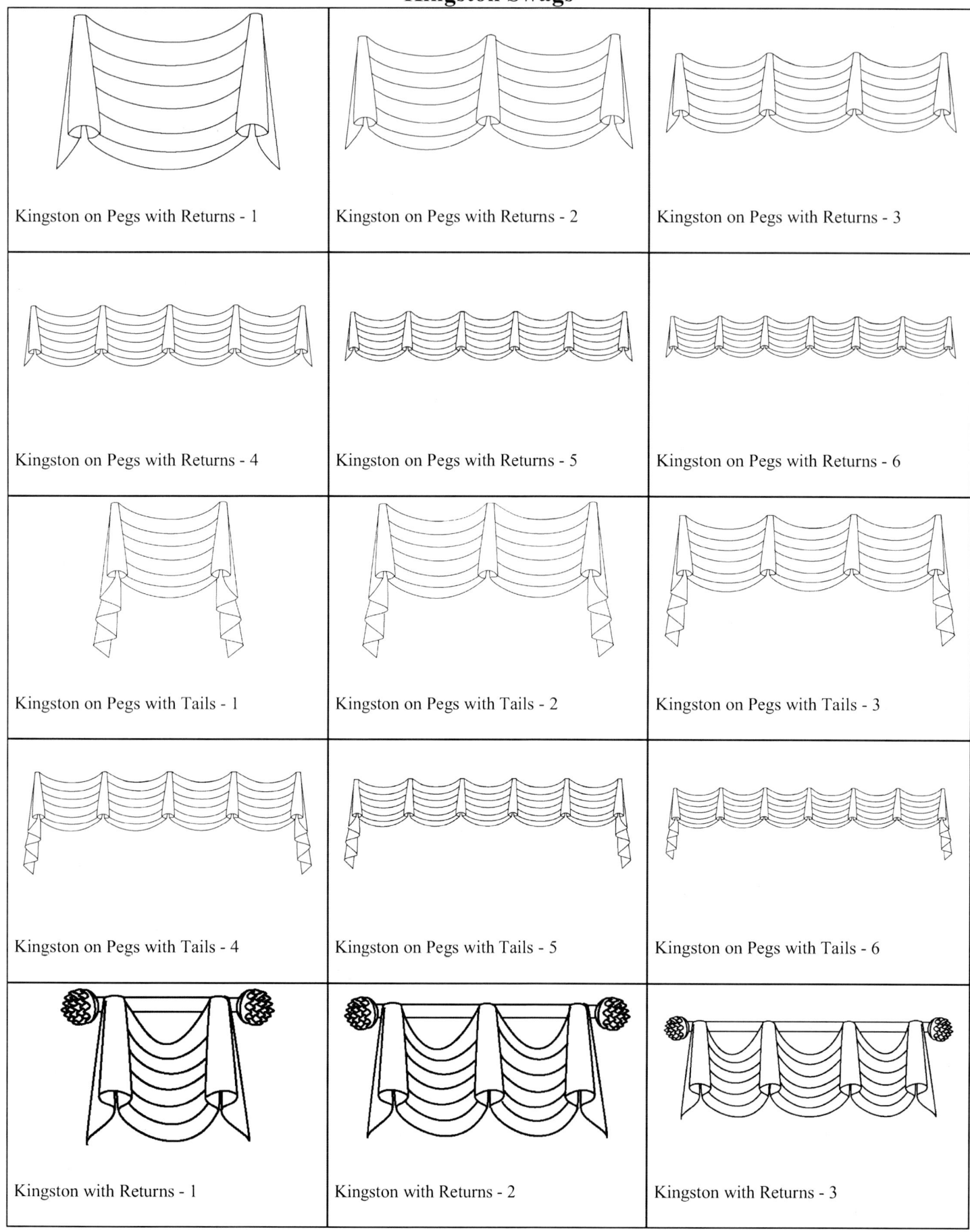

Kingston on Pegs with Returns - 1	Kingston on Pegs with Returns - 2	Kingston on Pegs with Returns - 3
Kingston on Pegs with Returns - 4	Kingston on Pegs with Returns - 5	Kingston on Pegs with Returns - 6
Kingston on Pegs with Tails - 1	Kingston on Pegs with Tails - 2	Kingston on Pegs with Tails - 3
Kingston on Pegs with Tails - 4	Kingston on Pegs with Tails - 5	Kingston on Pegs with Tails - 6
Kingston with Returns - 1	Kingston with Returns - 2	Kingston with Returns - 3

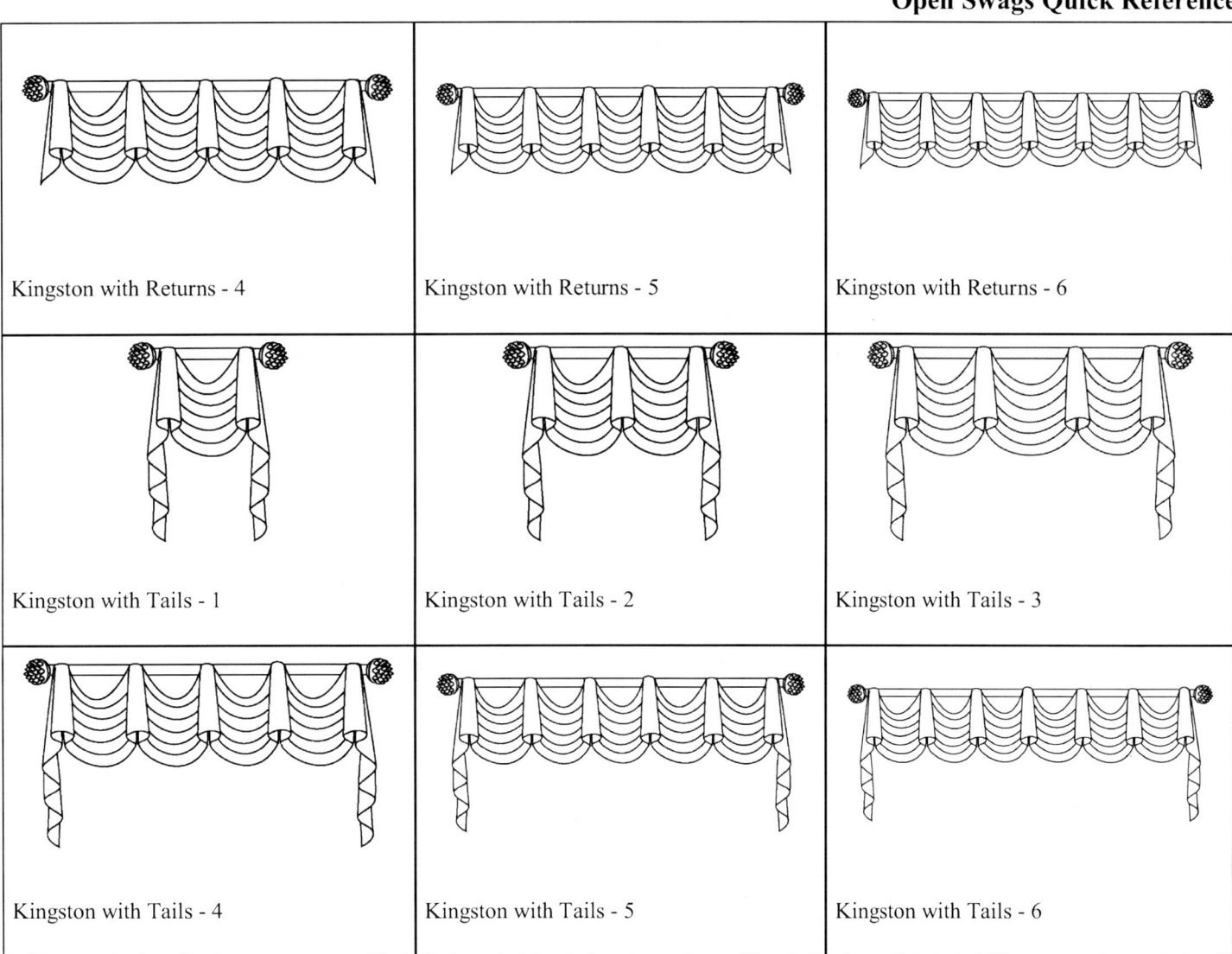

Open Swags Quick Reference

Kingston with Returns - 4	Kingston with Returns - 5	Kingston with Returns - 6
Kingston with Tails - 1	Kingston with Tails - 2	Kingston with Tails - 3
Kingston with Tails - 4	Kingston with Tails - 5	Kingston with Tails - 6

Elements of Soft Treatments

Open Swags Quick Reference

Empires Swags

Empire with Returns - 1	Empire with Returns - 2	Empire with Returns - 3
Empire with Returns - 4	Empire with Returns - 5	Empire with Returns - 6
Empire with Tails - 1	Empire with Tails - 2	Empire with Tails - 3
Empire with Tails - 4	Empire with Tails - 5	Empire with Tails - 6

Open Swags Quick Reference

Bell Swags

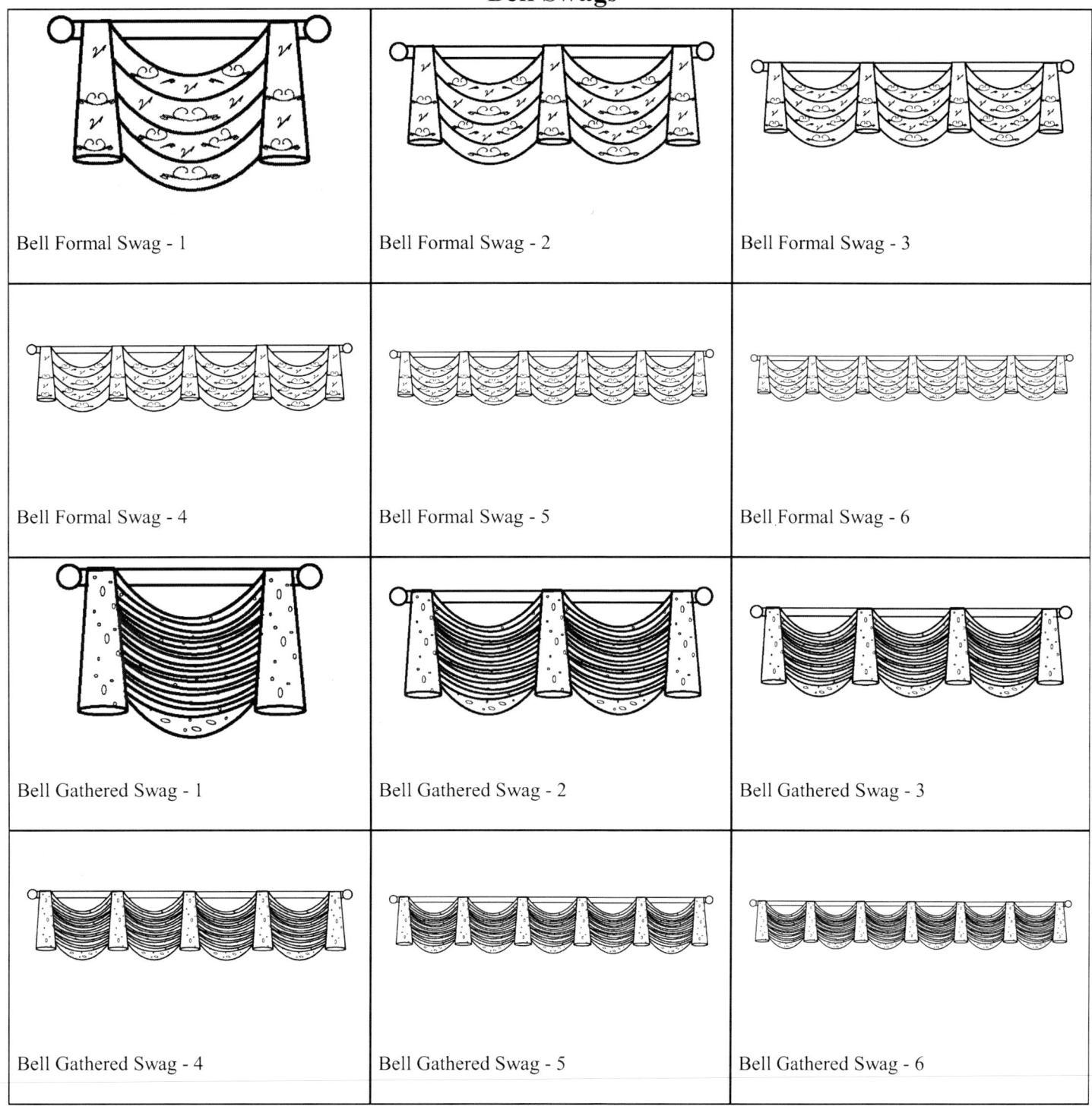

Bell Formal Swag - 1	Bell Formal Swag - 2	Bell Formal Swag - 3
Bell Formal Swag - 4	Bell Formal Swag - 5	Bell Formal Swag - 6
Bell Gathered Swag - 1	Bell Gathered Swag - 2	Bell Gathered Swag - 3
Bell Gathered Swag - 4	Bell Gathered Swag - 5	Bell Gathered Swag - 6

Elements of Soft Treatments

Window Scarfs Quick Reference

Scarf Holders

Single Throw	Tube Swag on Medallions	Tube Swag with Knots on Arch

Tube Swag with Knots		

Pole Wraps

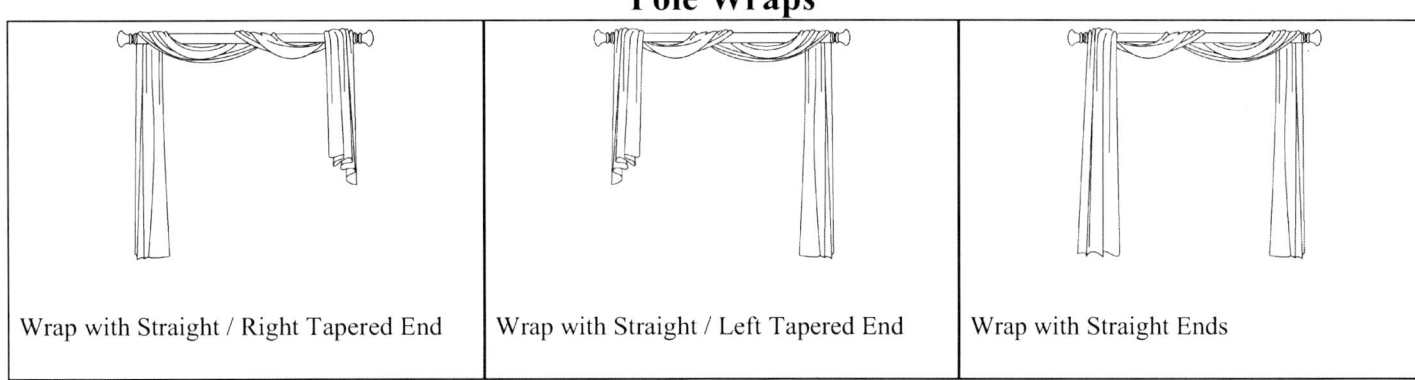

Wrap with Straight / Right Tapered End	Wrap with Straight / Left Tapered End	Wrap with Straight Ends

Rod Pocket Wraps

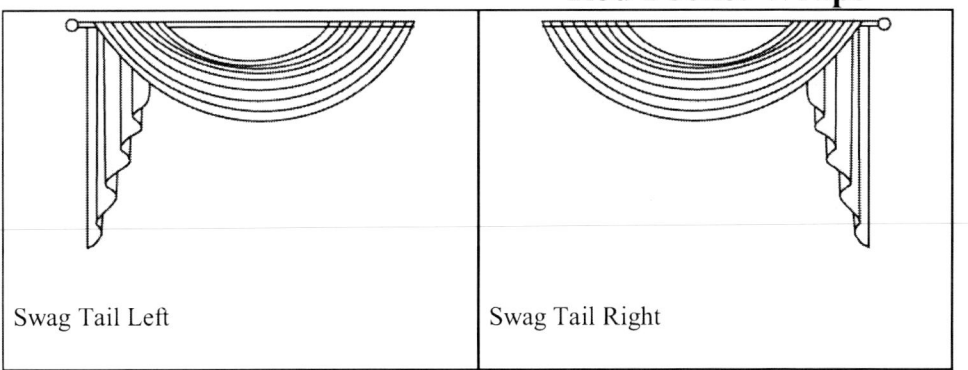

Swag Tail Left	Swag Tail Right

Elements of Soft Treatments

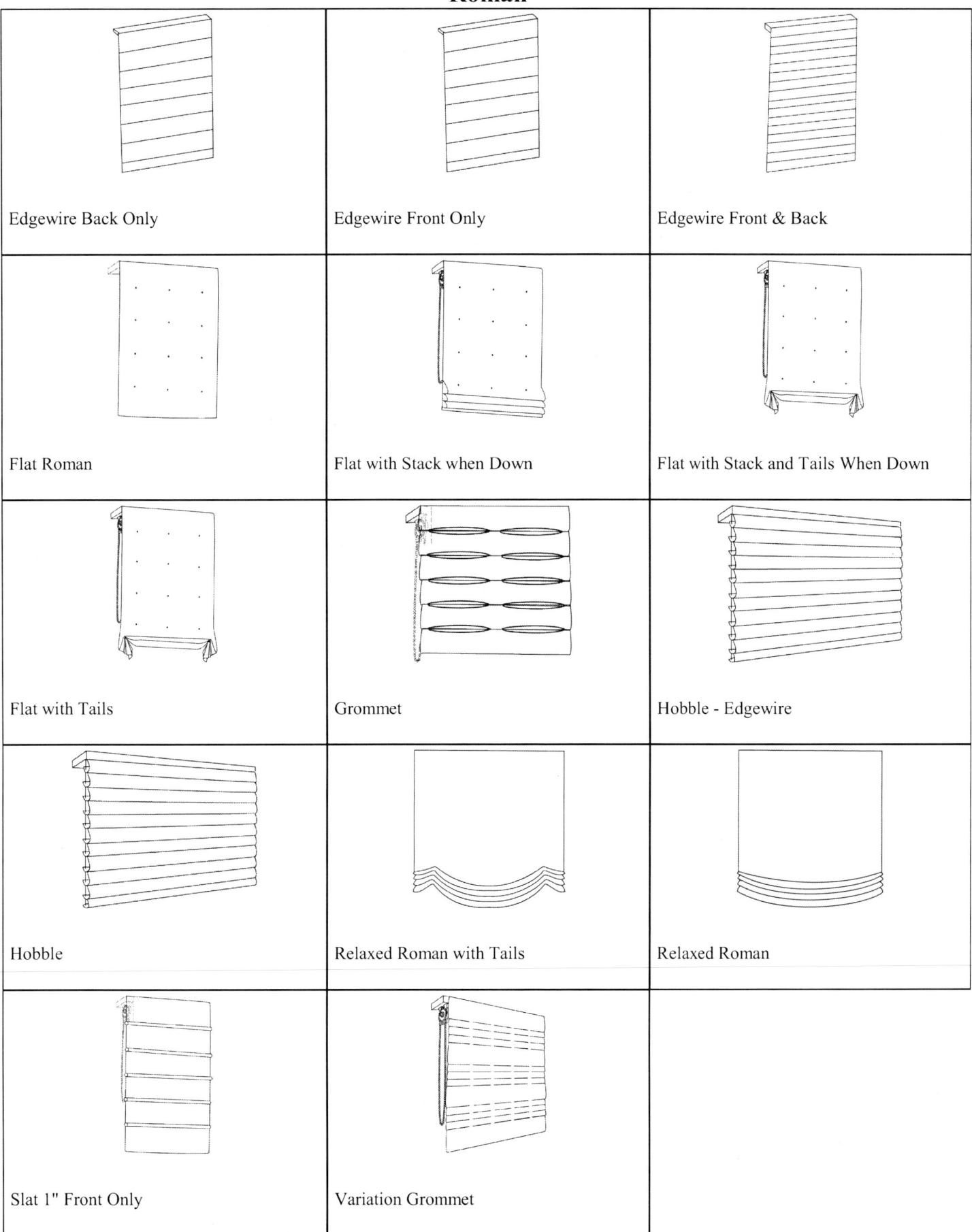

Fabric Shades Quick Reference

Roman

Edgewire Back Only	Edgewire Front Only	Edgewire Front & Back
Flat Roman	Flat with Stack when Down	Flat with Stack and Tails When Down
Flat with Tails	Grommet	Hobble - Edgewire
Hobble	Relaxed Roman with Tails	Relaxed Roman
Slat 1" Front Only	Variation Grommet	

Elements of Soft Treatments

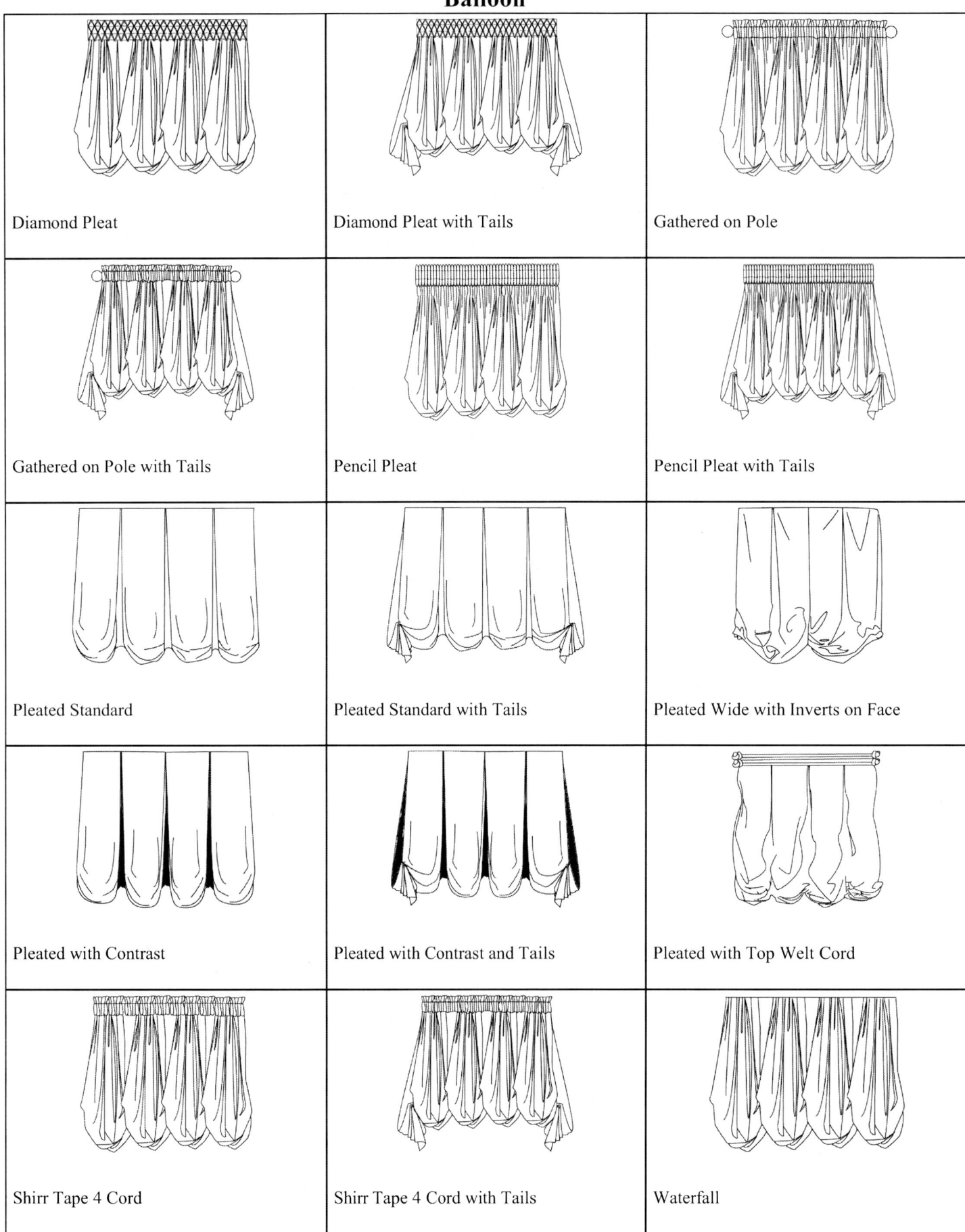

Fabric Shades Quick Reference

Balloon

Diamond Pleat	Diamond Pleat with Tails	Gathered on Pole
Gathered on Pole with Tails	Pencil Pleat	Pencil Pleat with Tails
Pleated Standard	Pleated Standard with Tails	Pleated Wide with Inverts on Face
Pleated with Contrast	Pleated with Contrast and Tails	Pleated with Top Welt Cord
Shirr Tape 4 Cord	Shirr Tape 4 Cord with Tails	Waterfall

Fabric Shades Quick Reference

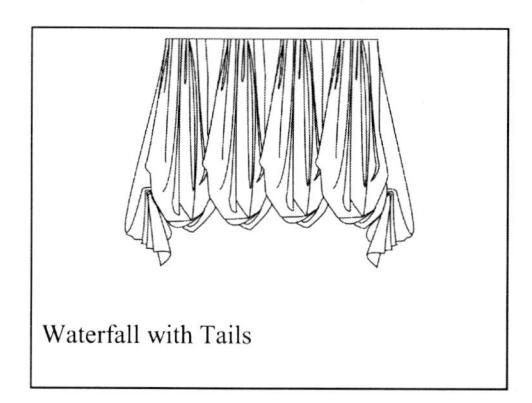

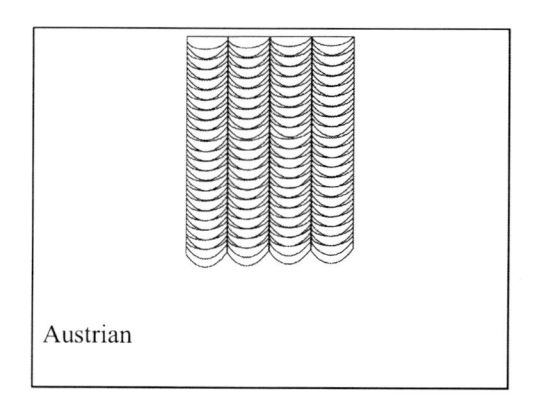

Waterfall with Tails

Austrians

Austrian

Sunburst Quick Reference

Frame

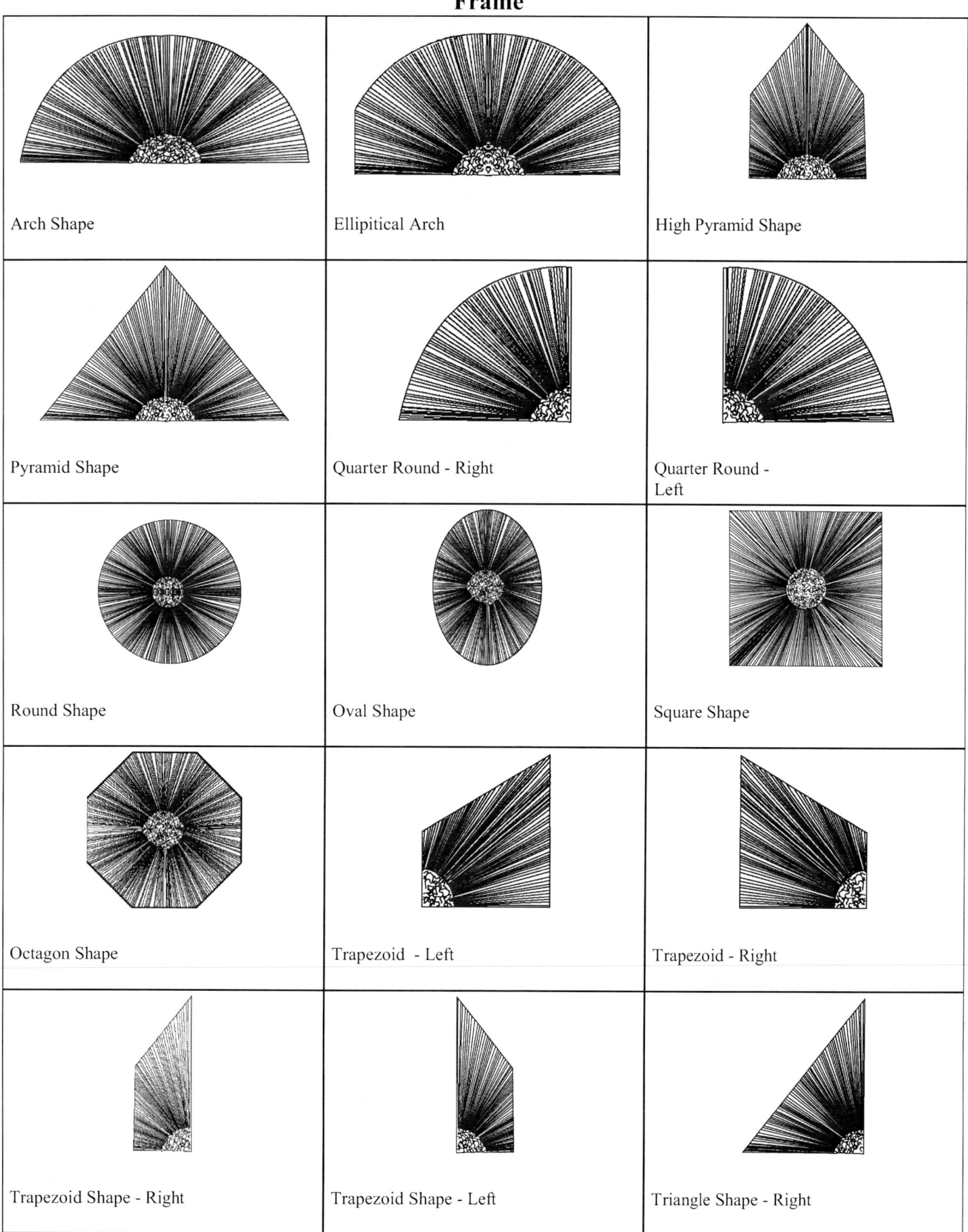

Arch Shape	Ellipitical Arch	High Pyramid Shape
Pyramid Shape	Quarter Round - Right	Quarter Round - Left
Round Shape	Oval Shape	Square Shape
Octagon Shape	Trapezoid - Left	Trapezoid - Right
Trapezoid Shape - Right	Trapezoid Shape - Left	Triangle Shape - Right

Elements of Soft Treatments

Sunburst Quick Reference

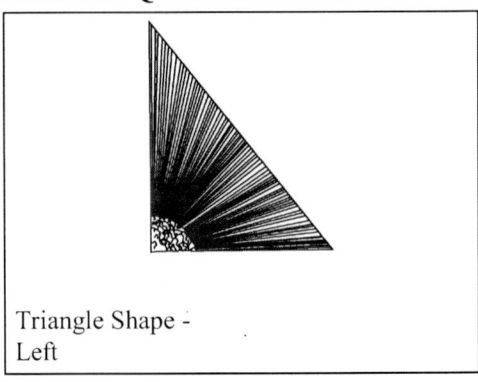

Triangle Shape - Left

Rod Pocket

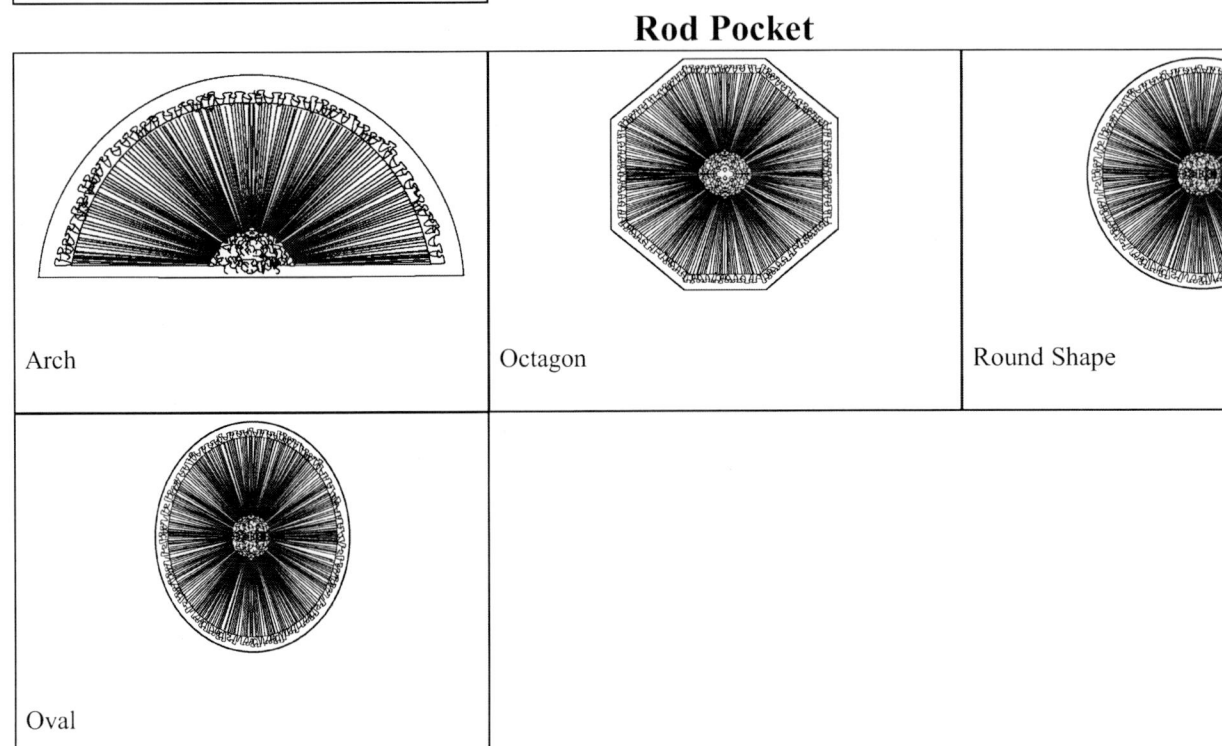

Arch

Octagon

Round Shape

Oval

Bedding Quick Reference

Bed Skirts

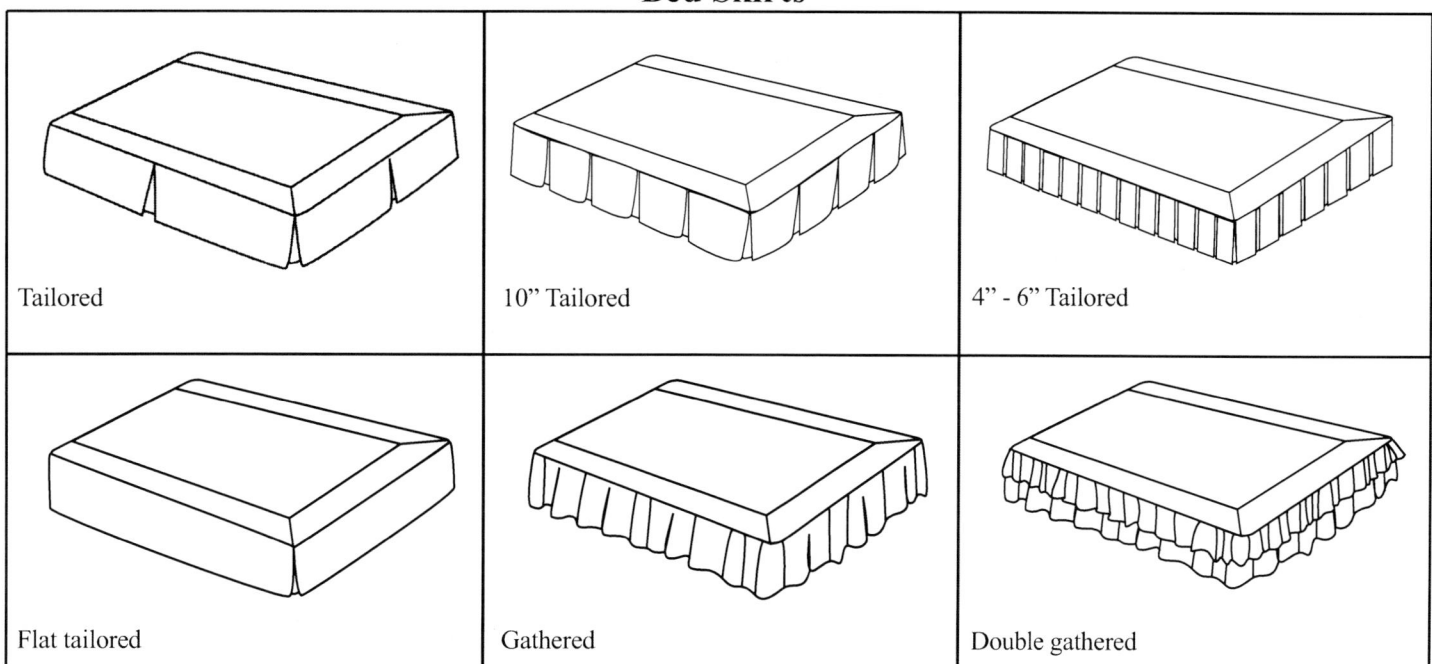

Tailored	10" Tailored	4" - 6" Tailored
Flat tailored	Gathered	Double gathered

Bedspreads

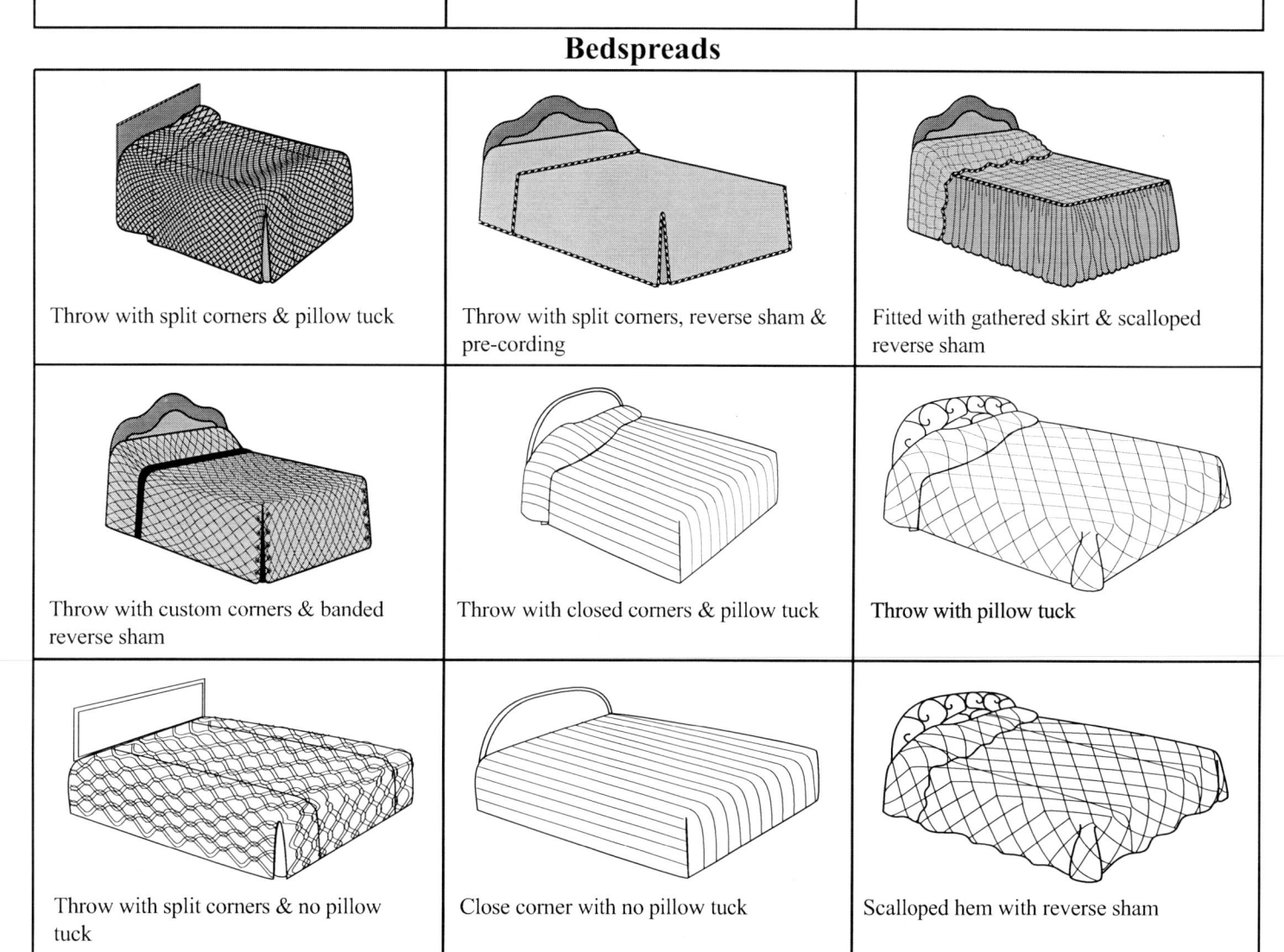

Throw with split corners & pillow tuck	Throw with split corners, reverse sham & pre-cording	Fitted with gathered skirt & scalloped reverse sham
Throw with custom corners & banded reverse sham	Throw with closed corners & pillow tuck	Throw with pillow tuck
Throw with split corners & no pillow tuck	Close corner with no pillow tuck	Scalloped hem with reverse sham

Elements of Soft Treatments

Bedding Quick Reference

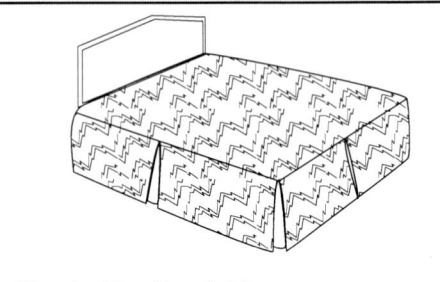

Fitted with tailored skirt	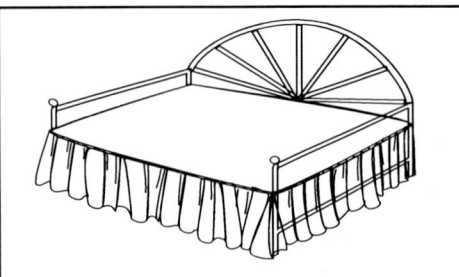 Fitted with gathered skirt on a daybed	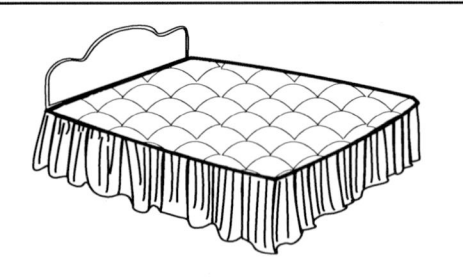 Fitted with gathered skirt & no pillow tuck

Coverlets

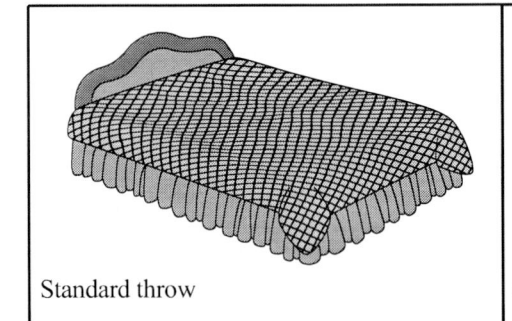

Standard throw	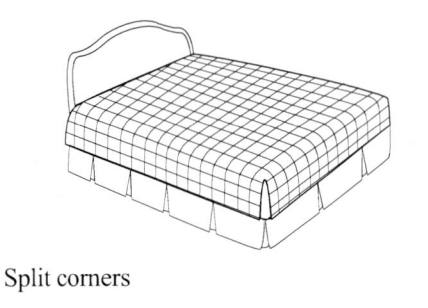 Split corners	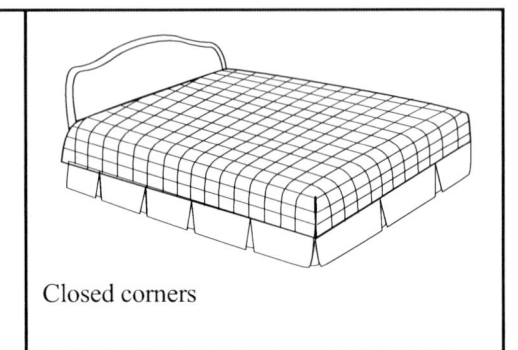 Closed corners

Comforters

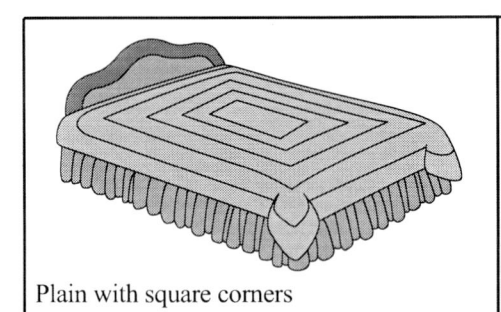

Plain with square corners	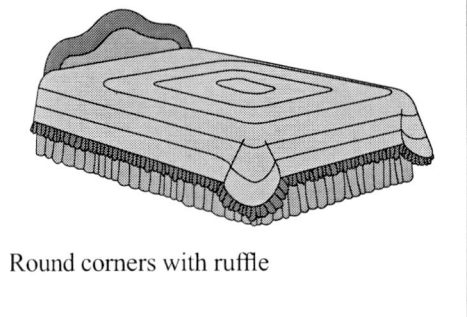 Round corners with ruffle

Duvet Covers

Knife edge on bed	Knife edge with zipper	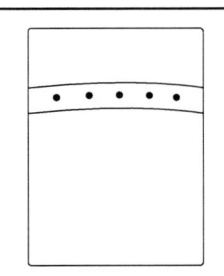 Envelope with buttons

Bedding Quick Reference

Knife edge with mitered border	Scalloped flange	Knife edge with ruffle
Knife edge with double ruffle	Mitered flange inset pre-cording	

Elements of Soft Treatments

Pillows Quick Reference

Knife edge

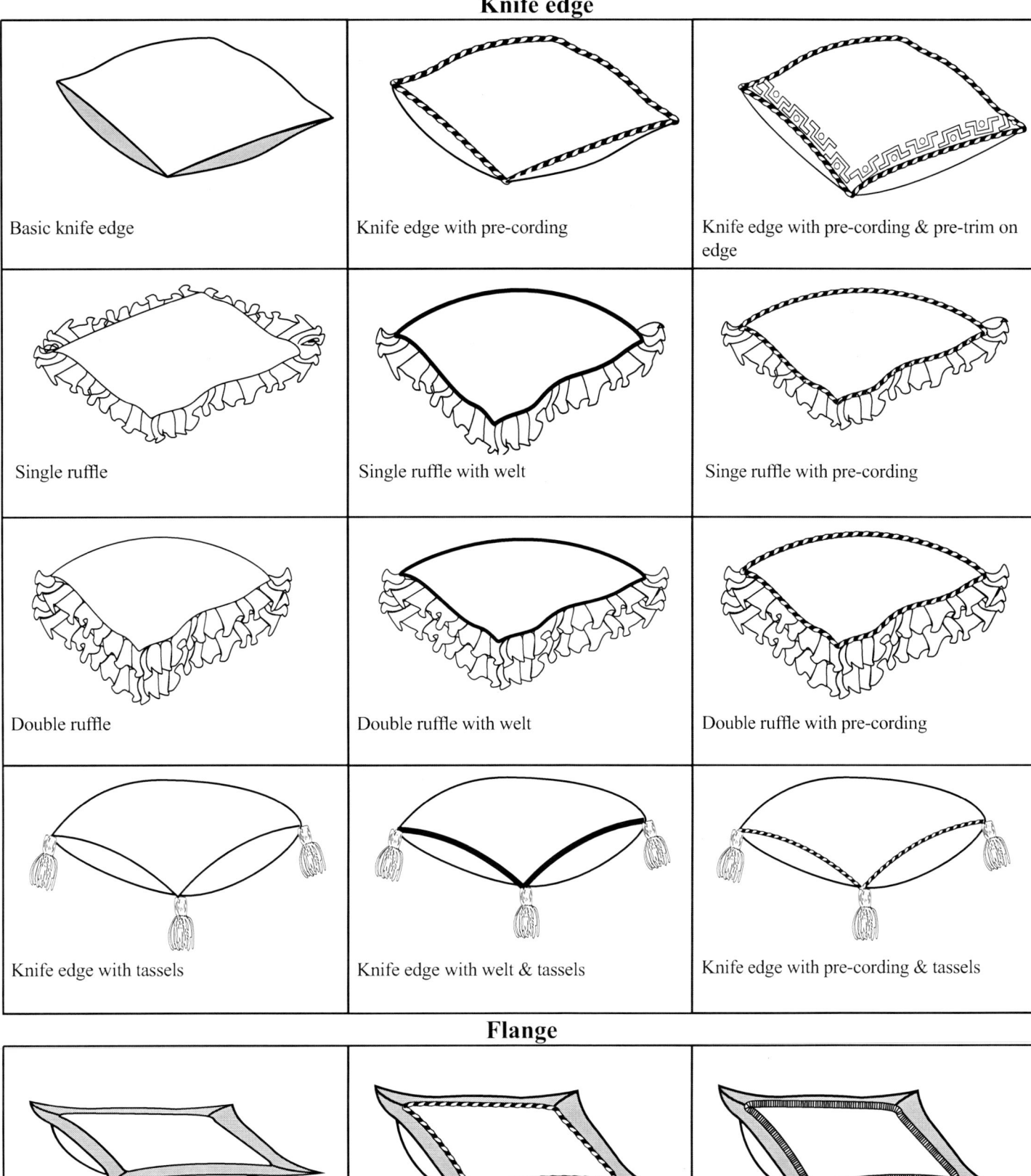

Basic knife edge	Knife edge with pre-cording	Knife edge with pre-cording & pre-trim on edge
Single ruffle	Single ruffle with welt	Singe ruffle with pre-cording
Double ruffle	Double ruffle with welt	Double ruffle with pre-cording
Knife edge with tassels	Knife edge with welt & tassels	Knife edge with pre-cording & tassels

Flange

Mitered flange	Mitered flange with pre-cording	Mitered flange with shirred welt

Elements of Soft Treatments

Pillows Quick Reference

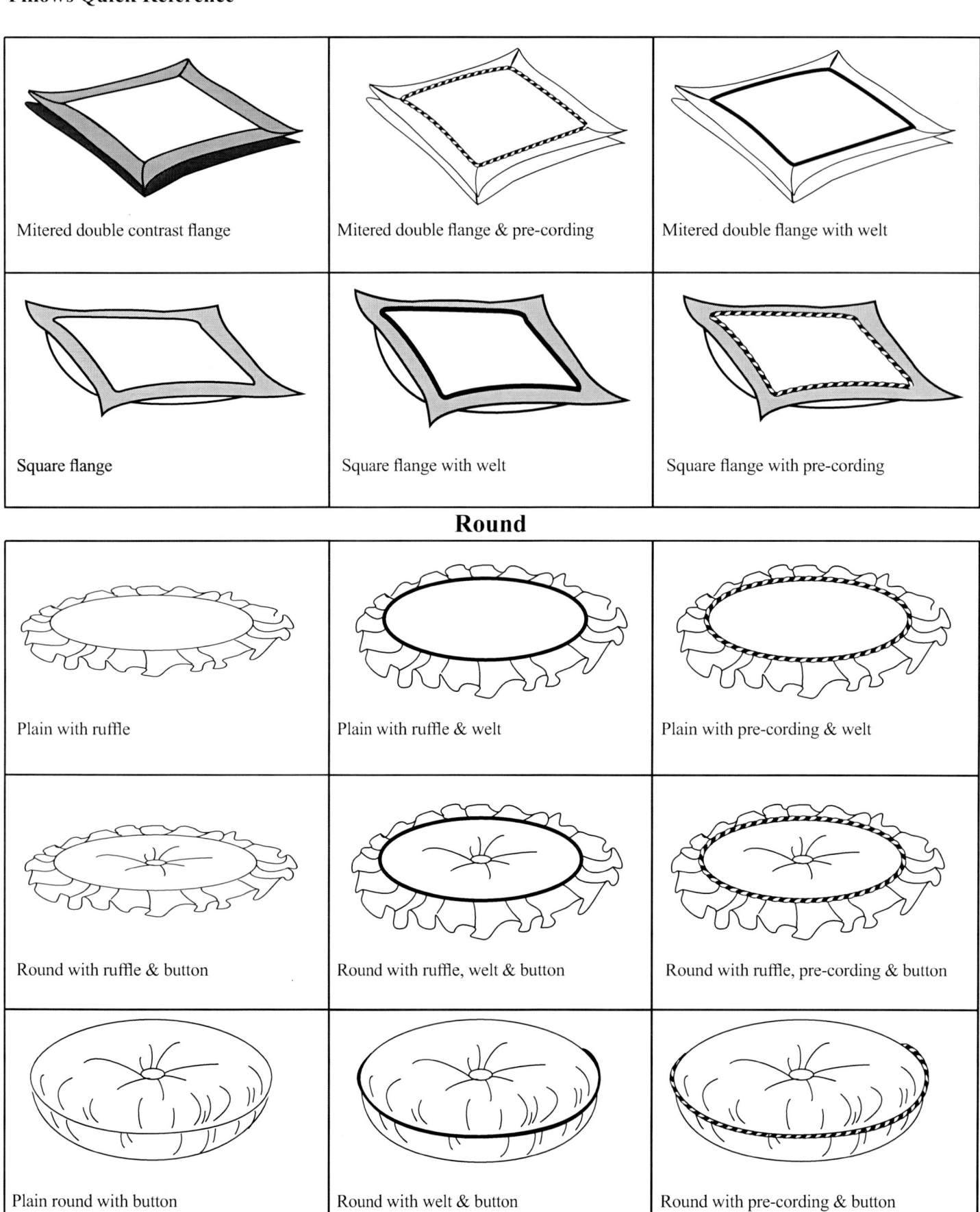

Mitered double contrast flange	Mitered double flange & pre-cording	Mitered double flange with welt
Square flange	Square flange with welt	Square flange with pre-cording

Round

Plain with ruffle	Plain with ruffle & welt	Plain with pre-cording & welt
Round with ruffle & button	Round with ruffle, welt & button	Round with ruffle, pre-cording & button
Plain round with button	Round with welt & button	Round with pre-cording & button

Pillows Quick Reference

Boxed

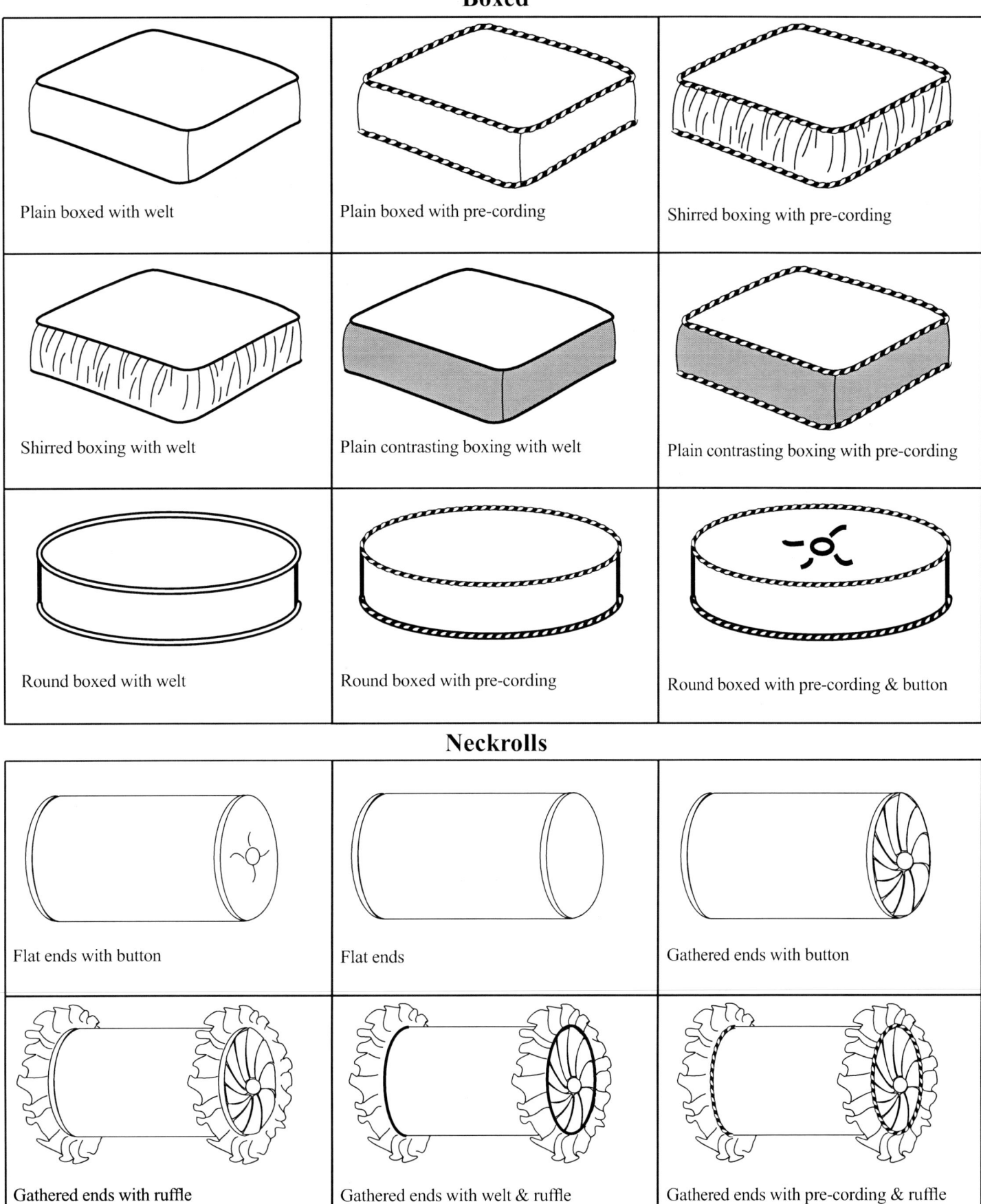

Plain boxed with welt	Plain boxed with pre-cording	Shirred boxing with pre-cording
Shirred boxing with welt	Plain contrasting boxing with welt	Plain contrasting boxing with pre-cording
Round boxed with welt	Round boxed with pre-cording	Round boxed with pre-cording & button

Neckrolls

Flat ends with button	Flat ends	Gathered ends with button
Gathered ends with ruffle	Gathered ends with welt & ruffle	Gathered ends with pre-cording & ruffle

Elements of Soft Treatments

Pillows Quick Reference

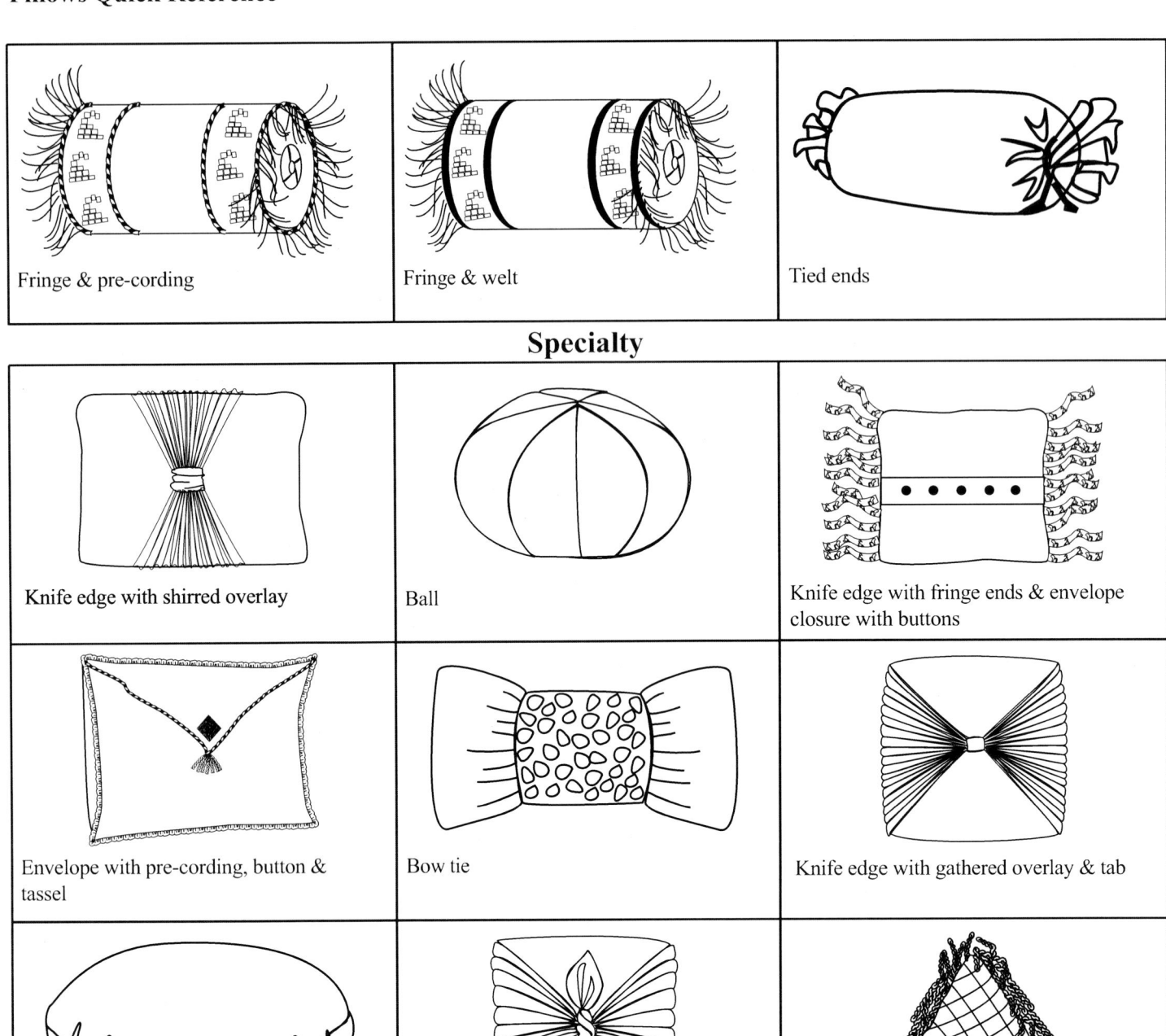

Fringe & pre-cording	Fringe & welt	Tied ends

Specialty

Knife edge with shirred overlay	Ball	Knife edge with fringe ends & envelope closure with buttons
Envelope with pre-cording, button & tassel	Bow tie	Knife edge with gathered overlay & tab
Large round floor pillow	Knife edge with gathered overlay & tie	Triangle with fringe

Soft Accessories Quick Reference

Canopies

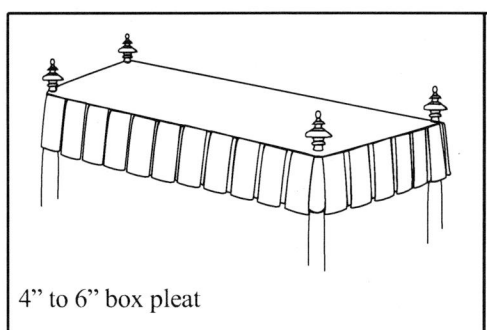

4" to 6" box pleat

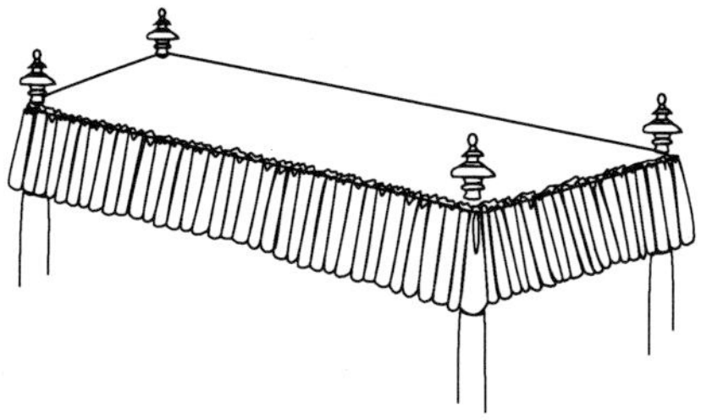

Gathered

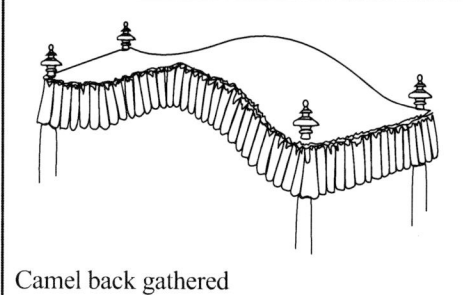

Camel back gathered

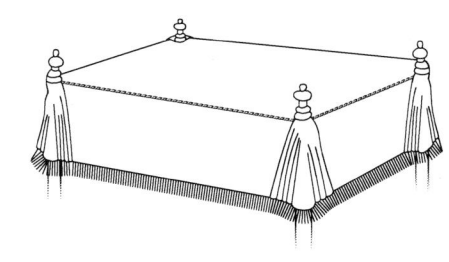

Gathered corners with fringe

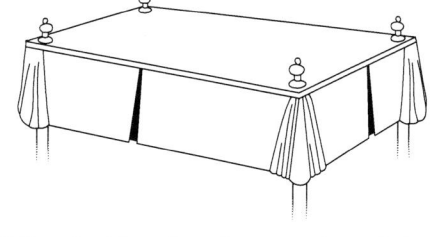

Tailored with gathered corners & corded top

Headboards

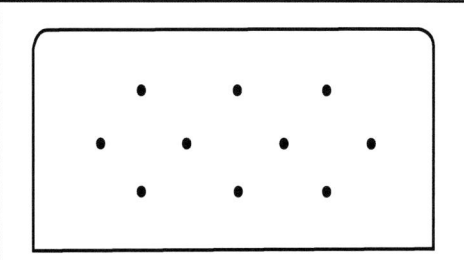

Rectangular button tufted

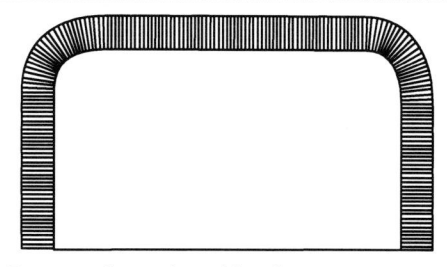

Rectangular gathered border

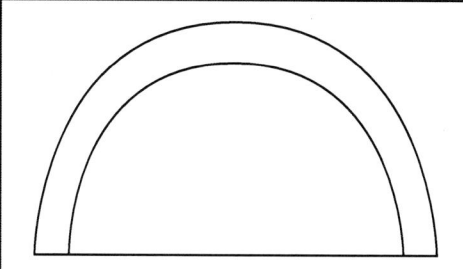

Half circle with plain border

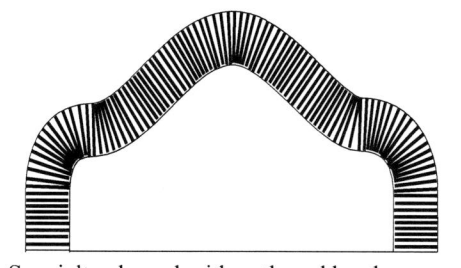

Specialty shaped with gathered border

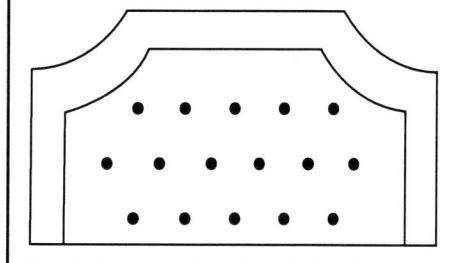

Specialty shaped with plain border & button tufted

Decorative Throws

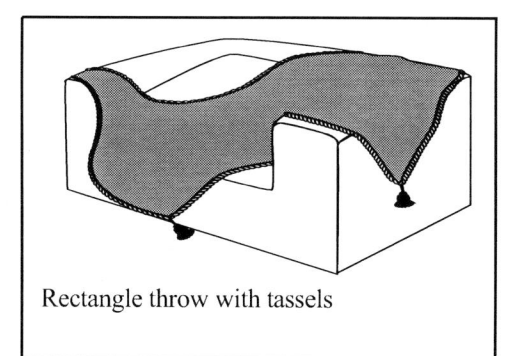

Rectangle throw with tassels

Elements of Soft Treatments

Soft Accessories Quick Reference

Table rounds

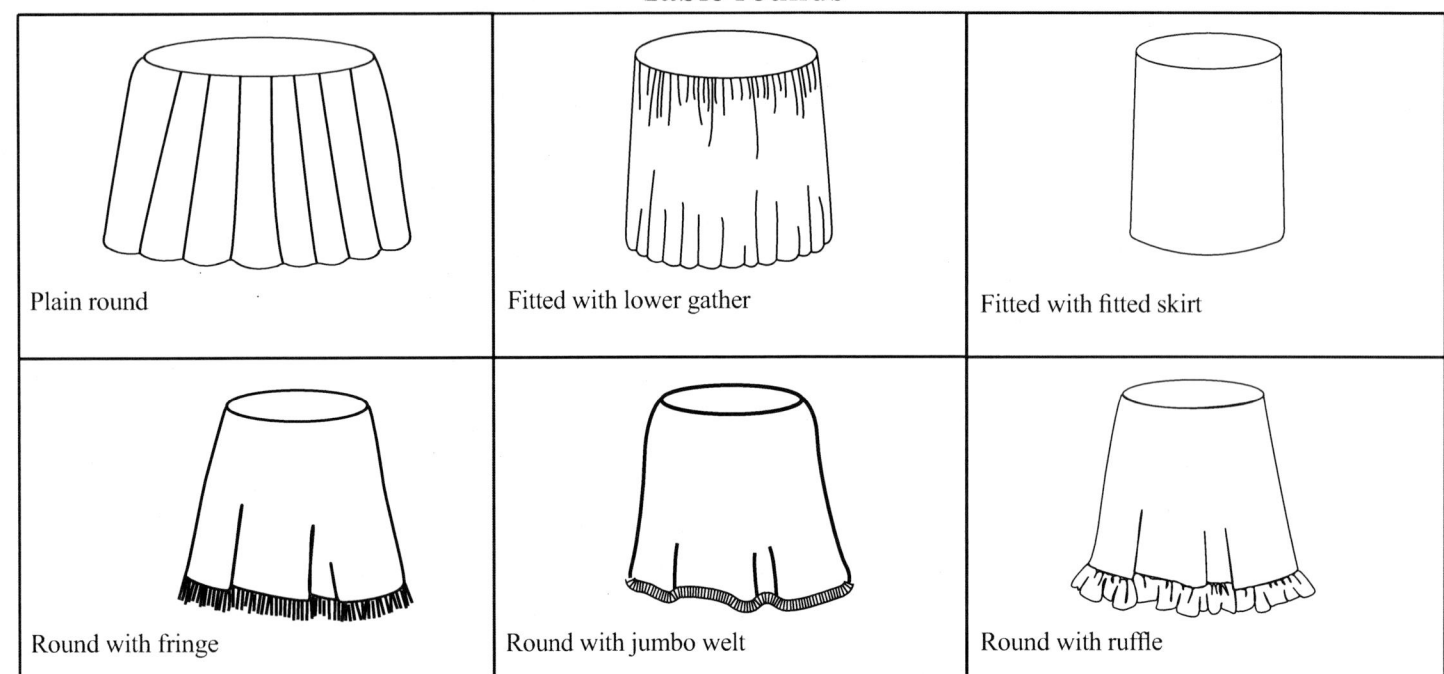

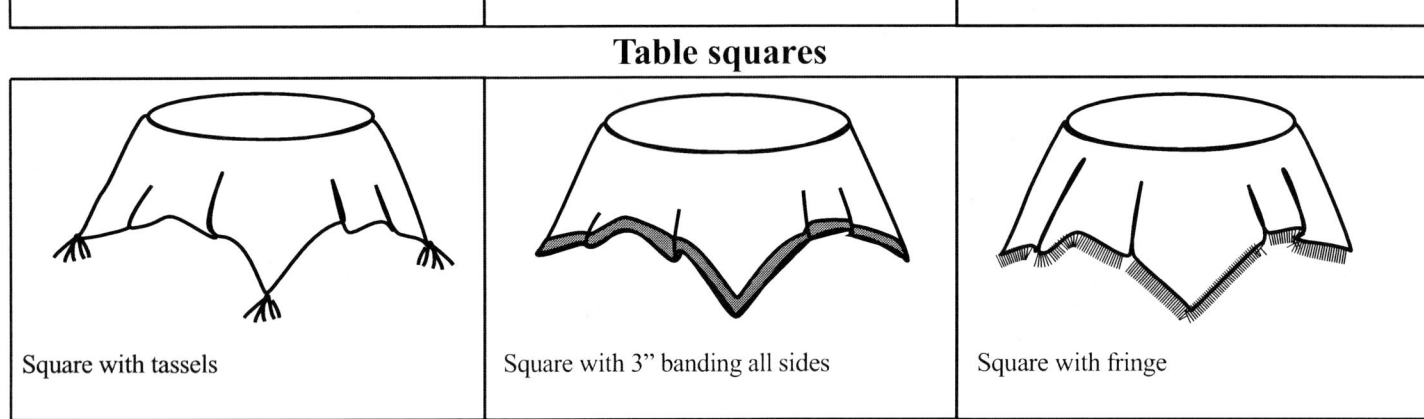

Plain round	Fitted with lower gather	Fitted with fitted skirt
Round with fringe	Round with jumbo welt	Round with ruffle

Table squares

Square with tassels	Square with 3" banding all sides	Square with fringe

Table Cloths

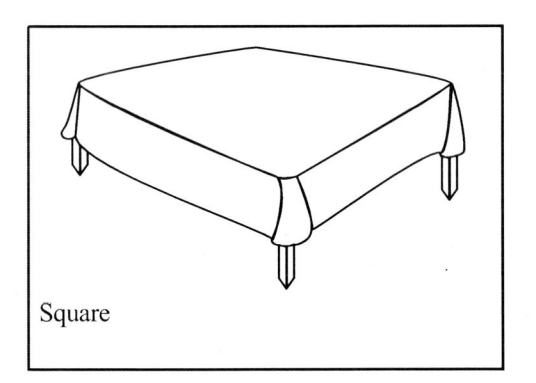

Square

Soft Accessories Quick Reference

Napkins

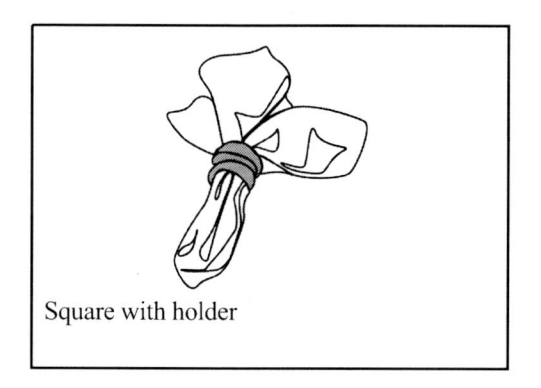

Square with holder

Table Runners

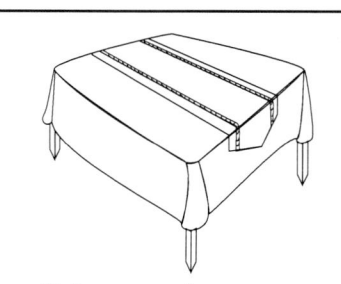

Runner with inset pre-trim

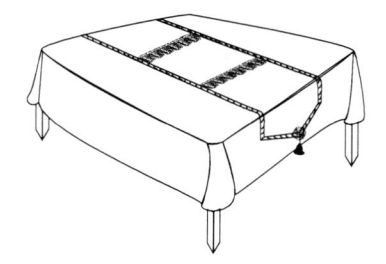

Runner with inset banding

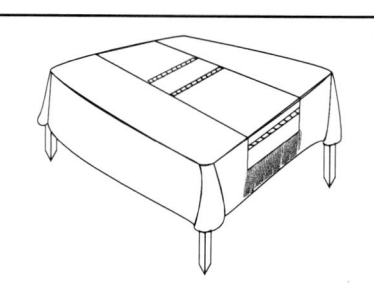

Runner with end bullion

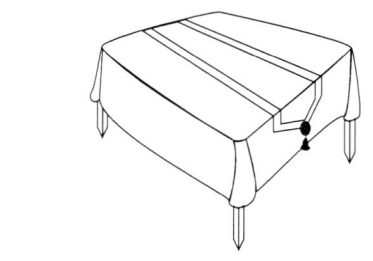

Runner with edge banding & tassels

Placemats

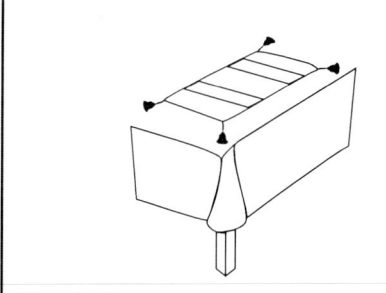

Tassels four corner

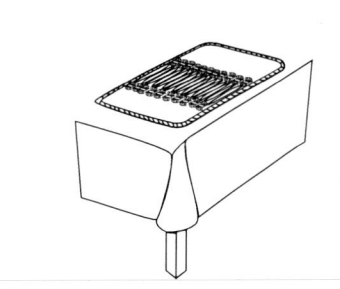

Applique in center

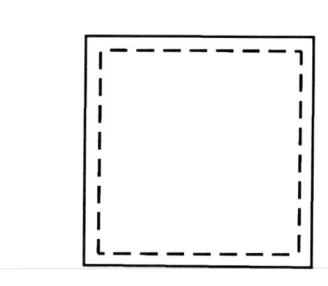

Square

Elements of Soft Treatments

295

Soft Accessories Quick Reference

| Rectangle | Oval | Cut corners |

Custom shape

Chair Pads

Knife edge with welt & ties

Knife edge with ruffle & ties

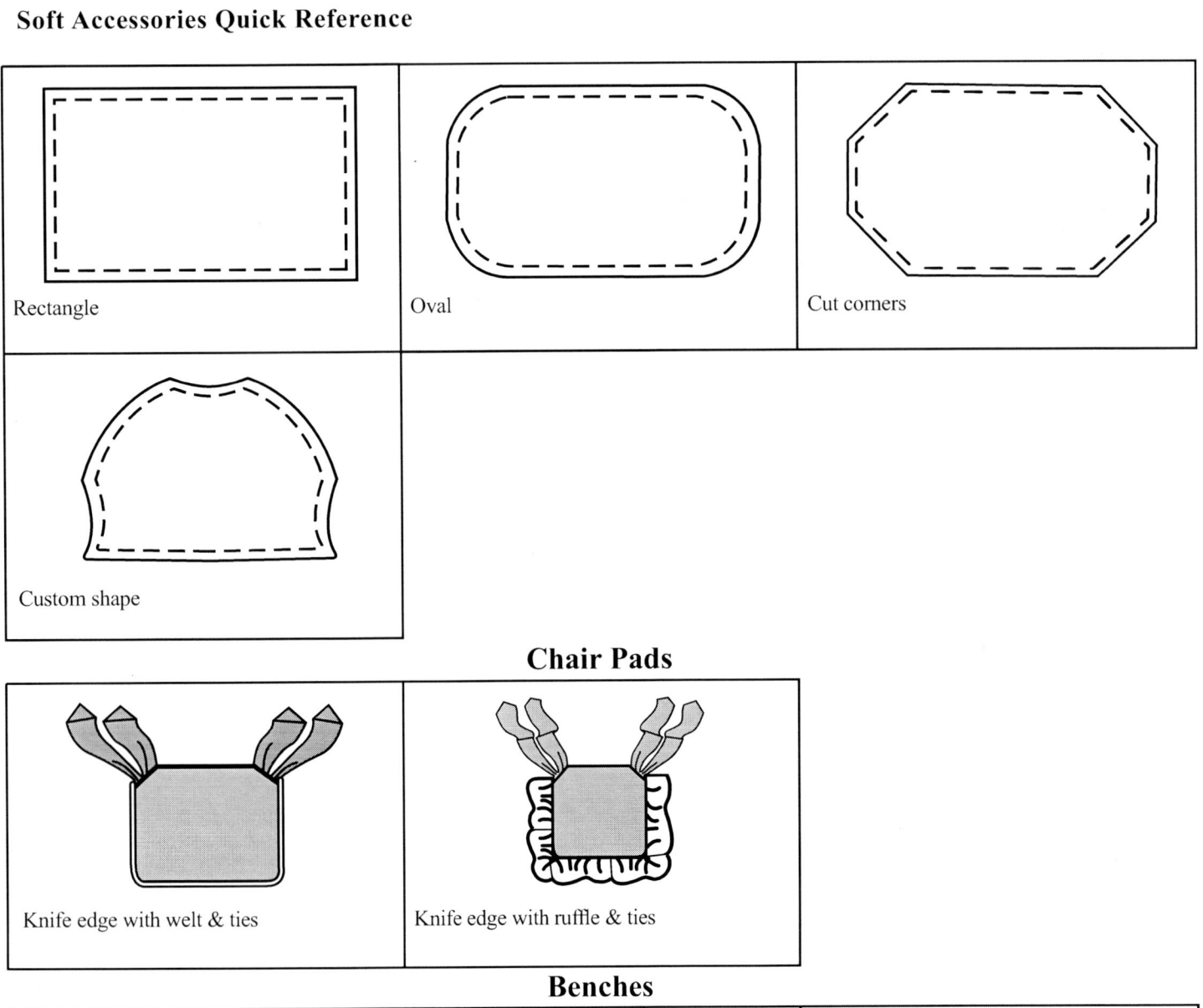

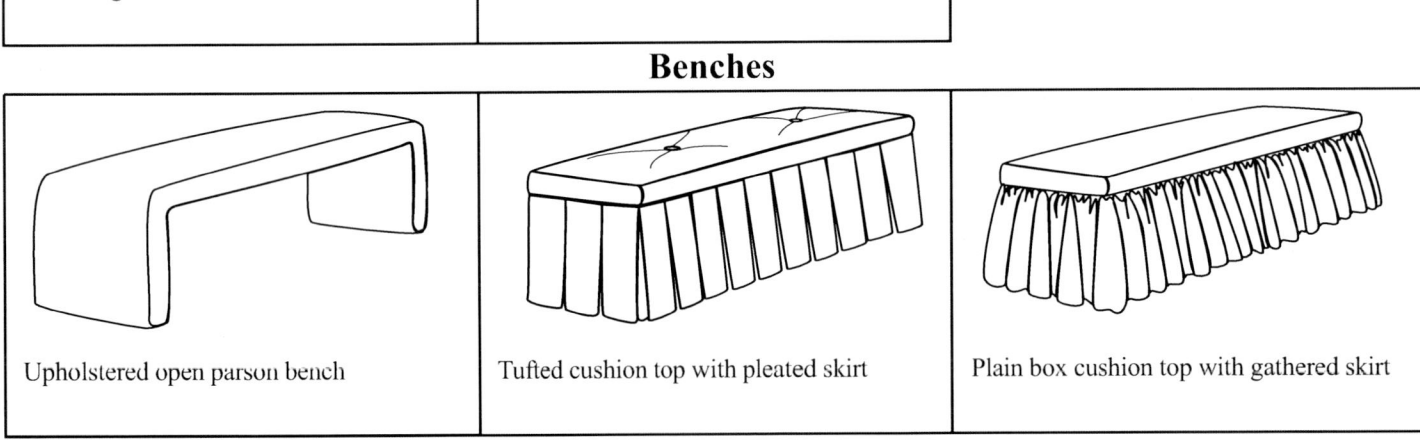

Benches

Upholstered open parson bench

Tufted cushion top with pleated skirt

Plain box cushion top with gathered skirt

Soft Accessories Quick Reference

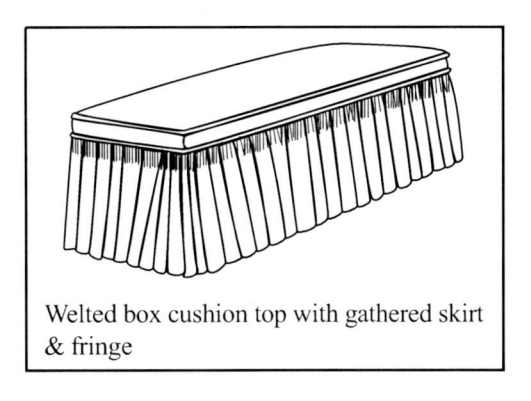

Welted box cushion top with gathered skirt & fringe

Foot Stools

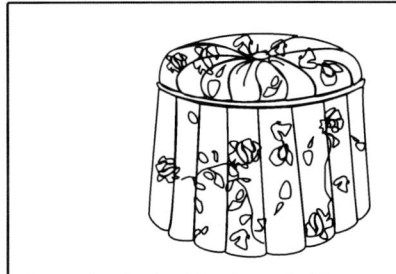

Round tufted with pleated skirt

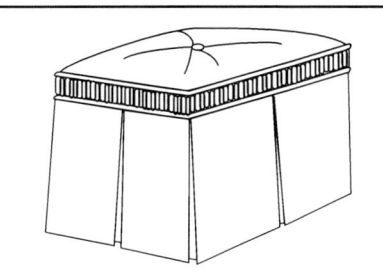

Welted with gathered boxing, button tufted & pleat skirt

Cushions & Bolsters

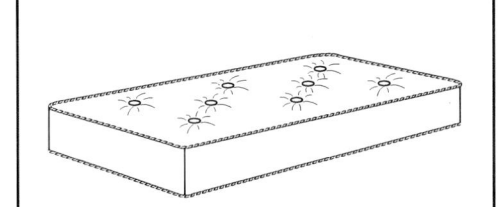

Box with pre-cording & button tufted

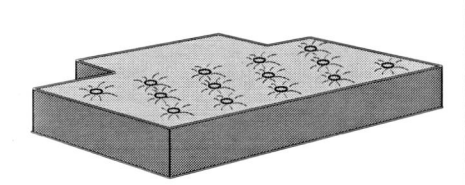

Custom cut outs

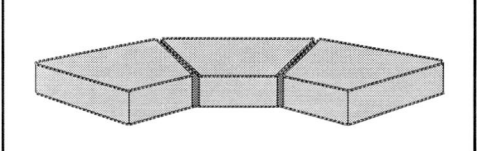

Bay window seats

Round boxed with welt

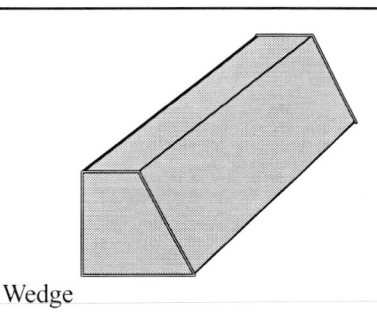

Wedge

Elements of Soft Treatments

Soft Accessories Quick Reference

Slip Covers

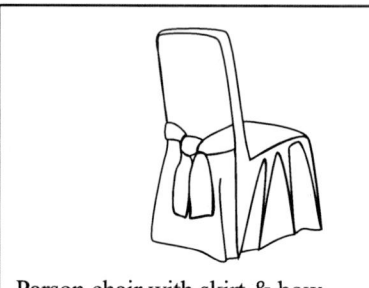

Parson chair with skirt & bow

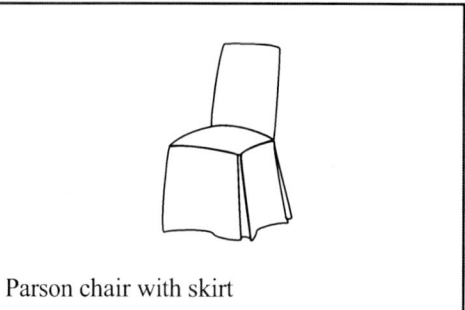

Parson chair with skirt

Furniture

Upholstered sofa

Add-on Quick Reference

Banding

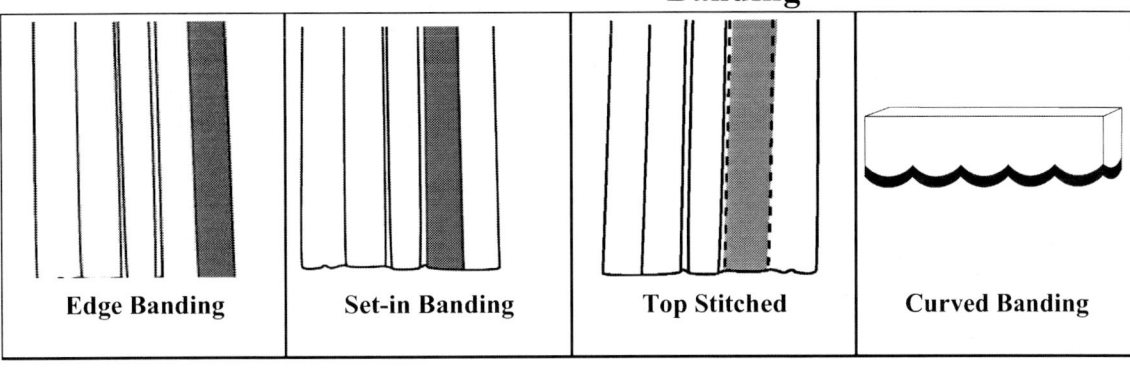

| Edge Banding | Set-in Banding | Top Stitched | Curved Banding |

Build Ups

| Standard Box Pleat | Box Pleat Center Only | Box Pleat Ends Only | Box Pleat Center & Ends | Box Pleat 3 Panel |

| Box Pleat 4 Panel | Invert Box Pleat | Inverted Box Pleat with Scallops | Box Pleat with Scallops | Pleated Balloon |

| Gathered Balloon | Austrians Types | Self Valance |

Elements of Soft Treatments

Add-on Quick Reference

Buttons/Similar Items

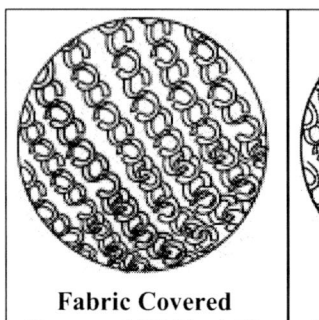

Fabric Covered Buttons 1/2" To 1.5"	Fabric Covered Buttons 1-7/8" To 3"	Decorative Nail Head(You Supply)	Pre-made Buttons(You Supply)	Tassel & Rosettes

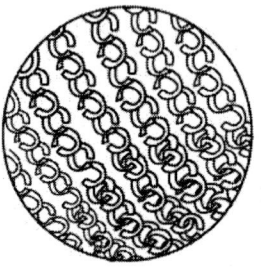

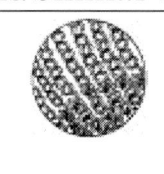

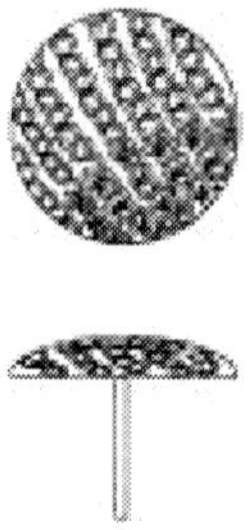

Tassel

Caps

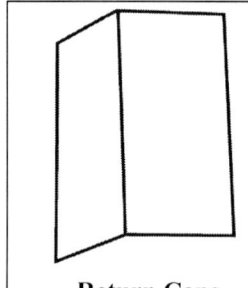

Return Caps	Return Cap with End Pleats

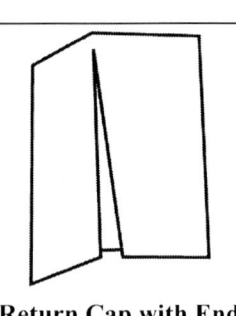

Add-on Quick Reference

Cascades

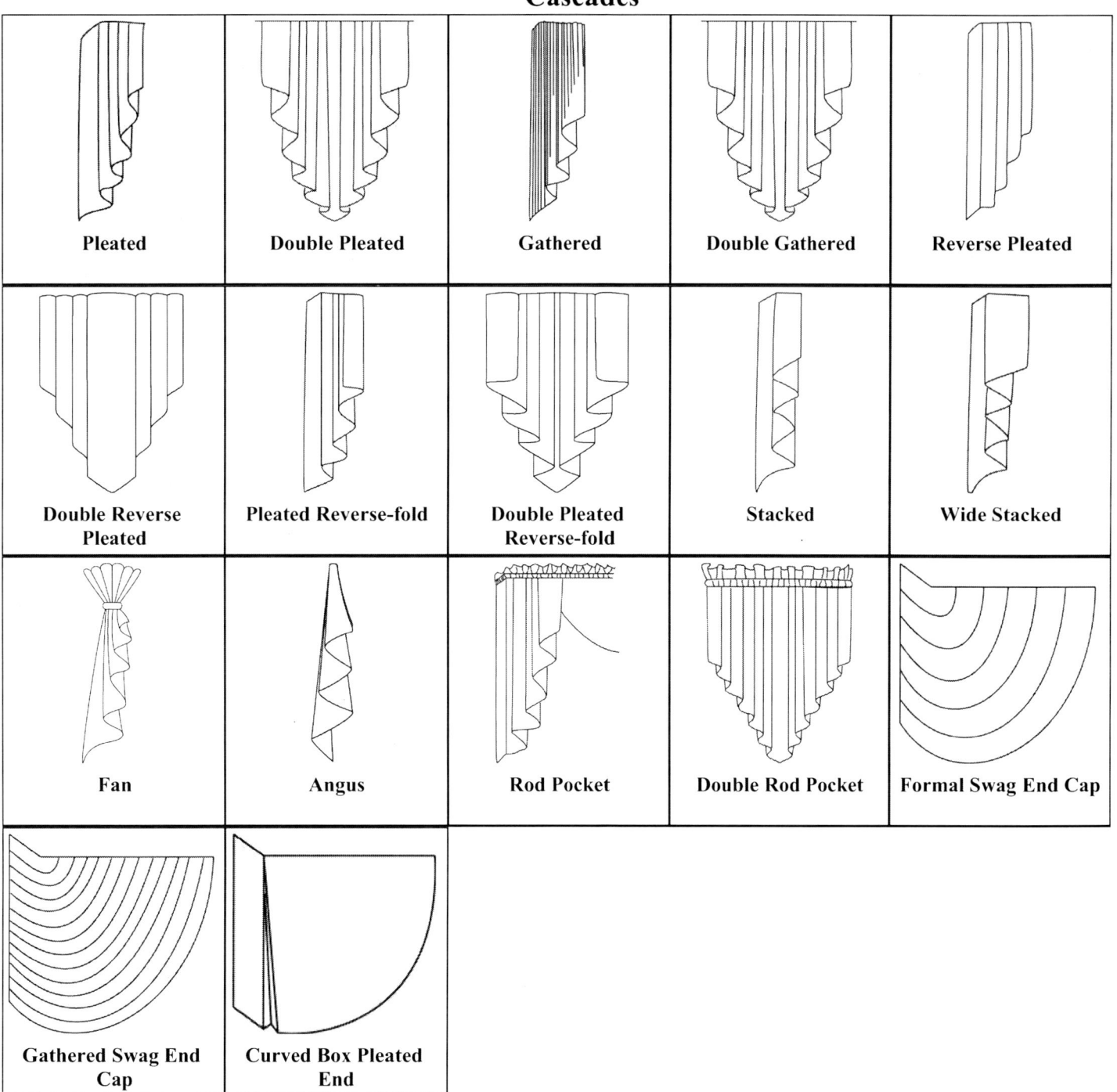

Pleated	Double Pleated	Gathered	Double Gathered	Reverse Pleated
Double Reverse Pleated	Pleated Reverse-fold	Double Pleated Reverse-fold	Stacked	Wide Stacked
Fan	Angus	Rod Pocket	Double Rod Pocket	Formal Swag End Cap
Gathered Swag End Cap	Curved Box Pleated End			

Elements of Soft Treatments

Add-on Quick Reference

Contrast

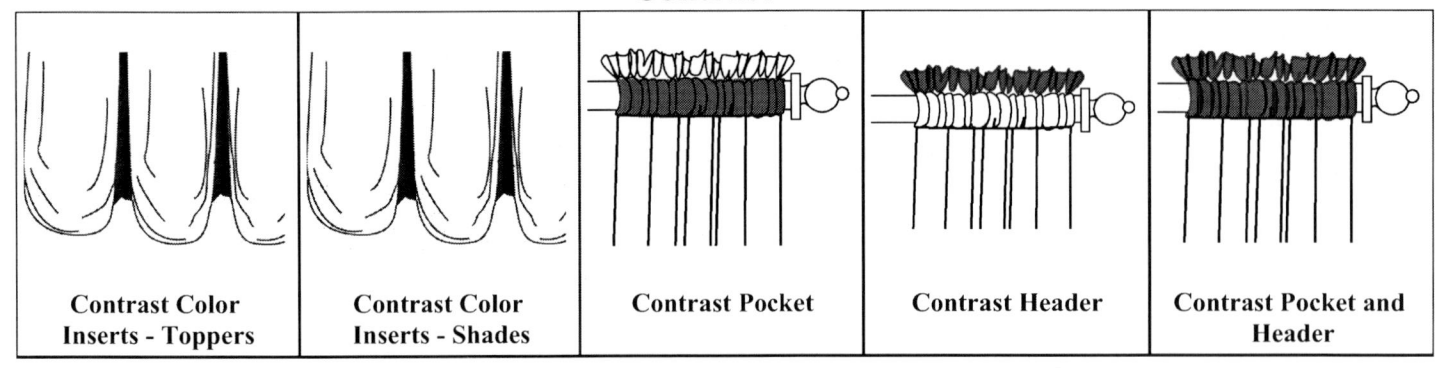

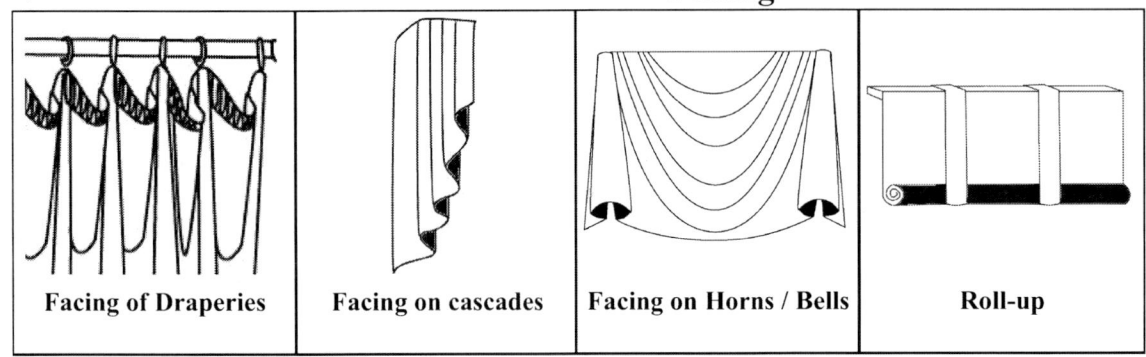

| Contrast Color Inserts - Toppers | Contrast Color Inserts - Shades | Contrast Pocket | Contrast Header | Contrast Pocket and Header |

Facing

| Facing of Draperies | Facing on cascades | Facing on Horns / Bells | Roll-up |

Fringe

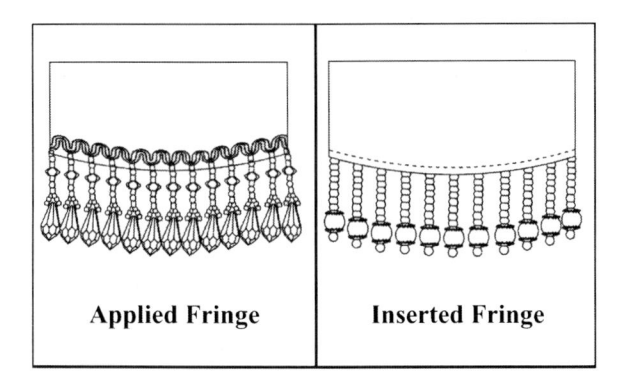

| Applied Fringe | Inserted Fringe |

Add-on Quick Reference

Inlays or Overlays

Inlay Curved	Inlay Straight Egdes	Inlay Window Flat (shaped)	Inlay Window Shirred (shaped)	Inlay Window Pleated (shaped)
Inlay Diamond Effect	Inlay Diagonal	Inlay Vertical Shirred	Underlayer Square or Rectangle	Overlay Gathered
Overlay Square or Rectangle Piece	Overlay Flat (shaped)	Overlay Shirred (shaped)	Overlay Pleated (shaped)	Overlay Patch Work

Elements of Soft Treatments

Add-on Quick Reference

Jabots

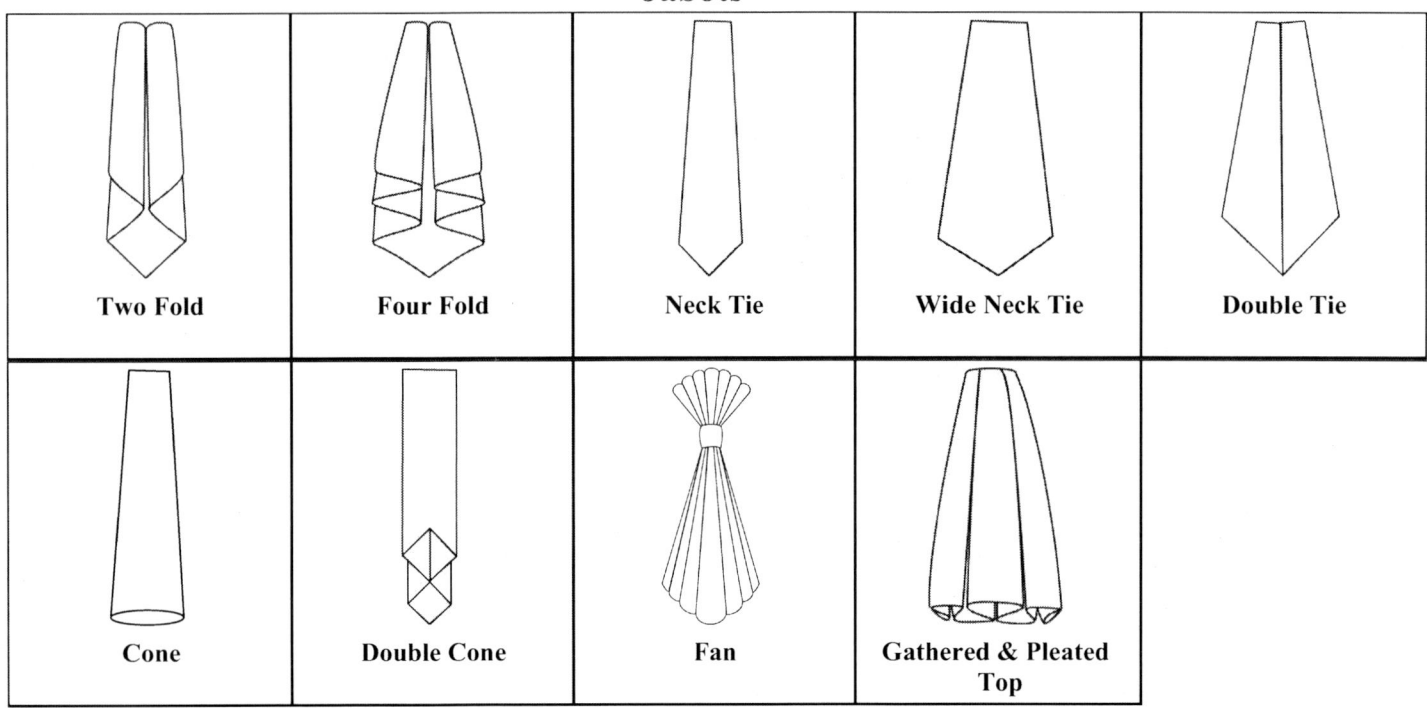

Two Fold	Four Fold	Neck Tie	Wide Neck Tie	Double Tie
Cone	Double Cone	Fan	Gathered & Pleated Top	

Miscellaneous

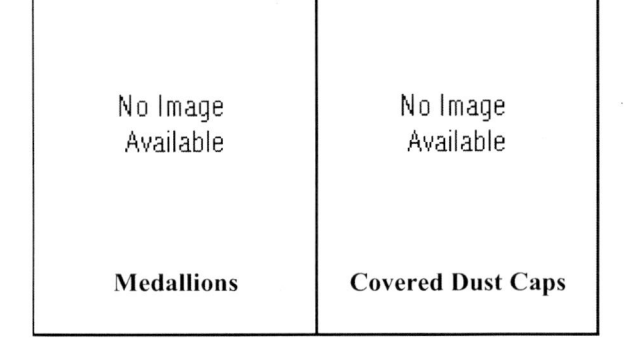

Medallions (No Image Available)	Covered Dust Caps (No Image Available)

Panels

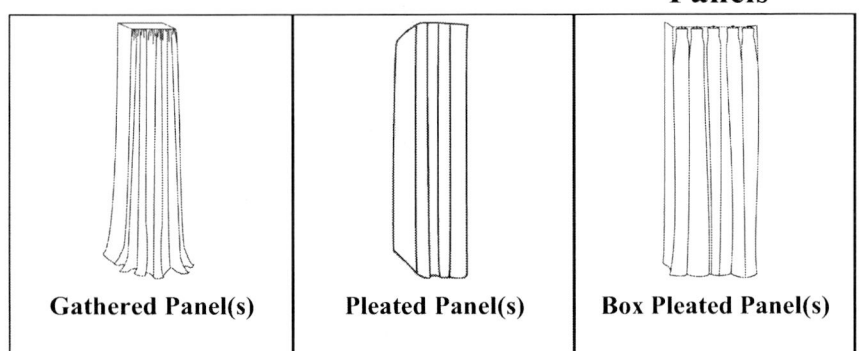

Gathered Panel(s)	Pleated Panel(s)	Box Pleated Panel(s)

Add-on Quick Reference

Pelmets

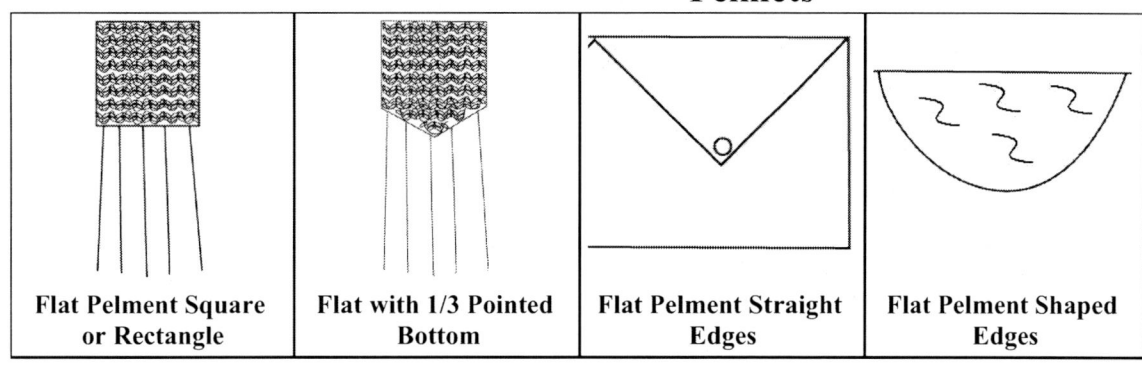

| Flat Pelment Square or Rectangle | Flat with 1/3 Pointed Bottom | Flat Pelment Straight Edges | Flat Pelment Shaped Edges |

Petticoats

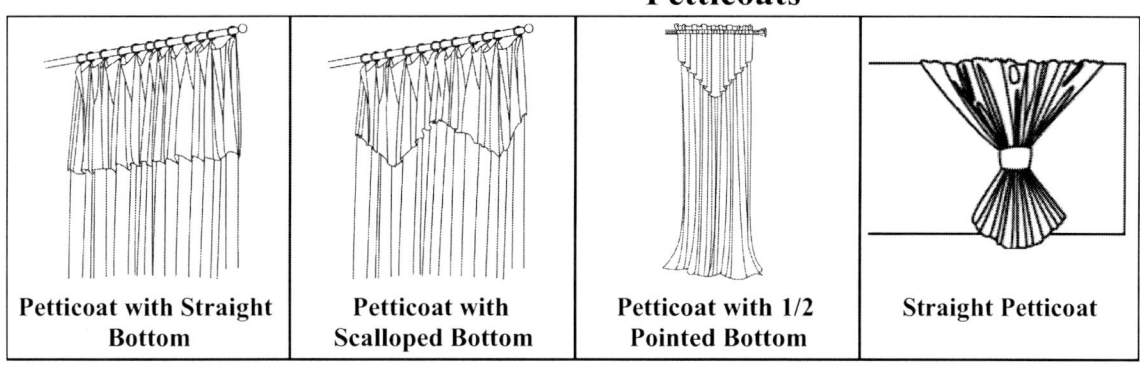

| Petticoat with Straight Bottom | Petticoat with Scalloped Bottom | Petticoat with 1/2 Pointed Bottom | Straight Petticoat |

Pre-cording

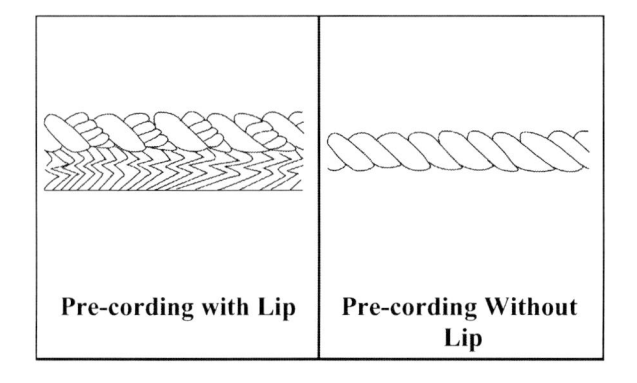

| Pre-cording with Lip | Pre-cording Without Lip |

Pre-trims

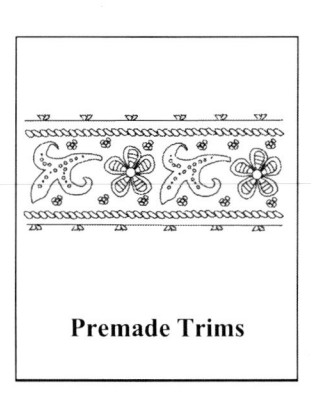

Premade Trims

Elements of Soft Treatments

305

Add-on Quick Reference

Rosettes/Knots/Bows

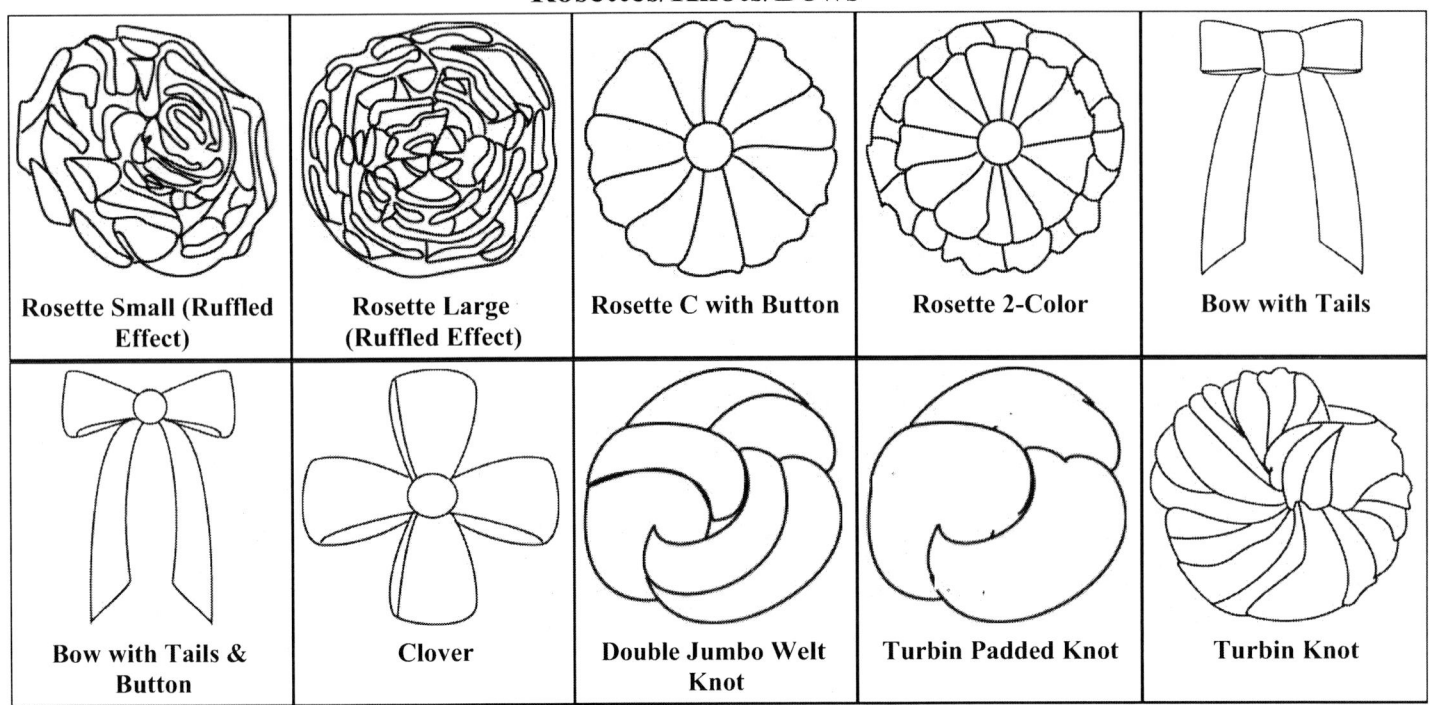

Rosette Small (Ruffled Effect)	Rosette Large (Ruffled Effect)	Rosette C with Button	Rosette 2-Color	Bow with Tails
Bow with Tails & Button	Clover	Double Jumbo Welt Knot	Turbin Padded Knot	Turbin Knot

Ruffles

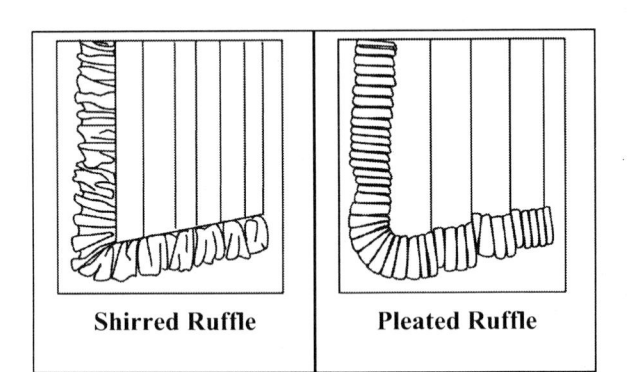

Shirred Ruffle	Pleated Ruffle

Add-on Quick Reference

Swags - For Draperies

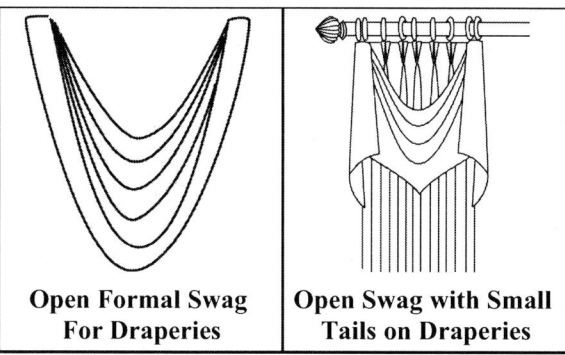

| Open Formal Swag For Draperies | Open Swag with Small Tails on Draperies |

Swags - Medallions

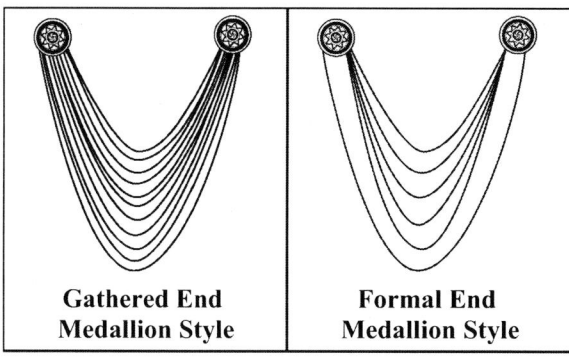

| Gathered End Medallion Style | Formal End Medallion Style |

Swags - Open Tops

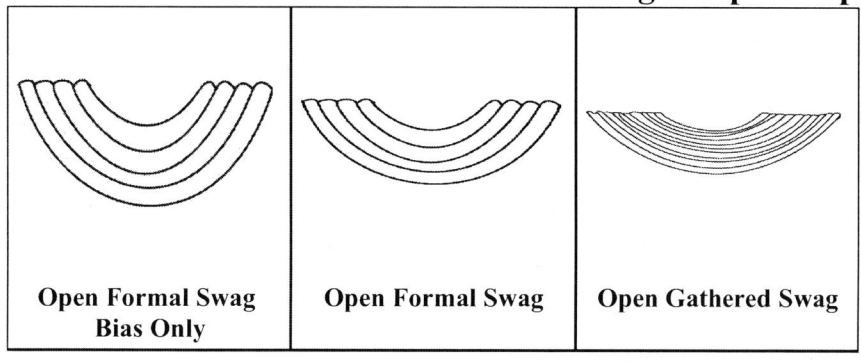

| Open Formal Swag Bias Only | Open Formal Swag | Open Gathered Swag |

Swags - Tabs

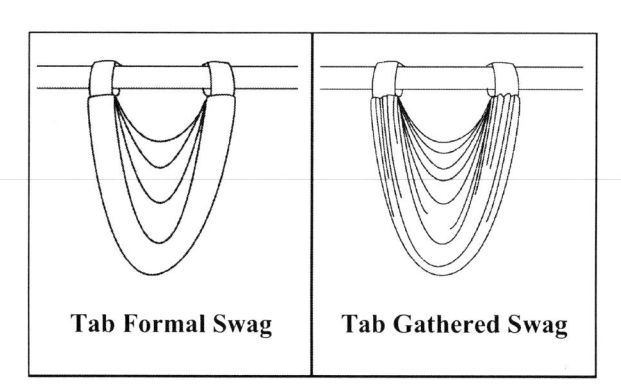

| Tab Formal Swag | Tab Gathered Swag |

Elements of Soft Treatments

Add-on Quick Reference

Swags - Traditional Formal

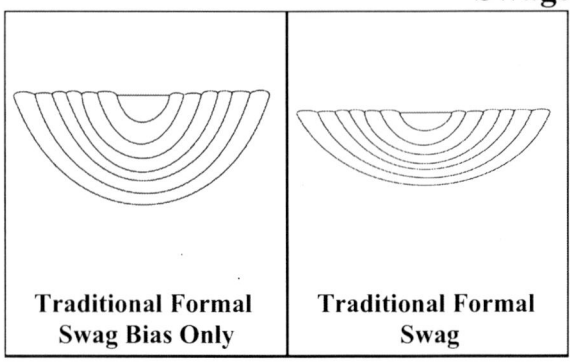

Traditional Formal Swag Bias Only

Traditional Formal Swag

Swags - Traditional Gathered

Traditional Gathered Swag

Add-on Quick Reference

Tabs

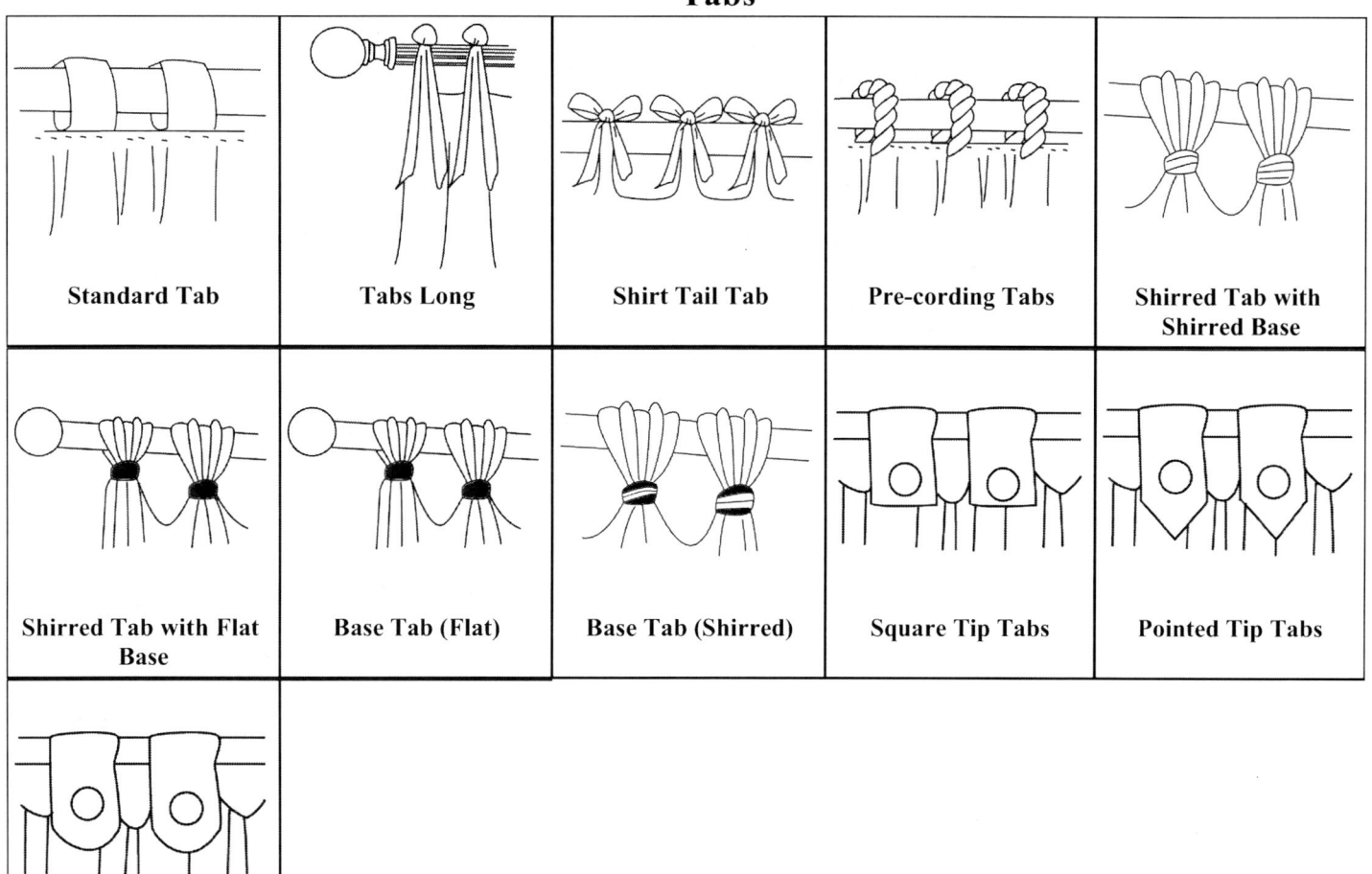

Standard Tab	Tabs Long	Shirt Tail Tab	Pre-cording Tabs	Shirred Tab with Shirred Base
Shirred Tab with Flat Base	Base Tab (Flat)	Base Tab (Shirred)	Square Tip Tabs	Pointed Tip Tabs
Curved Tabs				

Elements of Soft Treatments

Add-on Quick Reference

Tiebacks

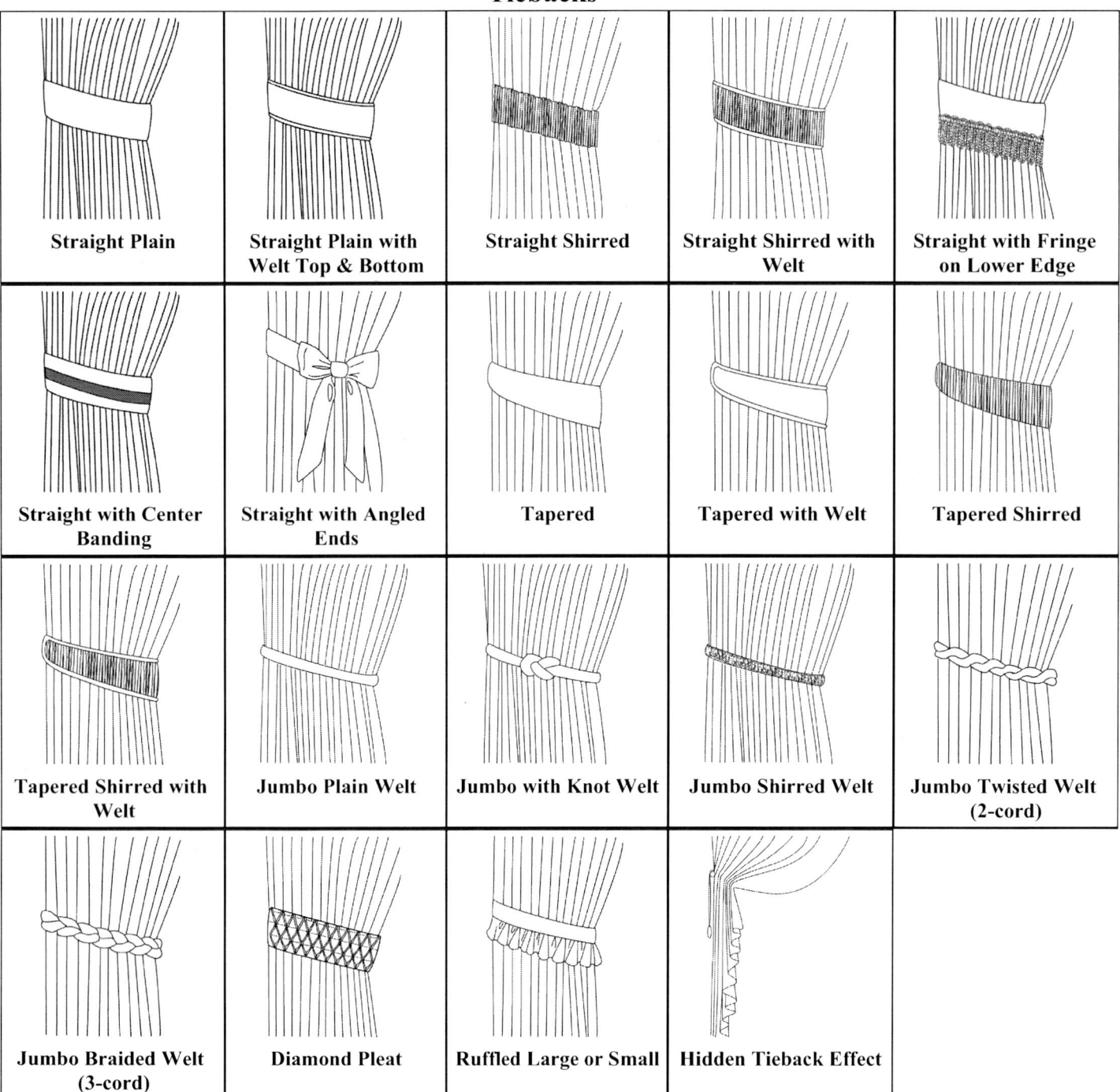

Straight Plain	Straight Plain with Welt Top & Bottom	Straight Shirred	Straight Shirred with Welt	Straight with Fringe on Lower Edge
Straight with Center Banding	Straight with Angled Ends	Tapered	Tapered with Welt	Tapered Shirred
Tapered Shirred with Welt	Jumbo Plain Welt	Jumbo with Knot Welt	Jumbo Shirred Welt	Jumbo Twisted Welt (2-cord)
Jumbo Braided Welt (3-cord)	Diamond Pleat	Ruffled Large or Small	Hidden Tieback Effect	

Add-on Quick Reference

Ties

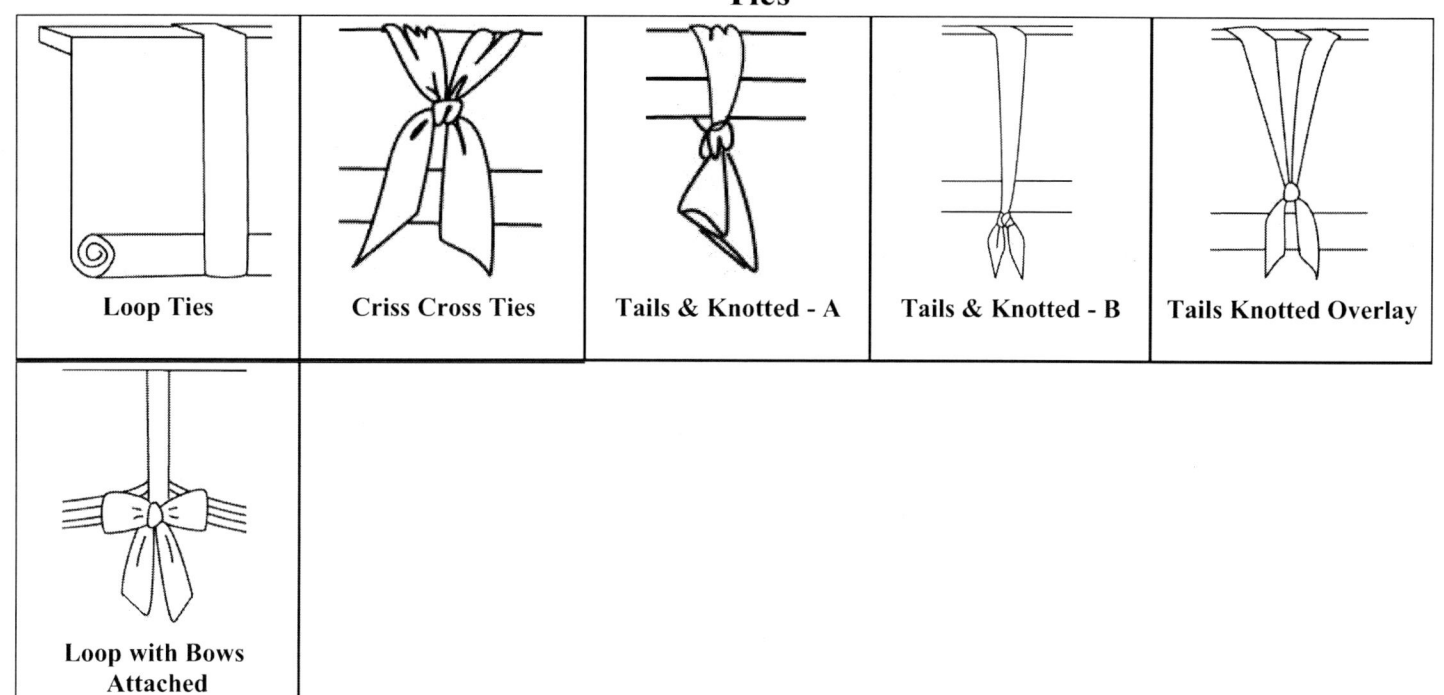

Loop Ties	Criss Cross Ties	Tails & Knotted - A	Tails & Knotted - B	Tails Knotted Overlay

Loop with Bows Attached

Upholstery Items

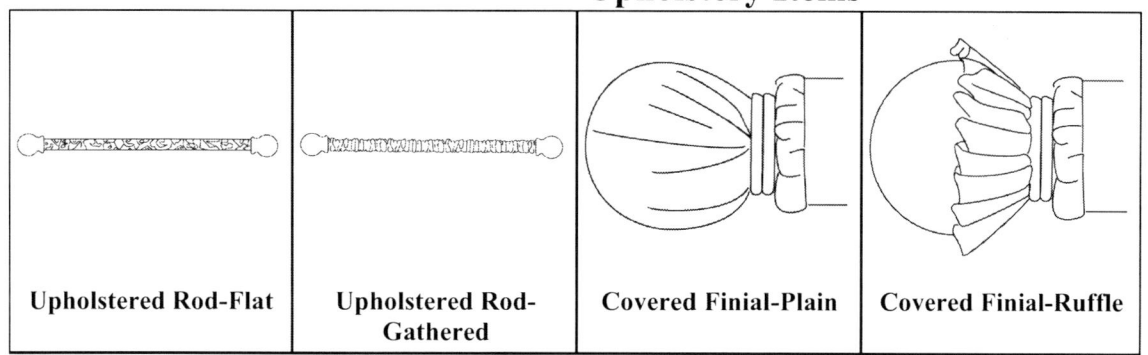

Upholstered Rod-Flat	Upholstered Rod-Gathered	Covered Finial-Plain	Covered Finial-Ruffle

Elements of Soft Treatments

Add-on Quick Reference

Welts

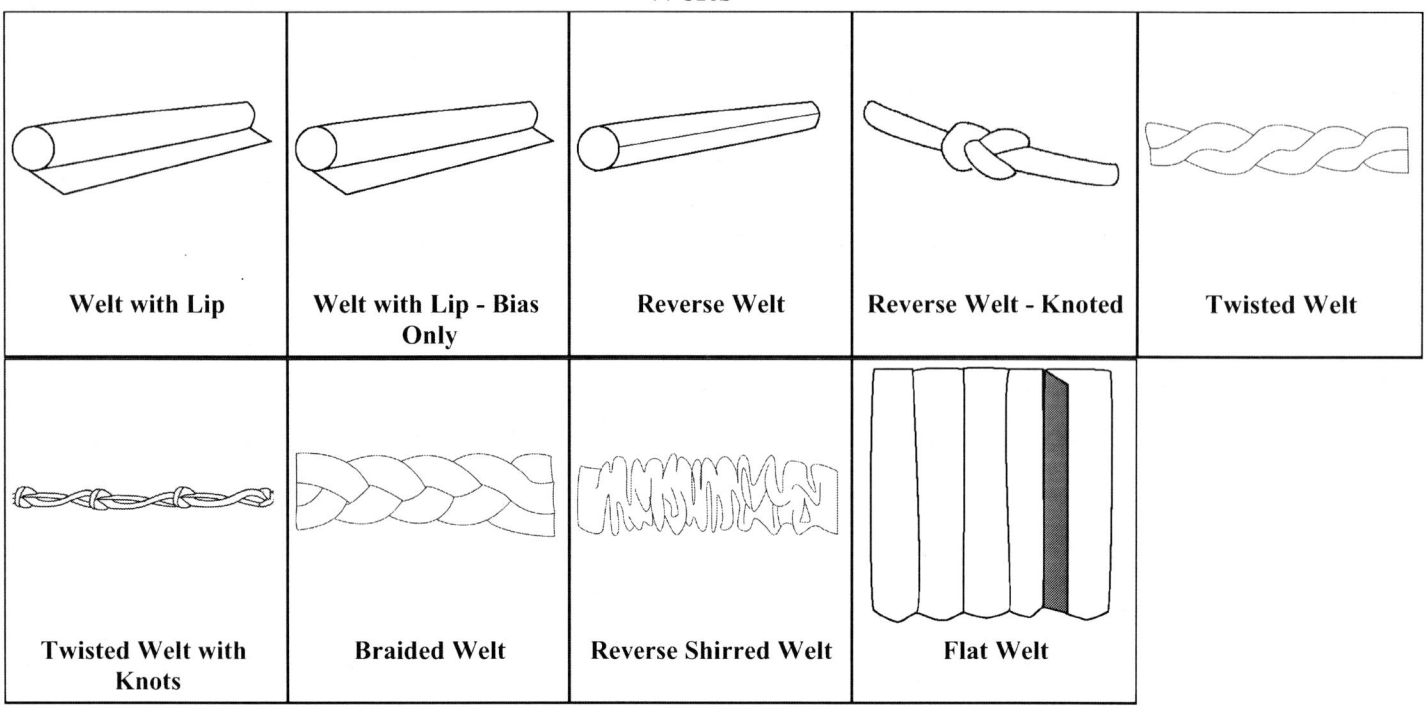

Welt with Lip	Welt with Lip - Bias Only	Reverse Welt	Reverse Welt - Knoted	Twisted Welt
Twisted Welt with Knots	Braided Welt	Reverse Shirred Welt	Flat Welt	

APPENDIX D
Work Orders

Here is a collection of work orders that can be used for each treatment category.

DRAPERIES
WORK ORDER FORM

BILL TO: _____ P.O.# _____ ORDER # _____ PAGE _____ OF _____

FIRM NAME _____ QUOTE ☐ # _____ NEED BY: _____ TODAY'S DATE _____

YOUR NAME _____ WORKORDER ☐ SHIP VIA _____

STREET _____ SAVE FABRIC ☐ CUSTOMER _____

CITY _____ STATE _____ ZIP _____ STREET _____

PHONE _____ FAX _____ CITY _____ STATE _____ ZIP _____

PHONE _____ FAX _____

QUOTE—LABOR ☐ YARDAGE ☐ HARDWARE ☐ INSTALL ☐ MEASURE ☐

REFERENCE
X = WHERE APPLIED

#	ITEM #	QUANTITY	ROOM	STYLE #	PAIR	PANEL	LEFT STACK	RIGHT STACK	CTN. PANEL	# OF WIDTHS	FULLNESS	ROD WIDTH	FIN. LENGTH	RETURNS	OVERLAPS (OL)	PIN/HOOK SET	THERMAL	SATIN SHEEN	BLACKOUT	SELF	C.O.M.	OTHER	WHITE	IVORY	TRIM SIZE / OTHER	PLACEMENT
1																										
2																										

	VENDOR/PATTERN	WIDTH / RPT	VENDOR/PATTERN	WIDTH / RPT	VENDOR/PATTERN	WIDTH / RPT
Fabric #A						
Fabric #B						
Fabric #C						

TIEBACKS

	QTY	STYLE	WIDTH	LENGTH
#1				

FABRIC # _____
OTHER _____

	QTY	STYLE	WIDTH	LENGTH
#2				

FABRIC # _____
OTHER _____

HARDWARE	QTY

INSTALLATION INSTRUCTIONS

PLACEMENT

ITEM #	#1	#2
CEILING		
ABOVE TRIM		
ON TRIM		
SILL		
APRON		
FLOOR		
PUDDLE		
OUTSIDE MT		
INSIDE MT		
SIDE HANGS INTO WINDOW		
TIEBACK INTO WINDOW		

#1 OPTIONS / SPECIAL INSTRUCTIONS / DRAWINGS

#2 OPTIONS / SPECIAL INSTRUCTIONS / DRAWINGS

☐ Check here if DRAPERIES is to match (cut from the same bolt of fabric)
Swags, Cornices, rod pockets, shades, etc. which accompany this order

Authorization signature _____ Date _____

REV. 12/05

ROD POCKETS PANELS ORDER FORM

BILL TO:
- FIRM NAME
- YOUR NAME
- STREET
- CITY _____ STATE _____ ZIP _____
- PHONE _____ FAX _____
- QUOTE—LABOR ☐   YARDAGE ☐   HARDWARE ☐   INSTALL ☐   MEASURE ☐

P.O.# _____   QUOTE ☐ #_____   SAVE FABRIC ☐
WORKORDER ☐

ORDER # _____   PAGE _____ OF _____
NEED BY: _____ TODAY'S DATE _____
SHIP VIA _____
CUSTOMER _____
STREET _____
CITY _____ STATE _____ ZIP _____
PHONE _____ FAX _____

REFERENCE X = WHERE APPLIED

ITEM	QUANTITY	ROOM	BOARD MOUNT	STYLE	FULLNESS	PAIR	PANEL	LEFT STACK	RIGHT STACK	CTN. PANEL	# OF WIDTHS	ROD WIDTH	FINISHED LENGTH	RETURNS	RETURN CUT-OUT	HEADING	POCKET	TOP & BOTTOM	THERMAL	SATIN SHEEN	BLACKOUT	SELF	C.O.M	OTHER	WHITE	IVORY	TRIM SIZE / OTHER	PLACEMENT

1
2

#1   Fabric #A   VENDOR/PATTERN   WIDTH / RPT

#2   Fabric #B   VENDOR/PATTERN   WIDTH / RPT

Fabric #C   VENDOR/PATTERN   WIDTH / RPT

#1 OPTIONS / SPECIAL INSTRUCTIONS / DRAWINGS

#2 OPTIONS / SPECIAL INSTRUCTIONS / DRAWINGS

TIEBACKS

	STYLE	WIDTH	LENGTH
#1 QTY			
FABRIC #			
OTHER			
#2 QTY	STYLE	WIDTH	LENGTH
FABRIC #			
OTHER			
QTY	HARDWARE		

INSTALLATION INSTRUCTIONS PLACEMENT

ITEM #	#1	#2
CEILING		
ABOVE TRIM		
ON TRIM		
SILL		
APRON		
FLOOR		
PUDDLE		
OUTSIDE MT		
INSIDE MT		
SIDE HANGS INTO WINDOW		
TIEBACK INTO WINDOW		

☐ Check here if ROD POCKET PANEL is to match (cut from the same bolt of fabric) Swags, Cornices, Draperies or shades etc. which accompany this order

REV. 12/05

Authorization signature _____   Date _____

TOPPERS
WORK ORDER FORM

BILL TO: _____ P.O.#_____ QUOTE ☐ #_____ ORDER #_____ PAGE_____ OF_____

FIRM NAME_____ WORKORDER ☐ NEED BY:_____ TODAY'S DATE_____

YOUR NAME_____ SAVE FABRIC ☐ SHIP VIA_____

STREET_____ STATE_____ ZIP_____ CUSTOMER_____

CITY_____ STATE_____ STREET_____

PHONE_____ FAX_____ CITY_____ STATE_____ ZIP_____

QUOTE—LABOR ☐ YARDAGE ☐ HARDWARE ☐ INSTALL ☐ MEASURE ☐ PHONE_____ FAX_____

REFERENCE   X = WHERE APPLIED

ITEM #	ROOM	QUANTITY	STYLE	FACE WIDTH	RETURNS	REDUCED HEADER	FINISHED LENGTH	MEDIUM POINT	SHORT POINT	FULLNESS	# OF WIDTHS	ROD POCKET (IF NEEDED)	HEADER (IF NEEDED)	UPRIGHT (SEAMS)	RAILROAD	SEE TOP OF DUSTCAP	OUTSIDE MT	INSIDE MT (WKRM MAKE ALLOWANCES)	THERMAL	BLACKOUT	SATIN SHEEN	SELF	C.O.M.	OTHER	WHITE	IVORY	SIZE TRIM / OTHER	PLACEMENT
1																												
2																												

Fabric #A	VENDOR/PATTERN	WIDTH / RPT	Fabric #B	VENDOR/PATTERN	WIDTH / RPT	Fabric #C	VENDOR/PATTERN	WIDTH / RPT

#1 OPTIONS / SPECIAL INSTRUCTIONS / DRAWINGS

#2 OPTIONS / SPECIAL INSTRUCTIONS / DRAWINGS

INSTALLATION INSTRUCTIONS
PLACEMENT

ITEM #	#1	#2
CEILING		
ABOVE TRIM		
ON TRIM		
LEFT (inches)		
BOARD EXTENSION		
RIGHT (inches)		
OUTSIDE MT		
INSIDE MT		
REMOVE OLD		
HARDWARE PAGES		

☐ Check here if TOPPER is to match (cut from the same bolt of fabric) Swags, Cornices, rod pockets or pinch pleats… etc which accompany this order

Authorization signature_____ Date_____

REV. 12/05

DRAPERY VALANCE WORK ORDER FORM

BILL TO:
- P.O.#
- FIRM NAME
- YOUR NAME
- STREET
- CITY _____ STATE _____ ZIP
- PHONE _____ FAX
- QUOTE—LABOR ☐ YARDAGE ☐ HARDWARE ☐ INSTALL ☐ MEASURE ☐

ORDER # _____ **PAGE** _____ **OF** _____
NEED BY: _____ **TODAY'S DATE** _____
SHIP VIA
CUSTOMER
STREET
CITY _____ **STATE** _____ **ZIP**
PHONE _____ **FAX**

QUOTE ☐ WORKORDER ☐ # _____ SAVE FABRIC ☐

REFERENCE X = WHERE APPLIED ← X →

ITEM #	ROOM	QUANTITY	STYLE	FULLNESS	ROD WIDTH	RETURNS	# OF WIDTHS	FINISHED LENGTH	MIDDLE POINT	SHORT POINT	PIN / HOOK SET	UPRIGHT (SEAMS)	RAILROAD	THERMAL	SATIN SHEEN	BLACKOUT	SELF	C.O.M.	OTHER	WHITE	IVORY	SIZE TRIM / OTHER	PLACEMENT
1																							
2																							

#1 Fabric #A VENDOR/PATTERN WIDTH / RPT Fabric #B VENDOR/PATTERN WIDTH / RPT Fabric #C VENDOR/PATTERN WIDTH / RPT

#1 OPTIONS / SPECIAL INSTRUCTIONS / DRAWINGS

#2 OPTIONS / SPECIAL INSTRUCTIONS / DRAWINGS

INSTALLATION INSTRUCTIONS PLACEMENT

	ITEM # #1	#2
CEILING		
ABOVE TRIM		
ON TRIM		
LEFT (inches)		
RIGHT (inches)		
ROD EXTENSION		
OUTSIDE MT		
INSIDE MT		
REMOVE OLD		
HARDWARE PAGES		

QTY	HARDWARE

☐ Check here if DRAPERY VALANCE is to match (cut from the same bolt of fabric) Swags, Cornices, rod pockets or pinch pleats… etc which accompany this order

REV. 12/05

Authorization signature _____ Date

ROD POCKET VALANCE
WORK ORDER FORM

BILL TO: _____ P.O.# _____ QUOTE ☐ # _____ ORDER # _____ PAGE _____ OF _____

FIRM NAME _____ WORKORDER ☐ NEED BY: _____ TODAY'S DATE _____

YOUR NAME _____ SAVE FABRIC ☐ SHIP VIA _____

STREET _____ STATE _____ ZIP _____ CUSTOMER _____

CITY _____ STREET _____

PHONE _____ FAX _____ CITY _____ STATE _____ ZIP _____

QUOTE—LABOR ☐ YARDAGE ☐ HARDWARE ☐ INSTALL ☐ MEASURE ☐ PHONE _____ FAX _____

REFERENCE   X = WHERE APPLIED

Fabric #A	ITEM #	ROOM	QUANTITY	STYLE	FULLNESS	ROD WIDTH	RETURNS	RETURN CUT-OUT + FINISHED LENGTH	MIDDLE POINT	SHORT POINT	FULLNESS	# OF WIDTHS	ROD POCKET	HEADER	UPRIGHT (SEAMS) / RAILROAD	THERMAL / SATIN SHEEN / BLACKOUT	SELF / C.O.M. / OTHER	WHITE / IVORY	SIZE TRIM / OTHER	PLACEMENT
1																				
2																				

Fabric #A VENDOR/PATTERN _____ WIDTH / RPT _____
Fabric #B VENDOR/PATTERN _____ WIDTH / RPT _____
Fabric #C VENDOR/PATTERN _____ WIDTH / RPT _____

#1 OPTIONS / SPECIAL INSTRUCTIONS / DRAWINGS

#2 OPTIONS / SPECIAL INSTRUCTIONS / DRAWINGS

INSTALLATION INSTRUCTIONS

PLACEMENT	ITEM #	#1	#2
CEILING			
ABOVE TRIM			
ON TRIM			
LEFT (inches)			
ROD EXTENSION			
RIGHT (inches)			
OUTSIDE MT			
INSIDE MT			
REMOVE OLD			
HARDWARE PAGES			

HARDWARE	QTY

☐ Check here if ROD POCKET VALANCE is to match (cut from the same bolt of fabric) Swags, Cornices, rod pockets or pinch pleats… etc which accompany this order

_____ _____
Authorization signature   Date

REV. 12/05

CORNICES ORDER FORM

BILL TO:
- FIRM NAME _____
- YOUR NAME _____
- STREET _____
- CITY _____ STATE _____ ZIP _____
- PHONE _____ FAX _____

QUOTE—LABOR ☐   YARDAGE ☐   HARDWARE ☐   INSTALL ☐   MEASURE ☐

QUOTE ☐   WORKORDER ☐   SAVE FABRIC ☐

P.O.# _____   # _____

ORDER # _____   PAGE _____ OF _____
NEED BY: _____   TODAY'S DATE _____
SHIP VIA _____
CUSTOMER _____
STREET _____
CITY _____ STATE _____ ZIP _____
PHONE _____ FAX _____

REFERENCE X = WHERE APPLIED

ITEM	QUANTITY	ROOM	STYLE	FACE WIDTH	INSIDE / OUTSIDE	RETURNS	REDUCED HEADER	COVER TOP	LONG POINT	MIDDLE POINT	SHORT POINT	UPRIGHT (SEAMS)	RAILROAD	ALL SIDES WELT	TOP WELT	BOTTOM WELT	CUSTOM WELT	WELT SIZE (3/8) STD	TRIM SIZE / OTHER	PLACEMENT FOR TRIM / OTHER
1																				
2																				

#1

FACE FABRIC VENDOR/PATTERN	WIDTH / RPT	BANDING / OTHER) VENDOR/PATTERN	WIDTH / RPT	WELT VENDOR/PATTERN	WIDTH / RPT	BANDING / OTHER) VENDOR/PATTERN	WIDTH / RPT	CASCADES VENDOR/PATTERN	CASCADE LINING VENDOR/PATTERN WIDTH / RPT

OPTIONS / SPECIAL INSTRUCTIONS / DRAWINGS

#2 OPTIONS / SPECIAL INSTRUCTIONS / DRAWINGS

CASCADES INFO

LONG POINT | SHORT POINT | UNDER / OVER | FACED | CASCADE STYLE

INSTALLATION INSTRUCTIONS

PLACEMENT	ITEM #	#1	#2
CEILING			
ABOVE TRIM			
ON TRIM			
LEFT (inches)			
RIGHT (inches)			
BOARD EXTENSION			
OUTSIDE MT			
INSIDE MT			
REMOVE OLD			
HARDWARE PAGES			

☐ Check here if CORNICES is to match (cut from the same bolt of fabric) Swags, rod pockets or pinch pleats... etc. which accompany this order

REV. 12/05

Authorization signature _____   Date _____

SWAGS ORDER FORM
TRADITIONAL SWAGS
&
OPEN SWAGS

BILL TO: _____ P.O.# _____ QUOTE ☐ # _____ ORDER # _____ PAGE _____ OF _____

FIRM NAME _____ WORKORDER ☐ NEED BY: _____ TODAY'S DATE _____

YOUR NAME _____ SAVE FABRIC ☐ SHIP VIA _____

STREET _____ STATE _____ ZIP _____ CUSTOMER _____

CITY _____ STATE _____ ZIP _____ STREET _____

PHONE _____ FAX _____ CITY _____ STATE _____ ZIP _____

QUOTE—LABOR ☐ YARDAGE ☐ HARDWARE ☐ INSTALL ☐ MEASURE ☐ PHONE _____ FAX _____

REFERENCE X = WHERE APPLIED

STYLE: QUANTITY | ROOM | TRADITIONAL | OPEN

SWAG INFORMATION — FINISH LENGTH
FACE WIDTH | RETURNS | # OF SWAGS | LONG POINT | SHORT POINT | BIAS | UPRIGHT (SWAGS) RAILROADED | REDUCED TIDE COVER TOP | CASCADE STYLE (LEFT/RIGHT)

CASCADE / PANELS INFORMATION — FINISH LENGTHS
CASCADE WIDTH | # OF WIDTHS | LONG POINT (LEFT/RIGHT) | SHORT POINT (LEFT/RIGHT) | UNDER SWAG (LEFT/RIGHT) | OVER SWAG (LEFT/RIGHT) | STRAIGHT MITERED (LEFT/RIGHT) | FACED RETURNS (LEFT/RIGHT) | PLACEMENT

JABOT STYLE	# OF JABOTS	UNDER SWAG	OVER SWAG	LONG POINT	SHORT POINT	FINISHED WIDTH	# OF KNOTS	# OF ROSETTES	TRIM SIZE	PLACEMENT
SWAG FABRIC	VENDOR/PATTERN	VENDOR/PATTERN	WIDTH / RPT	CASCADE FACE	VENDOR/PATTERN	WIDTH / RPT	WIDTH / RPT	JABOT FACE	VENDOR/PATTERN	WIDTH / RPT
SWAG LINING	VENDOR/PATTERN	VENDOR/PATTERN	WIDTH / RPT	CASCADE LINING	VENDOR/PATTERN	WIDTH / RPT	WIDTH / RPT	JABOT LINING	VENDOR/PATTERN	WIDTH / RPT

OPTIONS / SPECIAL INSTRUCTIONS / DRAWINGS

INSTALLATION INSTRUCTIONS
PLACEMENT
- CEILING
- ABOVE TRIM
- ON TRIM
- LEFT (inches)
- BOARD EXTENSION
- RIGHT (inches)
- OUTSIDE MT
- INSIDE MT
- REMOVE OLD
- HARDWARE PAGES

QTY	HARDWARE			

☐ Check here if SWAG is to match (cut from the same bolt of fabric) Swags, Rod Pockets, Draperies or shades which accompany this order

REV. 12/05

Authorization signature _____ Date _____

WINDOW SCARFS
ORDER FORM

BILL TO:

FIRM NAME _____

YOUR NAME _____

STREET _____

CITY _____ STATE _____ ZIP _____

PHONE _____ FAX _____

QUOTE—LABOR ☐   YARDAGE ☐   HARDWARE ☐   INSTALL ☐   MEASURE ☐

P.O. # _____   QUOTE ☐   SAVE FABRIC ☐
WORKORDER ☐ #_____

ORDER # _____   PAGE _____ OF _____
NEED BY: _____   TODAY'S DATE _____
SHIP VIA _____
CUSTOMER _____
STREET _____
CITY _____ STATE _____ ZIP _____
PHONE _____ FAX _____

REFERENCE   X = WHERE APPLIED

ITEM #	ROOM	QUANTITY	STYLE	(A) LEFT SIDE	(B) ROD WIDTH	(C) RIGHT SIDE	# OF SWAGS	FLAT WIDTH	FLAT LENGTH	# OF WIDTHS	ROD POCKT (IF NEEDED)	HEADER (IF NEEDED)	THERMAL	SATIN SHEEN	BLACKOUT	SELF	C.O.M	OTHER	WHITE	IVORY	SIZE, TRIM / OTHER	PLACEMENT
1																						
2																						

← X →

Fabric #A | VENDOR/PATTERN | WIDTH / RPT | Fabric #B | VENDOR/PATTERN | WIDTH / RPT | Fabric #C | VENDOR/PATTERN | WIDTH / RPT

#1 OPTIONS / SPECIAL INSTRUCTIONS / DRAWINGS

#2 OPTIONS / SPECIAL INSTRUCTIONS / DRAWINGS

INSTALLATION INSTRUCTIONS

PLACEMENT	#1	#2
ITEM #		
CEILING		
ABOVE TRIM		
ON TRIM		
LEFT (inches)		
RIGHT (inches)		
ROD EXTENSION		
TAIL LENGTHS (A) LEFT		
(C) RIGHT		
OUTSIDE MT		
INSIDE MT		
REMOVE OLD		
HARDWARE PAGES		

☐ Check here if WINDOWSCARF is to match (cut from the same bolt of fabric) Swags, Cornices, rod pockets or pinch pleats... etc which accompany this order

REV. 12/05

Authorization signature _____ Date _____

FABRIC SHADE
WORK ORDER FORM

BILL TO:

P.O.# _____ QUOTE ☐ # _____ ORDER # _____ PAGE ___ OF ___

FIRM NAME _____ WORKORDER ☐ NEED BY: _____ TODAY'S DATE _____

YOUR NAME _____ SAVE FABRIC ☐ SHIP VIA _____

STREET _____ CUSTOMER _____

CITY _____ STATE ___ ZIP ___ STREET _____

PHONE _____ FAX _____ CITY _____ STATE ___ ZIP ___

QUOTE—LABOR ☐ YARDAGE ☐ HARDWARE ☐ INSTALL ☐ MEASURE ☐ PHONE _____ FAX _____

REFERENCE _____   X = WHERE APPLIED

ITEM #	ROOM	QUANTITY	STYLE	FACE WIDTH	RETURNS (more than 1.5")	FINISHED LENGTH (Long or short point: Lp or Sp)	UPRIGHT (Stans) / RAILROAD	ROD POCKT SIZE	HEADER SIZE	# OF WIDTHS	FULLNESS (if different)	STANDARD	FLAT	CUSTOM SEE TOP OF HEADRAIL	OUTSIDE MT / INSIDE MT	MOUNT TYPE	THERMAL (wkrm make allowances) / SATIN SHEEN / BLACKOUT	SELF / C.O.M. / OTHER	WHITE / IVORY	SIZE TRIM / OTHER	PLACEMENT
1																					
2																					

Fabric #A	VENDOR/PATTERN	WIDTH / RPT
Fabric #B	VENDOR/PATTERN	WIDTH / RPT
Fabric #C	VENDOR/PATTERN	WIDTH / RPT

#1 OPTIONS / SPECIAL INSTRUCTIONS / DRAWINGS

#2 OPTIONS / SPECIAL INSTRUCTIONS / DRAWINGS

INSTALLATION INSTRUCTIONS

	PLACEMENT	
ITEM #	#1	#2
CEILING		
ABOVE TRIM		
ON TRIM		
SILL		
APRON		
FLOOR		
OUTSIDE MT		
INSIDE MT		
REMOVE OLD		

#1 CORD PLACEMENT
QTY ___ RIGHT ☐
QTY ___ LEFT ☐
MECHANISM
CLEAT ☐ LOCK ☐
CLUTCH ☐ WHITE ☐ NICKEL ☐
BRASS ☐

#2 CORD PLACEMENT
QTY ___ RIGHT ☐
QTY ___ LEFT ☐
MECHANISM
CLEAT ☐ LOCK ☐
CLUTCH ☐ WHITE ☐ NICKEL ☐
BRASS ☐

☐ Check here if FABRIC SHADE is to match (cut from the same bolt of fabric) Swags, Cornices, rod pockets or pinch pleats... etc. which accompany this order

Authorization signature _____ Date _____

REV. 12/05

SUNBURSTS
WORK ORDER FORM

BILL TO:
FIRM NAME _____
YOUR NAME _____
STREET _____
CITY _____ STATE _____ ZIP _____
PHONE _____ FAX _____

P.O.# _____
QUOTE ☐   WORKORDER ☐   # _____
QUOTE ☐   SAVE FABRIC ☐

ORDER # _____   PAGE _____ OF _____
NEED BY: _____   TODAY'S DATE _____
SHIP VIA _____
CUSTOMER _____
STREET _____
CITY _____ STATE _____ ZIP _____
PHONE _____ FAX _____

QUOTE—LABOR ☐ YARDAGE ☐ HARDWARE ☐ INSTALL ☐ MEASURE ☐

REFERENCE   X = WHERE APPLIED   ← X →   ← X →

| ITEM # | ROOM | QUANTITY | STYLE | FACE WIDTH | FINISHED LENGTH | FULLNESS | # OF WIDTHS | ROSETTE | BUTTON | UPRIGHT (SEAMS) | RAILROAD | OUTSIDE MT | INSIDE MT (WKRM MAKE ALLOWANCE) | THERMAL | SATIN SHEEN | BLACKOUT | SELF | C.O.M. | OTHER | **WHITE** | **IVORY** | SIZE TRIM / OTHER | PLACEMENT |

#1

| 1 | | | | | | |
| 2 | | | | | | |

Fabric #A	VENDOR/PATTERN	WIDTH / RPT
Fabric #B	VENDOR/PATTERN	WIDTH / RPT
Fabric #C	VENDOR/PATTERN	WIDTH / RPT

OPTIONS / SPECIAL INSTRUCTIONS / DRAWINGS

#2

OPTIONS / SPECIAL INSTRUCTIONS / DRAWINGS

INSTALLATION INSTRUCTIONS

ITEM #	PLACEMENT #1	#2
OUTSIDE MT		
INSIDE MT		
REMOVE OLD		
HARDWARE PAGES		

☐ Check here if SUNBURST is to match (cut from the same bolt of fabric) Swags, Cornices, rod pockets or pinch pleats…. etc which accompany this order

REV. 12/05

Authorization signature _____   Date _____

MISCELLANEOUS ORDER FORM

BILL TO: _____ P.O.# _____ QUOTE ☐ # _____ ORDER # _____ PAGE _____ OF _____

FIRM NAME _____ WORKORDER ☐ NEED BY: _____ TODAY'S DATE _____

YOUR NAME _____ SAVE FABRIC ☐ SHIP VIA _____

STREET _____ CUSTOMER _____

CITY _____ STATE _____ ZIP _____ STREET _____

PHONE _____ FAX _____ CITY _____ STATE _____ ZIP _____

QUOTE—LABOR ☐ YARDAGE ☐ HARDWARE ☐ INSTALL ☐ MEASURE ☐ PHONE _____ FAX _____

| FABRIC (A) FRONT | ☐ PATTERN PLACEMENT | WIDTH /RPT | FABRIC (B) | ☐ PATTERN PLACEMENT | WIDTH /RPT | FABRIC (C) | ☐ PATTERN PLACEMENT | WIDTH /RPT |

ROOM _____

☐ Check here if rod order is to match (cut from the same bolt of fabric)
☐ Swags, Cornices, Draperies or shades which accompany this order

REV. 12/05

Authorization signature _____

BED SKIRTS ORDER FORM

QUOTE ☐   WORKORDER ☐   # _____

BILL TO: P.O.# _____   ORDER # _____ PAGE ____ OF ____

FIRM NAME   _____   NEED BY: _____ TODAY'S DATE: _____

YOUR NAME   _____   SHIP VIA _____

PHONE _____ FAX _____   CUSTOMER _____

                                                 STREET _____

☐ CHECK HERE IF DUSTRUFFLE ARE CUT FROM THE SAME   CITY _____ ST. _____ ZIP _____
   BOLT OF FABRIC AS YOUR DRAPERIES, BEDDING. ETC.

QTY	STYLE	LINED ☐ UNLINED ☐	BED STYLE	SIZE
	BOX PLEAT 4-6" ☐ GATHERED ☐		CAL. KING ☐ TWIN ☐	WIDTH LENGTH DROP
	BOX PLEAT 10" ☐ GATHERED CORNERS ☐		KING ☐ CRIB ☐	
	FAN PLEAT ☐ TAILORED ☐		QUEEN ☐ DAY BED ☐	
	TWO LAYER GATHERED ☐		FULL ☐ 4-SIDED ☐	

FABRIC (A) FRONT ☐ PATTERN PLACEMENT WIDTH /RPT	FABRIC (D) ☐ PATTERN PLACEMENT WIDTH /RPT
FABRIC (B) ☐ PATTERN PLACEMENT WIDTH /RPT	FABRIC (E) ☐ PATTERN PLACEMENT WIDTH /RPT
FABRIC (C) ☐ PATTERN PLACEMENT WIDTH /RPT	FABRIC (F) ☐ PATTERN PLACEMENT WIDTH /RPT

Check off what add-ons you would like.

Drawn details by labeling with arrow and letters as to where they go.

_____ ☐ WELT (1)   SIZE _____ . BIAS, RR, SEAMS
_____ ☐ WELT SHIRRED _____
           PLACEMENT EDGE   # _____
                      INSET # _____ INCHES _____
_____ ☐ BUTTONS (DETAILS NEEDED)
_____ ☐ CONTRAST PLEATS (DETAILS NEEDED)
_____ ☐ DECKING (BANDED) 5"
_____ ☐ FRINGE
_____ ☐ IVORY LINING
_____ ☐ PRE-CORDING
_____ ☐ RUFFLE   SIZE _____ (1) BIAS, RR, SEAMS
_____ ☐ RUFFLE DBL. SIZE _____ (2) BIAS, RR, SEAMS
_____ ☐ RUFFLE (BANDED) SIZE _____ BIAS, RR, SEAMS
        ☐ SPLIT CORNER (2) ☐ SPLIT CORNER (4)
_____ ☐ TASSELS EA.
_____ ☐ TIE ....SIZE _____
_____ ☐ TRIM / BANDS   SIZE _____ BIAS, RR, SEAMS
           PLACEMENT ..TOP ☐ (DETAILS NEEDED)
           ....BOTTOM ☐
           INSET _____ INCHES
_____ ☐ VELCRO MOUNT (DETAILS NEEDED)
_____ ☐ OTHER

CAL. KING	78W X 84L	STD. KING	78W X 80L
QUEEN	60W X 80L	FULL	54W X 75L
TWIN	36W X 80L	DAY BED	80W X 36L

REV.2/06

SIGNATURE _____ DATE _____

BEDSPREADS / COVERLETS
ORDER FORM

QUOTE ☐   WORKORDER ☐   # _____

BILL TO: P.O.# _____

FIRM NAME _____

YOUR NAME _____

PHONE _____ FAX _____

SHIP VIA _____

ROOM _____ PAGE _____ OF _____

NEED BY: _____ TODAY'S DATE: _____

CUSTOMER _____

ADDRESS _____

CITY _____ STATE _____ ZIP _____

☐ CHECK HERE IF BEDSPREADS/ COVERLET ARE CUT FROM THE SAME BOLT OF FABRIC AS YOUR DRAPERIES, BEDDING. ETC.

ONE OF THESE MUST BE MARKED

QTY	BED STYLE	LINING	CUSTOM SIZE			TYPE		
	☐ CAL. KING ☐ DAY BED	WHITE (STD) ☐	WIDTH	LENGTH	DROP	REVERSE SHAM ☐	THROW ☐	CONTOURED ☐
	☐ KING ☐ 4-SIDED					PILLOW TUCK ☐	GUSSET ☐	WITH ELASTIC ☐
	☐ QUEEN	IVORY ☐				STOP AT	WATERFALL ☐	SQUARED ☐
	☐ FULL					HEADBOARD ☐	CAPED	(COVERLET ONLY)
	☐ TWIN						CORNERS ☐	

CHOOSE BADDING

☐ 3.75 OZ. LIGHT   ☐ 6 OZ. STANDARD   ☐ 9 OZ. MEDIUM   ☐ 12 OZ. BEST   ☐ 18 OZ. HEAVY

FABRIC (A) FRONT ☐ PATTERN PLACEMENT WIDTH /RPT	FABRIC (D) ☐ PATTERN PLACEMENT WIDTH /RPT
FABRIC (B) ☐ PATTERN PLACEMENT WIDTH /RPT	FABRIC (E) ☐ PATTERN PLACEMENT WIDTH/RPT
FABRIC (C) ☐ PATTERN PLACEMENT WIDTH /RPT	FABRIC (F) ☐ PATTERN PLACEMENT WIDTH /RPT

FABRIC #   **REVERSE SHAM OPTIONS**
_____ ☐ SCALLOPED EDGE
_____ ☐ STRAIGHT EDGE
_____ ☐ WITH 1/2" 3/4" WELT (CIRCLE ONE) BIAS, RR, SEAMS
_____ ☐ WITH SHIRRED 1/2" 3/4" WELT   BIAS, RR, SEAMS
_____ ☐ WITH JUMBO WELT   BIAS, RR, SEAMS
_____ ☐ WITH SHIRRED JUMBO WELT   BIAS, RR, SEAMS
_____ ☐ PRE-CORDING
_____ ☐ FRINGE

QUILTED OPTION
☐ NON-QUILTED (WORKROOM APPROVAL)
☐ QUILTED   STYLE _____

Draw details by labeling with arrows and letters as to were they go.

FABRIC #   **OTHER OPTIONS**
_____ ☐ WITH SHIRRED DROP
_____ ☐ WITH TAILORED DROP
_____ ☐ WELT 1/2" AROUND MATTRESS   BIAS, RR, SEAMS
_____ ☐ WELT ON BOTTOM 1/2" TO 3/4"   BIAS, RR, SEAMS
_____ ☐ JUMBO WELT ON BOTTOM
_____ ☐ SHIRRED WELT AT BOTTOM 1/2" TO 3/4" BIAS, RR, SEAMS
_____ ☐ SHIRRED JUMBO WELT AT BOTTOM   BIAS, RR, SEAMS
_____ ☐ WELT ON SEAMS SIZE _____ BIAS, RR, SEAMS
_____ ☐ SCALLOPED HEM
_____ ☐ ROUNDED HEM
_____ ☐ RUFFLE SIZE _____ (1) BIAS, RR, SEAMS

_____ ☐ RUFFLE ....SIZE _____ (2) BIAS, RR, SEAMS

_____ ☐ BUTTONS SIZE_____ WE MAKE OR PRE-MADE

_____ ☐ BANDING SIZE _____ (DETAILS NEEDED) BIAS, RR, SEAMS
_____ ☐ FRINGE
_____ ☐ PRE-CORDING
_____ ☐ OTHER

PLEASE MEASURE BED TO VERIFY

SIGNATURE _____ DATE _____

REV.12/06

COMFORTERS ORDER FORM

QUOTE ☐   WORKORDER ☐   # _____

BILL TO: _____ P.O.# _____

FIRM NAME _____

YOUR NAME _____

PHONE _____ FAX _____

☐ CHECK HERE IF COMFORTER ARE CUT FROM THE SAME BOLT OF FABRIC AS YOUR DRAPERIES, BEDDING. ETC.

SHIP VIA _____

ROOM _____ PAGE ____ OF ____

NEED BY: _____ TODAY'S DATE: _____

CUSTOMER _____

ADDRESS _____

CITY _____ STATE _____ ZIP _____

QTY	BED STYLE	CUSTOM SIZE			QUILTING OPTIONS	CORNERS
	☐ CAL. KING ☐ DAY BED ☐ KING ☐ 4-SIDED ☐ QUEEN ☐ FULL ☐ TWIN	WIDTH	LENGTH	DROP	NON-QUILTED ☐ QUILTED ☐ STYLE _____ (Must have style)	ROUNDED ☐ SQUARE ☐

CHOOSE BADDING

☐ 3.75 OZ. LIGHT   ☐ 6 OZ. STANDARD   ☐ 9 OZ. MEDIUM   ☐ 12 OZ. BEST   ☐ 18 OZ. HEAVY

FABRIC (A) FRONT ☐ PATTERN PLACEMENT WIDTH /RPT	FABRIC (D) ☐ PATTERN PLACEMENT WIDTH /RPT
FABRIC (B) ☐ PATTERN PLACEMENT WIDTH /RPT	FABRIC (E) ☐ PATTERN PLACEMENT WIDTH/RPT
FABRIC (C) ☐ PATTERN PLACEMENT WIDTH /RPT	FABRIC (F) ☐ PATTERN PLACEMENT WIDTH /RPT

OPTIONS

____ ☐ WELT ON BOTTOM 1/2" TO 3/4"   BIAS, RR, SEAMS

____ ☐ JUMBO WELT ON BOTTOM   BIAS, RR, SEAMS

____ ☐ WELT ON SEAMS SIZE _____ BIAS, RR, SEAMS

____ ☐ GATHERED WELT AT BOTTOM 1/2" TO 3/4" BIAS, RR, SEAMS

____ ☐ GATHERED JUMBO WELT AT BOTTOM   BIAS, RR, SEAMS

____ ☐ BUTTONS SIZE _____ WE MAKE OR PRE-MADE
____ ☐ FRINGE
____ ☐ PRE-CORDING
____ ☐ RUFFLE (SIZE) _____ (1) BIAS, RR, SEAMS

____ ☐ RUFFLE (SIZE) _____ (2) BIAS, RR, SEAMS
____ ☐ OTHER

Drawn details by labeling with arrows and letters as to were they go.

PLEASE MEASURE BED TO VERIFY   REV.2/06

SIGNATURE _____ DATE _____

DUVETS ORDER FORM

QUOTE ☐   WORKORDER ☐   # _____
BILL TO: P.O. # _____

FIRM NAME _____

YOUR NAME _____

PHONE _____ FAX _____

SHIP VIA _____

ROOM _____ PAGE _____ OF _____

NEED BY: _____ TODAY'S DATE: _____

CUSTOMER _____

ADDRESS _____

CITY _____ ST. _____ ZIP _____

☐ CHECK HERE IF PILLOW / SHAMS ARE CUT FROM THE SAME BOLT OF FABRIC AS YOUR DRAPERIES, BEDDING. ETC.

QTY	BED STYLE	STYLE	SIZE			CHOOSE CLOSURE	CLOSURE PLACEMENT	FIBERFILL INSERT	QUILTED
	☐ CAL. KING	RD EDGE ☐	WIDTH	LENGTH	DROP	BUTTON ☐	TOP ☐	9 OZ. ☐	QUILTED ☐
	☐ STD. KING	SQUARE ☐				FLAP ☐	TOP INSET ____	12 OZ. ☐	STYLE
	☐ QUEEN	3 SIDED ☐				ZIPPER ☐		18 OZ. ☐	
	☐ FULL	4 SIDED ☐				VELCRO ☐	BTM ☐	24 OZ ☐	
	☐ TWIN	☐ CRIB					BTM INSET ____	CHAN. ONLY	

FABRIC (A) FRONT   ☐ PATTERN PLACEMENT   WIDTH /RPT

FABRIC (D)   ☐ PATTERN PLACEMENT   WIDTH /RPT

FABRIC (B) BACK   ☐ PATTERN PLACEMENT   WIDTH /RPT

FABRIC (E)   ☐ PATTERN PLACEMENT   WIDTH/RPT

FABRIC (C)   ☐ PATTERN PLACEMENT   WIDTH /RPT

FABRIC (F)   ☐ PATTERN PLACEMENT   WIDTH /RPT

Check off what add-on's you want.

FABRIC #   (CIRCLE ONE)

_____ ☐ WELT (1)   SIZE _____ . BIAS, RR, SEAMS
_____ ☐ WELT (2)   SIZE _____ BIAS, RR, SEAMS
_____ ☐ WELT SHIRRED (3)
             PLACEMENT EDGE ☐ # _____
                        INSET ☐ # ____ INCHES ____
_____ ☐ WELT (FLAT) (4) SIZE ____ BIAS RR, SEAMS
_____ ☐ WELT (FLAT) (5) SIZE ____ BIAS RR, SEAMS
_____ ☐ BORDER APPLICATION
_____ ☐ BUTTONS (DETAILS NEEDED)
_____ ☐ FAN PLEAT
_____ ☐ FLANGE........SIZE _____ (1)
_____ ☐ FLANGE DOUBLE .... SIZE _____ (2)
_____ ☐ FLANGE (INTERIOR)
_____ ☐ FLANGE CONTRAST .... SIZE _____
_____ ☐ FLANGE PADDED   ☐ FLANGE PELLON
_____ ☐ FLANGE MITERED
_____ ☐ FLANGE SCALLOPED
_____ ☐ FRINGE
_____ ☐ INTERIOR TIES
_____ ☐ PATCH WORK
_____ ☐ PRE-CORDING
_____ ☐ QUILTED   STYLE _____
_____ ☐ RUFFLE / FRONT SIZE ____ (1) BIAS, RR, SEAMS
_____ ☐ RUFFLE 2-COLOR SIDED (BACK)
_____ ☐ RUFFLE DBL. _____ SIZE _____ (2)
             BIAS, RR, SEAMS
_____ ☐ RUFFLE (BANDED) SIZE ____ BIAS, RR, SEAMS
_____ ☐ SHIRRED FRONT (DETAILS NEEDED)
_____ ☐ SHIRRED BACK (DETAILS NEEDED)
_____ ☐ TASSELS EA.
_____ ☐ TIES .... SIZE _____

Drawn details by labeling with arrow and letters as to were they go.

PLEASE MEASURE BED TO VERIFY

SIGNATURE _____ DATE _____

REV.12/05

PILLOW / SHAM / NECKROLL ORDER FORM

QUOTE ☐   WORKORDER ☐   # _____
BILL TO: P.O.# _____
FIRM NAME _____
YOUR NAME _____
PHONE _____ FAX _____

☐ CHECK HERE IF PILLOW / SHAMS ARE CUT FROM THE SAME BOLT OF FABRIC AS YOUR DRAPERIES, BEDDING. ETC.

SHIP VIA _____
ROOM _____ PAGE _____ OF ___
NEED BY: _____ TODAY'S DATE: _____
CUSTOMER _____
ADDRESS _____
CITY _____ STATE _____ ZIP _____

QTY	STYLE OR SHAM # SELF-LINED ☐	WIDTH	LENGTH	DROP/BOX	DIAM.	CHOOSE FORM	CHOOSE CLOSURE
						STANDARD ☐ HANDSTITCH ☐ FLAP ☐
						OTHER ☐ MACHINE ☐ BUTTON ☐
						DOWN 10/90 ☐ VELCRO ☐ ZIPPER ☐
						CUSTOMERS ☐ FLAP/VELCRO TAB ☐

FABRIC (A) FRONT   ☐ PATTERN PLACEMENT   WIDTH /RPT
FABRIC (D)   ☐ PATTERN PLACEMENT   WIDTH /RPT

FABRIC (B) BACK   ☐ PATTERN PLACEMENT   WIDTH /RPT
FABRIC (E)   ☐ PATTERN PLACEMENT   WIDTH/RPT

FABRIC (C)   ☐ PATTERN PLACEMENT   WIDTH /RPT
FABRIC (F)   ☐ PATTERN PLACEMENT   WIDTH /RPT

Check off what add-ons you want.

FABRIC #   (CIRCLE ONE)
_____ ☐ WELT (1)   SIZE _____ . BIAS, RR, SEAMS
_____ ☐ WELT (2)   SIZE _____ BIAS, RR, SEAMS
_____ ☐ WELT SHIRRED (3)
            PLACEMENT   EDGE ☐ # _____
                        INSET ☐ # _____ INCHES _____
_____ ☐ WELT (FLAT) (4)   SIZE _____ BIAS RR, SEAMS
_____ ☐ WELT (FLAT) (5)   SIZE _____ BIAS RR, SEAMS
_____ ☐ BORDER APPLICATION
_____ ☐ BUTTONS (DETAILS NEEDED)
_____ ☐ BOXED (FLAT)
_____ ☐ BOXED (SHIRRED)
_____ ☐ ENVELOPE/FLAP
_____ ☐ WELT ON ENVELOPE/FLAP SIZE ____ BIAS, RR, SEAMS
_____ ☐ FAN PLEAT
_____ ☐ FLANGE........SIZE _____ (1)
_____ ☐ FLANGE DOUBLE.............SIZE _____ (2)
_____ ☐ FLANGE (INTERIOR)
_____ ☐ FLANGE CONTRAST....... SIZE _____
_____ ☐ FLANGE PADDED one / both   FLANGE PELLON
_____ ☐ FLANGE MITERED
_____ ☐ FLANGE SCALLOPED
_____ ☐ FRINGE
_____ ☐ KNOTTED CORNERS (INCLUDES WELT)
_____ ☐ PATCH WORK
_____ ☐ PRE-CORDING
            PLACEMENT   EDGE S _____
                        INSET _____ INCHS
_____ ☐ QUILTED   STYLE _____
_____ ☐ RUFFLE / FRONT   SIZE _____ (1) BIAS, RR, SEAMS
_____ ☐ RUFFLE DBL. SIZE _____ (2) BIAS, RR, SEAMS
_____ ☐ RUFFLE 2-COLOR SIDED (BACK) _____
            BIAS, RR, SEAMS (CIRCLE ONE)
_____ ☐ RUFFLE (BANDED) SIZE _____ BIAS, RR, SEAMS
_____ ☐ SHIRRED FRONT (DETAILS NEEDED)
_____ ☐ SHIRRED BACK (DETAILS NEEDED)
_____ ☐ TASSELS EA. PLACEMENT _____
_____ ☐ TIES...........SIZE ____ (PLACEMENT NEEDED)
_____ ☐ TURKISH CORNER
_____ ☐ TRIM / BAND .. SIZE _____ BIAS, RR, SEAMS

Drawn details by labeling with arrow and letters as to where the fabric letters go.

REFERENCES:
KING   36W X 20L
QUEEN   30W X 20L
FULL/STD   26W X 20L
EURO   26W X 26L

SIGNATURE _____ DATE _____

REV.12/05

TABLECLOTHS / RUNNERS ORDER FORM

QUOTE ☐   WORKORDER ☐   # _____

BILL TO: P.O.# _____

FIRM NAME _____

YOUR NAME _____

PHONE _____ FAX _____

SHIP VIA _____

ROOM _____ PAGE _____ OF _____

NEED BY: _____ TODAY'S DATE: _____

CUSTOMER _____

ADDRESS _____

CITY _____ STATE _____ ZIP _____

☐ CHECK HERE IF DUSTRUFFLE ARE CUT FROM THE SAME BOLT OF FABRIC AS YOUR DRAPERIES, BEDDING. ETC.

QTY	TYPE	STYLE	SIZE	LINING
	TABLECLOTH ☐ RUNNER ☐	☐ ROUND ☐ SQUARE ☐ CUSTOM	WIDTH / LENGTH/DROP / FULL DIAMETER	WHITE ☐ INTERLINING ☐ IVORY ☐ OTHER ☐

FABRIC (A) FRONT   ☐ PATTERN PLACEMENT   WIDTH /RPT   FABRIC (D)   ☐ PATTERN PLACEMENT   WIDTH /RPT

FABRIC (B)   ☐ PATTERN PLACEMENT   WIDTH /RPT   FABRIC (E)   ☐ PATTERN PLACEMENT   WIDTH/RPT

FABRIC (C)   ☐ PATTERN PLACEMENT   WIDTH /RPT   FABRIC (F)   ☐ PATTERN PLACEMENT   WIDTH /RPT

FABRIC #

_____ ☐ WELT   SIZE _____ BIAS, RR, SEAMS
_____ ☐ WELT SHIRRED
           PLACEMENT   EDGE ☐
                       INSET ☐   INCHES _____

_____ ☐ WELT (FLAT)   SIZE _____ BIAS RR, SEAMS
_____ ☐ BORDER APPLICATION
_____ ☐ BUTTONS (DETAILS NEEDED)
_____ ☐ FRINGE
           PLACEMENT   EDGE ☐
                       INSET ☐   INCHES _____

_____ ☐ PATCH WORK
_____ ☐ PRE-CORDING
           PLACEMENT   EDGE ☐
                       INSET ☐   INCHES _____

_____ ☐ QUILTED   STYLE _____

_____ ☐ RUFFLE ....SIZE _____ (1) BIAS, RR, SEAMS

_____ ☐ RUFFLE DBL. SIZE _____ 2) BIAS, RR, SEAMS

_____ ☐ RUFFLE (BANDED) SIZE _____ BIAS, RR, SEAMS
_____ ☐ TASSELS EA.
_____ ☐ TIES ....SIZE _____
_____ ☐ TRIM / BAND SIZE _____

Drawn details by labeling with arrow and letters as to were they

SIGNATURE _____ DATE _____

REV.12/05

GLOSSARY

Add-on An additional item that is applied to the main treatment design. Examples include banding, pre-cording, welting, cascades, knots, rosettes, ruffles, panels, jabots, etc.

Allowance Established guidelines used to figure yardages for window covering treatments. Examples of allowances are bottom hem, top hem, side hems, add to width, add to length, fullness, etc.

Apron The wood trim molding below the window sill.

Banding This is a narrow length of fabric which is applied to the treatment for contrast.

Baton A stick, rod, or wand used to hand draw draperies to an open or closed position.

Bay window A configuration of more than two windows which are set at angles from each other forming a cove or protrusion from a room.

Bias The diagonal direction of fabric. The true bias is at a 45° angle to the straight grain of a woven piece of goods.

Blackout lining A lining used in draperies to block light, which usually consists of two or more layers bonded together, one of which is a black, light blocking material.

Bleed through This occurs when the front fabric is thin or is of a light color and the back layer or lining is a darker color. The light passing through the back fabric causes the front fabric to appear to change color and look darker or muddy looking.

Bow window A configuration of more than three windows which are set at very slight angles from each other forming a rounded shape cove or protrusion from a room.

Buckram See Crinoline.

Cable ties A plastic device that has teeth on a strip which then slips into an opening on the tie. When the tooth side is inserted into the hole, the teeth keep it from slipping. These are also known as holding wires or wire ties.

Casing 1) Also known as a pocket, and is stitched in the fabric to allow for a curtain rod to pass through; 2) The framing in the wall around a window opening into which the window is set.

Casement 1) A hinged window or part of the window; 2) A type of fabric that is very loosely woven.

Clearance Space required between treatment layers to allow them to hang freely or operate comfortably without rubbing on walls or adjacent layers.

Cleat (cord) A piece of hardware that is mounted to the wall around which the cords of a window treatment are wrapped. These will secure the position of a shade or prevent cords from dangling and causing a potential safety hazard.

Cord lock A piece of hardware that is attached to a blind or shade to lock the cords in place and secure the position of the shade.

Corner window Two windows located in close proximity to each other in the corner of a room, usually set at a 90° angle from each other.

Elements of Soft Treatments

Glossary

Crinoline   A stiff textile product that is used as a foundation for pleats in draperies, which causes the top to become stiff.

Deck banding   A narrow band of the bed skirt material which is applied to the edge of the deck of the skirt, so that if the mattress shifts, the fabric of the skirt is visible and not the lining.

Dust board   The mounting board or cornice top to which the legs and/or the face are attached.

Face width   The width measurement across a treatment or rod from right to left as you are facing it.

Facing   A strip of fabric stitched along an edge of an item which folds over and lays toward the reverse side. This is done to help provide stability to the edge of the item.

Finished length   The length of an item measured from top to bottom when it is completed.

Finished width   The width of an item measured from right to left when it is completed.

Flat mounted   Used on Roman shades where the board is set up so the projection is only ¾". The widest part of the board is set vertically.

Flat welt   Similar to welting, but there is no cord inside, which gives it a flat look. Used where the welt is too stiff for the treatment to hang freely.

Fullness   This refers to how much fabric is added to the rod width, face width, or length measurement in order to create the desired effect. Fullness can be added to the item width or length depending on the type of treatment being made.

Half drop repeat   See Drop repeat.

Header   The ruffled edge that extends above a rod pocket.

Hourglassing   When a shade bows inward along its sides and creates an hourglass shape.

Hybrid Mount (HBM)   Combination of inside mount and outside mount for fabric shades.

Inside Mount (ISM)   Treatment is mounted inside the window casing or between two walls.

Interlining   Any plain fabric which is stitched between the face fabric and the lining fabric.

Leading edge   See Overlaps.

Loft   This is fluffiness of quilt batting or fill.

Long point   Longest point of the design when referring to length.

Memory stitch   A stitch used to hold the lining and face fabric together and to help keep draperies hanging in their proper folds. Very useful if drapery is very long and is full working.

Middle point   Any middle point of a design when referring to length.

Outside Mount (OSM)   Treatment is mounted on the outside of the window casing onto the window frame or wall.

Pair   A drapery treatment where there are panels on the left and right of the window. Also, two of any item that are exact mirror images of each other, such as tie backs.

Panel   A drapery treatment where there is only one fabric panel on a window. It will stack to one side only.

Pattern placement Instructions to place a specific motif of the material at specified points on the treatment.

Pattern repeat The measure of a pattern on a fabric that repeats itself horizontally or vertically

Picture Frame Mount (PFM) When a fabric shade is mounted to the window trim and a small border of the trim frames the shade.

Pillowcasing A fabric joining technique where the face fabric and the lining fabric are stitched together, usually with a ½" seam, then turned and pressed so the seam becomes the very edge of the item.

Piping See Welting.

Pocket See Casing.

Pre-cording with lip Pre-made trim from a supplier which is braided or twisted. It comes with a small fabric flap which is used for sewing, gluing, or bonding onto a treatment.

Pre-cording without lip Pre-made cording from a supplier which is braided or twisted. It is made without a fabric flap so it can be applied to the outside of the treatment or draped loosely over the treatment.

Projection Distance from the front edge of an item to the wall.

Proportion The size relationship of one part of an object to other parts of the object.

Rabbet A joint used in wood working, to notch out a lip which fits into a corresponding groove, and is used to obtain a flush surface when other objects are installed onto a wood frame. Examples are picture frames with glass inserts, padded or painted sunburst frames, etc.

Railroad A manufacturing technique where the lengthwise grain (warp) runs in a horizontal manner across the window treatment, making vertical seams unnecessary, or where the selvage edges are used at the top and bottom of the treatment rather than the sides.

Reduced header The top, wall edge of a board has a cut out to allow for obstacles at the desired installation height, i.e. for a cornice over a ceiling mounted traverse rod, or ceiling mounted mini blinds, or for mounting over window trims.

Return The distance on a drapery panel from the finished edge to the last pleat, or the distance from the face of a rod or board to the wall.

Return cut out The return part of the drapery or valance is cut out to allow the return to wrap around to the wall. This happens on rod pocket items where the rod has a finial on the end or on items where returns will interfere with architectural trims or mouldings.

Reverse welting A cord covered with a fabric. It is made so the seam is inside the pocket with the welt.

Rod width This is the measurement across the face of a rod from the outside of the left bracket to the outside of the right bracket, or the amount of a rod that a panel will cover.

Roping A term used to describe the rippling effect that can happen when bias cut fabric is shirt tail hemmed, or is turned and stitched as sometimes occurs when bias cut welt is made.

Self-lined The face fabric is also used for the back side as a lining.

Glossary

Selvage The finished edge of textile goods.

Shirt tail hem When the fabric edge is double rolled approximately ¼"-½" and then top stitched to give it a small hem look.

Short point Shortest point of the treatment design when referring to length.

Shrinkage This happens when fabric is rolled out and then allowed to relax to its natural state before sewing.

Side hem A vertical hem on the side of the treatment.

Sidelight These are small narrow windows that are placed either side of an opening such as a door or pair of doors.

Sill The horizontal ledge that is at the bottom of a window.

Stack The thickness of a fabric shade when it is opened. It also applies to the space occupied by draperies when they are opened and drawn back.

Take up As the fabric is gathered the width or length will shrink due to the gathering.

Tip to tip measurement The finished width measurement of a single swag.

Transom window This is a small window running horizontally across the top of another window or window combination.

Traverse The action of moving a drapery from its open to closed position or from its closed to open position. Draperies can be manually traversed through the use of a baton or operated with a pull cord through the use of a traversing rod.

Traversing rod This is a drapery rod with rings or carriers from which working draperies are hung that allows them to be opened and closed through the use of a pull cord.

Upright Method of manufacturing where the item is made with the lengthwise grain (warp) of the fabric running vertically, or up and down.

Warp These are the threads that run the length of the bolt of fabric that the weft threads weave under and over.

Weft These are the threads which run backward and forward across the loom, wrapping around the end warp threads to form the selvage and they create the fill of the fabric between warp threads.

Welt (reverse) See Reverse welting.

Welting Also known as piping. A cord covered with fabric, made with a lip or small fabric flap to allow for attachment into a treatment.

Width 1) Refers to a treatment's finished width; 2) When referring to fabric, one width is equal to one cut of fabric at the cut length. When multiple cuts of fabric are sewn together they are referred to as widths, i.e. 3 widths = 3 cuts of fabric sewn together.

Window type A description of the type of window. Examples: corner, bay, curved, arched, etc.